BORDERS IN RED

A volume in the NIU Series in

Slavic, East European, and Eurasian Studies

Edited by Christine D. Worobec

For a list of books in the series, visit our website at cornellpress.cornell.edu.

BORDERS IN RED

MANAGING DIVERSITY IN THE EARLY SOVIET UNION

Stephan Rindlisbacher

NORTHERN ILLINOIS UNIVERSITY PRESS
An imprint of
CORNELL UNIVERSITY PRESS
Ithaca and London

The prepress stage of this publication was supported by the Swiss National Science Foundation to promote scientific research.

Copyright © 2025 by Cornell University

The text of this book is licensed under a Creative Commons Attribution-NonCommercial-NoDerivatives 4.0 International License: https://creativecommons.org/licenses/by-nc-nd/4.0/. To use this book, or parts of this book, in any way not covered by the license, please contact Cornell University Press, Sage House, 512 East State Street, Ithaca, New York 14850. Visit our website at cornellpress.cornell.edu.

First published 2025 by Cornell University Press

Library of Congress Cataloging-in-Publication Data

Names: Rindlisbacher, Stephan, author.
Title: Borders in red : managing diversity in the early Soviet Union / Stephan Rindlisbacher.
Description: Ithaca : Northern Illinois University Press, an imprint of Cornell University Press, 2025. | Series: NIU series in Slavic, East European, and Eurasian studies | Includes bibliographical references and index.
Identifiers: LCCN 2024028900 (print) | LCCN 2024028901 (ebook) | ISBN 9781501780530 (hardcover) | ISBN 9781501780585 (paperback) | ISBN 9781501780547 (epub) | ISBN 9781501780554 (pdf)
Subjects: LCSH: Territory, National—Soviet Union. | Nationalism—Soviet Union. | Soviet Union—Boundaries. | Soviet Union—Politics and government—1917-1936. | Soviet Union—Ethnic relations.
Classification: LCC DK46 .R56 2025 2025 (print) | LCC DK46 (ebook) | DDC 320.1/20947—dc23/eng/20241114
LC record available at https://lccn.loc.gov/2024028900
LC ebook record available at https://lccn.loc.gov/2024028901

https://doi.org/10.7298/fcn6-jn89

For my parents

Contents

List of Maps and Illustrations   ix

Acknowledgments   xi

Note on Terminology, Abbreviations, Transliteration, Calendar, and Maps   xiii

Introduction	1
1. The Leninian Moment: Making the Soviet State	13
2. Gosplan: How to Achieve Spatial Homogeneity	32
3. Ukraine and the RSFSR: How to Find a Common Border	63
4. Central Asia: How to Discuss a Common Border	93
5. Armenia and Azerbaijan: How to Search for a Common Border	126
6. How to Contextualize "Khrushchev's Gift"?	156
Conclusion	172

Glossary   183

Notes   187

Bibliography   243

Index   268

Maps and Illustrations

1. Political borders of the Soviet state, 1 July 1924. xviii
2. Political borders of the Soviet state, 15 April 1929. xix
3. Political borders of the Soviet state, 1 July 1975. xx
4. Contemporary administrative map of the RSFSR, 10 December 1920. 41
5. Economic raiony according to the scheme proposed by Gosplan in November 1921. 42
6. Map of the gubernii (hubernii) of the UkrSSR in 1921. 47
7. Map of the okruga (okruhy) of the UkrSSR in 1928. 48
8. Map of the oblasti of the UkrSSR in August 1937. 49
9. Ukrainian borders between 1917 and 1924. 66
10. Map of border revisions in Kursk Guberniia, 1924–1928. 70
11. Ukrainian borders between 1924 and 1928. 78
12. Contemporary map of the border in the region of Milove/Chertkovo, 1926. 84
13. Political map of Central Asia, 1923. 97
14. Picture of the Territorial Commission for Delimitation of the Central Asian Republics, 1924. 107
15. Political map of Central Asia, 1926. 115
16. Political map of the Fergana Valley, 1940. 118
17. Adapted map of Kyrgyz Botkan-Budzhuk Volost and Uzbek Sokh and Vorukh Volosti, 1928. 120
18. Adapted map of Kyrgyz Isfana Volost, 1928. 121
19. Adapted map of a border revision between Proletarian (Tajik) and Liailiak (Kyrgyz) Raiony, 1938. 123
20. Political map of the South Caucasus region at the end of 1921. 133
21. Delimitation of the republican borders in the region around Bashkend, 1930. 135

MAPS AND ILLUSTRATIONS

22. Political map of the South Caucasus at the end of 1936.   145
23. Map of the winter and summer pastures of the Azerbaijan SSR, 1 June 1924.   149
24. Location of Putivl' Volost within Russian imperial Kursk Guberniia.   158
25. Political map of Central Asia, 1975.   167

Acknowledgments

This book is the result of a long and intricate process. I would like to express my gratitude to all the people who took part in it. In particular, I would like to thank the Swiss National Science Foundation (SNSF) for financing research in various post-Soviet archives. The *Advanced postdoc.mobility* program allowed me to discuss my ideas with colleagues all over the world. The SNSF then made it possible to publish this book in open access. I am also thankful to the German Historical Institute in Moscow, the Ilia State University in Tbilisi (there, in particular, to Ketevan Gurchiani), the Institute of East and Southeast European Studies in Regensburg (especially Ulf Brunnbauer, Luminita Gatejel, and Cindy Wittke), as well as the University of Wisconsin-Madison for hosting me while I worked on this project. Particular thanks go to the Viadrina Center of Polish and Ukrainian Studies for making the completion of this book possible.

Furthermore, I would like to mention the many librarians and archivists across Armenia, Belarus, Georgia, Kazakhstan, Kyrgyzstan, Russia, and Ukraine who provided crucial assistance. The development of the book manuscript was an interesting but sometimes painstakingly long process. Therefore, I would like to express my gratitude to all the people who read the manuscript and provided the necessary input and feedback to bring the book to its present form. This group includes Jörg Baberowski, Nick Baron, Fabian Baumann, Werner Benecke, Yelena Borisënok, Ray Brandon, Philipp Casula, Marina Cattaruzza, Victoria Clement, Vitalij Fastovskij, Falk Flade, Felix Frey, Frank Grelka, Arsen Hakobyan, Francine Hirsch, Anton Liavitski, Dagmara Jajeśniak-Quast, Martin Jeske, Robert Kindler, Harrison King, Johannes Kleinmann, Rustem Kubeyev, Gero Lietz, Fabian Lüscher, Arpine Maniero, Ibrahim Mirzayev, Olena Palko, Julia Richers, Benjamin Schenk, Sanela Schmid, Anna-Konstanze Schröder, Nicholas Seay, Sebastian Steiner, Alun Thomas, Dimitri Tolkatsch, Paul Werth, Kristina Wittkamp, and Lidia Zessin-Jurek.

Special thanks go to Silke Dutzmann, who drew the many maps for this volume, and to Bogdan Zawadewicz, with whom I had the chance to visit almost all of the border regions discussed here in 2016 and 2017.

With the generous permission of the original publishers, this book incorporates material that has appeared in my articles and book chapters: "From Space to Territory: Negotiating the Russo-Ukrainian Border, 1919–1928," *Revolutionary Russia* 31, no. 1 (2018): 86–106; "Contested Lines: The Russo-Ukrainian Border, 1917–1929," in *Making Ukraine: Negotiating, Contesting and Drawing the Borders in the Twentieth Century*, ed. Constantin Ardeleanu and Olena Palko (Montreal: McGill-Queen's University Press, 2022), 189–209; and "National Forms with Economic Content? Gosplan's Expertise on Territorializing the Soviet State, 1921–1930," in *Spatial Entrepreneurs: Actors and Practices of Space-Making under the Global Condition*, ed. Steffi Marung and Ursula Rao (Berlin: De Gruyter, 2023), 39–57.

Note on Terminology, Abbreviations, Transliteration, Calendar, and Maps

In any book about the Soviet Union, it is all but impossible to avoid using dozens of abbreviations and acronyms. The Soviet Union rested on a state bureaucracy and the Communist Party apparatus, and these institutions in Moscow were replicated throughout the Soviet republics. State structures were run by a Central Executive Committee (Tsentral'nyi ispolnitel'nyi komitet, TsIK) that decided administrative territorial issues until the 1936 constitutional reform. From 1923 until 1936, the All-Union TsIK was the formal head of the Soviet state. In turn, the Russian Socialist Federative Soviet Republic (RSFSR) had its All-Russian Central Executive Committee, the VTsIK (Vserossiiskii tsentral'nyi ispolnitel'nyi komitet); and the Ukrainian Socialist Soviet Republic (UkrSSR) had its All-Ukrainian Central Executive Committee, the VUTsVK (Vseukraïns'kyi tsentral'nyi vykonavchyi komitet).[1]

Within each TsIK were various subcommissions, whose work was supervised by the TsIK secretary. Likewise, each government (Sovet narodnykh komissarov, Sovnarkom or SNK) had its own set of commissions. Of these, the most important here is the State Planning Commission (Gosudarstvennaia planovaia komissiia, Gosplan). Gosplan, too, had regional and local commissions throughout the Bolshevik realm. The UkrSSR, for example, had UkrDerzhplan, while Kursk Guberniia had Kursk Gubplan.

State institutions within the Transcaucasian Federation (Zakavkazskaia sotsialisticheskaia federativnaia sovetskaia respublika, ZSFSR) mediated between the center in Moscow and the Soviet republics of Georgia, Armenia, and Azerbaijan from 1922 to 1936. Abbreviations for these institutions can easily be identified by the prefix Zak- for *zakavkazskii* (Transcaucasian), as in ZakTsIK, ZakSovnarkom, ZakGosplan, etc.

The Soviet Union's ruling communist party renamed itself several times. From 1918 to 1925, it was the Russian Communist Party

xiii

(Bolshevik) (Rossiiskaia kommunisticheskaia partiia [bol'shevikov], RKP[b]). Republican parties, such as the one in Ukraine, the KP(b)U (Komunistychna partiia [bil'shovykiv] Ukraïny), were formally independent. Between 1925 and 1952, the Soviet party called itself the All-Union Communist Party (Bolshevik) (Vsesoiuznaia kommunisticheskaia partiia [bol'shevikov], VKP[b]), which included the national parties of all the republics within the Soviet state, save for the RSFSR. There was no "Russian" branch of the party. The RSFSR had only the VKP(b). From 1952 to 1991, the party was known as the Communist Party of the Soviet Union (Kommunisticheskaia partiia Sovetskogo soiuza, KPSS), with branch parties in all the union republics except for the RSFSR.

Within the party, the Politburo (Politicheskoe biuro, Political Bureau) that rose to prominence during the Civil War was formally a commission of the Central Committee (Tsentral'nyi komitet, TsK), the governing organ of the party. It was during this period that the TsK in Moscow began to establish intermediate organs to supervise Soviet functionaries in remote regions. These organs were also often renamed, and their scope of action modified. For the Caucasus, especially the South Caucasus, there was the Kavbiuro (Kavkazskoe biuro TsK RKP[b]) and later the Zakkraikom (Transcaucasian Regional Committee, Zakavkazskii kraevoi komitet TsK RKP[b]) and for Central Asia the Turkkomissiia and later the Turkbiuro and the Sredazbiuro (Central Asian Bureau, Sredneaziatskoe biuro TsK RKP[b]). Both were dissolved during the 1930s. In addition, each Soviet Republic had its own Central Committee and Politburo—Ukrainian, Georgian, Belarusian, and so on.

Often reference is made to the different administrative units of the Soviet state during a period of transition. Between 1923 and 1929, old imperial designations for administrative units coexisted with new Soviet ones. The Russian Empire and the early Soviet state both used a three-tier administrative system. The Russian Empire had *gubernii* (provinces, governorates), *uezdy* (pre-reform counties) and *volosti* (shires), which the Soviet state replaced with *oblasti* (regions), *okruga* (post-reform counties) and *raiony* (districts). The old regime also had particular territorial entities such as the *namestnichestvo* (viceroyalty) in the Caucasus or Turkestan Krai in Central Asia. Under Soviet rule, the administration also used designations such as *krai* (border region). For administrative-territorial terms, I generally use Russian equivalents because Russian served as the lingua franca in policy debates. When necessary, I refer to administrative-territorial units using transliterations from the titular language of the republic at issue in brackets, for instance, the Ukrainian *povit* for uezd, the Armenian *šejan* for raion, or the Georgian *olk'i* for oblast.

Names of individuals reflect the multinational and multilingual Soviet state and change depending on a source's original language. For example, the first head of the Uzbek government can appear as Faizulla Khodzhaev in transliteration from Russian or as Fayzulla Xo'jayev in modern Uzbek, while the Azerbaijani commissar for agriculture in the 1920s is sometimes Dadash Buniat-Zade, transliterated from Russian, and sometimes Dadaş Bünyadzadə, as it appears in modern Azerbaijani. The head of the All-Union Commission for Raionirovanie appears as Saak Ter-Gabrielian in Russian or Sahak Ter-Gabrielyan in Armenian. To avoid confusion, I stick to the way names appear in the documents I consulted. I limit myself to romanization from Russian as well as Ukrainian (which the UkrSSR managed to introduce as an administrative language in the 1920s) according to a slightly adapted ALA-LC framework. The ZSFSR also used Russian as its lingua franca, as did Central Asia, but in the case of the latter, the national languages were still undergoing codification during the 1920s. For the names of towns and villages, I stick to the same approach. I use the spellings found in a document. The capital of the Georgian SSR, for example, was called Tiflis up to 1936. Only at that point did the city receive the name Tbilisi. The town that later became the capital of the Kyrgyz SSR was called Pishpek until 1926, Frunze between 1926 and 1991, and Bishkek after 1991. The current name of a locality is provided in parentheses when that appears potentially helpful.

The Soviet government moved from the Julian calendar to the Gregorian calendar in February 1918. For January 1918 and before, double dates indicate Old Style and (marked) New Style.

This book includes several historical maps. The process of border making is depicted as accurately as the underlying documents allow. However, factual errors cannot be excluded. Their sole purpose is to illustrate the debates analyzed. They have no legal value whatsoever. Please contact me if you find any mistakes.

Table 1. Administrative-territorial units in the Early Soviet Union

RUSSIAN	ARMENIAN	AZERBAIJANI	BELARUSIAN	GEORGIAN	KAZAKH	KYRGYZ	TAJIK	TURKMEN	UKRAINIAN	UZBEK	ENGLISH
губерния gubernia (gubernii)	նահանգ nahang	quberniya	губерня hubernia	გუბერნია gubernia	губерния guberniia	губерния guberniia	губерния guberniia	guberniya	губернія huberniia	guberna	province
уезд uezd (uezdy)	գավառ gavaŕ	qəza	павет pavet	მაზრა mazra	уезд uezd	уезд uezd	уезд uezd	uezd	повіт povit	uyezd	pre-reform county
волость[1] volost' (volosti)	տեղամաս[2] teġamas[2]	nahiyə	воласць volasts'	საბამასახლისო[3] samamasaxliso[3]	болыс bolys	болуш bolush	кент kent	volost	волость volost'	volost[4]	shire
область oblast' (oblasti)	մարզ marz	vilayəti	вобласць voblasts'	ოლქი olk'i	облыс oblys	облус oblus	вилоят viloiat	welaýat	область oblast'	viloyat	region
округ okrug (okruga)	օկրուգ okrug	daira[5]	акруга akruha	ოლქი olk'i	округ okrug	округ okrug	округ okrug	etrap	округа okruha	okrug	post-reform county
район raion (raiony)	շրջան šejan	rayon	раён raën	რაიონი raioni	аудан audan	район raion	ноҳия nohiia	raýon	район raion	rayon	district
край krai (kraia)	երկրամաս yerkranas	diyar	край krai	მხარე[6] mxare[6]	аймақ aimaq	край krai	кишвар kishvar	gyra or sebit	край krai	o'lka	border region

теми (груз.) temi	თემი t'emi	temi (Georg.)
кантон (кырг.) kanton	кантон kanton	canton (Kyrgyz)
участок (арм.) uchastok	գավառակ gavaṙak	uchastok (Arm.)

Note: Written in current orthography. The designation of administrative territorial units differed in the languages of the union republics. This table provides a comprehensive collection of these terms in all eleven official republican languages of the USSR in 1936 and their English translation.

1. The Caucasian Viceroyalty had a three-tier administrative-territorial order of *guberniia*, *uezd*, and *politseiskii uchastok* (police district). In addition, there was also a set of particular oblasti and okruga that were under military rule, e.g., Batum Oblast or Sukhum Okrug.
2. Before 1917 *politseiskii uchastok* could be called either ոստիկանական տեղամաս (ostikanakan teġamas) or simply տեղամաս (teġamas).
3. The terms თემი (t'emi) and სამამასახლისო (samamasaxliso) were used before 1917 as synonyms; the term ვოლოსტი (volosti) was also used in rare cases as a synonym.
4. Other Uzbek variants are *volust* and *bolost*.
5. In the 1920s Azerbaijan had a two-tier administrative-territorial order of qəza (uezd) and daira.
6. At least in the 1920s, the Russian term *krai* was also translated as ოლქი (olk'i).

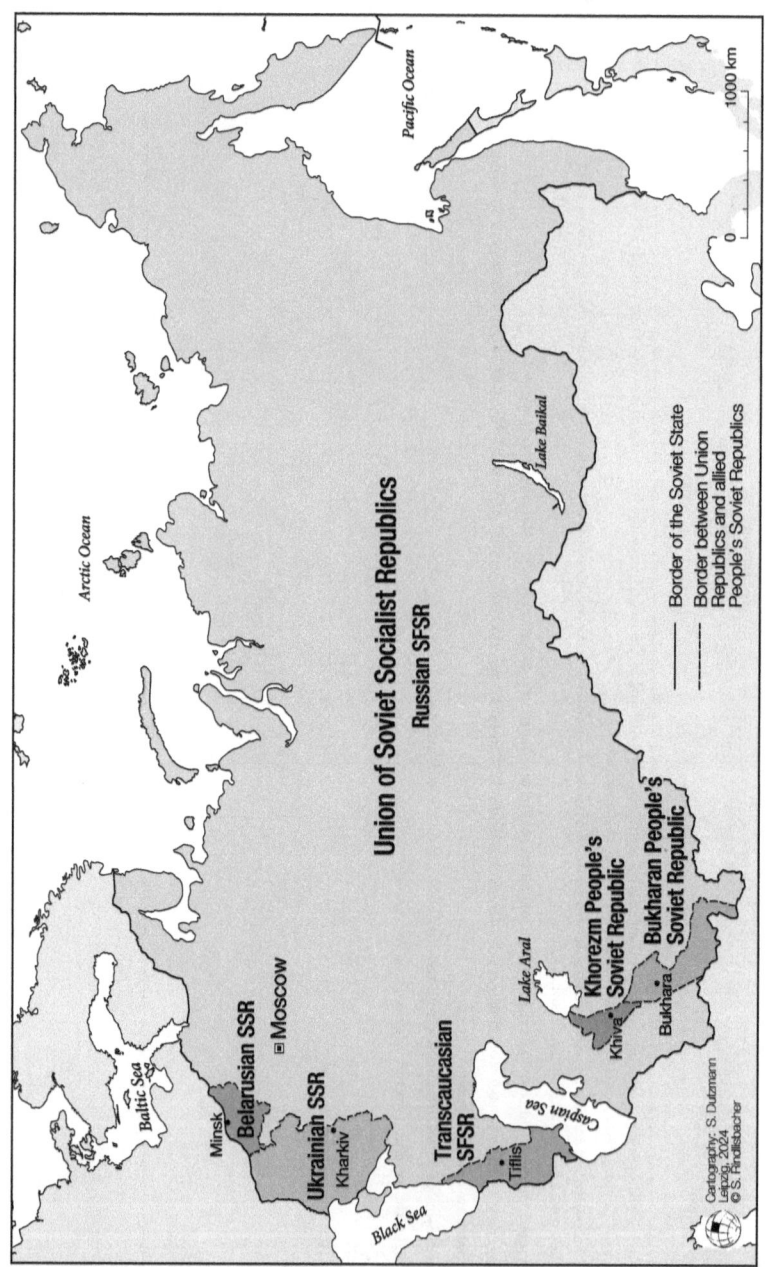

Figure 1. Political borders of the Soviet state, 1 July 1924.

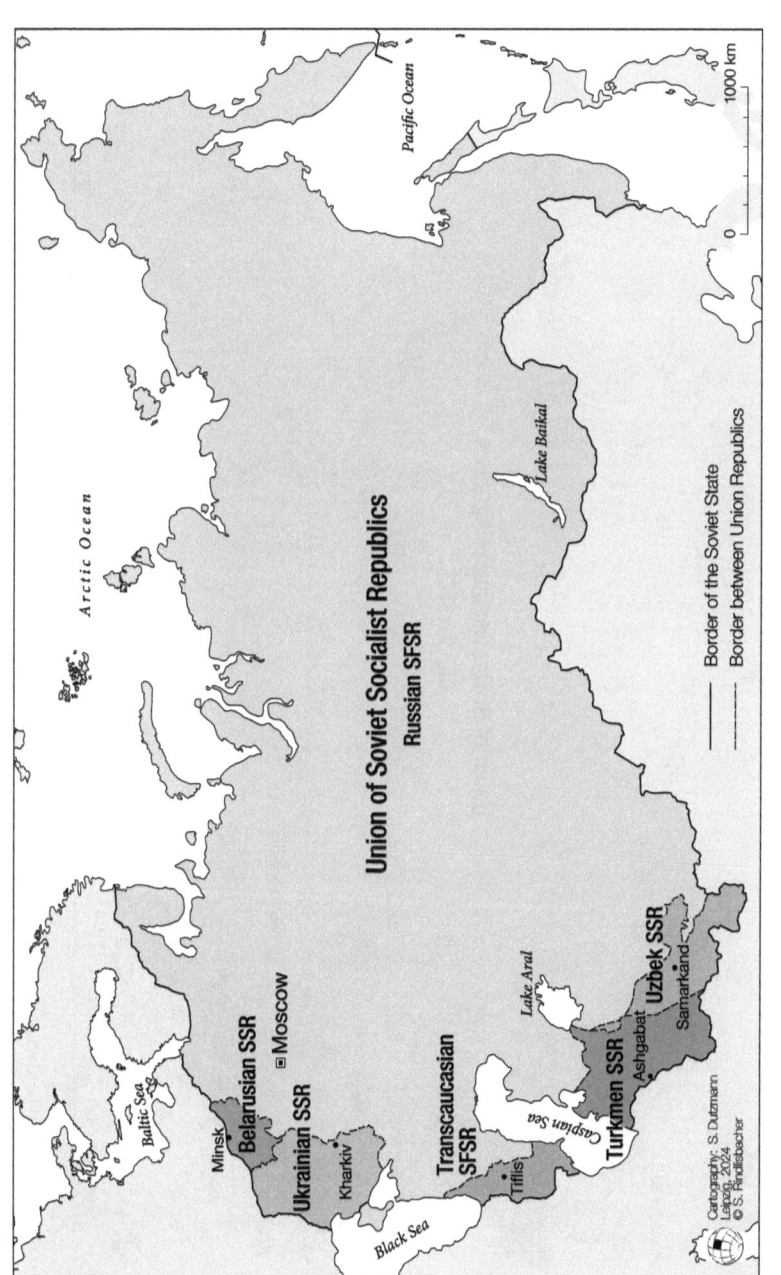

FIGURE 2. Political borders of the Soviet state, 15 April 1929.

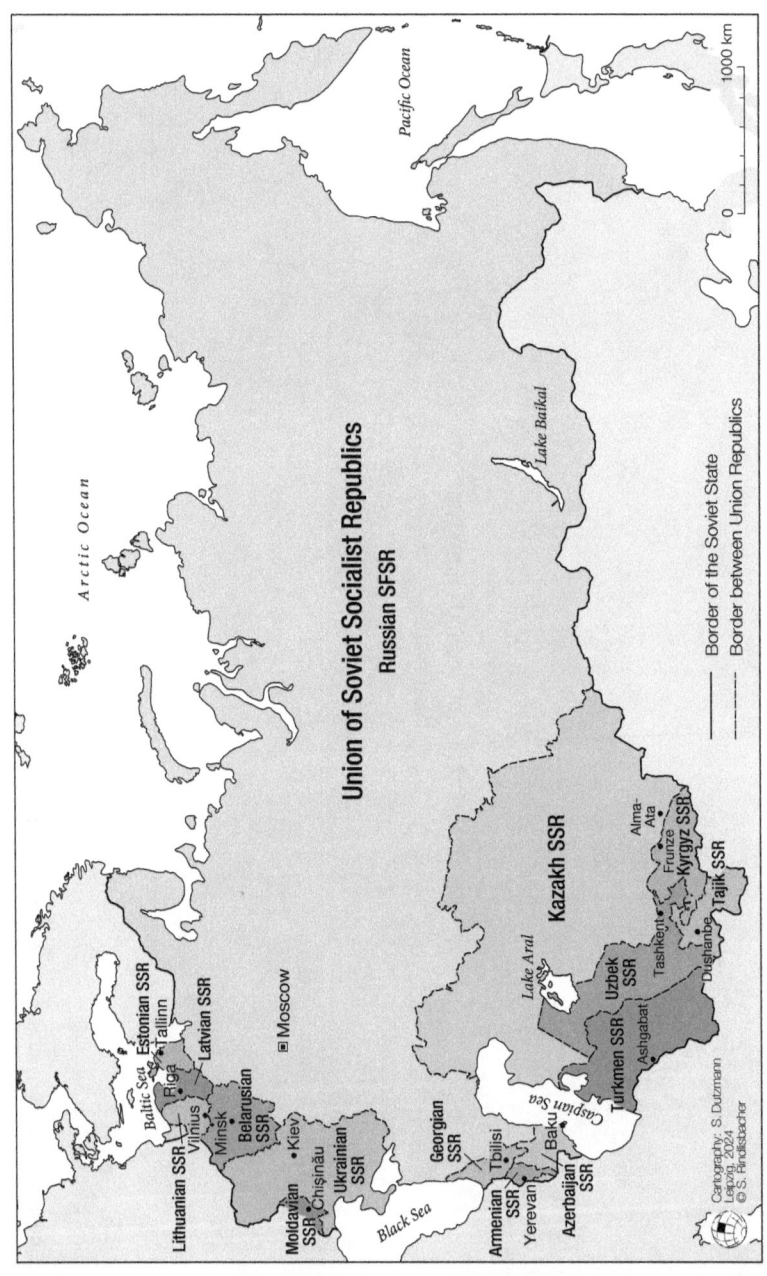

FIGURE 3. Political borders of the Soviet state, 1 July 1975.

Introduction

> They tell us that Russia is falling apart and is fracturing into separate republics, but we have nothing to fear. However, as many separate republics there may be, we will not be afraid. For us, it is not important where a state border runs, but that the union of the workers of all nations is preserved for the struggle against the bourgeois of any nation whatsoever.
>
> —Vladimir Lenin [Ul'ianov], 1917

> When it comes to the historical destiny of Russia and its peoples, Lenin's principles of state development were not just a mistake; they were worse than a mistake, as the saying goes. This became patently clear after the dissolution of the Soviet Union in 1991.
>
> —Vladimir Putin, 2022

In the settlement of Milove/Chertkovo, divided between Ukraine and Russia, the border caused difficulties in inhabitants' everyday lives. It mostly followed the railroad tracks and crossed right through the railway station. The local market on the Ukrainian side attracted many people, and for a while, the Ukrainian authorities were able to collect all the local market taxes. Subsequently, the Russian authorities lowered the taxes on their side to attract customers and sellers. The first party secretary in Starobil's'k District (*okruha*), where Milove was located, complained to his superiors that the bazaar had moved next to the railroad tracks and led to a lot of border—and by default track—crossings. "One day, an accident occurred when a steam engine hit somebody. The legs of the body were found on our side, while the head fell on the side of the North Caucasus [in Russia]. Engulfed by a huge crowd, our [Ukrainian police] and the police forces from the North Caucasus plunged into an argument. They were arguing over responsibility for writing the report and taking care of the body."[1]

This border incident, which happened in 1926, shows how, under Soviet rule, territorial issues mattered to different bureaucratic entities as well as to customers and sellers at the local bazaar. Ukraine and the Russian Socialist Federative Soviet Republic (RSFSR) were not only struggling over the location of the bazaar but also over the question of who would eventually control the railway station. It goes without saying that both sides tried to revise the republican border in their favor.

In principle, borders between Soviet republics could be crossed without much ado, yet problems nonetheless arose as soon as economic assets were involved.[2] These borders divided tax systems, official languages, and access to state property and institutions. Furthermore, they had an impact on career opportunities. Population groups previously assumed to be indifferent to nationalism began to adopt national frames as a strategy for defending daily interests.[3]

The authorities of Ukraine and the RSFSR as well as the party and state leadership in Moscow were aware of such border troubles. After the foundation of the Soviet Union in 1922, committees and commissions were tasked with establishing and revising borders between member republics: they were supposed to preclude such situations as in Milove/Chertkovo and ease the day-to-day functioning of local administrations. With some notable exceptions, these Soviet politicians and experts as well as engaged local citizens found viable solutions. National borders were, in their majority, defined in the 1920s and the beginning of the 1930s, and in 1991 the Soviet Union would break apart along these lines.

Territory and statehood in the post-Soviet space seem more uncertain than ever. Since 2022 Russia has been trying to revise borders that date back to the early days of the Soviet state. The Russian president has condemned Bolshevik nationality policies as a historical mistake.[4] This book shows not only why Lenin and his Bolshevik government embraced the nationality question, but also why and how they institutionalized it as a viable means of governance.[5] The making of national borders can be used as a lens through which to examine the Bolsheviks' fundamental shift from proletarian internationalism to ethnonational federalism sui generis. Creating, revising, and maintaining national territories proved to be a viable tool for structuring the Soviet state and managing its linguistic, economic, and cultural diversity.[6] In creating official maps, the communist government addressed the nationality question with borders in "red." Many state structures were initially improvised. The developing Soviet order was a product of trial and error.

The Soviet ruling elite of dedicated party cadres governed a heterogeneous realm. Marxism-Leninism served as a foundation for the stated mission to end the exploitative economic system and establish a universal, just, and rational order where humankind could realize its potential to the fullest extent.[7] Intending to expand the Soviet state until this new type of civilization would encompass the whole globe, the Bolsheviks established and maintained the instruments necessary to pursue such a mission—the internationalist cadre party, the Red Army, and the state bureaucracy.[8]

This universalist civilizational mission as well as the large heterogeneous territory the Bolsheviks ruled provide the core criteria of what can be understood as "imperial."[9] Whereas "nation-states" are ideally defined as homogeneous in linguistical and cultural matters, "empires" are defined by their social heterogeneity.[10] The perspective of "new imperial history" viewed large asks about the practices of managing conflicting interests that ensue from social heterogeneity and asymmetries of power.[11] Questions of belonging, administration, or territoriality—as they surfaced in Milove/Chertkovo—provide starting points for further analysis.[12]

In comparison to failed traditionalist, universalist empires such as the Ottoman Empire or China under the Qing dynasty, the Soviet state was inspired by a progressivist, rationalist mission, grounded in the European tradition of enlightenment. The Soviets shared this regard for the Enlightenment with the United States, their mightiest competitor on a global scale after the Second World War. In contrast to their American rivals, the Bolsheviks assumed that state and party institutions had to direct social development. Instead of an "invisible hand" of the market, an avant-garde elite were to realize this new social order with scientific precision.[13]

This Bolshevik political project ultimately failed, but its legacy continues to trouble the current world. Its way of nation building and border making is one of its most prominent legacies. After the Civil War, the Bolsheviks had to deal with the challenges of political, economic, and cultural heterogeneity. They had to find answers to what they perceived as economic backwardness, low cultural development, and national secessionism, and they developed a strategy that Francine Hirsch has described as "state sponsored evolutionism."[14] In searching for and implementing feasible solutions to conflicting interests, they had to adapt their universalist ideology to achieve—like the overseas empires of that time—higher-ranking goals of developing a "backward" economy.[15] In general, these solutions found and implemented in the 1920s were rationally elaborated and could improve exigencies of governance. This provided tantalizing opportunities. By creating, revising, and maintaining national-territorial entities, the Soviet state efficiently institutionalized its power and secured its reign over the margins.

Paul Werth has proposed that studying borders and their evolution allows us to "elucidate the place of Russia and the USSR in the wider world."[16] This book is a further step in that direction. The Bolsheviks' teleological presuppositions, their dialectical materialism, and all related intricate discussions had only a moderate impact on policy making in the different regions. The ban on factions, the ideal of party discipline, and the failure to perform it in practice are only examples of this gap between plan and reality.[17] The Bolsheviks developed a territorial structure according to the principles of "national self-determination," economic dependencies, and exigencies of governance. These principles were often in conflict with each other, and the politicians and experts involved had to find feasible settlements.[18]

We can contextualize these settlements from two different perspectives. On one hand, we can see them in a line with the internal reorganization of the European overseas empires in the late nineteenth and early twentieth centuries. On the other, we can connect them with the new ordering of Central and Southeastern Europe in the aftermath of the First World War.

All rising empires extend their outside borders, but by sheer necessity they must also create an internal structure. After the "Scramble for Africa" in the late nineteenth century, the European colonial powers, the French and British in particular, had to structure the administration of their new realms.[19] Whereas the borders between empires were defined at the green table in Berlin in 1885—such as those of today's Democratic Republic of the Congo—the territories within a given empire were compartmentalized differently. For instance, the borders French authorities drew between Algeria and Tunisia or those of Niger have political relevance up to the present day.[20]

Such intra-imperial borders share certain similarities with those drawn between Soviet republics as particular commissions were installed and tasked with finding feasible solutions. In the African colonial context, their creation was far from arbitrary and often involved expertise in ethnography, geography, and economy, but the colonialized populations and their representatives were excluded from the decision-making process. However, deliberate involvement of local representatives in the ruling elites and at the very center sets the Soviet cases clearly apart from those in colonial Africa.²¹ The deliberate cooptation of natives—as long as they promised not to be anti-communist—into the field of power serves as a crucial argument against the use of the term "colonial" in the Soviet context.²² This is not simple formalism, as excluding regional and local elites from the higher echelons of power appears to be a major driver for emancipatory movements in colonized societies.²³ Today some researchers expand the term "colonial" to define a "fundamental matrix of power, operating through the control of four interrelated domains: economy, authority or governmentality, gender and sexuality, and production of knowledge and subjectivity."²⁴ However, such a far-reaching approach encompasses every asymmetrical relationship—including, for instance, that between urban and rural communities—and is thus barely helpful as an analytical category.

In modern colonial empires such as the British, Spanish, Portuguese, Belgian, or Dutch, the colonialized were deliberately "othered" and *by law* excluded from the field of power. Moreover, the metropole considered itself culturally superior and opened the colonized economies up to imperial exploitation.²⁵ For the early Soviet case, these two basic criteria are questionable. All people living on Soviet soil shared the same citizenship. The center in Moscow subscribed at least to the ideal of developing all regions equally and not exploiting one region for the sake of another. Moreover, as Terry Martin has shown in his *Affirmative Action Empire*, "backwardness" even became a valuable asset for regional activists when including and binding them within the state and party structures.²⁶

In addition to similarities to intra-imperial structuring, the Bolsheviks' claim for "national self-determination" resembles the restructuring of Central and Southeastern Europe at the Paris Peace Conference in 1919–1920. Here the victorious powers took that slogan as a guiding theme for the new order. In Paris, the victorious powers developed a set of tools for reshaping Europe after the horrors of the First World War. The nation-state was perceived as the new ideal, while minorities had to be protected by special legislation. In defining borders, the Entente diplomats considered whether a certain nation was among the winners, like Poland, or the vanquished, like Hungary. Furthermore, they talked about aspects of cultural superiority and geostrategy. Finally, they also discussed and organized plebiscites in contested areas.²⁷

The Bolsheviks refused to adopt the categories used by the Paris delegates because they could neither distinguish between victorious and vanquished nationalities nor refer to aspects of cultural superiority.

They would also not risk mobilizing the population for plebiscites. Even worse, their dialectical categories (bourgeoisie/proletariat, oppressive/oppressed, and instinctive/rational) were of no practical use. Of course, the politicians and experts involved established categories for "efficient" solutions to territorial issues such as nationality, economy, or exigencies of governance.[28] They understood their decisions were being closely observed abroad, especially in Eastern Europe. The practical results would showcase Soviet policy making in general and thus had the potential to attract or repel populations beyond the Bolshevik realm.[29] Terry Martin condensed this approach in his famous idea of the "Piedmont Principle."[30] Studying bordering practices allows us to explore how the Soviet state evolved as a "work-in-progress" while the Bolsheviks discussed and evaluated different tools of power.[31]

Research on Soviet nationality policies has undergone a decisive shift in the last forty years. Political scientists and historians such as Robert Conquest, Olaf Caroe, and Hélène Carrère d'Encausse once suspected the Bolsheviks of using the slogan of "self-determination" to simply play the Soviet nationalities against one another; some post-Soviet historians, such as Rahim Masov or Arslan Koichiev, have continued to adhere to such narratives.[32] Kate Brown later suspected some sort of "gerrymandering" during the creation of Soviet national territories.[33] Since the opening of the archives in almost all of the post-Soviet republics, hundreds of academic works have appeared to challenge this one-sided approach.

Revisionist historians including Jeremy Smith, Ronald G. Suny, and Gerhard Simon have detached themselves from simplistic assumptions. They have explored such questions as how Soviet nationality policies culminated in *korenizatsiia* (indigenization).[34] In particular, Terry Martin, Francine Hirsch, and Juliette Cadiot have revealed the mechanisms of how the realization of national narratives was closely linked to the promotion of national languages and the all-union census of 1926.[35] Hirsch even speaks of a process of "double assimilation," as the party's intention behind all the affirmative policies was to Sovietize the population by nationalizing culture and language.[36] However, these revisionist scholars could not explain why the Bolsheviks ultimately embraced the concept of nationality and tied it to territoriality, despite having an alternative concept in the drawer. Hirsch and Martin emphasize that multiple actors were engaged, and both historians point primarily to the meso-level—the agency of regional officials and experts—but not to the micro level in the margins. Here I show how the creation, revision, and maintenance of national territories offered a viable tool to perform and institutionalize state power—a solution much more pragmatic than the alternative "Austromarxist" concept of *raionirovanie* (commonly translated as "regionalization").

There is no shortage of insightful regional studies on Soviet external and internal border making. Studies on the evolution of the Soviet Union's external borders depict the intricate interplay between modernizing state authorities and local strategies of subversion.[37] Those on internal border making all point to the broad agency of regional party and state actors. Here politicians and experts relied on national and economic rationales as well as exigencies of governance in solving territorial issues. The latter all focus on a particular case—be it Uzbekistan, Karelia, or Bessarabia.[38] By default, these analyses do not compare the territories they study with other regions of the Soviet state. Their regional foci show an imbalance: Central Asia has attracted the most attention, in part because of the intricate nature of the borders established there. Except for works published in the languages of the republics concerned, there are few, if any, studies of how national-territorial questions in the South Caucasus or the western part of the union were resolved.[39] However, a comparison of how the party and state managed issues of national diversity in the core regions of Soviet federalism—Ukraine, the South Caucasus, and Central Asia—provides insights not only into their policy making but also into the roots of current territorial conflicts.[40] In addition, such a comparison underlines the particularly problematic position of the South Caucasus region within the Soviet state.

Two particular issues concerning the creation of the Soviet empire are still disputed. The first is whether experts had any impact on early policy making. Whereas Francine Hirsch and Juliette Cadiot have highlighted the experts' influence, Adeeb Khalid has contended that Bolshevik politicians often chose to ignore them.[41] My comparison of the three core regions of Soviet federalism offers a more inclusive and intricate approach that demonstrates contradictions in policy. Soviet ethnographic and economic experts enjoyed greater agency in the decision-making process in Eastern Europe than in the South Caucasus or Central Asia.

The second issue revolves around whether the Bolsheviks "artificially" created national territories. Christian Teichmann has asserted that the party leadership under Stalin invented nationalisms and nations where none had existed before, whereas Adeeb Khalid and Gero

Fedtke have countered that such nationalisms grew out of an authentic response of progressivist indigenous elites to the challenges of modernization.[42] I show that nationalism was nowhere a foreign idea. However, in the most contentious case, that of Central Asia, the party leadership began to support one faction of indigenous communists, which promoted a strict national delimitation, and to ignore the one that favored alternative, federalist approaches.

In the 1920s Soviet institutions on various levels put a lot of effort and money into solving the problem of territoriality and adopted its product as a valuable power tool. Their debates were not staged by the party leadership, nor was any universal blueprint employed. Party directives provided a rough discursive framework. Some Soviet territorial solutions may seem awkward: for example, the profusion of enclaves in the Fergana Valley, where several Uzbek and Tajik villages and even small towns are surrounded by Kyrgyz territory, whereas some Kyrgyz villages are completely encapsuled by Uzbek territory. These border-making processes and the rationales behind them are not absurd but grounded in certain rationales. Some early Soviet politicians and experts considered nationality a necessary but transient phenomenon in history, and initially, they thought it would fade away like the state itself.[43] Within the first decade of Soviet rule, this initial assumption changed. The state and party leadership realized that national entities and their maintenance eased the performance and institutionalization of party and state.[44]

Contrary to previous assumptions, Stalin was not the driving force behind the demarcation of borders, but he was the one who brought an end to the seemingly boundless debates over territoriality. He then used the institutionalized national-territorial structure as one of his power tools. "National deviations"—that is, questioning the national-territorial status quo—appeared to him as particularly harmful to the all-encompassing modernization policy, as they diverted resources and attention from the main objective.

To tackle the complexity of the Soviet order, I use the term "territory" as a basic concept. Like time, space is a fundamental category of human perception, and by these two categories humans relate to themselves and others. Perceptions of space are by-products of social interaction. Territory is logically derived from space. Whereas space as a general term is diffuse and vague (like the term "Eastern Europe"), territory is clearly defined by recognized (or contested) boundaries for the actors involved.[45] Territorialization is the result of epistemological processes that create a territory within a space whereupon structures of power receive a seemingly fixed geographic shape. As a result, borders define what or who is inside and outside a territory, providing the frames for official responsibilities. In cases of bad border drawing, this can lead to conflicts like the one in Milove/Chertkovo. Hence looking at territorialization always means examining political practices, power structures, and their asymmetries.[46]

Such an understanding of territory provides a viable conceptual link to the "new imperial history." Soviet politicians and experts solved functional problems and simultaneously identified them as pragmatic ways to institutionalize their power. Analyzing such political practices shows that the early Soviet state was more than simply a "façade federation" or "pseudo federation."[47] Even though the Bolshevik party structure was authoritarian, territorialization not only involved party elites but included regional experts as well, and they even offered windows of opportunity for local agency. They thus included the margins—that is, regional and local activists—into the imperial power structures.

The ideas of natural and artificial borders dominated the older literature. In the last five decades, this essentialist perception has successfully been called into question. It is almost superfluous to state that all political borders, national ones included, are human-made.[48] Soviet functionaries projected borders mainly on physical markers that facilitated the economic exploitation of a certain area. In the RSFSR-Ukrainian borderland this was local use of fields and pastures, with the option to adapt the republican border if land use among neighboring villages changed. In the South Caucasus mountain ridges helped to define republican borders; in Central Asia the dividing line would be set between steppe and irrigated oases. In barely inhabited steppe or desert regions around the Aral Sea republican borders were simply drawn with a ruler on the map.

The terms "central," "regional," and "local" serve to distinguish macro, meso, and micro perspectives. Central stands for the party and state leadership in Moscow and its experts; they shared the greater vision of constructing socialism in a backward country. Territorialization meant for them first and foremost finding a convenient structure to advance modernization. At the regional level—that is to say, at the level of the union republics, such as Ukraine, or the greater regions (oblasti or gubernii) of the RSFSR, such as the Urals or the North Caucasus—things already looked different. Regional functionaries and their experts also propagated the construction of socialism, of course, but they justified it in terms of meeting regional or national demands, such as Ukrainization or promoting certain sectors of their production base. At the local level, the lowest and smallest of the three, the demarcation of borders between republics affected land use among neighboring villages. There peasants feared that they might lose access to the fields, pastures, and forests that they had previously used if they happened to be on the "wrong" side of an envisioned boundary. Thus they began to link basic needs for subsistence with national frames.[49]

From this micro perspective, the modes of demarcating borders under Soviet rule were comparable to considerations unfolding in Central and Southeastern Europe at the same time. Several studies offer valuable insights. Laura Di Fiore depicts the dialectical interaction between state institutions and local populations when borders were defined and implemented and concludes that the "actual act of mapping [borders] had a performative power, since it did not merely reproduce what was real, having also the capacity to create it."[50] Relying on documents from post-World War I boundary commissions, Peter Haslinger and Catherine Gibson have provided case studies of such local mobilizations in the Hungarian-Czechoslovak and the Estonian-Latvian borderlands.[51] In a study focusing on Western Europe, Jacobo García-Álvarez and Paloma Puente-Lozano further elaborate that such border commissions act by default as arbiters between different groups, contexts, and levels of power.[52] These commissions thus have the potential to settle local conflicts and thus perform state power over the margins.

The general perspective of this book is synchronic, focusing on the 1920s and early 1930s. Krista A. Goff's *Nested Nationalism: Making and Unmaking Nations in the South Caucasus* analyzes the recursive interplay of state-sponsored promotion and discrimination and the long-term effects on national identities, focusing on the example of Soviet Azerbaijan. There the policies implemented by the Azerbaijani government led eventually to the marginalization of dispersed communities such as the Talysh.[53] Internal Soviet border making had a decisive impact on minorities. In a long-term perspective, these decisions contributed to the marginalization of herders migrating between summer and winter pastures divided by republican borders in the South Caucasus and in Central Asia. This aspect will be problematized, but its comprehensive analysis remains a topic for further research.

To discuss Soviet efforts to resolve territorial issues, I start chapter 1 with the ambiguous slogan of "national self-determination." In contrast to Woodrow Wilson, who considered the nation-state a fundamental building block for a liberal international order, Lenin saw in this slogan a useful antidote to national secessionism within a unitary socialist state. In 1917 it was not yet clear what this slogan could mean in practice. The RSFSR thus became an experimental field with trial and error in national-ethnographic and economic territorialization. Chapter 2 then tracks the subsequent institutional competition between supporters of national self-determination and the "Austromarxist" concept of raionirovanie. Experts at Gosplan promoted an administrative-territorial structure following economic considerations because they saw non-territorial solutions for the nationality question as most apt for the Soviet state. During the 1920s this alternative lost more and more support because ethnonational structuring had much greater practical success in mobilizing party cadres and the masses.

In the main three chapters, I analyze and compare regional case studies of regulating national border issues. I begin chapter 3 with the process of determining and revising the RSFSR-Ukrainian border, where the party leadership kept a tight control over the decision making and where the Piedmont Principle had little effect on the result. The decision makers even feared to mobilize the population too much. In chapter 4, in contrast, the delimitation of Central Asia in 1924, directed by party functionaries, had a key effect in mobilizing first political elites and then the population for the Soviet project. Whereas in chapters 3 and 4 the party leadership played a major role in directing how territorialization would proceed, chapter 5 shows how Moscow deliberately kept itself out of the border revision in the South Caucasus. The state and party were well aware of the tensions among the three Transcaucasian republics and avoided taking sides. They thus tasked regional politicians with searching for solutions. However, one side or the other often obstructed their implementation. In the end, large parts of the borders, especially those between Armenia and Azerbaijan, remained badly defined. This made the South Caucasus the odd region out within the Soviet federal system.

After 1929, the Stalinization of party and state led to a fundamental change in decision making and documentation. Whereas there are several bookshelves of archival documents on territorial questions in the 1920s, there is an acute scarcity of such materials after Stalin's rise to power. Most top-down orders were given orally and remained undocumented. Chapter 6 puts the transfer of Crimea in 1954 in this context and deconstructs the still popular myth of Crimea as simply being "Nikita Khrushchev's gift" to Ukraine. Gifts were no category of Soviet policy making. Throughout Soviet history, the once-established considerations of economic dependencies, nationality, and exigencies of governance remained the pivot of territorial thinking.

Within the first decade of the Soviet state, nationality became a pragmatic tool in everyday policy. Nationalized institutions did a good job of exerting Soviet power in non-Russian regions. Other than the party, which had relatively few members, and the Red Army, these institutions provided viable conduits between the population and the imperial center in Moscow. As the first decade gave way to the second, a decisive majority of Soviet state and party functionaries realized this potential and thus began to make it a core policy. This book tells the story of this slow, almost subliminal shift.

Chapter 1

The Leninian Moment
Making the Soviet State

> Russia is a prison house of nations not only because the tsarist government has a belligerent-feudal character ... but also because the Polish and other bourgeoisies have sacrificed national freedom and democracy [*demokratizm*] in general for the interests of capitalist expansion.
>
> —Vladimir Lenin, 1915

"It is not possible to establish the projected new state border according to the principle of nationality. To satisfy one part of the population means an unsatisfactory decision for the other part of the population."[1] This is how Sergei Vvedenskii concluded an expert opinion on border revisions between Soviet Ukraine and Soviet Russia in 1924. Acting as an expert for Gosplan, the state's economic planning agency, he summed up the fundamental problem that had been troubling the eastern part of Europe, particularly since the end of the First World War.[2] Once national belonging was supposed to define statehood and territory, conflicts were inevitable, as ethnographically and linguistically homogeneous regions are rare. Regions rich in diversity present a particular challenge to political leaders who base their policy for a new universal order on slogans of national self-determination. The Bolsheviks closely followed the debates at the Paris Peace Conference. However, they refrained from approaches developed there, such as ideas of "cultural superiority," minority rights, or referenda in contested areas. When structuring the early Soviet state, they deliberately opted for alternatives such as raionirovanie. Minority issues were addressed by unique form of compartmentalization.

National Self-Determination—a Challenging Promise

It is rather surprising that the Bolsheviks, as outspoken Marxists and thereby proletarian internationalists, adopted a stance on the nationality question that did not aim for indifference but for categorization. Before the Great War, Josef Stalin, became engaged in the debate on nationality and helped to define the Bolshevik mainstream approach on this matter. In 1913 he was a minor activist in underground circles. Nevertheless, while in Viennese exile, he entered the debate over so-called Austromarxist approaches.

In Vienna Austrian social democrats—Otto Bauer, Max Adler, and Karl Renner among others—tried to mitigate the nationality issues within the Habsburg Empire. State institutions were expected to counteract centrifugal tendencies arising from national movements by creating new paths to unity in a diverse polity. In a context of imperial compromises, these Austromarxists claimed that national and economic conflicts should be solved by means of personal autonomy. Diverse communities should live on the same territory, but they should have access to autonomous education and separate cultural institutions. Such ideas propagated territorial inclusion instead of division.[3] Under such circumstances, Bauer concluded that socialism would eventually emerge from the working class itself. National self-determination was not a contradiction to class consciousness but its useful supplement.[4]

Stalin rejected such considerations, at least superficially. In his famous article on "Marxism and the Nationality Question," he linked the concept of nationality with that of territoriality. In response to the Austromarxist position, he produced a set of prerequisites for defining a group of people as a nationality (*natsiia*). To do so, they had to share a common language, culture, economic way of life, *and* territory.[5] In essence, he thus pivoted the Bolshevik stance in nationality policies toward approaches of territorial division instead of inclusion. Refusing inclusive approaches such as those proposed by the Jewish Bund, Stalin took arguments from opponents of Austromarxism, namely from Czech and Polish social democrats.[6] Consciously or not, Stalin shared his essentialist perception of nationality with Bauer as the latter considered it as a biological as well as a cultural phenomenon.[7] Moreover, they both highlighted a politically advantageous connection between class consciousness and nationality.

The leader of the Bolshevik Party, Vladimir Lenin, adopted this idea of national categorization when he soon after reflected on national self-determination. However, his conception was theoretical. He never intended to contribute to its realization.[8] In his view, the formal right to secession and independence in a socialist state would preclude national oppression. In contrast to Austromarxists like Bauer as well as his Menshevik rivals, Lenin was convinced that the popular masses, the proletariat, would never gain appropriate class consciousness on their own. They had to be instructed by a vanguard party.[9]

Lenin also insisted on another principle: in a future socialist republic, there would be no compulsory state language. Even if he agreed that there had to be a lingua franca, no one would be forced to learn it, because compulsion would lead only to rejection, resistance, and ultimately secessionism. Every community could conduct schooling and local administration in its own language, and a common, universal language would be taught solely as an elective.[10] The "leader of the global proletariat" would stick to this principle until his very last conscious moments.[11]

The Bolsheviks did not act in an intellectual vacuum. During the First World War, all sides began to sympathize with the idea of basing the postwar order in Europe on the principle of nation-states. Germany, for instance, recreated a Polish statehood in 1916 to mobilize Polish nationalism for its war effort.[12] US President Woodrow Wilson presented a new order for Europe in his Fourteen Points in January 1918. Whereas Wilson was not clear about the fate of Austria-Hungary, his vision would lead multinational empires to yield to liberal, democratic, and independent nation-states.[13] After the Entente's victory, such ideas would have a tremendous impact on the 1919–1920 peace negotiations in Paris. Manela Erez coined the trope of the "Wilsonian moment" when analyzing the global impact of these negotiations.

However, Erez, together with Larry Wolff and Leonard V. Smith, have stressed that Wilson's calls for national self-determination had to compete with Lenin's. Both were similar in their influence on postwar Europe.[14] Even though their views on European and global politics mutually excluded each other, they nonetheless shared the same anti-imperialist slogans such as the need to put an end to "secret diplomacy."[15] Yet despite numerous works about the impact this "Wilsonian moment" had on Central and Southeastern Europe, there are few comprehensive studies on its "Leninian" counterpart.[16] This is even more surprising because the Bolsheviks faced challenges similar to those of the delegates in Paris.

Despite the similar wording, an ideological abyss separated Wilson's and Lenin's ideas of national self-determination. Wilson's concept was grounded in a liberal order where different nations would organically govern themselves and would take part in a global regime under a league of nations. However, Wilson restricted this self-determination to "civilized" nations, deliberately excluding non-European, colonized communities. In contrast to Wilson, Lenin promised self-determination to all communities without discrimination, notwithstanding their level of social development, but he expected that ideologically firm activists would lead them toward the communist future.

In Paris, mostly at the Quai d'Orsay, the victorious allied powers met in January 1919 for months of negotiations over how to redraw the borders of Central and Southeastern Europe after the collapse of the Habsburg, Ottoman, and Romanov empires. Nation-states were to replace the old imperial order, and the Bolshevik revolution had to be contained. The representatives of new states met with those of the established Entente powers.[17] Together, they expected to found a new order in Europe along the lines of Wilson's Fourteen Points.[18] The statesmen arrived with a host of ethnographers, geographers, and economists, who provided expertise about one party or another party to the discussion.[19] The hierarchy was more or less set, as the Big Four (the United States, the United Kingdom, France, and Italy) could dictate their terms to Austria, Hungary, the Ottoman Empire, Bulgaria, and in particular Germany. Because Central and Southeastern Europe constituted a rag rug in ethnographic terms, establishing state borders proved extremely difficult. Every possible outcome produced new majorities and minorities.[20]

The decision makers in Paris had two basic tools: on one hand, preferential and discriminatory treatment and, on the other, regional plebiscites. The division of countries into winner and vanquished nations served as the basis for preference and discrimination. Whereas Hungarian politicians and their experts had little reason to believe their claims would receive a fair hearing vis-à-vis the Western allies, Romanian or Polish delegates and their aides could be sure that the Big Four would pay attention to their concerns.[21] In ambiguous cases, the victorious powers organized plebiscites, as they did in Schleswig, Upper Silesia, or Carinthia. Although the framework of such referenda was often designed to favor one side, the Entente powers as a rule respected the outcome of such popular votes.[22] Furthermore, the Big Four deliberately dismissed population resettlements. The new nation-states had to provide legal protection to minority populations, guaranteed by the peace treaties and then by the League of Nations.[23]

In Paris, problems arose when plebiscites or the system of winners and losers could not provide an answer. This was the case in Istria and Dalmatia—which Italy and the Kingdom of Serbs, Croats, and Slovenes both claimed—or in the Polish-Czechoslovak border region around Teschen. In the case of Burgenland, the delegates in Paris had to decide which vanquished nation should be awarded this territory: Austria or Hungary. Even though the order created during the Paris conference appeared highly unsatisfactory to certain parts of the population, the framework of the delegates' deliberations appeared transparent.[24]

The February Revolution in Petrograd and the fall of Nicholas II led not only to a spring of the soviets but also to a spring of national movements in the margins of the Russian Empire. With the rupture of central authority after March 1917, regional forces gained momentum. These included the Ukrainian movement with its institutionalization in the form of the Central Rada, the Belarusian movement in the west, the Ozakom in the South Caucasus, the Alash movement in the Kazakh steppe, and the Jadids in Central Asia. Although a party rooted in a class-based ideology, the Bolsheviks had to make at least some conceptual offers to the non-Russian population. When aspiring for state power, their party showed a great deal of political pragmatism, at least in words.[25]

In November 1917, after the Bolsheviks had seized state power, the new government proclaimed national self-determination one of its core policies.[26] What this meant in practice, however, had by no means been resolved. Moreover, leading party members such as Gleb Krzhizhanovskii, Martin Latsis, and Nikolai Bukharin subjected the entire notion to constant fire on ideological grounds. They argued that national divisions would be detrimental to a future socialist state.[27] Their "internationalist" approach may have been appropriate for debates among comrades, but it would prove counterproductive to winning over potential allies in a civil war.

With the dramatic failure of the Baku Commune and the problems of ethnic tensions in Soviet Central Asia the Bolsheviks learned the hard way to comprehensively address the issue of nationality.[28] As a result, "internationalist," class-based political ideas began to lose much of their appeal. This does not mean, however, that the advocates of affirmative nationality policies had closed ranks in unanimity. Most issues in this regard remained open to debate. Should national self-determination mean formal independence or just some sort of cultural autonomy? What was the function of the Bolshevik Party within this new framework? The party and state leadership had to find answers to what they considered as the nationality question (*natsional'nyi vopros*). Thus they had to formulate and revise "nationality policies" in a set of administrative, propagandistic, and cultural measures. In the wake of the October Revolution in 1917, Stalin became commissar for nationality affairs, and his essentialist conceptions began to influence the new order. During the Russian Civil War, the Bolsheviks succeeded in keeping large parts of the shattered Russian Empire together.[29]

As noted, Lenin viewed the formal right of national self-determination and rejection of a compulsory state language as preconditions for cooperation among people of different linguistic and cultural backgrounds. In the first years after the Bolshevik coup, the structure of the Soviet empire remained a work-in-progress, subject to constant change day in and day out. In practice, too, party leaders showed a great deal of flexibility in their dealings with regional actors. This became apparent in the evolution of the institutional framework of the Russian Socialist Federative Soviet Republic (RSFSR).

When dealing with national-ethnographic issues, leading Bolsheviks relied exclusively on their own activists, politicians, and experts. In stark contrast to the expertise on hand in Paris, the Communist Party directed the production of knowledge in the Soviet state. Even though not all Soviet experts had to be party members, they were expected to think within a technocratic framework that did not contradict the Bolsheviks' teleological weltanschauung.[30] They rejected out of hand any ideologically wayward approaches or "deviations" submitted by experts and intellectuals. "Philosophy steamers" bound for the West in 1922 were the most spectacular expression of the Bolsheviks' rejection of expertise that failed to conform.[31] As mentioned above, the Bolsheviks could not distinguish between winning and losing nations as the delegates in Paris had. Of course, they could differentiate between "oppressing," "advanced" and "oppressed," "backward" nations, and they did reject "Great Russian chauvinism," but in practice, such categories proved to be of little help. In principle, the party considered all nationalities equal.[32]

Ideally, a territory would be associated with only one nationality.[33] All of the other population segments would count as minorities. These minorities could form an autonomous subunit only if they lived compactly in one area, because minority rights were—with a few exceptions—associated with a given territory. Thus decisions to attach certain territories to one or another national unit could give rise to secondary issues.

From the start, the RSFSR was an awkward federal republic. To analyze the formation and evolution of its intricate structure would require a separate book.[34] Here it is possible only to provide a general outline so that readers have necessary background information for the chapters that follow. Due in particular to Lenin's constant exhortations, the party accepted that "Great Russian chauvinism" posed the greatest danger to cohesion within the Bolshevik power structure. In the early Soviet state, Russians were considered the only fully developed nationality with their own proletariat and bourgeoisie.[35]

Borrowing a metaphor from Iosif Vareikis, one of those dedicated party activists, Yuri Slezkine has described the structure of the Soviet state as a communal apartment. There all of the families have separate rooms according to their size, and they all share common spaces such as the kitchen, corridors, and bathrooms.[36] Drawing on this metaphor, it was possible to designate each separate Soviet territory by the name of a nationality. Because the party promoted all of the previously "oppressed" nationalities in their historical development, each and every one of them was expected to get its own territory. Any space that was not claimed by a nationality was left undesignated. Within the Soviet framework, this space was simply called the RSFSR. As members of the developed nationality, Russians were denied party support and thus had nothing to claim in their name. The RSFSR occupied the large space in the middle of Slezkine's communal apartment as well as shared rooms such as the kitchen and the bathroom. But even if this metaphor may seem insightful for us today, it is nonetheless a description post factum. We must turn it upside down to better understand the making of Soviet nationality policies.

In January 1918, the Bolshevik government declared Soviet Russia (i.e., the territory of the former Russian Empire without Finland) to be a federation of "free nations," but it was unclear how this federative form would be filled in terms of content.[37] Once this great expanse descended into civil war, Bolshevik territory was in a state of constant flux. Political entities, such as the Lithuanian-Belarusian Socialist Soviet Republic (Litbel) or the Donetsk-Krivoi Rog Soviet Republic, split off from the RSFSR, enjoyed a fleeting moment in the sun, and then disappeared as quickly as they had appeared. Other national entities, such as the Volga German Workers' Commune (Trudovaia kommuna nemtsev Povolzh'ia) or the Bashkir Republic in the Urals, proved more stable. Over time, however, such political concessions led to the creation of a certain routine and the establishment of patterns for dealing with the nationality question. Thus the initial Soviet state was made up of improvisations that over time crystallized into long-term institutions. In retrospect, Lenin saw the beginning of his government as a work-in-progress. He expressed this with a bon mot that he ascribed to Napoleon—"*on s'engage, et puis on voit*" (first we engage [in a battle] and then . . . we will see [what happens]).[38]

Lara Douds has analyzed this structural crystallization in much greater detail. The party, in particular the Politburo, achieved its dominance over state affairs only after 1919. The centralized party structure was, like the heterogeneous Soviet state, the result of a formation process that unfolded under the harsh conditions of civil war and economic crisis.[39] Douds argues that the Central Executive Committee (VTsIK), the nominal head of the RSFSR, and the Council of People's Commissars (Sovnarkom)—that is, the government—began to lose the political initiative after Yakov Sverdlov died in early 1919 and Lenin fell ill in 1921.[40] However, state institutions, particularly the TsIKs in the union republics, maintained at least some agency during the 1920s.

The first basic distinctive feature in Soviet federalism, one that would endure until 1991, came in response to the question whether a given entity should be considered legally separate from RSFSR structures. In 1918 Soviet Ukraine, the Provisional Polish Revolutionary Committee, and Soviet Finland were clearly excluded. Only in the first case were the Bolsheviks able to maintain their dominance. The other former western parts of the Russian Empire succeeded in suppressing domestic revolutionary efforts, expelling the Red Army with German and Entente support, and creating internationally recognized independent states.

The first constitution of the RSFSR, adopted on 10 June 1918, formally granted the possibility of creating territorial entities with autonomous status.[41] However, amid the state decay, mutinous armies, foreign interventions, and secession movements in the border regions, the Soviet government was engaged in a daily struggle for its political survival. Despite the criticism from Nikolai Bukharin and others, the government felt an affirmative national policy afforded them an advantage in fighting the White Army.[42] In the border regions, it helped them turn the imperial Whites' Russian nationalism against them.

Creating New Rooms in the Soviet Apartment

The People's Commissariat for Nationality Affairs (Narkomnats) was *the* instrument of power for addressing nationality issues and organizing support from the non-Russian population. There each significant non-Russian nationality had its own commissariat or department. In turn, each of those departments had to mobilize its national elites for the Soviet cause and at the same time represent those elites vis-à-vis the government in Moscow. This dual function often led to conflict and confusion, but it also enabled the establishment of the first autonomous territories within the RSFSR. As time went on, these national bureaucracies, once installed, would continue to call for more funding and provide arguments for their continued existence.[43] According to experts within Narkomnats, the creation of each national territory would be determined by numbers and statistics.[44] However, this soon proved problematic, as the experts and politicians found they lacked reliable statistical data. This scarcity of reliable information would continue to disrupt the Soviet Union's abilities to govern until the 1926 census.[45]

The first entities to gain "autonomous" status within the RSFSR in 1918 paved the way for a broad spectrum of what the term could mean in practice. The Turkestan Autonomous Socialist Soviet Republic (Turkestanskaia avtonomnaia sotsialisticheskaia sovetskaia respublika, TASSR) and the Volga German Workers' Commune were among the first. They were explicitly designated parts of the RSFSR, unlike Litbel. The political rights of these territorial entities depended on circumstances. In 1918 and 1919 the TASSR was largely cut off from the other territories controlled by the Bolsheviks. Regional activists had to rely on their own means. Russian and Ukrainian settlers dominated Turkestan's soviets, and their political actions often discriminated against the indigenous Muslim population. Unsurprisingly, this triggered local resistance to Soviet power, which in turn contributed to the emergence of insurgents labeled as Basmachi.[46] The party and state leadership in Moscow tried to counter the dominance of the Slavic settlers by lending support to Muslim activists. The resulting close alliance with local progressively minded activists such as the Jadids—initially a designation for Muslim educational reformers—would ultimately help to shape Moscow's Central Asia policies from late 1919 until the mid-1930s.[47] While regional party and state activists in Turkestan enjoyed broad agency, the Germans in the Volga Commune remained under the close supervision of Moscow. In practice, Volga German institutions initially gained little more than the right to appeal to the government in Moscow without intermediaries.[48]

Bashkiria provides an example of the Bolsheviks' pragmatism with national representatives who were ideologically opposed to the Communist Party. In this case, the Bolsheviks were able to turn the Russian nationalism of White Admiral Aleksandr Kolchak against himself. Kolchak's forces included a sizable contingent of Bashkir troops, but repeated humiliations at the hands of Russians within the ranks had alienated these Bashkirs. The Bolsheviks exploited their grievances and convinced the latter to change their allegiance. They promised their leader Akhmet-Zaki Validov Bashkir self-rule within Soviet Russia. Thus, in 1919, the Bashkirs came to help the Red Army gain the upper hand against Kolchak in western Siberia. Even though later conflicts between Validov and the Soviet government were almost preprogrammed and eventually led to a parting of ways in 1920, the Bashkir example provided a viable blueprint for the national autonomies that would soon flourish within the RSFSR.[49]

Toward the end of the Civil War, the state and party leadership saw the support of oppressed Muslims as a means of promoting revolution in Asia and the Middle East, a possible opportunity to make up for the failures in the West.[50] The Congress of the Peoples of the East, held in Baku in September 1920, produced a landmark change in Bolshevik politics. Instead of the proletariat of the industrialized West, the peoples of the colonialized East were expected to continue the World Revolution. Hence the communist movement gained a decisively anti-colonialist turn and the Soviet approaches of how to deal with modernization of "backward" society would be discussed in liberation movements all over the world.[51]

Mirsaid Sultan-Galiev, who between 1918 and 1923 headed the Muslim Commissariat (Muskom) at Narkomnats, was particularly active in promoting such emancipatory ideas. Originally from Ufa Guberniia, Sultan-Galiev had joined the Bolsheviks in 1917 and agitated on their behalf for the unity of all Turkic speakers in the former Russian Empire. With Lenin's explicit support, he was able to sidestep party discipline in efforts to mobilize the Muslim population for the Soviet cause. Such inclusive ideas were hardly awkward, as the Soviet administration initially considered the term "Muslim" an ethnonym for non-Christian indigenous populations of Eastern Europe, Siberia, Central Asia, and the South Caucasus. The same applied with respect to the term "Jewish," which could refer to an ethnicity as well as a religious affiliation.

This is why Narkomnats had branches like Muskom. Official differentiation of the "Muslim" population along linguistic, economic, and cultural lines was just getting underway.[52]

The creation of a joint Tatar-Bashkir Autonomous Republic was Sultan-Galiev's pet project in 1918 and 1919. However, this political undertaking failed to materialize due to two contradictory factors. On one hand, the members of the Bashkir government that already existed opposed the project, seeing in it a threat to their own political privileges.[53] On the other, from the Bolsheviks' point of view, national belonging was supposed to be nothing more than a means of mobilizing the non-Russian peoples. That is to say, for the Bolsheviks, the emancipation of the Muslim population was a means, not an end. There was a crucial dividing line between the Bolshevik leadership and activists such as Sultan-Galiev. Despite this, activists at Narkomnats continued to advocate ideas that ran contrary to those of the Communist Party's mainstream: for example, discussing Austromarxist approaches of personal autonomy and national inclusion in the commissariat's own periodical *Zhizn' natsional'nostei* (Life of the Nationalities).[54]

At the same time, the fundamental opposition to nationally defined polities within the Bolshevik realm did not by any means simply fade away. Mikhail Vladimirskii, deputy head of the People's Commissariat for Internal Affairs (NKVD RSFSR), promoted a class-based restructuring of Soviet space. He therefore planned to strengthen the proletarian centers—that is, towns with a working-class majority. These loyal centers would guarantee implementation of Soviet policies within the different regions.[55] Other party activists took up such ideas and developed them further. In 1921, Timofei Sapronov not only planned to strengthen these proletarian centers, but he also called for expanding the competences of the gubernii. In other words, he wanted the imperial-era gubernii to form the backbone of the Soviet federal structure.[56]

Despite such rival approaches, the distinction between autonomous oblasti and republics became increasingly common within the growing federal system of the RSFSR—something that would last until 1991. Even though there were no precise rules governing which nationality could gain what status, smaller and more "backward" nationalities tended to receive oblast status, while larger ones achieved that of a republic. The differences between these two levels were considerable. Autonomous republics, such as Bashkiria, had their own commissariats and could act independently in certain areas, such as education. Autonomous oblasti, such as Komi, initially had no more administrative power than any other guberniia of the RSFSR. The sole exception was that an autonomous oblast did have direct access to the central government in Moscow. Both kinds of autonomy, however, included particular policies in cadre recruitment, education, and implementation of official languages.[57] Hence, within the emerging federalist framework, national-territorial status came with a set of privileges. The Twelfth Party Congress would go on to institutionalize them in 1923.

The coexistence of a centralizing party and a federalizing state seems at first glance counterintuitive, but they must be seen in their dialectical relationship. The RSFSR took a federal form in order to preempt secessionist movements and mobilize the entire population. This goal could be realized only if representatives of state and party institutions could speak the languages of all their citizens throughout the Bolshevik realm. However, the party, particularly the secretariat of the Central Committee, strictly supervised the promotion of national cadres. The Eighth Party Congress in 1919 formally stated that they were bound to the party discipline—that is, orders from the Central Committee in Moscow.[58] The form of the autonomous state institutions was federal, but the party decided the content, meaning which people received key positions. Stalin, first as commissar of nationality affairs and then as general secretary of the Central Committee, quickly learned how to make use of these instruments of power.[59]

To keep a tight rein on the chains of command, the Central Committee formed regional sections and sent plenipotentiaries wherever and whenever it needed them. The Kavbiuro was expected to supervise all party activists in the North and South Caucasus regions, the Turkbiuro those in Turkestan. Not only could these party institutions overrule decisions made by state institutions, but their scope of action also crossed existing state borders. The Kavbiuro at one point had to supervise the North Caucasus, which lay within the RSFSR, as well as the formally independent South Caucasian Soviet republics. The Turkbiuro had to deal with the TASSR and then also with the formally independent entities of Khorezm and Bukhara.[60] Later, these regional sections were renamed but continued to act as the main intermediaries between Moscow and functionaries in the different regions. It is not surprising that these conduits were where internal party conflicts became visible and regional policies were made.

Adding a New Floor to the Soviet Building

In 1921 and 1922, as the Bolsheviks were asserting their control over large swaths of the former Russian Empire, they began to develop, with far greater precision, the still improvised structure of their new state. In the eyes of the Moscow leadership, the Soviet republics outside the RSFSR were constantly causing problems. Even though their cadres were bound to the Communist Party, they kept acting like politicians from independent states. This was particularly true when they tried to establish formal relations with other states, as the Georgian or Bukharan governments did in 1921 and 1922. Moscow saw its authority challenged by such moves and intervened.[61] However, this further damaged Moscow's already weak reputation in the margins, as such interventions strengthened the impression of foreign rule. The Bolshevik leadership thus searched for other forms that would best fit their needs.

In this urgent matter, Stalin proved to be the right man at the right place. After the Civil War, he made his mark as a diligent administrator within the party apparatus. It is no wonder that, in September 1922, he came to head a Central Committee commission to overhaul the Soviet state's structure. This commission decided to include all of the still formally independent parts of the Soviet realm into the RSFSR. Dmytro Manuïl's'kyi, the first secretary of the Ukrainian party, was a particularly energetic supporter of Ukraine's entry into the framework of the RSFSR. In his opinion, direct subordination to Moscow's rule would overcome the factional divides among Ukrainian communists.[62]

Now Stalin had to sell this idea to Lenin, who was still recovering from his first stroke. In his report, Stalin again emphasized that the current situation had led to administrative chaos. The party had two options: grant these Soviet republics either "real independence" or "real unification." Of course, this was rhetorical posturing, because the first option was hardly realistic from the party's point of view. Stalin depicted the goal of the whole discussion quite bluntly: "[we must] replace fictitious independence with the real autonomy of a republic in the sense of language, culture, justice, internal affairs, agriculture, and so on."[63] He went even farther: "We are now experiencing such a pace of development that we cannot ignore the form, law, and constitution, when the young generation of communists in the border regions refuses to understand the game of independence as a game [*molodoe pokolenie kommunistov na okrainakh igru v nezavisimost' otkazhetsia ponimat' kak igru*]. They persistently take the word 'independence' at face value, and they persistently demand that we act according to the letter of the republics' constitutions."[64]

While agreeing with the general framework of the project, Lenin proposed changing the form slightly. All of the Soviet republics together with the RSFSR should form a new kind of union state—the Union of Soviet Republics of Europe and Asia. Lenin detested the idea of endowing Ukraine and Georgia with the same level of "autonomy" as Tatarstan or Bashkiria. In a letter to Lev Kamenev, who was also a member of the commission, he made his thinking quite clear: "It is important that we do not provide oxygen to the 'independists,' that we do not destroy their *independence* but create a *new floor*, a federation of equal republics."[65] This new floor would have its own Sovnarkom and its own TsIK. "Russia" would no longer appear in the state's name. The Central Committee commission would go on to include Lenin's suggestion in its draft.

In October 1922, the party leadership was more or less in agreement as to how to proceed with constitutional reform, but sudden resistance from their comrades in Tiflis (today Tbilisi) led to a crisis that later became known as the "Georgian affair." Rivalries between the Zakkraikom (the successor to the Kavbiuro) and Georgian party leaders lay at the source of this matter. Relations between Sergo Ordzhonikidze, head of the Zakkraikom, and his Georgian comrades had turned sour, as they were not playing the "game" according to Ordzhonikidze's expectations. For example, in 1921, they opposed giving up an independent Georgian currency.[66] The Georgian Bolsheviks agreed in principle to enter into a closer union with other parts of the Soviet state, but they asked for more time and protested the Zakkraikom's constant interference in their internal affairs.[67] Ordzhonikidze's impulsive and undiplomatic character did not ease the situation. Things began to get out of hand when the Zakkraikom demanded that the Georgian leadership join the new union state by means of a Transcaucasian Federation (ZSFSR). Most Georgian communists rejected the idea that Georgia was not an automatic member of the proposed union but only in the form of a federation with Armenia and Azerbaijan. They saw themselves as marginalized. Subsequently, in November 1922, a majority of the Georgian Central Committee resigned in protest. This scandal drew the attention of Moscow, prompting the Central Committee there to send a commission to Tiflis to investigate. The party leadership was eager to introduce the new state order as soon as possible. Thus the commission's conclusions backed the Zakkraikom and criticized the Georgian comrades for their behavior.[68]

The "Georgian affair" would have remained a footnote, if Lenin had not then intervened in favor of the Georgian Bolsheviks. As Jeremy Smith shows in detail, the affair was not so much a struggle between Lenin and Stalin on the issue of "centralism" versus "autonomism"—something Richard Pipes, Gerhard Simon, and to some extent Stephen Blank previously highlighted—but rather an issue of manners within the party.[69] In the course of events, Lenin learned of Ordzhonikidze's erratic and even brutal behavior when dealing with other party members. Brutality toward the enemy was nothing unusual for Bolsheviks, but it was not the way to treat dissenting comrades (yet). Lenin viewed Ordzhonikidze's behavior not as an isolated incident but as a symptom of "Great Russian chauvinism."[70] However, his intercession on behalf of the Georgian comrades came to naught. A second severe stroke on 15-16 December disabled him from performing any further duties of office. Moreover, other party leaders, Stalin in particular, obstructed his effort to remedy the situation. Thus the Soviet Union came into being on 30 December 1922. Even though Lenin's vision of a federal state beyond Russia prevailed, Stalin could fit its institutions to tighten his own power position.[71]

To analyze the Soviet Union in action, Jeremy Smith also provides an important distinction between the form of the state and the party's national policy. The forms, the institutions, nationalism, and economic considerations were different layers within the game of power all the party activists had to learn how to play. Despite flowery slogans of "independence," "self-determination," or later "socialist construction," they all had (in theory) to adhere to party discipline and maintain political unity, once the Tenth Party Congress in 1921 formally enacted a ban on internal factions. National policies were aimed at winning over populations and mobilizing them for the Soviet project. Within this game, "Great Russian chauvinism" endangered the realization of the party's tactics toward the non-Russian people—that is, nationality policies—whereas "national deviation" by non-Russian party members posed a threat to party discipline, the very essence of Bolshevik power.[72] From the party's point of view, Ordzhonikidze had upset the implementation of certain policies in the South Caucasus, whereas the Georgian communists put Bolshevik rule as such in jeopardy.

The Twelfth Party Congress: Carrot and Stick for National Activists

The Russian Communist Party tried to institutionalize the way it managed the problems that arose from the nationality question. At its Twelfth Congress in April 1923, it adopted a comprehensive program to deal with the non-Russian nationalities. The delegates at this congress again condemned "Great Russian chauvinism" as "oppressive" and "imperialist," and they introduced a set of measures designed to promote "non-imperial," "backward" nationalities such as the Ukrainians, Tatars, or Kirgiz.[73] These policies were later called korenizatsiia. Tied to a titular territory, they were to guarantee the mobilization of the "backward" population for the Soviet project. Institutionalized promotion of previously "oppressed" nationalities in state and party offices lay at the very core. Depending on the territory in question, it could take specific designations such as *Ukrainization, Belarusification,* or *Uzbekization*.[74]

Despite the condemnation of "Great Russian chauvinism" and the institutionalization of korenizatsiia, it did not take the party leadership long to provide a demonstration of what would happen if someone failed to play the game. Immediately after the Twelfth Party Congress, they made an example of the well-known Muslim activist Mirsaid Sultan-Galiev. Among the numerous faults party officials would find, chief among them was the fact that Sultan-Galiev had previously promoted the idea of forming a single Soviet republic that would include all the Turkic peoples of the Soviet state, and he was a vocal opponent of all manifestations of "Great Russian chauvinism." In May 1923 the Central Committee of the RKP(b) accused him of having organized a conspiracy against Soviet power. Subsequently, he was arrested and expelled from the party. In the years to come, "sultangalievism" would serve as a synonym for national deviation.[75]

The Twelfth Party Congress made Stalin a visible member of the party leadership. He was able to present himself as Lenin's most dedicated pupil and thus he strengthened his powerbase, while his opponents Leon Trotsky and Grigorii Zinov'ev lost some of their influence. As commissar of nationality affairs as well as general secretary of the Central Committee, Stalin was in charge of recruiting and promoting national cadres. He would make extensive use of this bureaucratic power.[76]

After the Sultan-Galiev affair, the party organized a convention with regional national activists in June 1923. The new rules of the game should be publicly performed. Stalin, as representative of the Politburo, gave the concluding speech after the discussions. Whereas he praised the Georgian and Armenian comrades for their successes, he severely criticized the Ukrainian and Turkestani communists as they had failed to mobilize larger parts of the population.[77] This is why he repeated the urgent need for "affirmative" policies: "it is necessary to create favorable conditions in order to attract local people to the party and promote them into executive positions, even if they are of less educated and possibly less proletarian nationalities [*menee kul'turnykh i mozhet byt' menee proletarskikh natsional'nostei*]."[78]

The new constitution of the USSR was still in the making, but Stalin underlined the necessity for a centralized command structure. The union republics should not have their own foreign policies because this would create disunity and waste precious state funds in parallel structures. Vis-à-vis the still formally independent republics of Khorezm and Bukhara, he urged the necessity of purges in their party and state administrations before they could join the Soviet Union. The right to join had "to be earned."[79] This was more than a euphemistic wording. Through these purges, Bukharan and Khorezmian politicians eventually lost much of their agency and became increasingly forced into the multilayered game of power.[80]

In drafting this new constitution of the new union state, party leaders also had to determine how border revisions between Soviet republics were to be addressed. A commission of the All-Union TsIK raised such issues in mid-April 1923. Among the commission's members were numerous figures who would later play important roles in resolving territorial issues: Mykhailo Poloz and Mykola Skrypnyk of Ukraine, Saak Ter-Gabrielian of Armenia, Avel' Yenukidze, secretary of the TsIK and VTsIK, and finally General Secretary Stalin himself. After discussing the possibility of border revisions between union republics, this commission decided that all republics affected by any revision, as well as the All-Union TsIK, had to approve such territorial changes. Hence every republic had to give formal consent to changes in its territorial structure.[81] If necessary, they could be forced to consent by party discipline. The party and state leadership would take on the role of arbiter if necessary.[82]

In 1923 and 1924 the framework of the game was taking shape. If possible, every nationality on Soviet territory would receive an autonomous territorial unit that would bear its name. When a nationality formed a coherent majority within the territory of another nationality, then the state administration would create a national sub-entity. In the 1920s and early 1930s all kinds of territories bearing the name of a nationality kept popping up throughout the Soviet space. Even the smallest nationalities could form autonomous raiony (districts) and rural soviets. On paper, the administration of such a unit was to function in its national language.[83] The matryoshka, the nesting doll, can serve as a metaphor: the Ukrainian Republic contained in its territory a Moldovan Autonomous Socialist Soviet Republic (MASSR). Further down, within the MASSR, was a German rural soviet in Glikstal' (Glückstal). In this way, a German rural soviet could be part of a Moldovan entity, which was itself part of a Ukrainian entity, which was, of course, part of the union state.[84]

Even though Austromarxist approaches of cultural autonomy and national inclusion were not that popular within the party, in certain cases, there was no alternative. Examples are the short-lived Mountain Republic and the much more enduring Dagestani Republic in the North Caucasus. There the ethnic composition appeared too diverse to form national units. Thus the Soviet administration gave such ethnically diverse territories a collective autonomous form.[85]

After Lenin's death in 1924, "Marxism-Leninism" would become the guiding ideology within the Communist Party. "Leninism" as an amendment to "Marxism" stood for radical political pragmatism. Political problems like the nationality question would not miraculously fade away; they had to be managed by a chosen vanguard party. Its members had to thoroughly engineer and supervise social development.

Even though the smaller national rural soviets and raiony fell victim to Stalinist rationalizations at the end of the 1930s, the larger administrative units would remain until 1991.[86] This "party state" was built on conflicting ideas of universalistic socialism and particularistic nationalism. Their synthesis was at the core of the Soviet polity.[87] Nationality, cadre selection, and territorialization merged into a pragmatic way of institutionalizing Soviet power.

As a result of this expansive set of autonomous oblasti and republics, as well as the creation of the USSR, Narkomnats itself became redundant. Since 1917, it had been an intermediary between different nationalities within the RSFSR and the state leadership. Now these nationalities had defined autonomous territories and institutionalized access to Moscow. Despite resistance from its activists, the Soviet leadership dissolved Narkomnats on 9 April 1924.[88]

In the emerging federal system, the RSFSR remained the odd one out. The danger of "Great Russian chauvinism" seemed to be formally banned, but in the years that followed, new union institutions grew to become the Siamese twins of their RSFSR equivalents. Many of the RSFSR's institutions were identical with those of the union or were filled with the same party cadres.[89] For instance, Mikhail Kalinin was simultaneously chairman of the TsIK and the VTsIK; Avel' Yenukidze was his secretary at the TsIK as well as at the VTsIK.

Despite all the territorial diversity and conflicts of interests that existed at the outset of the 1920s, party and state functionaries knew all too well that the Politburo of the Communist Party had ultimate authority in political decisions. However, the Politburo was limited in its capacities. It could not regulate every detail within a territory that stretched across one-sixth of the planet's landmass.[90] In the 1920s political leaders like Lenin and Trotsky or later Stalin could not simply materialize a certain idea with the snap of their fingers. Administrative structuring according to national-ethnographic criteria or the rival concept of raionirovanie offered practical solutions to the existing challenges. Mid-level politicians and experts had then to settle disputes arising from such territorial issues. Their agency grew when the decisions of the Politburo and the Central Committee left room for interpretation, when the center intentionally declined to provide detailed instructions, or when it simply delegated problem management to subordinate levels.

Chapter 2

Gosplan

How to Achieve Spatial Homogeneity

> From an economic point of view, this state will be centralized until the mighty impulse of the proletarian revolution erases national borders once and for all.
>
> —Konstantin Yegorov, 1922

The statement by Konstantin Yegorov, a young and dedicated expert for administrative affairs, reflected the general mood within the State Planning Commission's Section for Raionirovanie (Sektsiia po raionirovaniiu) in 1922.[1] This commission, known as Gosplan, was founded in 1921. After the Civil War, the Soviet government had to manage the diverse territorial structure it had inherited from the Russian Empire. For dedicated Marxists, divisions along national lines belonged to the bourgeois past, not the socialist future. However, the Bolshevik government had to find a feasible means of organizing and governing the enormous expanses under its control, in particular because, from a long-term revolutionary point of view, this space would come to encompass the whole globe.[2] The state and party institutions exhibited two contradictory tendencies. On one hand, Gosplan—especially its Section for Raionirovanie—sought to order Soviet space according to inclusive economic characteristics. On the other, Lenin and his comrades had loudly expressed their support for national self-determination to all the peoples of the former Russian Empire. Functionaries at Narkomnats and party officials in Ukraine, as well as in the Caucasus and Central Asia, insisted that this promise be kept.[3] Thus the early Soviet state faced conflicting aims. At the same time, these new ideas had to grapple with holdover imperial administrative structures, such as Kursk or Voronezh Gubernii, where political leaders were promoting regional identities.

Older historical research on Soviet nationality policy focused on the tug-of-war between the "centralists" around Stalin and the "autonomists" around Lenin.[4] However, this approach provides only limited and biased insight into what was a much broader, more complex debate over nationality, economy, and territoriality during the 1920s. In *Empire of Nations*, Francine Hirsch provides a detailed analysis of the debate over the territorial models proposed by Gosplan and Narkomnats between 1921 and 1924. Both sides agreed on the need to eliminate economic backwardness and resolve the nationality question, but they differed on how to achieve these goals. Gosplan's experts emphasized economic matters. Their colleagues from Narkomnats put ethnographic considerations front and center.[5] Whether this debate among the experts in Moscow had any tangible effect on the ground in the various regions remains unclear. Hirsch ends her analysis with the dissolution of Narkomnats in 1924. The demise of Narkomnats deprived its experts of most of their institutional funding and their periodicals such as *Zhizn' natsional'nostei*, but their colleagues at Gosplan were able to continue promoting their ideas throughout the 1920s. I therefore focus on Gosplan's ideas and their reception in the medium term as the debates related to this reception provide hints as to why the Bolshevik government adopted an affirmative stance toward nationalism instead of economic materialism in administrative practice.

Though the experts at Gosplan did not succeed with their materialist concepts, their terminology, which focused on the economy, greatly influenced the general debate and produced results on the ground. Drawing on this framework and their terminology, I explore the choices experts considered as possible answers and what they had in mind with their "national-ethnographic" and, in particular, "economic" arguments. At first glance, both terms seem to be self-evident, but if we look more closely, we see that they covered a number of different, even contradictory approaches in the Soviet debates. Experts struggled ardently over how to define their content.

Konstantin Yegorov will not only accompany us throughout this chapter but also make repeated appearances later. Throughout the 1920s, he was one of the most prominent and productive men at Gosplan and was widely admired by his colleagues for his dedication and energy.[6] Yegorov's career was meteoric. After three years of study, he left university without a diploma in 1918, when the Bolshevik government offered him a number of tantalizing opportunities. Initially, Yegorov was active in the local soviet in Simferopol. After becoming a member of the Communist Party, he started to work with the NKVD RSFSR in 1919. There he dealt with the organization of Soviet power at the local level. Not long thereafter, the commissariat appointed him secretary of the newly established Administrative Commission (AK VTsIK), where he was responsible for the formation of new territorial entities. Moreover, he helped establish the NKVD's cartographic branch.[7] Of course, during the 1920s Yegorov's ideas—like those of his colleagues—evolved from strictly "economic" approaches to more pragmatic ones. At the end of the 1920s, the concepts developed by such experts became highly effective tools in the hands of those who wielded power.

Ambitious experts, such as Yegorov, were respected by their peers, and the Soviet government often turned to them for policy advice. With their expertise, they could influence and shape, as well as channel, the full scope of the debate. Alun Thomas appropriately called them "intellectuals whom the party consulted but could choose to disregard."[8] Unlike their colleagues in Central and Southeastern Europe, they were bound by the policy lines set by the Communist Party.[9] Nonetheless, their conceptions of territoriality were the subject of controversies and as a result always in flux. Their most important terms were *razmezhevanie* (delimitation) and *raionirovanie* (territorialization or, depending on the context, regionalization or discretization).[10] Whereas *razmezhevanie* referred to the formation of national borders, *raionirovanie* was applied to the formation of economic and administrative territories. Even though national-ethnographic and economic considerations influenced both types of territorialization, and both types also tended to overlap in practice, the experts were well aware of the fundamental differences between them.

The term *raion* itself, from which *raionirovanie* originated, was highly ambiguous and confusing, even for the experts involved.[11] In early Soviet discourse, it could signify the largest territorial unit (i.e., region), but at the same time also the smallest administrative entity above the rural soviets (i.e., district).[12] Thus it seems necessary to clarify in which sense experts and politicians used the term *raion*. In doing so, I add regional scale or district scale in brackets.

In their daily work, Yegorov and his colleagues could draw from a long tradition of ideas and concepts about how to organize Russian imperial space into manageable units. Since the eighteenth century, research on the Russian Empire and its geography and climate had been a growing field. In the mid-nineteenth century, the debate became more sophisticated when geographers such as Konstantin Arsen'ev and later Pëtr Semënov-Tian'-Shanskii proposed ordering imperial space according to a bundle of economic, demographic, linguistic, or natural criteria.[13] Aleksandr Chuprov popularized the idea of stimulating economic growth by reordering the territorial structure. The famous chemist Dmitrii Mendeleev also explored such ideas and proposed a model according to which the regions of the Russian Empire were to be conceived as proceeding from a central point. Such centers were to serve as the loci for any territorial reconfiguration so that they could drive economic development.[14] The terms *raion* (derived from French *rayon*—i.e., honeycomb) and *raionirovanie* had been widely used among experts since the early 1890s.[15] On the eve of the twentieth century, Veniamin Semënov-Tian'-Shanskii, Pëtr's son, popularized the idea of dividing the Russian Empire into agricultural and industrial raiony. He also submitted a plan that called for these regions to be implemented from the bottom up, not the top down.[16]

Russia's imperial experts also had a long tradition of studying how to manage the empire's territory, including its colonies in Central Asia.[17] Altogether, this discourse had created a specific body of knowledge by the time the Bolsheviks seized power.[18] Prior to the revolution, the discourse among imperial experts had exerted little influence on "real" policy, but the new regime was much more open to implementing the experts' models on the ground.[19] The prerevolutionary debates were hardly isolated from the rest of the world either. Russian imperial experts had been in close contact with their colleagues in Western Europe and North America. Moreover, the models of spatial planning developed by the German agrarian scientist Johann Heinrich von Thünen and the economist Alfred Weber had influenced the Russian imperial discourse, as they offered approaches to describing and prescribing space.[20] These last two scholars would also influence Walter Christaller and his theory of central localities. This theory later shaped spatial thinking not only in Nazi Germany but also on both sides of the Iron Curtain during the Cold War.[21] Christaller's model had certain similarities with the approaches discussed in the early Soviet state. However, it is unlikely that the Soviet debate greatly influenced Christaller's 1933 thesis.[22] Both models rather coevolved.

Energetic Plans

The Bolshevik regime's first foray into territorial matters created a mess. On 18 January 1918 (31 January 1918, New Style), the Sovnarkom decreed that local soviets could change administrative borders of their own accord. They only had to inform the central authorities of these changes.[23] The new government even proclaimed: "[We] give every population, every volost, every uezd, etc., the opportunity to regroup around the natural centers to which they feel attracted. [We offer them the opportunity] to satisfy their needs for the recovery, prosperity, and relief of their economy."[24] The local soviets heard this call and went straight to work. The result was unprecedented administrative chaos. This did not much affect the Soviet war effort, but as the Red Army gained the upper hand, such administrative-territorial issues became more pressing. From the point of view of the Bolsheviks' ability to govern, this situation could not last.[25] In the meantime, the Soviet economy was in a state of complete turmoil. Economic regulation during the Civil War had proven to be highly inefficient. Nonetheless, the party still sought to establish a new kind of economy that would be one "vast people's workshop," where production would be rationally organized according to an all-encompassing plan.[26]

In Lenin's eyes, the management of the German economy during the First World War provided a model for the future Soviet order.[27] However, in the face of economic collapse, even the most dogmatic Bolshevik had to realize that reliable statistical data and rational administrative structures were preconditions for governing such a planned economy. Experts would have to provide a plan for making Soviet space and all its resources "legible" for the regime.[28] This was one reason why the government over time increasingly curtailed certain elements of local autonomy. After 1920 local and regional soviets within the RSFSR could no longer decide their territorial structure. Every change had to be approved by the center in Moscow.[29]

The revolutionary state tried to acquire geographic, economic, demographic, and ethnographic expertise by funding well-equipped research commissions. It relied on experts who had made their careers under tsarist rule as well as dedicated young people such as Yegorov.[30] The Imperial Academy of Sciences, in particular its Commission for the Study of the Country's Natural Productive Forces (Komissiia po izucheniiu estestvennykh proizvoditel'nykh sil strany, KEPS), was transformed into a Soviet institution. The government also funded new agencies to search for an "efficient" order, such as Narkomnats or the Supreme Soviet of the National Economy (Vysshii sovet narodnogo khoziaistva, VSNKh), which was trying to organize the economy in the wake of the Civil War. As many of these committees and commissions had proven unfit to deal with the challenges of economic collapse since the war, the Soviet government dissolved them, changed their designation, or fired their employees.[31] At the same time, the Soviet regime used the most convenient (and only) method it had to address the challenge of establishing governance: it simply created new bureaucratic structures—and hired people who seemed better qualified. As Lara Douds has shown in much greater detail, commissions and study groups were set up as was politically necessary during early Soviet period. They remained active for as long as their task seemed urgent. When they had carried out their task, or failed to do so, they disbanded themselves or a higher authority liquidated them. In some cases, they ceased work without being formally disbanded.[32]

The first large-scale campaign on behalf of the economy that Lenin and the VSNKh pushed—the GOELRO project—became highly attractive to qualified and dedicated people alike.[33] Relying on existing plans, its main goal was to provide electricity to the population in the European part of the Soviet state.[34] Initiated in February 1920, GOELRO could go back to plans and expertise developed in late tsarist Russia, in particular to the achievements of KEPS. Gleb Krzhizhanovskii, an Old Bolshevik and one of Lenin's friends, supervised the project.[35] Ivan Aleksandrov, a highly respected geographer and railway engineer, provided the blueprint for its administrative implementation. According to this plan, the existing territorial structure of the European part of the Soviet state would be reorganized according to criteria necessary for energy self-sufficiency. This would come to define the structure of new raiony (regional scale).[36] Thus, when territorial experts discussed "economic efficiency" in the early 1920s, they primarily had in mind self-sufficiency in terms of resources for electricity production.[37]

Revolutionary elan was one of the forces driving people such as Konstantin Yegorov. In January 1921, after the Sovnarkom had tasked the Administrative Commission with collecting all of the available data on the Soviet space and developing plans for its territorial restructuring, Yegorov even declared he would create a new order within two months.[38] Unsurprisingly, he failed to keep such an ambitious promise, but this failure was at the same time the starting point for a more comprehensive approach toward this territorial challenge. And Yegorov was still able to make his mark for his expertise and his zeal.

Over time, the party leadership had to accept that there was no instant solution for the territorial issue on the lower level and economic management writ large. Faced with famine and an uprising in Kronstadt, the party adopted a radical change in economic policy at its Tenth Congress in March 1921—later known as the New Economic Policy (NEP).[39] During the NEP era, Bolsheviks abandoned the economic measures applied under War Communism and reintroduced a limited legal framework for free markets and private enterprise. The party maintained control only over the "commanding heights," such as large-scale industry and foreign trade.[40] At the very same moment, however, the Soviet government also created Gosplan. The implementation of the GOELRO project was the new committee's first big task.[41] Krzhizhanovskii became its first head. The leading Bolsheviks thus demonstrated their newfound awareness that basic infrastructure and coherent data were needed to organize a planned economy.[42] It was for this reason that Lenin put so much effort into GOELRO. In their work on this project, the experts involved would also be able to generate valuable statistical data for further planning.

In the spring of 1921, Gosplan hired the most promising experts it could find, including Konstantin Yegorov. In no time, he was one of the most prominent members within Gosplan's Section for Raionirovanie. Aleksandrov became its head. Following the latter's ideas, the section developed a framework whereby Soviet space was divided into territories that facilitated the exploitation of local resources and the production of electricity: be it wood, peat, water, coal, or oil. Aleksandrov expected this territorial structure of energy efficiency to lay the foundation for any future political order.[43] Leaning on ideas laid out by Mendeleev and others, every raion (regional scale) would have an administrative-economic center and a certain population that would allow for the best possible exploitation of the available potential for energy. Densely populated raiony would be smaller in size, sparsely populated ones larger.[44] This concept of the raiony was organic. They were to take the shape that would best advance their development of energy efficiency.

At the time, the VTsIK and the Sovnarkom were willing to provide ample funding to encourage lively debate within the Section for Raionirovanie. At regular biweekly meetings, experts from different fields—geographers, engineers, statisticians, and economists—were to share, evaluate, and discuss data related to the Soviet space and improvement of governance.⁴⁵ This concentration of expertise promised the most effective form of problem management. Despite all the official attention they received, Gosplan's experts both cooperated and competed with other institutions, such as VSNKh, Narkomnats, and the Central Statistical Administration (TsSU), in their efforts to accumulate and produce knowledge concerning the Soviet space. The Section for Raionirovanie formally existed from 1921 to 1930, but regular staff meetings appear to have ceased after 1924. However, experts such as Yegorov and Aleksandrov often took part in follow-up expert commissions on raionirovanie organized by the VTsIK or the Sovnarkom.⁴⁶

Alongside considerations of energy efficiency, ideas of improving governance became increasingly important in the section's debates. On one hand, old territorial entities inherited from the Russian Empire— for instance, Kursk and Voronezh Gubernii—did not cease to exist but continued to function as administrative structures in the early Soviet state. On the other hand, the Bolshevik government had created ad hoc autonomous territorial entities within the RSFSR, as we saw in the previous chapter. Furthermore, the fate of the formally independent Soviet republics such as Ukraine was not yet clear.⁴⁷ In the eyes of Gosplan's experts, this chaotic administrative structure was ill-suited to any kind of social progress. Hence they proposed replacing the existing administrative-territorial framework completely. The *guberniia* (province), *uezd* (pre-reform county), and *volost'* (shire) structure as well as the national-territorial entities were to give way to designed entities of energy efficiency: *oblast'* (region), *okrug* (post-reform county), *raion* (district), and *sel'sovet* (rural soviet). The number of entities were to be reduced at every level. According to Yegorov, about two old volosti would form a new raion (district scale).⁴⁸ Thus the administrative staff in the regions could be reduced and simultaneously professionalized. Gosplan proposed a radical solution to address the administrative-territorial mess. Chaotic diversity could be replaced by homogeneous raiony (regional scale) or oblasti.⁴⁹ According to this plan, Soviet Ukraine would be divided into two parts, whereas all three of the formally independent Soviet republics in the South Caucasus were merged with the North. Such plans had zealous supporters but also dedicated opponents in the highest ranks.⁵⁰

A closer look reveals that the new, "efficiently" structured oblasti promoted by the Section for Raionirovanie were in large part a cheap marketing trick. In the case of the envisioned Central Black Earth

Oblast, the imperial Kursk, Voronezh, Orël, and Tambov Gubernii were simply merged into one unit with their existing borders. The same happened with the gubernii in the northeast.[51] The Caucasian Viceroyalty (*namestnichestvo*), an extraordinary administrative-territorial entity within the Russian imperial framework in the southern margin, was simply transformed into a "new" oblast.[52] However, neither the proponents nor the opponents of raionirovanie pointed out this fact. They all silently acquiesced to this borrowing from the imperial administrative system, as they did with the terminology. The imperial military often used the terms *okrug* and *oblast'* to designate zones under special military rule like those in Batum Oblast or Sukhum Okrug.

Initially, Gosplan's experts ignored objections to their territorial vision. At the first meeting of the Section for Raionirovanie on 26 May 1921, Mikhail Vladimirskii, an Old Bolshevik and chairman of the Administrative Commission, made his position quite clear: "The most important principle of how to build up the oblasti is the development of industry and the exploitation of resources. . . . The nationality question somehow impedes the whole thing and demands a revision of the borders. [Officially] the principle of nationality should be fundamental, but after a certain time, our work will demonstrate the necessity of an economic foundation."[53] After Gleb Krzhizhanovskii interrupted him and asked what was to be done with the existing national entities, Vladimirskii replied that "from an economic point of view, a national entity as such is hardly rational. Perhaps it will be possible to separate national and cultural entities from economic raiony [regional scale]."[54] Vladimirskii saw no contradiction in the coexistence of national autonomy and economic territorial entities. In this way, he came close to Austromarxist ideas of separating national from territorial issues, promoting an inclusive attempt to deal with the nationality question.

The majority at the Section for Raionirovanie did not neglect national aspects or the idea of a federation per se, even though their mental map of "Russia" encompassed not only the RSFSR but also the South Caucasus and Ukraine.[55] In their eyes, the existence of national-territorial entities was a historically transient phenomenon. The Soviet state had to respect the right of self-determination, but at the same time, all territorial units had to follow a much more important goal: the construction of socialism. As it proved difficult to unite scattered national communities into a functional administrative unit, section experts gave energy self-sufficiency and aspects of governance priority over national-ethnographic considerations.[56] Aleksandrov made this clear with regard to Soviet Ukraine when he told his colleagues that

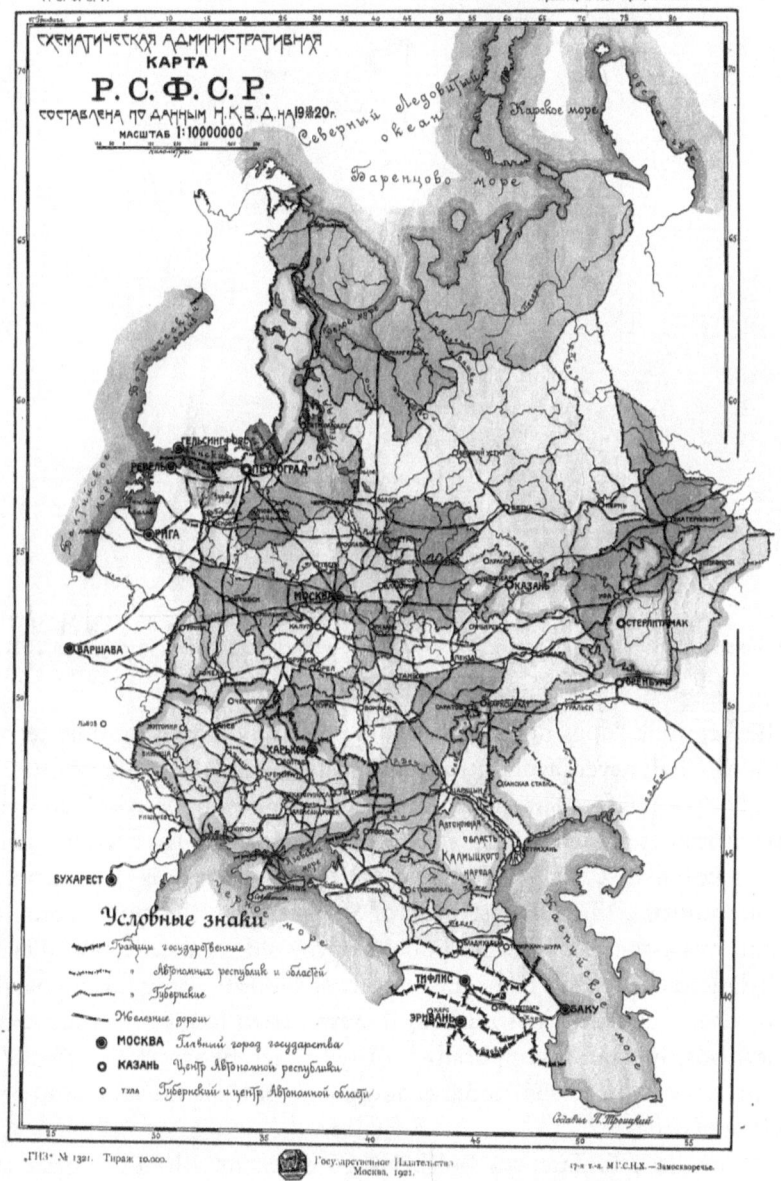

FIGURE 4. Contemporary administrative map of the RSFSR, 10 December 1920.

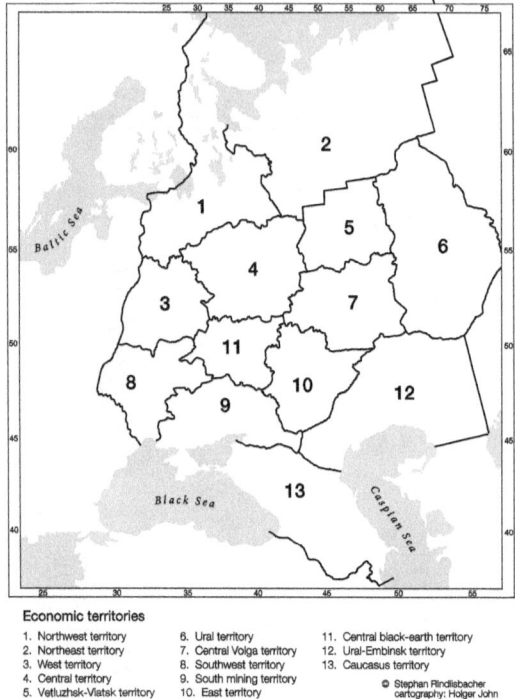

FIGURE 5. Economic raiony according to the scheme proposed by Gosplan in November 1921.

this republic "does not have anything to unify it in economic terms, and we shall never favor national interests instead of economic ones."[57]

The section faced particular opposition from supporters of national-territorial approaches. The latter even declared that the section's ideas were colonialist and exploitative of local populations and national communities.[58] In the first years of Soviet power, the word "colonialism" was associated with the policies of the old regime. The Bolsheviks distanced themselves from any notions of subordinating certain people to others.[59] Experts like Yegorov, however, tried to give the old term a new, positive spin. As opposed to former times, he saw raionirovanie as a program of state-sponsored economic development that would benefit everyone.[60]

With little fanfare, the Bolshevik government solved the basic territorial problem. Against broad opposition, it brought up the section's territorial plans for internal discussion.[61] In a joint Commission for Raionirovanie under VTsIK Chairman Mikhail Kalinin, experts from Gosplan and Narkomnats, as well as various representatives from the regions, met to discuss the issue between November 1921 and February 1922. In light of certain constitutional barriers, they concluded that national entities could not be split between two economic raiony (regional scale).[62] The representative of Narkomnats on this commission, Gustav Klinger, put this quite bluntly: "Soviet power has proclaimed the principle of self-determination, and [this principle] must be preserved. Raionirovanie provides the base for the utmost prosperity of autonomous national entities in economic affairs."[63] Hence national considerations were formally prioritized over economic ones. This decision had a long-lasting effect. Ukraine would remain a single administrative unit. Moreover, representatives from both Georgia and the Kuban region opposed the plan to unite the whole Caucasus region within a single unit like that of the old imperial viceroyalty.[64]

The Momentum of the Margins

The months and years that ensued were particularly productive for the Section for Raionirovanie, but it had to deal with growing opposition to its initial ideas of energy efficiency. Its staff accumulated statistical materials and supervised territorial restructuring first in the RSFSR and then throughout the entire Soviet state. In these first years, section members produced a remarkable number of publications. However, party support for the section's plans was starting to wane. After a prolonged and heated debate within the party leadership, the Twelfth Party Congress in 1923—where korenizatsiia policies were institutionalized—accepted the new territorial structure, but only halfheartedly: "The introduction of a new system of administrative-territorial division needs a careful approach and a long time for its implementation. . . . The [congress] considers the plan . . . that Gosplan and the Administrative Commission of the VTsIK have developed a preliminary working hypothesis. Based on practical experience, it needs further revision and development."[65]

One of the areas where the new, scientific way of ordering Soviet space could undergo further revision and development was the Ural region.[66] Gosplan's experts had planned to base energy production on coal and hydroelectric dams as a means of developing the local metallurgical industry.[67] Raionirovanie started here in November 1923 and ended in March 1924. The newly formed oblast encompassed about 1,450,000 square versta (1,300,000 square kilometers, roughly the size of today's France, Germany, and Poland combined) and had slightly more than six million inhabitants. By reducing the number of administrative units, the state could save huge sums on salaries, at least on paper. All heavy industry came under the auspices of a single conglomerate (*trest*) that could supervise resource exploitation and electricity production. It almost goes without saying that Ural Oblast was not realized fully in accordance with Gosplan's original vision. Its experts had to adapt their plans due to the existence of ethnonational entities. The Bashkir Republic refused to join this Ural Oblast. So section experts had to reconfigure the territory of this oblast several times. This solution for the basic territorial problem in favor of ethnonational considerations led to new challenges in practice.[68]

The North Caucasus was another area where Gosplan, together with regional party and state institutions, introduced a new territorial framework in 1924. Here the experts planned to base the territorial entity's economy on petroleum and coal.[69] Even more so than in the Ural region, the result differed drastically from the original vision. In the first draft, the Caucasus region was to form a single economic unit. However, the South Caucasus was never part of any real discussion, as even the party leadership favored the option of leaving the South Caucasus separate within the Transcaucasian Federation.[70]

The experts made adaptations within the "rational" four-tier administrative frame of Gosplan when they added the krai as a particular kind of oblast. This term was directly borrowed from the old imperial vocabulary. There it signified "borderland," as in Turkestan Krai. Initial draft plans for the Southeastern Oblast (Iugo-vostochnaia oblast') shattered when they faced the topographical challenges and ethnic diversity on the ground.[71] In 1924 the politicians and experts came up with this new-old term and concept when they presented the idea of the North Caucasus Krai (Severo-Kavkazskii krai). The designation should indicate that this was no ordinary oblast, but an entity with certain privileges, including autonomous national territories.[72] The North Caucasus was—in ethnographic terms—the most diverse within the Soviet state. Thus, in the first attempt to rationalize this space, the government created several national entities, such as the Karachaevo-Cherkes or the Chechen Autonomous Oblasti, but then subordinated them to the krai center in Rostov-na-Donu.[73] Dagestan was not attached to the North Caucasus Krai until 1931. In the end, the krai's borders resulted from a merger of economic and national-ethnographic considerations.

In the years to come several other kraia took shape within the RSFSR: for instance, the Siberian and the Far Eastern ones. In cultural, economic, and political matters they could virtually gain the same rank as the union republics.[74] In the case of the North Caucasus Krai, their leaders and experts would be the main agents competing with the Ukrainian representatives for assets and territory. As we will see below, the former often had better ties to Moscow.

People and space emerged as clay that Gosplan's experts could shape, even if this was not their primary intent. In practice, regional experts could not take part in the planning in Moscow. This lack of mobilizing appeal outside of Moscow-based expert circles would be one of this concept's key weaknesses. This was in stark contrast to the nationalist party activists who constantly circulated between the center and the margins. Though the experts in Moscow tried to distance themselves from the old regime, their attitude toward the people on the ground remained the same. Before 1917, the division between gubernii, uezdy, and volosti had been established top-down out of strategic, fiscal, and judicial considerations.[75] This basic structure went back to the reign of Peter I (1689–1725) and was later extensively reformed under Catherine II (1762–1796), as the tsaritsa tried to establish an enlightened administration for her empire with gubernii and uezdy. The basic assumption behind their formation was that a certain number of people should live in each territory, and the regional administration would have to levy taxes. The military, stationed in the central town, was supposed to be able to deploy anywhere within a given entity in a certain amount of time.[76] However, a plethora of various other territorial schemes for postal services and telegraphs, education or water management later coexisted alongside this imperial administrative structure. Moreover, certain parts of the empire, like the Kingdom of Poland, the Grand Duchy of Finland, the large Caucasian Viceroyalty, or the Turkestan Krai were under particular types of administration.[77] In the early Soviet debate on raionirovanie, demographic and strategic factors still played a role, but these were not mentioned any more than the borrowings from the old framework of gubernii. The major difference between the old and the new regime—and all the experts involved highlighted this—was that economic aspects played a subordinate role in the old imperial administrative-territorial structure. Now governance, economic development, and resource extraction within a certain territory stood front and center. Soviet power had to be brought closer to the people so as to better manage and mobilize all productive forces. The party later adopted this approach for the slogan "face the village" (*litsom k derevne*).⁷⁸

The Bolsheviks created the Soviet Union as a federal state at the end of 1922, but the number of constituent entities, as well as their administrative hierarchy, remained unsettled. Initially, there were only four union subjects: the Belarusian Republic (BSSR), Ukraine (UkrSSR), the RSFSR, and the Transcaucasian Federation. With the decision to form a federal union, the party leadership made concessions to the periphery.

Even though Gosplan experts in Moscow favored a close economic union between the RSFSR and Ukraine, their Ukrainian colleagues reformulated territorial ideas in their own way.⁷⁹ In June 1925, the chairman of the Ukrainian Administrative Commission, Ivan Cherliunchakevych, was invited to give a presentation to colleagues in Moscow. There he once again rejected Aleksandrov's idea of dividing Ukraine politically into two large territorial "energo-economic" entities: "No variants of such a division of Ukraine are feasible due to national and political considerations. They divide it into an industrial [i.e., Russian-speaking] and an agricultural [i.e., Ukrainian-speaking] part. This would create a split between the [Russian] proletariat and the [Ukrainian] peasantry and pose an obstacle to developing the political line of the peasantry."⁸⁰

The Ukrainian leadership was seeking to organize its territory's economy around a single administrative center, namely the capital of the UkrSSR in Kharkiv (Kiev became the capital only in 1934). But Ukraine's experts did introduce their own territorial order inspired by Gosplan's ideas. From 1923 to 1925, the old administrative units inherited from the Russian Empire were completely dissolved and gradually replaced by what Ukrainian planners considered rational and feasible for their republic: a system of okruga (okruhy), raiony, and rural and urban soviets (*sil'rady/mis'rady*). Before the reforms, the UkrSSR had had twelve gubernii (hubernii), 102 uezdy (povity), and 1,989 volosti; after the reforms, it had forty-one okruga (okruhy) and 632 raiony.⁸¹ The population of an okrug was usually 400,000 to 600,000 people; exceptions were made for regions around large urban centers such as Kharkiv or Kiev. The size of the raiony depended on their economic function: agricultural ones were bigger than mixed or industrial/urban ones.⁸² Though the territory of the Ukrainian SSR was completely restructured in accordance with concepts developed by Gosplan, it endured as a national entity—and that is the most important point.⁸³

The idea of raionirovanie was also discussed in the Transcaucasian Federation by Gosplan's local branch, ZakGosplan. According to its

FIGURE 6. Map of the gubernii (hubernii̇̈) of the UkrSSR in 1921.

chairman, Filipp Makharadze, the okrug would also be the central feature: "In drawing the okruga, we should take into consideration not only the current economic situation and forms of economy but also plans for its further development and restructuring. Thus raionirovanie on a large scale has to consider the general okrug framework of an economic plan, as if it were its territorial expression."[84] Despite this reasonable assertion, ZakGosplan produced comparatively few tangible results, and it faced stubborn resistance from the three Transcaucasian republics. Its own Section for Raionirovanie proved to be particularly feeble.[85] In this situation, regional experts stepped in and proposed their own approaches.[86]

Georgian experts like A. Gegechkori—though grateful to Moscow for the "brotherly advice"—preferred homegrown models of territorialization: "The Russian example has not been able to convince us in every detail. This is why we cannot simply copy it. We have reduced its broad framework, its scale a little. We took only the principle and basis for its modeling from the other parts of the [Soviet] Union."[87] Due to Georgia's geography, regional experts and politicians in 1925-1926 introduced their own two-tier administrative system of uezdy (*mazra*) and temi (*t'emi*) instead of Gosplan's four-tier system of oblast, okrug, raion, and rural soviet.[88] According to the plans of Georgian experts,

FIGURE 7. Map of the okruga (okruhy) of the UkrSSR in 1928.

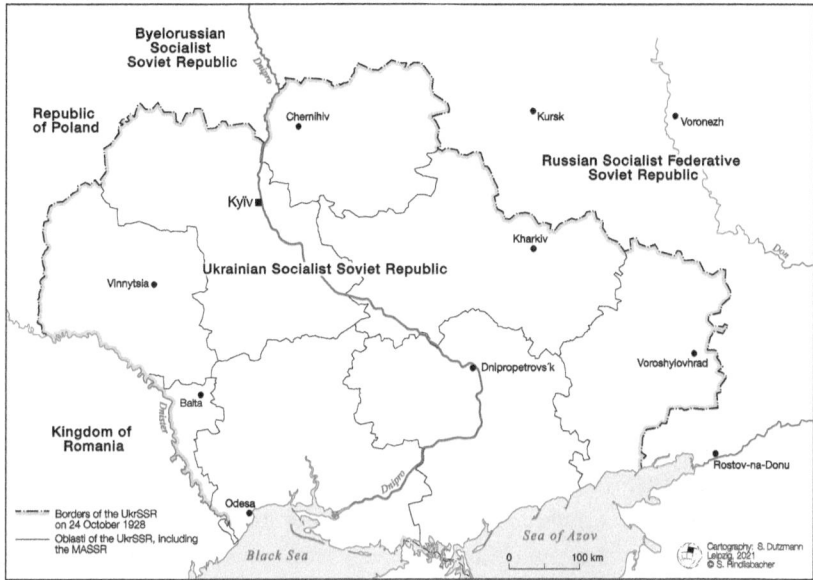

FIGURE 8. Map of the oblasti of the UkrSSR in August 1937.

temi would combine the functions of the raiony and the rural soviets, as they would better fit Georgia's mountainous topography.[89] Thus geographic considerations, not energy production, took center stage in Georgian experts' debates. For instance, the villages in a certain valley that had traditionally formed a "natural" unit were merged and designated as temi.[90]

Armenian experts also proposed their own model, seeing uezdy (*gavar̄*) and uchastki (*gavar̄ak*) as ideal for their republic. They highlighted the fact that configuration of the territory had to take into account the general lack of economic capital. Therefore, experts here felt the approaches taken in Ukraine or the RSFSR were not really that helpful. Furthermore, they emphasized that a unified approach was not at all desirable for the South Caucasus region. The temi might appear useful in Georgia, but such a structure would make no sense for Armenia. Thus they concluded that "all of the [Transcaucasian] republics must have the possibility of finding their own solution to this important question."[91]

Whereas in Eastern Europe and the South Caucasus regional Gosplan experts struggled over how to order state administration, their colleagues in the Kyrgyz ASSR worried about how to create such structures from scratch. In this remote region of Central Asia created after the national delimitation in 1924, the experts tasked with raionirovanie did not dare discuss electricity production. In the southern and the western part of Kyrgyzstan only larger settlements had access to the mail and telegraph networks. Thus it seemed impossible to maintain and improve steady contact between the capital in Frunze (today Bishkek) and most of the volost administrations, never mind rural soviets, in a reasonable amount of time.[92] Furthermore, the administrative borders before 1917 had been deliberately fluid, as they were structured around aspects of tribal belonging. As the local population was mobile and tribal networks flexible, the Russian imperial administrative structure had been in constant motion.[93]

"The aspect of kinship is key for the realization of raionirovanie."[94] This was the main statement by Vladimir Dublitskii, the leading expert for Kyrgyzstan in 1926. He therefore proposed a three-tier system of *kanton—volost—rural soviet* as most appropriate. In such an administrative division, at least the centers of the kantony would have access to postal and telegraph services.[95] On a volost level, Dublitskii then proposed to separate Kyrgyz and "European" entities to avoid "misunderstandings" between the communities and to enable access to secluded Kyrgyz communities in order to mobilize them for the Soviet project.[96]

In this remote region of the Soviet state, aspects of geography, nationality, and aspects of governance completely eclipsed the once purely economic considerations of raionirovanie. Dublitskii considered the three-tier structure of *kanton—volost—rural soviet* as temporary and to be ultimately replaced by a two-tier of *raion—rural soviet*.[97] However, governmental structures had to be built first. Therefore, he openly told his colleagues that raionirovanie in Kyrgyzstan needed more state spending, not less.[98]

Experts like Dublitskii projected that successful raionirovanie would take at least twenty-five years in Kyrgyzstan. They identified two decisive factors for this long-term state-building. On one hand, there were not enough Kyrgyz cadres to fill the administrative positions. They had to be trained first. On the other hand, in many regions there were simply no settlements where a local administration could establish itself. Field surveyors and geographers had first to find spots suitable for development into a regional center, and then such prospective centers had to be connected with the basics of modern statehood: roads, postal stations, and telegraph stations.[99]

The cases of Ukraine, the South Caucasus, and Kyrgyzstan demonstrate how regional experts reformulated Gosplan's concepts of raionirovanie in the mid-1920s. This process did not represent a simple "degeneration" of Gosplan's initial concepts, as Z. Mieczkowski once claimed, but rather its successful adaptation by a heterogeneous polity.[100] At first, raionirovanie had been closely related to GOELRO, but then the concept evolved into a much broader debate, one involving numerous voices, over how to master the multitude of spatial challenges. Experts in Moscow had little choice at the time but to adapt to this development.[101]

When the implementation of raionirovanie got underway in 1923, regional actors saw a chance to revise the existing territorial framework in pursuit of their own interests.[102] Their goal was to enhance the productive forces under their control, even if doing so came at the expense of neighboring Soviet territory.[103] Belarusian politicians were the first to successfully exploit Gosplan's designs for their own ends. After the Peace of Riga in 1921, the Belarusian SSR had shrunk in size to only six uezdy of the former Minsk Guberniia.[104] With support from experts such as Yegorov, Belarusian politicians laid claim to parts of the Vitebsk, Gomel', and Smolensk Gubernii, all of which were in the RSFSR. Their main argument was not national affiliation or language but sustainability in terms of energy efficiency as propagated by Gosplan. The BSSR was supposed to encompass what Gosplan had proposed in 1921 as the Western Economic Oblast.[105] The RKP(b) Politburo supported these Belarusian claims not only for economic but also for propagandistic reasons: to promote Soviet national policies among the Belarusian minority in Poland. Thus territories from the RSFSR were added to the BSSR in two phases, one in 1924 and another in 1926. The Politburo merely stipulated that the BSSR should respect the rights of the Russian and Jewish "minorities" in the areas in question, meaning schools should not be the target of Belarusification.[106] This border drawn in the mid-1920s later evolved into the international border between Belarus and Russia we know today.

Observing this promotion of Belarusian territoriality, experts at the Ukrainian Planning Commission (UkrDerzhplan) seized the opportunity to call for revisions as well. For instance, they proposed attaching Putivl' Uezd, then in Kursk Guberniia, to Ukraine, as this territory nearly formed an RSFSR enclave between Hlukhiv and Sumy.[107] Furthermore, Ukrainian experts proposed the transfer of Millerevo Uezd from Voronezh Guberniia in the east, as geologists had recently discovered a large field of black coal there.[108] The Industrial Section at Gosplan in Moscow even considered adding the southern parts of Kursk Guberniia to Ukraine. The thinking here was to unite the regional sugar industry within a single union republic.[109] Their colleagues in Ukraine swiftly adopted this idea with gratitude.[110] The regional experts of Kursk Guberniia, for their part, tried to make use of the raionirovanie vocabulary to oppose such a territorial change at the expense of "their" economic assets.[111]

Soon the Ukrainian republic and Russian regional administrations were engaged in a contest over territory. Ukrainian state and party institutions, the Ukrainian Central Executive Committee (Vseukraïns'kyi tsentral'nyi vykonavchyi komitet, VUTsVK) in particular, promoted a large-scale border revision, while the regional administrations of the RSFSR in Kursk and Voronezh opposed these proposals. The functionaries in the North Caucasus Krai even lobbied to attach some parts of the Ukrainian Donbas to the RSFSR. The party and state leadership had to intervene and partly decree and partly negotiate solutions for these territorial claims and counterclaims. In the end, both sides could realize at least some of their initial plans at the expanse of the other side. Overall, however, Ukraine drew the poorer hand in this contest for territory. We will see in much greater detail in the next chapter why the party leadership would show itself much less sympathetic to Ukrainian claims than those from the Belarusian side.

After 1923 raionirovanie affected the peripheral regions of the Soviet state, whereas the core around Leningrad and Moscow continued with the old imperial administrative system. The historian Vladimir Kruglov suspects that this delay was also due to the ongoing power struggle at the top of the party. In 1924 Lev Kamenev and Grigorii Zinov'ev were heads of the regional party structures in the Moscow and Leningrad Gubernii respectively. Through raionirovanie they would have had the chance to broaden their power base, posing a dangerous challenge to other party leaders.[112] Thus the administrative-territorial reforms were introduced in the core regions only after the struggle for power had been decided in Stalin's favor.

The Evaluation of Raionirovanie

In 1925 Gleb Krzhizhanovskii considered the results of raionirovanie a success, even though regional actors had adapted Gosplan's original concepts to suit their own prerogatives. He concluded: "Gosplan's project provided the basic principles for dealing with the national structure of the Union. We have established a framework that—if the system of raionirovanie is correctly implemented—allows the national autonomies and republics to keep their rights and gain a firm ground for their individual development, as well as to fulfill their functions as members of the Union."[113] Despite this rather positive assessment, Gosplan's experts could not keep all of the promises once so loudly proclaimed.

Konstantin Yegorov had an insatiable hunger for data on the raionirovanie process. To feed this hunger, he initiated a large survey of the newly created raiony (district scale) in early 1926. He developed a questionnaire and sent it to the oblast executive committees (oblastnoi ispolnitel'nyi komitet, OIK) in the RSFSR and to the union republics' administrative commissions, which in turn saw to its dissemination down to the local level.[114] The questionnaire contained seventeen specific items regarding the functioning of each raion administration. The raion executive committees (raionnyi ispolnitel'nyi komitet, RIK) first had to provide information about their staff and offices and explain the changes that had taken place vis-à-vis the previous volost administration. Then the RIKs were asked about their connection to the okrug center and other state institutions. Finally, the RIKs were to describe how they had prepared and carried out raionirovanie. They were also to discuss its impact on daily life and indicate whether there had been cases of discontent among the population and whether the raion borders and the center of the raion were adequately and clearly defined.[115] The set of questions reveals just how much Yegorov gave priority to the functionality of the new administrative units and the improvement of local governance.

While examples of replies have yet to turn up in the central archives of Soviet-era records in Moscow, responses from twenty-one of the twenty-seven raiony have been found in the records of Kharkiv Okruha (Okrug), held in the State Archive of Kharkiv Oblast.[116] Most depict a positive mood. They confirm that raionirovanie went well, that the administration was functioning, and that the population was content with raion administration services, including education, health care, libraries, veterinary medicine, and so on. However, some RIKs pointed out that, due to the poverty of their raion, cultural projects required larger subsidies from the center. In everyday practice, such budgetary dependency on higher authorities (i.e., Moscow) was an important feature of Soviet federalism.[117] A comparison of the responses from the raiony of Kharkiv Okruha shows that they tended to fulfill Yegorov's expectations.

That said, a closer reading also provides indications that one of the main goals of raionirovanie—to save funds by rationalizing the administrative structure—was not realized. Even though most RIKs in Kharkiv Okruha reported that fewer people were working in the local administration compared to the volost era, they openly said that new, better-qualified raion personnel earned about 50 percent more than former volost employees. Other data indicated a similar pattern throughout the union.[118]

Sometimes, the responses provided deeper insights into how the Soviet administration worked. Answering a question about local participation in raionirovanie, the report from Bol'she-Pisarevskii Raion humbly stated: "The [Ukrainian] Central Administrative-Territorial Commission carried out raionirovanie in 1923. Raionirovanie was not decided within the raion. It was not a decision of the local assemblies. The population perceives raionirovanie as the correct way to strengthen the Soviet apparatus."[119]

After reading such replies, Yegorov began to realize that the original idea of raionirovanie had not achieved its goal of mobilizing the population for the Soviet project. Nationally organized entities were much more successful when performing transformative power. Like the national politicians who had adapted to the structuring ideas of raionirovanie, Yegorov began to alter his approach to nationalism and its role in the Soviet state.[120] He concluded that central administration and national autonomy had to go hand in hand.[121]

Konstantin Yegorov's new, more decentralizing approach to raionirovanie faced strong institutional opposition. The Bolshevik administration had certain misgivings about measures that could lead to decentralization, directly or indirectly. They saw too much local autonomy as a potential threat to Soviet rule. Some local actors might forget how to play the multilayered game of power. Thus representatives from the Commissariat for Post and Telegraph Services, and from within Gosplan, argued against any dispersal of authority.[122] This concern prompted the All-Union Commission for Raionirovanie (Komissiia po raionirovaniiu TsIK SSSR), chaired by Saak Ter-Gabrielian, to invite experts from throughout the union to share their views about raionirovanie at a conference in Moscow on 17 May 1926.[123] Konstantin Yegorov was also in attendance and stood out as one of the conference's most active participants.

The presentation on the territorial structure in Central Asia laid out the panoply of diversity that existed on the ground. Iosif Magidovich, an ethnographer and leading expert with the TsSU reported on his experiences. He first complained that experts like himself had no authority to make political decisions, as he and his colleagues were able only to "advise" regional politicians.[124] Even though these politicians had completely changed the map of the region during national delimitation, the territorial entities beyond the republic or oblast level remained the same. In the former region of Bukhara, the old vaialat were simply renamed *okrug*, while the old tuman received the designation *raion*; in the former Khorezm, the *shiro* was renamed *raion*.[125] The renamed units created confusion when they merged within the new Uzbek republic. According to Magidovich, the challenges were even more striking in Kyrgyzstan, where administrative structures in imperial times had relied on local kinship: "There volosti emerge spontaneously, and they split into parts spontaneously, depending on relations among the different Kyrgyz tribes. When these tribes want to unite in a volost, they unite. If you visit this volost for research, it could happen that they had decided to split into two volosti. I could provide you a list of such volosti that we only recently discovered. There are even more, about which we still have no idea."[126] During discussions of Magidovich's report, Yegorov and Ter-Gabrielian argued that the collection of more data was necessary before the commission could make any valid recommendations.

After the report on Central Asia, a heterogeneous delegation gave an account of raionirovanie within the Transcaucasian Federation. The first speaker from ZakGosplan, a certain Grigorian, started by directing attention to the lack of self-government under the old regime.[127] This stood in stark contrast to the zemstvo system of self-government in most European parts of the Russian Empire. According to Grigorian, it was for this reason that most people were distrustful of state institutions in the South Caucasus. Geography and a sparse population made the task even more difficult.[128] As discussed above, the heterogeneity of this region was already reflected in the terminology: Georgia was divided into a system of uezd (*mazra*) and temi, Armenia into one of uezd (*gavar*) and uchastki (*gavarak*), Azerbaijan into one of uezd (*qəza*) and daira (*dairə*).[129] This intricate territorial structure, Grigorian continued, was the result of history and nature. This heterogeneity and the funding spent on local administration were unique to the union. Maintenance of this administrative structure consumed 50–70 percent of the regional budget. Taken together, this posed a challenge to regional governance, as Grigorian concluded: "[It] makes the popularization of state power on the ground impossible, as this power does not possess any material means."[130]

Grigorian's claim that greater centralization was needed met with stiff opposition from his Transcaucasian colleagues. Barzian of Armenia and Ingorokva of Georgia defended their republics' existing administrative-territorial structures. Ingorokva again highlighted the temi-system as most suitable to Georgia's geography and went on to deny any connection between the territorial structure and the spending on local administration: "The example of Switzerland demonstrates this. As we all know, Switzerland has a complex territorial system with two levels: the municipality and the canton."[131] In effect, he was insisting that the existing structure, which relied on prerevolutionary administrative borders, would be able to advance Georgia's further development.[132] Concluding this discussion, Yegorov thanked the Transcaucasian participants for their comments and added that the main goal of raionirovanie was to strengthen Soviet power. The nomenclature used for territorial units seemed to him a secondary matter.[133]

Throughout the Soviet state, raionirovanie continued slowly but surely. In the autumn of 1926, experts and politicians developed a new territorial structure for Uzbekistan. The mixture of different entities was to be replaced with a threefold system of okruga, raiony, and rural soviets. The seven oblasti were replaced by ten okruga, the twenty-three uezdy by eighty-seven raiony. All volosti and their equivalents were dissolved.[134] Saak Ter-Gabrielian saw the new territorial units as "independent economic organisms," as they adhered to existing irrigation systems. Moreover, the new territorial configuration was expected to reduce the number of employees in the local administration from 14,000 to 13,500.[135] However, the whole Uzbek project was marred by a major incongruity: the Tajik ASSR—at that time still part of Uzbekistan—was not part of the reform. In this particularly remote region, the prerevolutionary units simply continued to exist.

From Moscow's perspective, this regional adaptation of raionirovanie portended growing chaos where dysfunctional local administrations wasted valuable state funds.[136] Some experts at Gosplan were especially disappointed with the results. One anonymous author complained in 1928 that national-ethnographic considerations had completely supplanted Gosplan's initial vision. Even though it was scientifically sound, opposition from Bashkiria, Ukraine, and the South Caucasus undermined its implementation.[137] Moreover, he complained that the

TsIK Commission for Raionirovanie in Moscow had no real power, and local opposition could easily obstruct its efforts. He concluded ironically: "We can hardly call raionirovanie of certain territories a process of economic raionirovanie, where the word *raionirovanie* itself is derived from *raion* in the sense of an entire economic oblast (krai). It is rather an administrative raionirovanie, where *raionirovanie* comes from the word *raion* in the sense of a small administrative-economic unit, between uezd and volost."[138] The crux of his argument was that the Soviet experts had replaced one inefficient administrative heterogeneity with another.[139] Such diversity could be understood as an obstacle. More discipline and more centralization were possible answers. According to this point of view, frustration with this chaotic and uncoordinated territorial policy contributed to the major shift in Soviet politics that would later become known as the Cultural Revolution.[140]

During the manifold adaptation of raionirovanie in the peripheries, spatial concepts of the Bolshevik leadership in Moscow evolved as well. The politicians in Moscow began to abandon ideas of an organic regional territorial structure in favor of more active central planning. Therefore, the state and party leadership would channel resources and people to develop a certain region not bottom-up but top-down. The state was expected to take a much more active role in developing the Soviet system as a whole.

These signals from the top provoked a shift in thinking among the territorial experts as well. Between 1926 and 1928 Yegorov, Aleksandrov, Vladimirskii, and others regularly organized discussions at the Institute of Soviet Construction (Institut sovetskogo stroitel'stva) within the Communist Academy (Kommunisticheskaia akademiia). There they reformulated their ideas of how to deal with the spatial diversity of the Soviet state. At the beginning of these discussions in May 1926, Yegorov openly admitted that Gosplan had been too eager to promote its idea of self-sufficiency in terms of energy efficiency. His colleagues agreed.[141] The challenge facing them now was to find an efficient, scientific way to deal with the existing economic, national-ethnographic, and geographic challenges. Nonetheless, they remained bound by a clear ideological perspective, as Vladimir Dosov, a representative of the Kazakh ASSR, demonstrated: "Autonomy is not an end in itself. Neither the soviets nor Soviet structures are ends in themselves. Our final goal is the withering away of the state, but obviously, current conditions demand the independent existence of separate kraia and raiony [regional scale]."[142]

The experts, however, had started to shift their focus from regional agency back to top-down governance. In the process, some of Yegorov's colleagues even threw their previous dogmas overboard. In February 1928 Vladimirskii openly asserted: "We will not be able to achieve raionirovanie based only on logical constructs and theories, however strong they are. They cannot create a country's administrative structure, especially not in the country where we are now. . . . We are faced with the conditions of a transition period, when all of the newly constituted raiony [regional scale] are again beginning to constitute themselves anew."[143] Vladimirskii further noted that such raiony should not be seen in terms of self-sufficient organic entities but as instruments, as means of transmitting orders for Soviet construction between planners in Moscow and workers on the ground. For him territorial units were now, first and foremost, to be the means of implementing the planned economy.[144]

Gosplan's institutional influence would reach its zenith with Stalin's rise to power. He wanted to catch up with the advanced capitalist states in the West within only ten years.[145] With the idea of a five-year plan, Gosplan offered him what he desperately needed—a blueprint for instant economic growth.[146] With Stalin's blessing, Gosplan became an almighty planning body. Its competitors in the field of expert policy advice were restructured (KEPS in 1930), dissolved (VSNKh in 1932), or attached to Gosplan (TsSU in 1930). Thus Gosplan played a key role in hollowing out the NEP and accelerating the forced collectivization of agriculture.[147]

Raionirovanie became one of the catchwords during the Cultural Revolution. Examination of the stenographs from the Fifteenth Party Congress in 1928 and the Sixteenth Party Congress in 1930 shows that almost everyone within the party leadership used the term. However, this widespread usage in party discourse was ambivalent. For Stalin, it provided a code for advancing his own policies as he consolidated his power. Hence he proclaimed in June 1930: "The aim of raionirovanie is to bring the party-soviet and economic-cooperative apparatus closer to the raion [district scale] and the village. Thus we have the means of deciding in a timely manner the biggest questions in agriculture—that is, its elevation, its restructuring [*rekonstruktsiia*]. In this sense—I repeat—raionirovanie has been a huge gain for our entire construction process."[148]

Given the fixation on rapid industrialization and collectivization, additional expert debates appeared as at best an obstacle. For this reason, territorial experiments and debates over the rational organization of territory came to an end. At the beginning of 1930, numerous expert committees were dissolved. After the Shakhty show trial against "bourgeois specialists" in early 1928, the GPU (political police) purged the "old" Gosplan of many of its experts. Gleb Krzhizhanovskii had to resign in 1930 and was replaced by Valerian Kuibyshev, one of Stalin's confidants.[149] In the midst of the Cultural Revolution, all of the territorial structures served the purpose of transmitting orders from the planners in the center to the people on the ground. National entities would serve as necessary interfaces. These were the guiding principles of the last major territorial restructuring.

Whereas the first attempt at raionirovanie took almost a decade, the second took only weeks. With the scratch of a pen, all of the okrug administrations were abolished throughout the union and their tasks transferred to the raiony in August 1930. A few large entities now governed a multitude of raiony. The state and party leadership sought to reallocate funding from administration to economic projects and to shorten the chain of command.[150] In the Ukrainian SSR, for example, the 40 okruga (okruhy) and 625 raiony from 1928 were replaced by 7 oblasti and 358 raiony in 1932.[151] This reorganization offered Stalin a priceless opportunity to reshuffle regional and local cadres and install his loyal followers on every level of state power.[152]

The abolition of the okruga was a top-down decision. This time, senior politicians, not experts, decided how to reshape the Soviet Union's administrative-territorial framework. Regional authorities received the order to introduce this reform with little opportunity for discussion. For instance, the Armenian Republic had been administered by a system composed of uezdy and uchastki between 1921 and 1929.[153] In 1929 the eight uezdy were replaced by five okruga. In 1930 Moscow entrusted a Zakkraikom commission with preparing and implementing a system that would considerably reduce the number of territorial entities in Armenia. As a consequence, a one-layer administrative system with twenty-seven raiony (šejan) was established.[154] It was no great surprise that this rushed restructuring only exacerbated the existing administrative chaos on the ground. It was often left unclear who had to carry out which responsibilities. For example, in Armenia and Georgia, village teachers had to wait months for their salaries. Another goal of this reform was to distribute the cadres from the okruga to the raiony, so that they could support the five-year plan on the ground, but most of them were hired by the administrations of the republican capitals instead.¹⁵⁵ Thus practical expertise became even more centralized, contrary to the designs of politicians in Moscow.

Within the "new" Stalinist Gosplan, there was no place for enthusiastic experts like Yegorov. In 1930 he lost his job and most of his influence. However, he did not fall victim to Stalinist repression but received a managing position in the rubber industry in Moscow.¹⁵⁶ When Stalinist experts used the term *raionirovanie* after 1930, they focused on the command economy. Thus their planning commissions saw the territorial structure as a means of transmitting orders to the locals. Each raion was to produce what seemed best to the politicians and experts.¹⁵⁷ Their goal was to increase output and support the industrialization effort. The needs of the people on the ground played a secondary role at best. In implementing this command economy, the planners in Moscow merged Turkmenistan, Uzbekistan, Tajikistan, and Kyrgyzstan into a region that was supposed to provide cotton for the growing industrial sector. Kazakhstan was designed as a single economic region that was to produce grain and breed livestock.¹⁵⁸ Combined with forced collectivization, such plans had tremendously adverse consequences for the population.¹⁵⁹

Anyone trying to initiate a new fundamental debate on territorial issues—be they economic or national—had to fear repression. The Ukrainian political elite faced this new hardline policy during the Kuban and Skrypnyk affairs in 1932, as did their comrades in the South Caucasus during the Great Terror four years later.¹⁶⁰ Nonetheless, changes in the territorial structure were possible and often carried out within Soviet republics and autonomous oblasti as long as they did not interfere with the borders of the national entities. Party and state organs regularly adapted administrative-territorial structures to projects related to needs of the planned economy.¹⁶¹ Thus raionirovanie as such did not end with the abolition of the okruga in 1930–1931. It remained a valuable administrative tool until the dissolution of the USSR in 1991.¹⁶²

At the beginning of the 1930s, however, the ideas behind raionirovanie ossified. Oblasti and raiony could be divided or merged according to the needs of the planned economy, but the productive debate over the criteria governing how the state could or should be structured faded away. In general, the number of oblasti grew after 1931 as their larger variants soon proved to be inefficient. For instance, the UkrSSR consisted of only seven oblasti in 1932 but had fifteen in early 1939. Whereas administrative borders within republics and autonomous units changed quite often, the Soviet state reconfigured or dissolved larger national territories only in exceptional cases as they served as the backbone of the Stalinist power structure. Nationality in the Soviet Union increasingly gained an essentialist quality. With the introduction of the passport system and the obligatory entry on nationality, every Soviet citizen was assigned a marker that proved nearly impossible to change.[163]

Under Nikita Khrushchev, the Soviet leadership transferred some types of economic planning back to the union republics and initiated an administrative-territorial reform. After his fall in October 1964, however, many of these reformist efforts were reversed. Thus the synthetic (economic and ethnonational) Soviet administrative-territorial framework endured (with minor changes) until the Soviet Union's demise a quarter of a century later.[164]

The Ossification of Soviet Modernization

At the outset of the 1920s, the Bolshevik government realized that it would not be able to govern the new Soviet state, its economy, its population, and its space without a well-developed plan based on accurate statistical data and a well-thought-out administrative structure. To obtain such data and produce a territorial framework for the new state, Moscow initially had to rely on Russian imperial expertise for raionirovanie. At the same time, with the introduction of the NEP, the Bolsheviks also created a nemesis to the free market—Gosplan. In the beginning, the GOELRO campaign and the debate on how to structure the Soviet state were intricately linked. In Gosplan's Section for Raionirovanie, well-paid experts collected and discussed data with the goal of managing the diversity of Soviet space with the greatest efficiency. They proposed a new model of homogenous territorial units that were to be self-sufficient in terms of energy production and to encourage local economic initiative. However, the experts wisely kept to themselves the fact that their "new" framework relied largely on the old imperial guberniia structure and its borders.

Regional and national politicians adapted the raionirovanie discourse to their own ends. In doing so, they offered viable conduits between the center and the margins in everyday practice. The experts in Moscow revised their ideas accordingly. Nevertheless, Gosplan's territorial vision had yet to exhaust itself. From a midterm perspective, the discourse on raionirovanie liberated itself from the GOELRO campaign and had a tremendous impact on the administrative-territorial restructuring of the early Soviet state. Gosplan's concepts materialized on a regional level. The Belarusian SSR, Ukraine, Georgia, Armenia, and Kyrgyzstan provided illustrative examples of this point. At the same time, experts from the center, such as Yegorov, continued to develop their ideas and plans. As many regional participants adapted the terminology provided by Gosplan to their needs, the experts in Moscow began to strengthen the role of the regions in economic development.

In the long term, the idea of a strong central institution like Gosplan regulating the whole economy gained the upper hand. Regional solutions conveyed the impression of administrative chaos and wasteful spending of state funding. People acting at various levels of the state bureaucracy and the party apparatus saw this administrative heterogeneity as an obstacle. Thus they grew more receptive to slogans for greater discipline and a "strong hand" at the helm. Under these conditions, raionirovanie mutated from a technocratic term into a convenient slogan for cadre reshuffling. Hence Stalin and his comrades were able to adopt this power tool for their own ends.

Chapter 3

Ukraine and the RSFSR
How to Find a Common Border

> Drawing on precise national-ethnographic data, we must conclude that the existing borders of the UkrSSR are hardly precise and justifiable.
>
> —Panas Butsenko, 1927

These pages are quite simply not the place for a discussion of Ukraine and the debates over its prospective territories in the nineteenth and early twentieth centuries. As intellectually stimulating and engrossing as the works on linguistics, ethnography, and cartography produced by experts such as Stepan Rudnyts'kyi, Eugeniusz Romer, or Yefim Karski may be, they had little influence on the people who had to negotiate and demarcate the border between Ukraine and the RSFSR in and after 1919.[1] This was even more true because local populations had a rather pragmatic approach to nationality before 1917.[2] At the Paris Peace Conference, representatives from the Ukrainian People's Republic (Ukraïns'ka narodna respublika, UNR) sought recognition from the victorious powers, but all their efforts were in vain. The Entente powers ultimately preferred Ukraine to be a part of a renovated Russian Empire. Thus all the petitions, studies, and debates concerning Ukrainian territory circulating during the conference were of almost no consequence in the founding of the sole Ukrainian territorial unit that survived the troublesome aftermath of the First World War—that is, Soviet Ukraine.[3]

Soviet Ukraine took shape outside the Entente's sphere of influence. According to western politicians, Poland and Romania were to contain the Bolshevik revolution. The outcome of the Polish-Soviet War and the Peace of Riga in 1921 defined most of Soviet Ukraine's western border, while Soviet commissions decided the Russian-Ukrainian border in the north and east.[4] According to the 1926 census, twenty-nine million people lived in Ukraine, about 20 percent of the population of the Soviet Union. Economically, Ukraine was the strongest of the republics after the RSFSR.[5]

Putting a Shattered Empire Together Again

After the collapse of the tsarist government in February 1917, the Ukrainian Central Rada (Ukraïns'ka tsentral'na rada), an assembly of Ukrainian political and social activists in Kiev, claimed to represent the interests of all Ukrainians within the Russian state. The Rada deputies initially preferred autonomy to independence. Due to requests from the Provisional Government in Petrograd, the representatives of the Rada accepted that a constituent assembly would establish Ukraine's borders. In the interim, the Rada was expected to function within five previously imperial gubernii: Kiev, Poltava, Podolia, Volhynia, and parts of Chernigov.[6] Following the Bolshevik revolution that same November, the Rada defined its territory unilaterally. In doing so, the deputies were prudent and supplied a preliminary list, according to which Ukraine would include the following imperial gubernii: Kiev, Podolia, Volhynia, Chernihiv, Poltava, Katerynoslav, Kherson, and Taurida (without Crimea). In Kursk, Kholm, and Voronezh Gubernii plebiscites should decide territorial affiliation.[7] Roughly two months later, the deputies formally proclaimed the independence of the UNR.

Throughout the Civil War that followed the Bolshevik revolution, the ideal of a united Ukrainian state with a defined territory remained a fiction. Over the course of 1918 and 1919, the armed forces of numerous states and movements battled for control of the Ukrainian lands: the German Empire, Austria-Hungary, General Skoropadskii's Hetmanate, the UNR, the Donetsk-Krivoi Rog Soviet Republic, tsarist loyalists under Anton Denikin, anarchists under Nestor Makhno, Poland, and of course the nascent Soviet state.[8] Borders were in a state of permanent flux. For example, the Hetmanate briefly occupied the region around Belgorod, a town in the southern part of Kursk Guberniia.[9] This town would become one of the stumbling blocks in Soviet debates over the RSFSR-Ukrainian border. Moreover, after the collapse of the Habsburg Empire in November 1918, Ukrainian activists, native to eastern Galicia, established a Western Ukrainian People's Republic.[10]

With that, a second Ukrainian state emerged outside the former Russian Empire, although the newly created Polish Republic would soon overrun it.[11]

Amid the chaos that unfolded after the withdrawal of German and Austro-Hungarian occupation forces, the Bolsheviks tried to export their revolution. With Moscow's support, Ukrainian communists in early 1919 created a satellite state in the south, the Ukrainian Socialist Soviet Republic (Ukraïns'ka sotsialistychna radians'ka respublika, UkrSSR).[12] When attempts to seize power in Kiev failed, this newly proclaimed Soviet government established itself in Kharkiv.[13] This town near the border with the RSFSR would remain the Ukrainian capital until 1934, even though Kiev was larger and seen as the historical center. Kharkiv was easier to access from Moscow.

In early 1919, the RSFSR and the UkrSSR began to consult officially over the future of their shared border. These negotiations were hastily arranged and did not last long. The result was a border convention signed on 25 February 1919. The Central Rada's definition of the Ukrainian lands, described above, served as a blueprint. Negotiators defined Ukrainian territory using the borders of the imperial gubernii. However, there were two major differences. Negotiators did not adopt the idea of plebiscites in contested areas, and they divided Chernigov Guberniia between them.[14] Nonetheless, the parties to the talks understood that these borders were preliminary and subject to later discussion.[15]

At first, Soviet space was not clearly compartmentalized. The eastern border between the UkrSSR and the RSFSR is a striking example. During the Polish-Soviet War, a first territorial transfer between the RSFSR and the UkrSSR took place in the early spring of 1920. The western parts of the Oblast of the Don Cossack Host (Oblast' voiska donskogo) were ceded to Ukraine. The idea behind this move was to bring the industry of the Donets Basin (Donets'kyi basein, Donbas), which had also been split between the RSFSR and the UkrSSR, under the administration of one Soviet republic. By doing so, the Soviets hoped this would improve coordination in the war effort against Poland.[16] The transfer took place not long after the Red Army defeated White forces in the region. Due to the ongoing war, the Soviet government did not discuss this territorial revision with local representatives. Here the ethnographic principle, which had played a decisive role in assigning gubernii the previous year, was now ignored. For similar economic and administrative reasons, the Cossack communities (*stanitsa*)

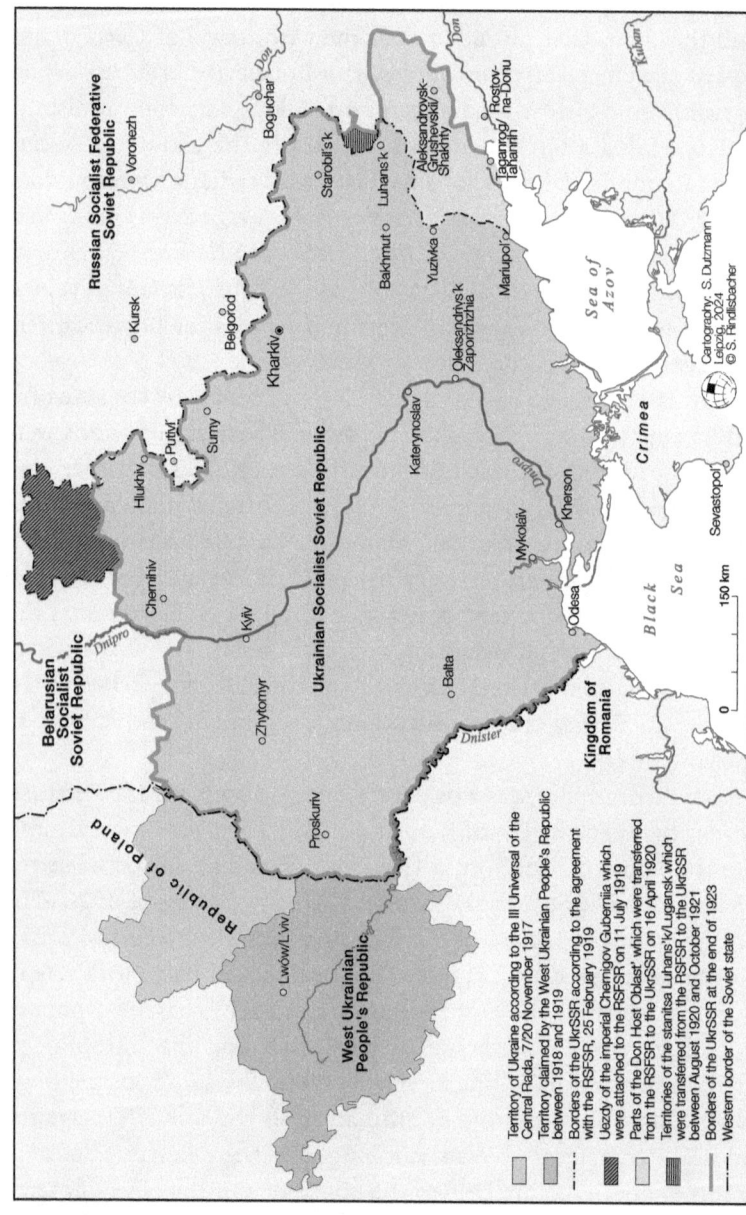

FIGURE 9. Ukrainian borders between 1917 and 1924.

around Lugansk were also added to the UkrSSR between August 1920 and October 1921.[17] In the west, the outcome of the war against Poland settled the borders of the UkrSSR. By the terms of the Peace of Riga, the Soviets had to surrender the western parts of Volhynia Guberniia to Poland in 1921.[18] Meanwhile, in the southwest, Romania occupied and annexed Bessarabia up to the Dniester River. The Bolshevik government never officially recognized this latter loss of territory. They chose instead to wait for a fitting opportunity to revisit the matter.[19]

After the Civil War, the Bolshevik leadership turned to the question of how to administer the space under the Red Army's control. As we have seen so far, the early Soviet state was quite chaotic with regard to territorial matters. Entities inherited from the old regime coexisted alongside new, nationally defined territories or formally independent Soviet republics such as Ukraine. As late as the mid-1920s, the internal structure of the Soviet state was still open for negotiation.

Internationalist and Austromarxist ideas in the upper party echelons went into steady decline as the Civil War drew to a close, even though some of Gosplan's experts continued to promote such inclusive approaches. The party leadership was leaning toward the formation of a federation or a union of states organized along national-ethnographic lines.[20] However, the Soviet discourse about "nation" and "nationality" was heterogeneous, to say the least. Even though Soviet experts emphasized slight but decisive differences, most of those engaged in such debates were politicians, and they used terms such as "ethnographic" (*etnograficheskii*), "national" (*natsional'nyi*), and "national-ethnographic" (*natsional'no-etnograficheskii*) or "nation" (*natsiia*) and "nationality" (*narodnost'* or *natsional'nost'*) interchangeably.[21] Thus the meaning of these terms often blurred, as they could refer to language, culture, or the organization of the economy among a certain part of the population when linking these factors with territory.[22] In short, the participants—the Ukrainian representatives among them—began to apply such terms to define a population group and their perceived interests as opposed to other communities within the Soviet state. Going forward, I use these words and phrases not as analytical terms but as they came up during this contentious political discourse.[23]

The Ukrainian communists were also far from homogeneous. Since their formation in 1918, they had split into three competing factions: the leftists, the centrists, and the "Yekaterinoslav group" or rightists.[24] The leftists were mostly convinced internationalists. They insisted on an independent Ukraine within the newly established Communist International but abstained from any "nationalist" policy. The Yekaterinoslav group promoted a close association with the Russian Communist Party. Whereas the rightists and leftists (each for their own reasons) were skeptical of Ukrainian nationalism, centrists such as Mykola Skrypnyk, an esteemed Old Bolshevik, saw in it positive potential. These centrists received a large boost of additional support in 1920, when the *borot'bisty*, left-wing Ukrainian Socialist-Revolutionaries, joined the ranks of the KP(b)U. Among them were activists like Oleksandr Shums'kyi and Mykhailo Poloz. In the first years of Soviet rule, these three factions of the KP(b)U competed fiercely for power and influence. The internal party tensions that resulted led to a series of Ukrainian first secretaries in quick succession.[25]

Shifts in politics among party leaders in Moscow allowed centrists in Kharkiv to gain more and more influence. In the mid-1920s, they grew to become the dominant faction.[26] The power struggle within the party leadership in Moscow weakened the Ukrainian party's leftists, who opposed the NEP. The centrists profited from korenizatsiia, which they then helped implement by pursuing Ukrainization within party and state institutions. Resolutions against "Great Russian chauvinism" would provide the discursive background for the debates to come.[27] The Sultan-Galiev affair, however, also made clear to all that there were red lines they had to observe.

The Ukrainian centrists' rise to power provided opportunities for younger party activists such as Panas Butsenko, an ardent follower of Skrypnyk and Shums'kyi and their Ukrainization policies. In July 1923, Butsenko became secretary of the Ukrainian Central Executive Committee (VUTsVK), which was the nominal head of the state administration. His responsibilities as secretary included overseeing territorial reforms, national minority affairs, and border revisions with the RSFSR. As part of his job, he promoted the formation of national rural soviets and raiony for Soviet Ukraine's Germans, Poles, Jews, and Bulgarians, among others, but he also publicly claimed the same rights for the Ukrainian-speaking population in the RSFSR.[28]

The Balancing Act of the Cherviakov Commission

Many regional and national actors thus saw opportunities to extend their influence and power. The heads of the newly established kraia within the RSFSR were in a rather privileged position. Nikolai Eizmont, party secretary in what would become North Caucasus Krai, laid claim to about 15,000 square versta (17,000 square kilometers) with approximately 600,000 inhabitants in eastern Ukraine.[29] The North Caucasus was one of the testing grounds for raionirovanie in the RSFSR and was still reconsolidating itself administratively. For support, Eizmont could rely on experienced experts like Vasilii Khronin, the head of Gosplan's local branch. In his memoranda, Khronin proposed adding the port of Tahanrih (today Taganrog) and the coalmines of Shakhty to the North Caucasus. He based his arguments on the fact that these towns were majority Russian-speaking. According to him, Tahanrih had the only deep-water port that was potentially available to the North Caucasus. The coalmines of Shakhty, in Khronin's view, would provide electricity and fuel.[30]

Party and state institutions in the North Caucasus launched a full-fledged propaganda campaign to reinforce their claims to Ukrainian territory. Vasilii Khronin edited a brochure with scientific studies summarizing all of the arguments for the region's transfer to the RSFSR.[31] The local newspaper *Sovetskii iug* (Soviet South) personified this campaign in a caricature that depicted Tahanrih as a weak old man who would profit from unification with the economically potent North Caucasus.[32]

Ukrainian representatives opposed such claims and sought to counter the "sinister" propaganda from the North Caucasus.[33] They pointed to the Ukrainian-speaking population in the surrounding villages and the role Tahanrih played in the development of industry in the Donbas.[34] Leading Ukrainian centrists were confident that they could easily foil these "Great Russian chauvinist" claims.

Quite to the contrary, Panas Butsenko and his comrade Mykhailo Poloz, the head of the Ukrainian State Planning Commission (UkrDerzhplan), sought to revise the northeast border in favor of the UkrSSR.[35] The volosti and uezdy along the southern rim of Briansk, Kursk, and Voronezh Gubernii were expected to be attached to Ukraine given their Ukrainian-speaking majorities. In the spring of 1924, the Section for Raionirovanie at UkrDerzhplan compiled a comprehensive dossier detailing their territorial claims.[36] UkrDerzhplan's experts had carefully analyzed the population of the gubernii in question. In addition, they were of the opinion that the regional sugar industry should be united under the Ukrainian republic. Most of the refineries were in the southern part of Kursk Guberniia, whereas the sugar beets were grown in Ukraine.[37] National-ethnographic considerations aside, they, too, were

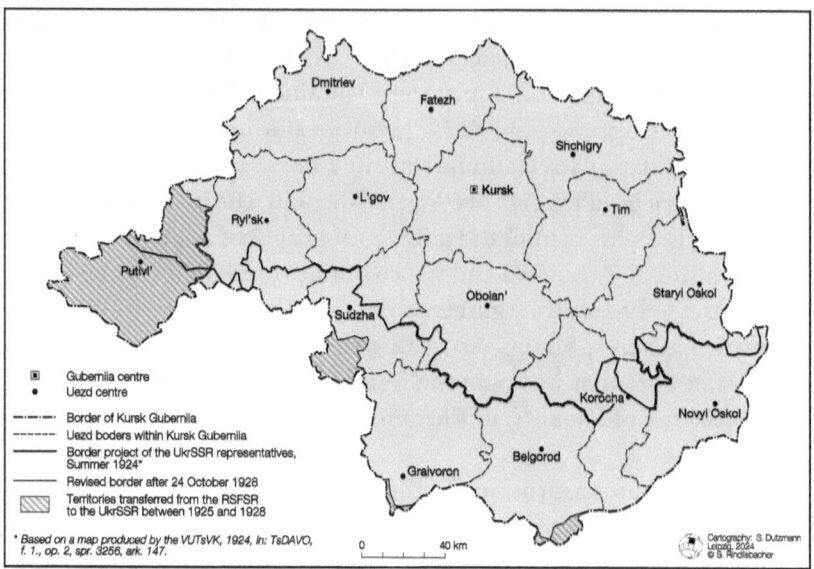

FIGURE 10. Map of border revisions in Kursk Guberniia, 1924–1928.

trying to improve "their" local economic base at the expense of their neighbors—much like the officials in the North Caucasus.

Some Ukrainian claims went much farther. In 1924 Mykhailo Hrushevs'kyi, a highly respected Ukrainian historian and statesman, wrote a memorandum for the Soviet Ukrainian government that called for the inclusion of the Kuban region in the UkrSSR as Ukrainian-speaking Cossacks lived in this area. His expert opinion became part of the Ukrainian side's official claims.[38]

The Ukrainian and Russian party leaderships agreed that they would have to discuss these territorial issues. Against the backdrop of the recent border revisions in favor of the Belarusian SSR in the spring of 1924, it initially seemed that the general political climate favored Ukraine rather than the RSFSR. Leading centrists lobbied successfully for the establishment of a bilateral Russian-Ukrainian border commission.[39] However, this commission would meet only behind closed doors because the topic under discussion could easily enflame nationalist sentiments within the Soviet state.[40]

A bilateral commission made up of representatives from the Russian and the Ukrainian Soviet republics had to find feasible solutions for conflicting territorial claims. Aleksandr Cherviakov, then chairman of the Belarusian TsIK, was assigned to head the commission in

April 1924. It was his job to play the role of a neutral broker and represent the interests of the union as a whole.⁴¹ On the eve of the first meeting, the Ukrainian representatives Butsenko and Poloz harbored great expectations. They had staked out claims on about 35,000 square versta (roughly 40,000 square kilometers) from the gubernii of Briansk, Kursk, and Voronezh.⁴² Almost two million people lived in the territories in question. According to their statistical data, the vast majority of the population in the border areas were Ukrainians.⁴³ The Politburo of the KP(b)U supported these claims in the northeast, but they gave Butsenko and Poloz strict orders not to raise the Kuban issue, including all claims toward North Caucasus Krai. These territories were taboo, even for discussions among comrades behind the scenes.⁴⁴

The Cherviakov Commission brought together party officials with contradictory approaches and aims. The lines of conflict were quickly exposed at the very first session on 1 July 1924. Both representatives of the RSFSR, Aleksandr Beloborodov and Martin Latsis, were leftist revolutionaries. Beloborodov had been commissar for internal affairs since 1923 and was one of Trotsky's close allies. Latsis had made his career within the Cheka. In 1919 he had even run the political police in Ukraine for a brief time. Even today, he remains infamous for his quip that, in times of revolution, the guilt or innocence of an individual is determined not by evidence but by class background.⁴⁵ In 1918 and 1919 Latsis also ranked among the critics of the party's nationality policies, favoring instead, like Bukharin and Georgii Piatakov, an "international" approach focused on the proletariat.⁴⁶ After the Civil War, Latsis had changed his line of work in constructing socialism and moved from the political police to agriculture and economics.

Both of the RSFSR representatives saw issues related to nationality as formalities, which stood in stark contradiction to the approach of their Ukrainian comrades. Beloborodov emphasized that the commission should organize the border revision according to economic considerations alone. He argued that adherence to ethnographic maps would produce inefficient, jagged borders.⁴⁷ The Ukrainian representatives insisted on the importance of national-ethnographic criteria. Hence finding agreement between the two sides was going to entail severe challenges. Even if Latsis and Beloborodov had not belonged to the party's leftists, they would have stuck to the economic line. They could not openly raise "Russian" national arguments without facing accusations of "Great Russian chauvinism."⁴⁸ Both sides tried to present their proposals as the most "efficient" (*tselesoobrazno*) way to deal with the issue. "Efficiency" was a Soviet buzzword. It was an empty, convenient shell that could be filled with any random content. Thus the central debate within the Cherviakov Commission revolved around what the most "efficient" solution would be.[49]

Some days after the commission's strained first meeting, the Ukrainian side had to accept its first major setback. The very nature of this blow reveals a great deal about decision making and power politics within the Soviet state. The Politburo in Moscow decided that the parts of eastern Ukraine around the towns Tahanrih and Shakhty had to be ceded to the RSFSR. In doing so, the Politburo not only bypassed the bilateral commission under Cherviakov. It made this decision even though Tahanrih and Shakhty had belonged to territories transferred from the RSFSR to the UkrSSR just four years previously. Relying exclusively on Khronin's expertise, the Politburo explained this re-revision by citing the North Caucasus's need for a deep-sea port and the ethnographic composition of these areas.[50] Representatives of the Ukrainian state and party apparatus protested in vain, but they had to stick to the rules of the game.[51]

Due to summer holidays and the need for further studies, the Cherviakov Commission did not meet until mid-October. Poloz and Butsenko expressed their displeasure with the Politburo's decision to the full extent permissible within the Soviet framework—they boycotted the commission's second session on 13 October 1924.[52] Cherviakov and the RSFSR representatives were left to plan the implementation of the border changes around Tahanrih and Shakhty on their own. They followed the Politburo's recommendations without hesitation and expressed their hope that there would be no "dissent from the representatives from the UkrSSR next time."[53] Butsenko and Poloz had to agree to the border revision at the next meeting on 21 October.[54] To make things worse, however, they had to give their assent to a fait accompli, since a bilateral regional commission had already demarcated the future border, and the territories in question had been transferred on 1 October.[55]

This setback did not discourage Butsenko and Poloz at first. They had also received some promising signals. They now turned self-confidently to their claims in the north. On 18 October Butsenko had been able to publish an article on the border issue in the all-union newspaper *Izvestiia*. There he publicly pointed to the necessity of considering ethnographic boundaries in negotiations over the Russian-Ukrainian border. He drew on resolutions from the Twelfth Party Congress and the legacy of Lenin's nationality policies.[56] In the commission meetings,

Poloz had taken the same line, repeatedly arguing that "the Ukrainian population forms a large majority in the border areas [of Kursk, Voronezh, and Briansk Gubernii]. The basis of our national policy is to serve the cultural needs of these people."[57] As a member of the board of directors at UkrDerzhplan, Poloz had also contributed to a memorandum in which he argued that the ethnographic principle should be fundamental, but that the border should meet regional economic needs. Thus the town of Belgorod, with sugar refineries in the outskirts, ought to belong to the UkrSSR.[58]

Within the Cherviakov Commission, two new factors emerged that seemed to dampen the prospects of Ukrainian success. First, representatives from Voronezh and Kursk Gubernii were invited to attend the next meeting. Even though they did not have a formal say in the proceedings, a majority of those sitting in the room were now against any major revisions to the borders.[59] Second, the Cherviakov Commission decided to create a subcommission of experts because the commission members saw themselves as ill-suited to evaluating all of the reports and statistical data each side had submitted. It should come as no big surprise that Cherviakov called on Konstantin Yegorov to head this subcommission.[60] As we have seen previously, Yegorov considered himself as an expert on wide array of matters, and he was still quite critical of "national-ethnographic" arguments in matters of territory, preferring instead arguments that addressed economic efficiency and exigencies of governance.[61]

After a meeting in Moscow on 23 October, Panas Butsenko grew increasingly pessimistic. In a report to the Central Committee of the KP(b)U, he complained about the general change in tone:

> we faced more and more difficulties from the representatives of the RSFSR, especially from the delegates from Kursk and Voronezh Gubernii, who showed up at the commission only to protest with a demonstrative walkout. We noticed a clear reluctance to discuss the project of the UkrSSR. Certain comrades even raised their voices and used terms like *Malorossiia* and *Velikorossiia*. They were referring to *malorossy* ... in Belgorod Uezd who do not want to join our republic. They also pretended that there were a lot of petitions from the population of the [Ukrainian] Novgorod-Seversk, Sumy, and Kharkov Okruga asking to join the RSFSR.[62]

In the wake of the setback involving Tahanrih and Shakhty, the Ukrainian representatives were now facing counterclaims in the north from the representatives of the RSFSR.⁶³ Butsenko, however, pressed forward in his struggle for a resolution of the border to Ukraine's advantage. He asked the TsK KP(b)U to appeal to its Russian counterpart to establish a binding line not only for the southeast but also in the north.⁶⁴ Furthermore, he urged UkrDerzhplan to counter the Russian claims and provide him with the best expertise they had: "Please prepare [the data] with all the attention required as the issue has taken on an extraordinarily serious character in the commission. For every village we claim, the Ukrainian government has to provide a precise economic and ethnographic foundation."⁶⁵

In the meantime, Yegorov's commission of experts had started work, and soon enough, the same divisions arose that existed within the Cherviakov Commission itself. Yegorov was assisted in his efforts by one Troitskii of Gosplan and a certain Vdovichenko of UkrDerzhplan. Together they had an effective say in matters. However, delegates from the border gubernii joined their sessions as well. During the first meeting at the main Gosplan building in Moscow, the experts agreed to use all of the materials available on the topic, in particular the census data of 1897 and 1920. Yegorov also promised that Gosplan would provide all of the publications and office supplies needed.⁶⁶ Ethnographic data remained highly contested and prone to bias. Every side collected and counted by its own methods and arrived at different figures.⁶⁷

The ongoing debates within Yegorov's subcommission mobilized the regional administrations as well. In October and November 1924 they issued a barrage of statements and counterstatements to promote their own cause and sent them to Yegorov or Cherviakov. Cheating and unfair arguments were not the exception but the rule. Neither regional nor local functionaries on either side of the border had the greater Soviet commonwealth in mind but solely "their" own territory. The border gubernii in the RSFSR were opposed to any changes, and the neighboring huberniï in the UkrSSR were claiming as many economically valuable assets as possible.

The chairman of the Gosplan branch office in Voronezh, D'iakonov, put together a memorandum in which he included every reason he could think of to contest any territorial transfer to Ukraine. First, he began with geological considerations: the current borders—in his view—corresponded to a layer of chalk and phosphate in the region. At the same time as his colleagues in Central and Southeastern Europe were trying to justify new borders with references to geology and climate,

D'iakonov was using similar considerations to support gubernii borders established under Catherine II.[68] He then went on to emphasize how much agricultural methods differed from one another in Voronezh and Kharkiv Gubernii. In doing so, he referred to the number of cattle and population density. Finally, according to D'iakonov, Voronezh's industry was further developed than Kharkiv's. In summarizing all of these economic reasons against any transfer, he felt it necessary to respond to Ukrainian claims based on national-ethnographic principles. In doing so, he tried to simply brush it aside, questioning whether it had any political validity at all: "The basic assumption of UkrGosplan, the ethnographic principle, is only a formality. Taking all of these facts into consideration, this principle cannot and must not have any decisive value."[69]

The Ukrainian side knew all too well about these efforts in Voronezh and allowed its regional administrations to respond to D'iakonov's arguments. Two experts, Rashin and Sliusarev, both members of the administration in Starobil's'k Okruha (Okrug), wrote a memorandum challenging D'iakonov's expertise, arguing that he had linked the uezdy in question with Kharkiv Huberniia, when they were supposed to be attached to Donets'k Huberniia. Thus all of D'iakonov's economic arguments comparing Voronezh with Kharkiv did not apply and were therefore irrelevant.[70] Then they went straight to the core argument, attacking the very assumption that the national-ethnographic principle was "only a formality." They outlined how the Soviet order was expected to function: "All of the policies of the USSR underscore the very significance [of this principle]. We do not have to say much about this. It is sufficient to recall the latest actions around the [delimitation] in Central Asia and the formation of the autonomous Mongolian SSR."[71] In short, Rashin and Sliusarev were arguing that federalism must be more than a façade and must be realized in political practice.

The guberniia executive committee in Voronezh went even farther and organized a demonstration of Ukrainian-speaking functionaries to agitate against any territorial revision. In doing so, the local functionaries mentioned that—even though the majority of the population in the southern part of Voronezh Guberniia was Ukrainian-speaking—Ukrainian schools and Ukrainian newspapers were not at all popular. Most of the local functionaries even stressed that they were *khokhly*, a pejorative designation for Ukrainians.[72] The chairman of the Boguchar Uezd executive committee, one Miroshnichenko, delivered a furious speech that particularly stood out: "Even though I am a *khokhol* and speak Ukrainian, I underscore that our uezd has no relationship to Ukraine. Surely, I am correct when I declare that the uezd does not want to join Ukraine at all."[73]

In the end, Yegorov's subcommission proved unable to produce a conclusive expert opinion based on the reports, memoranda, and tables it had evaluated. Its members tried to evade accountability. In their final report, they passed responsibility back up to the Cherviakov Commission, concluding, "within the greater framework, political considerations will have to solve this [territorial] issue."[74]

After the exchange of many contradictory reports and expert opinions, the Cherviakov Commission held three decisive sessions at the end of November 1924 where the Ukrainian representatives once more underlined their claims. Instead of reaching an agreement, the rivalry between the sides continued. The tone of the debate deteriorated. Butsenko, who had never concealed his antipathy for the old system of gubernii, declared with verve that these administrative units created under Catherine II should not define current political considerations.[75] State institutions must provide all Ukrainians within the Soviet state with the opportunity to develop their culture. They could do this best within the Ukrainian republic, and thus the southern parts of Briansk, Kursk, and Voronezh Gubernii should be transferred from the RSFSR to the UkrSSR.[76]

Such claims elicited resistance from the other side. Aleksandr Smirnov, people's commissar for agriculture, who had replaced Latsis for one session, sharply criticized his Ukrainian colleagues' statistics and tables: "I warn you, if you search by national criteria for Ukrainians, then you will not find any Ukrainians. We all know this very well, and we do not have to pretend; even in Ukraine, those who speak Ukrainian are a minority. It is a complete fantasy to assume that we can define the borders in these areas only by national criteria."[77]

Konstantin Yegorov now took a clearly anti-Ukrainian stance. In his role as adviser, he joined the three crucial sessions between 26 and 28 November 1924. As he summarized his opinion of the territories in question, he avoided any diplomatic banter and came to a clear recommendation. From a political point of view, he considered a transfer of large parts of Kursk and Voronezh Gubernii to be "not efficient."[78]

Whereas border revisions along the southern part of Briansk Guberniia did not present many difficulties, Cherviakov failed to negotiate an agreement between the two rival camps for the territories under consideration in Kursk and Voronezh Gubernii.⁷⁹ Because the commission consisted of five voting members—the two Ukrainian and two RSFSR representatives plus the Belarusian chairman—Cherviakov would be the deciding voice. Previously, he had argued that Soviet power had to support national minorities and provide an alternative model to the Versailles order in Central Europe. To establish a contrast to Poland, where Ukrainians and Belarusians were allegedly suppressed, it was incumbent on the Soviet Union to enact policy measures that supported its nationalities.⁸⁰ He thus used what Terry Martin would later describe as the "Piedmont Principle" as basic reasoning.⁸¹ Choosing to uphold an affirmative national policy toward non-Russians, Cherviakov adopted a large part of the Ukrainian position and voted in favor of a large-scale revision. Although he rejected Ukrainian claims in some cases, such as Sudzha Uezd in the southern part of Kursk Guberniia, he nonetheless promoted them in the overall framework.⁸² Among others, the town of Belgorod was to be attached to Ukraine due to its close economic ties and the predominance of Ukrainian-speaking inhabitants in the surrounding area.⁸³ In all, territories containing more than one and a half million inhabitants were supposed to be transferred from the RSFSR to the UkrSSR.⁸⁴

This was too much for the representatives of the RSFSR. They accused their Ukrainian colleagues of being insatiable and imperialist.⁸⁵ They resorted to the full arsenal of party invective to discredit the decision. Their protest was duly noted in the minutes.⁸⁶ The RSFSR commission members then promptly submitted an alternative solution, by which only minor parts of Kursk and Voronezh Gubernii would be transferred to Ukraine. According to the RSFSR representatives, only in these smaller areas, either national-ethnographic composition or administrative considerations presented clear grounds for border revision.⁸⁷

Cherviakov had relied on the official korenizatsiia line, but the RSFSR representatives had received unambiguous signals from the state and party leadership. The commission had not been expected to rule in favor of the Ukrainian side by very much. Avel' Yenukidze, secretary of the TsIK and VTsIK, as well as an intimate of Stalin's, had told them straight-out to make concessions only where the interests of the RSFSR were not at risk.⁸⁸ For instance, the RSFSR representatives should support the transfer of Putivl' Uezd. Despite its Russian-speaking majority, this entity was surrounded on three sides by Ukrainian territory and had close economic ties to the Ukrainian side.⁸⁹ Yenukidze also hinted

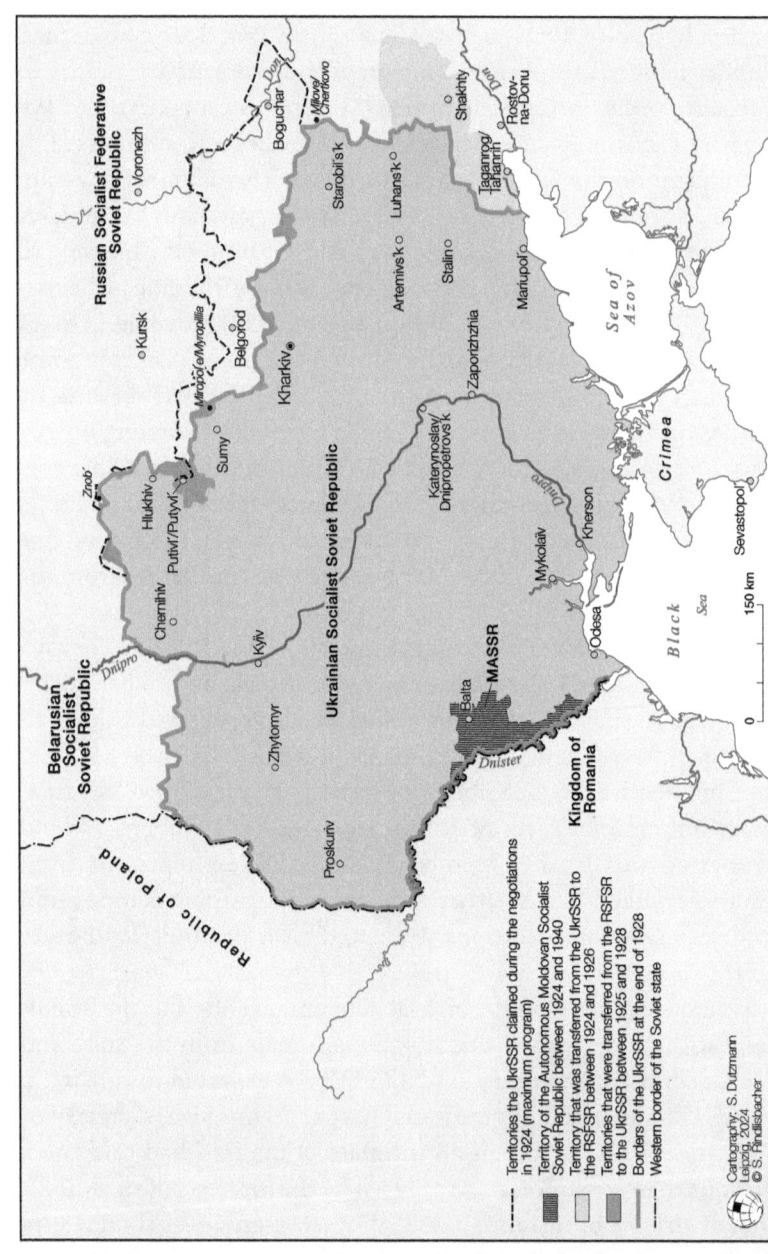

FIGURE 11. Ukrainian borders between 1924 and 1928.

that Ukraine was already powerful enough, and larger territorial transfers in its favor could prove detrimental to the stability of the entire union.[90] It was no coincidence that, from Yenukidze's point of view, the interests of the Soviet Union seemed congruous to those of the RSFSR.

Aleksandr Cherviakov now had to lobby the highest party echelons on behalf of his project. His efforts would be in vain. In a letter to the Politburo, he tried to explain the complexity of his commission's work. He also emphasized that his decision was not an easy one: "The position that I adopted after studying all the materials does not correspond with the position of one or the other side. It is clear that the solutions of the commission are my solutions. They support one side and at the same time encounter opposition from the other one."[91]

Notwithstanding these compelling arguments, the Politburo dismissed the recommendations of the Cherviakov Commission on 10 December 1924.[92] Despite all the catchy party slogans, the Ukrainian republic was not to be promoted. The argument of showcasing Soviet affirmative nationality policies could be used in the debate, but it had hardly any value against criteria based on economy and aspects of governance, as the Politburo's members upheld the claims of the RSFSR representatives. Cherviakov had to accept this second setback and adopted a downsized revision in January 1925.[93] The RSFSR representatives' proposal would serve as a roadmap in determining the new revisions.[94] A large share of the territories that were expected to go to Ukraine remained with the RSFSR. In the end, Ukraine "gained" about 4,000 square kilometers inhabited by approximately 300,000 people.[95] This was far less than the 13,000 square kilometers and 500,000 people it "lost" after the transfer of the territories around Shakhty and Taganrog in the southeast.[96] Butsenko complained that this new border made no sense, as it conformed to neither ethnographic nor economic considerations.[97]

Butsenko nonetheless had to submit to party discipline. In a separate letter, Cherviakov asked Ukrainian First Secretary Emanuïl Kviring to make sure that the commission's Ukrainian representatives received a party directive. If necessary, they would be forced to consent.[98] Although he had struggled so bitterly to prevent this kind of outcome, Butsenko now had to promote the final border revisions publicly, starting with an announcement about the territorial transfers between the UkrSSR and the RSFSR in the party's main newspaper, *Pravda*, on 8 August 1925. There he named all the uezdy and volosti that would soon be transferred. He also portrayed it so that, as in the case of Shakhty and

Taganrog, all of these changes went back to the initiative of the local population. However, Butsenko still managed to add that many Ukrainians were still living in the southern parts of Kursk and Voronezh Guberniï and concluded, "the state border between the UkrSSR and the RSFSR is far from regulated, and the fate of the Ukrainian population in Kursk and Voronezh Guberniï has yet to be determined."[99]

Lara Douds shows in her study *Inside Lenin's Government* the key role petitions from the population played in how the Soviet state functioned. Adopting traditions of paternalistic imperial rule, the government could bypass bureaucratic procedures and respond to local complaints. Mikhail Kalinin, since 1923 chairman of the TsIK and thus the nominal head of state, received the greatest share of such letters.[100] Depending on political utility, leading party and state officials could ignore them or make them a pretext for implementing their own policies.

In political practice, notions of "genuine" public involvement were anathema to Soviet functionaries. During the sessions of the Cherviakov Commission, Poloz had at times based his positions on popular initiatives. Smirnov at one point seized one such occasion to reprove the former *borot'bist* and explain the Soviet functionaries' view of petitions in unvarnished terms: "[Petitions] do not hold any meaning, as we have decided not to ask the population and to revise the borders otherwise. Thus, by relying on petitions, you are not only tactically but also politically wrong."[101] Smirnov was kindly reminding Poloz to stick to the game. This is why all of the politicians and experts involved in border revisions dismissed the idea of plebiscites in contested areas, as the party could hardly control the outcome.

Opportunities for Local Agency

As Butsenko had intimated in his article announcing the border revisions, territorial issues between Ukraine and Russia were not yet regulated with the formal handover of the above-mentioned 4,000 square kilometers in the spring of 1926. The TsIK installed a commission under Saak Ter-Gabrielian to supervise the implementation of this border revision. Here, too, the chairman, an Armenian, was an activist who was perceived to be "neutral" in the matter. Ter-Gabrielian's commission had to adjudicate problems, should it be necessary.[102] Among other things, it had to deal with petitions from different sides for or against a certain boundary.

Villages on the ground were often quite skeptical of the revisions, as they had to deal with the consequences. Rural soviets therefore submitted petitions and tried to mobilize officials within the state bureaucracy and the party apparatus for their cause. There were three possible responses to these apparently genuine initiatives from below. First, if neither republican administration took any interest in the locals' cause, nothing happened at all. Second, state institutions such as the VTsIK and the VUTsVK could react to local objections. In the best (and rarest) case, the RSFSR and the Ukrainian state administrations both agreed with a complaint from the locals. Then a revision was achieved with little ado. Third, when only one republican side supported a petition, a longer negotiation or delay began. However, the intensity of support or opposition could fluctuate. Here I provide examples from each of these three categories. I start with cases that both the Ukrainian and the Russian administrations ignored. Refusal to consider a local initiative was the most widespread outcome.[103] Then I analyze cases where both sides were able to reach agreement easily. Finally, I examine cases where both sides were competing for a solution to their advantage. Whereas I can address the two first scenarios rather briefly, the third scenario requires far more room for analysis.

The administrations of the RSFSR and UkrSSR ignored all petitions from the northern part of the former imperial Chernigov Guberniia. As mentioned at the outset, this guberniia had been divided between the two republics in 1919. Between May and July 1925, about 130 villages from the part that was attached to the RSFSR sent requests to join the UkrSSR. As their wording was in many cases similar or identical, one may assume that local activists had prompted them in some way. These petitions used certain standard phrases like: "We the citizens who sign this petition proclaim our solemn consent to join Chernigov Gub[erniia], as our fathers, grandfathers, and previous generations belonged to the Chernigov region."[104] Most of these petitions referred to the fact the villages north and south of the border had belonged to a Chernigov entity of some kind throughout history. As such categories had no place in Soviet spatial thinking, they went unanswered. These local perceptions fit neither the dominant national, economic, nor administrative framework.

However, if a local initiative addressed national, economic, and administrative issues, then the state bureaucracy lurched into motion. A petition from the village of Znob' corresponds with Soviet expectations in an almost ideal way. Here the Ukrainian as well as the Russian administrations agreed with the locals' line of argument and adopted it shortly thereafter. The village lay in the southernmost reaches of Briansk Guberniia. Previously, the Cherviakov Commission had decided that Znob' should be attached to Ukraine for administrative reasons, as the Russian village protruded relatively deep into Ukrainian territory.[105] The locals were decidedly against the plan. The chairman of the rural soviet argued that the new border would be disastrous for the village's economy. The main field of activity in Znob' was not the cultivation of grain but forestry. However, the forests where they worked were expected to remain within the RSFSR. Thus there was a real fear of losing access to the villagers' source of income. Moreover, the chairman also underlined that the peasants from Znob' were not Ukrainian at all, and they feared that they would have to pay higher taxes if they joined Ukraine. Finally, he also highlighted that the connection to the next administrative center in the RSFSR, Pocheb, was much better than to the next one in Ukraine, Hlukhiv.[106] The petition was forwarded to Ter-Gabrielian. After studying the details, all of the commission members sided with the petitioners. In the concluding statement, Ter-Gabrielian emphasized that the commission he chaired did not have to follow all decisions of the TsIK to the letter. In cases such as Znob', the border proposed made little sense on the ground and had thus to be changed.[107] Subsequently, the plan to include Znob' in the border revision was dropped.

In the region around Miropol'e/Myropillia, in the southwest area of Kursk Guberniia, the situation was the other way round. According to plans for the envisioned border, the fields, pastures, and forests of seven Ukrainian-speaking villages were to be attached to the UkrSSR, while the villages themselves were expected to remain within the RSFSR. As in Znob', the peasants feared that they might lose access to their source of income, and that neighboring villages in the UkrSSR might claim these fields for their use. In the end, peasants from these seven villages would go without straw. Thus local petitioners feared there might be bloodshed if no feasible solution was found.[108] They repeatedly urged state institutions at different levels to act.[109] First, the commission under Ter-Gabrielian accepted the request from Miropol'e/Myropillia. Then the VTsIK and the VUTsVK each gave their consent.[110] In 1927 the villages were able to change their republican affiliation.[111] Thus an additional territory of 200 square kilometers with a population of about 22,500 people was transferred from the RSFSR to the UkrSSR.[112] Together the examples of Znob' and Miropol'e/Myropillia show that the locals saw republican borders as something that had an immediate impact on their everyday lives. Here they were worried not so much about national belonging but rather about considerations of providing for their daily subsistence.

In other cases, support for one side or the other was not exceptionally strong—as, for instance, in the cases from Sudzha Volost in the southern part of Kursk Guberniia. Here local initiatives began in late February 1925, when Viacheslav Molotov visited the region. Stalin's right-hand man was on tour along the Russian-Ukrainian border to propagate the new party slogan "Face the village!" During his speech in Sudzha on 20 February 1925, he revealed that Sudzha Volost was expected to remain within the RSFSR. This news mobilized people from the area to direct several petitions to Kharkiv asking that they might nevertheless join Ukraine. For instance, 433 citizens of Zaoleshenka, right next to Sudzha, signed an appeal on 22 February to join the UkrSSR. As in Miropol'e/Myropillia the petitioners emphasized that their settlement was "100 percent Ukrainian," and that they had close economic ties to Sumy and Kharkiv. They also tried to master the party language: "the general assembly asks for the transfer of Zaoleshenka to the UkrSSR to improve economic and administrative ties. It [hereby] relies on LENIN's will regarding national self-determination, which the Twelfth Party Congress of the RKP(b) has [recently] confirmed. [Moreover,] the leaders of the workers and peasants have been proclaiming in the printed press the enhancement of the level of culture among the people of small nationalities."[113]

Even though the residents of Zaoleshenka tried to "speak Bolshevik," the Ukrainian institutions received their petition only halfheartedly.[114] Butsenko sent it together with others from Sudzha Volost to Ter-Gabrielian.[115] There they piled up and received no further attention. Such practices of delay and neglect provide us with hints as to the conditions needed to initiate a border change from below. It seems the petitioners did not so much have to master the dominant party discourse as to show practical interests related to their subsistence, such as forests for Znob' or fields for Miropol'e/Myropillia. If the petitioners could rely "only" on an abstract turn of phrase such as "national self-determination" or "historical connectedness," their chances of being heard by the Ter-Gabrielian Commission, the VTsIK, or the VUTsVK were rather small.

As already mentioned, some cases proved much more complicated because one side was for and the other against a petition. The ones that were the most complex and produced the most paperwork were those

CHAPTER 3

in which petitioners could point to economic concerns, as in Znob' or Miropol'e/Myropillia, but even in settling these, the RSFSR and the UkrSSR would try to revise the existing boundary to their advantage. The settlements of Uspens'ka/Uspenskaia and Milove/Chertkovo in the eastern border area provide the most controversial examples. In both cases, border issues merged with transportation issues.

The republican border established after the transfer of Taganrog and Shakhty in October 1924 separated the village of Uspens'ka on the Ukrainian side from the railway station Uspenskaia on the Russian side.[116] Because Uspenskaia was an important regional railway hub, both republics wanted it for their territory, arguing that their solution was more efficient than the other side's. The Ukrainians referred again to national-ethnographic makeup, while the RSFSR side highlighted the importance of the railway station for the local raion administration. In the end, both could agree that the existing situation was unsatisfactory, but neither was prepared to yield to their rival.[117]

In the deadlock over Uspens'ka/Uspenskaia, the RSFSR even stooped to fraud and unconstitutional actions. In March 1927 the Russian VTsIK presented a petition from Uspens'ka to the All-Union TsIK

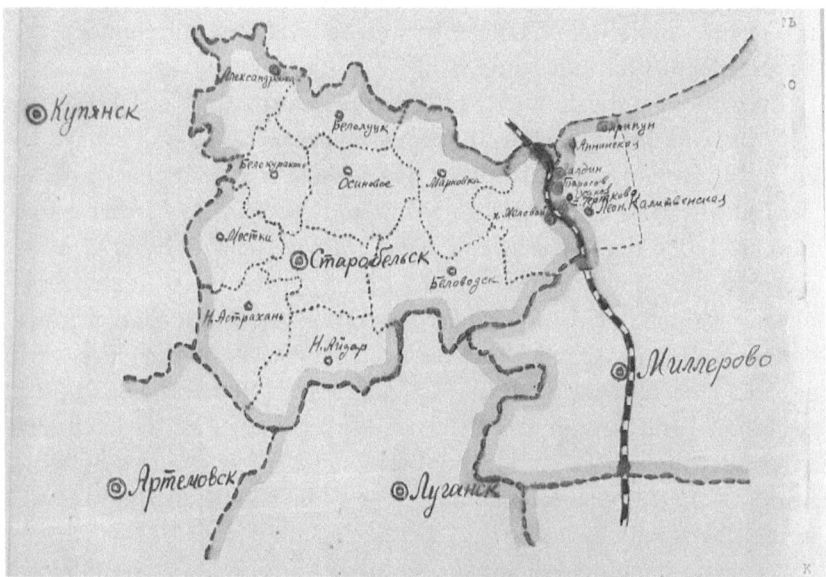

FIGURE 12. Contemporary map of the border in the region of Milove/Chertkovo, 1926. TsDAVOU, f. 1, op. 2, spr. 1809, ark. 26.

requesting discussion of a possible transfer to the RSFSR. In this petition a resident of Uspens'ka, named P. S. Vertelo, complained that the people of Uspens'ka wanted their village to be in the RSFSR, as their ties to Taganrog were closer than those to Stalino (today Donets'k) in the UkrSSR. Moreover, their village had fields on both sides of the border, and it would be better if the village and the land they used were in the same republic. He went on to state that the Ukrainian authorities had ignored all previously submitted complaints. As a result, the Russian side should take action.[118] Upon learning of this incident, Butsenko was infuriated, as the VTsIK and the TsIK had forgotten to inform the Ukrainian side that the village was now on the upcoming agenda. In a report to the KP(b)U leadership, Butsenko pointed out that Vertelo had no mandate at all, as nobody in Uspens'ka knew about his petition. Then Butsenko tried to undermine Vertelo's reputation by insinuating that he had once been a police sergeant under tsarist rule. Moreover, Butsenko charged that all of the actions taken by the Russian side concerning the matter ran contrary to the Soviet constitution—both sides had to consent to any territorial change. However, he also expressed his fear that the party might again decide in favor of the RSFSR.[119]

This time, Butsenko's fears did not come true, as Soviet state institutions usually observed formalities so long as the party did not interfere. Therefore, representatives of the RSFSR could not go through with their plan. After reconsidering the case, the TsIK sent the issue to the Politburo.[120] The party administration then delayed the Uspens'ka/Uspenskaia case and refused to decide in favor of one side or the other. The boundaries remained where they had been before.

The situation in Uspens'ka/Uspenskaia appeared messy enough, but things were even worse in Milove/Chertkovo, in the northeast border area. As noted above, the border there divided the settlement more or less along the railway tracks with Milove in Ukraine and Chertkovo in the RSFSR. The railway station itself was split between the two republics. On the outskirts of town, the railway tracks crossed the republican border several times. This strange territorial configuration dated back to the imperial guberniia and had provoked bureaucratic discord even before 1917.[121]

After the Soviets came to power in the region and gubernii borders became republican ones, the rivalry between the administrations got worse. The deterioration of the situation here serves as a showcase for the challenges facing Soviet federalism. The railway tracks presented an obstacle. Slepnev, the head of the railway administration in Chertkovo, complained that it was difficult to remove snow from the tracks in winter, as this had to be coordinated between two administrations. Furthermore, irregularities had arisen, as it was not clear which legal code, Ukrainian or Russian, was to be used for construction at the railway station. Some parts belonged to Ukraine and others to the RSFSR. The railway employees even had to pay different taxes depending on their place of residence. Slepnev thus concluded that this administrative mess could not endure.[122]

All of these inter-republican rivalries converged to create full-fledged administrative chaos at a local slaughterhouse. Both republics claimed this enterprise, which was located right at the border. The slaughterhouse paid taxes to the Ukrainian administration, while the Russian side administered the social security of its seventy-six employees as well as the trade union and the party cells on site.[123] This dualism also created opportunities for corruption. The RSFSR administration reported that purchasing agents from the slaughterhouse inflated prices in order to buy cattle for their own profit, while the company's management looked the other way.[124] In addition, after fire damaged the refrigerated warehouse in May 1922, the two sides had not been able to agree on how to repair it. Thus the enterprise had been forced to suspend operations until September 1924.[125] When the Ukrainian side launched a local Ukrainization campaign, some workers put up stubborn resistance. As the Ukrainian administration conducted all of its correspondence in Ukrainian, it expected responses to be in Ukrainian as well.[126] The employees and the Russian administration on the other side rejected this demand and began to make jokes about the Ukrainian language in public.[127]

The railway station and the slaughterhouse were not the only problems. They were not even the biggest ones. The bazaar mentioned at the beginning of this book posed a logistical challenge and led to a struggle among the authorities for who could collect the taxes and to the incident with the man killed by a steam train.[128] Moreover, in 1924, the harvested crop kept rotting in front of the railway station, as the two sides could not agree on how to process the shipment. Even criminals could profit, as local police forces were officially prohibited to follow a suspicious individual across the republican border.[129]

Even though the Cherviakov Commission never touched the Milove/Chertkovo issue in 1924, the RSFSR as well as the UkrSSR later tried to revise the border.[130] In this case, neither side was willing to give up territory, and from Moscow's perspective, the case looked terribly complex as well, since one side was going to suffer severe losses no matter the decision.[131] A territorial expert at the TsIK named S. Il'in presented the situation as follows. If Milove were transferred to the RSFSR, Starobil's'k Okruha would lose its only access to the railway and an important source of tax revenue. This was particularly unfortunate because this okruha was already one of the poorest in the UkrSSR and highly dependent on funding from the central administration. If, in contrast, Chertkovo were transferred to Ukraine, the surrounding region of Millerevo would lose an administrative center and a key transportation hub for its agricultural products. Having considered these factors, Il'in concluded that the less harmful solution would be to transfer Milove and all the rail tracks to the RSFSR.[132]

The All-Union TsIK discussed the matter of Milove/Chertkovo in two sessions but could not come to an agreement. As in Uspens'ka/Uspenskaia, Moscow remained neutral.[133] No solution appeared to be the best option. Starobil's'k could keep the tax revenue, and Millerevo retained an important regional center. The complexity of the situation would produce future challenges. Such problematic cases, however, were rather rare.

In establishing the revised borders on site, the politicians and experts involved were well aware of the implications in access to state property and institutions. Local field commissions surveying and demarcating republican borders paid close attention to the situation on the ground so as not to create any complications in the agricultural use of the areas where they were working. They adopted boundaries separating the fields, forests, and pastures of neighboring villages as prospective borders. In principle, they sought to ensure that peasants from a border village in the RSFSR would not have to worry about their fields or forests suddenly being located in the UkrSSR and vice versa.[134]

Local border commissions working on VUTsVK's and VTsIK's behalf even tried to install a mechanism for future border corrections. They had sound economic reasons for this, because in the mid-1920s the Soviet government encouraged measures aimed at land use amelioration (*zemleustroistvo*).[135] This policy foresaw, among other things, the "rectification" and rationalization of scattered holdings of land between neighboring villages. The experts involved expected that in future years fields might be exchanged between border villages. In such cases, the republican border would no longer conform to land use. Hence the local commissions surveying the border decided that every exchange of land between border villages would be considered a change in the border between two Soviet republics.[136]

On paper, both sides strove to avoid quarrels over field use between border villages, but in some cases, the same patterns as in Milove/Chertkovo and Uspens'ka/Uspenskaia emerged on a smaller scale. The woods known as Borki, located on the border between Chernihiv Okruha and Briansk Guberniia, were one such case. The village of Khoromnoe in the RSFSR claimed this area of about 0.4 square kilometers (374 desiatinas), but the woods were located in the UkrSSR.[137] The people of Khoromnoe had long used the woods and its clearings for grazing their cattle and gathering hay. In 1919, when Chernigov Guberniia was divided between the RSFSR and the UkrSSR, Borki came under Ukrainian administration and was attached to the forests of the village of Yeline without the villagers from Khoromnoe receiving notice. Written grievances from Khoromnoe went straight to the VTsIK, where they were approved and officially forwarded to the VUTsVK.[138]

The two sides proved unable to reach an agreement. The Ukrainian Forest Administration did not consider Khoromnoe's claims on Borki "efficient." They argued that these woods now made up a part of the greater forest zone and they could hardly be separated again.[139] Moreover, the VUTsVK emphasized that Borki was not directly positioned on the republican border. Thus a transfer would create an enclave of RSFSR territory inside the UkrSSR.[140] Avel' Yenukidze, secretary of the TsIK, was willing to agree on the transfer only if there was a consensus on both sides.[141] In the end, due to the resistance from the VUTsVK, Borki had to remain within the UkrSSR, and the RSFSR authorities had to compensate the people of Khoromnoe with a similar forest from the local state fund.[142]

In the case of the villages of Ohybne and Borisovka, the roles were reversed, and the situation was much more complicated. Before 1917 the two villages had been on the border between Khar'kov and Voronezh Gubernii. The peasants of Ohybne in Khar'kov Guberniia had leased about 560 desiatinas (0.6 square kilometers) of cropland for corn and hay from a large estate owner. This cropland was next to their village but lay within Voronezh Guberniia.[143] In 1919 the guberniia borders became inter-republican ones. Then the Voronezh Guberniia Executive Committee redistributed the nationalized fields that the villagers of Ohybne had used until 1920 to Borisovka, a nearby village in the RSFSR.[144] By way of compensation, the Ukrainian land administration offered other fields to the peasants from Ohybne, but these were faraway.

Ohybne's peasants refused to accept such a poor transaction and continued to insist on the fields next to their village.[145]

Relations between the two villages deteriorated dramatically in 1924, when peasants from Ohybne burned cornfields that were under Borisovka's care and severely wounded a policeman guarding the border between the villages.[146] Subsequently, the peasants of Borisovka sent letters and petitions to Moscow complaining about their neighbors.[147] In early 1927 Mikhail Kalinin, head of the All-Union TsIK, intervened and urged the local Ukrainian administration to put an end to such "vigilantism" (*samoupravstvo*).[148] In a note to the VUTsVK the peasants of Ohybne apologized for burning down the fields and beating the policeman. In doing so, however, they also pointed out the unfriendly behavior of their neighbors:

> In 1925, while children were guarding our cattle, about five or six head accidentally found themselves grazing on the fields of the Borisovtsy.... A policeman bribed by the Borisovtsy wounded our citizen Mikhail and took the cattle....
>
> Even if we want to keep our cattle on our side, this is hardly possible as the Borisovtsy's land is only two steps from our farmstead [*khutor*]. Our cattle will inevitably go there for pasture. The Borisovtsy's behavior is hostile. If they recognize one of us, they beat him. They do not let us take part in their yearly trade fair.[149]

Thus the peasants of Ohybne appealed to the VUTsVK to lobby for a revision of the border or to provide them with suitable fields on the Ukrainian side. Although I was unable to find out how the Ukrainian authorities finally resolved the matter, the case is revealing with regard to the challenges a republican border could pose. In the worst case, the peasants could lose their very means of subsistence.

The Decline of Korenizatsiia and the Fall of the Centrists in the UkrSSR

Confronted with many unsatisfactory cases, Panas Butsenko, in his capacity as VUTsVK secretary, continued to lobby for a large-scale border revision. After he received the results of the 1926 census, Butsenko kept sending reports to the Politburo of the KP(b)U asking for support. He argued that an honest nationality policy demanded the creation of precise borders between the different Soviet republics because it would act as a showcase in foreign affairs. How could Soviet officials complain about the harsh treatment of Ukrainians in Poland, Czechoslovakia, and Romania, when they failed to meet the needs of Ukrainians living in the RSFSR?[150]

As Stalin emerged as the unchallenged leader of the Soviet Union at the end of the decade, korenizatsiia went into decline throughout the union. In the wake of this development, ideas and petitions for the revision of republican borders were no longer on the political agenda. This became especially clear in February 1929, when Stalin invited Ukrainian writers to the Kremlin to discuss Soviet nationality policies. During this meeting, the Ukrainian writers mentioned the unsatisfactory border between the UkrSSR and the RSFSR, particularly in the east. The party leader first tried to avoid being drawn into the discussion. Nonetheless, when the Ukrainians persisted, Stalin explained: "We have discussed the [border issue] several times; but we've been changing the borders too often. . . . Too often, we change the borders—this makes a bad impression inside and outside our country."[151] Thus the Soviet Union's supreme leader gave an unambiguous signal as to how he wished to proceed in the matter. From his perspective, the revision of borders created unnecessary disputes between the Soviet republics and attracted unwanted attention from abroad. Hence it impeded the construction of socialism and industrialization. Those who called for border revisions in public could be easily accused of "nationalist deviation" and would soon have to fear repression.[152]

Starting with the 1927 campaign against Oleksandr Shums'kyi, the Ukrainian people's commissar for education, the political influence of the centrist faction in the UkrSSR entered into decline.[153] In 1928 Butsenko lost his position as VUTsVK secretary. Many more centrists lost their jobs. Loyal Stalinists began to replace them. Ukrainization slipped to the bottom of the political agenda. In December 1932 the Stalinists launched a full-blown campaign against the centrists, accusing them of being chauvinist nationalists. In the end, Mykola Skrypnyk, Shums'kyi's successor at the Ukrainian Commissariat of Education, was driven to suicide.[154] Many centrists would fall victim to the Great Terror four years later. Mykhailo Poloz was shot in 1937. Panas Butsenko was sent to Vorkuta. After Stalin's death, Butsenko was rehabilitated but did not return to politics.

Other party activists involved in the border talks between the UkrSSR and the RSFSR fared no better. Aleksandr Beloborodov, an ally of Trotsky, lost his position as commissar for internal affairs in 1927 and was shot in 1938. Martin Latsis tried to stay out of internal party struggles. He, too, ultimately fell victim to the Great Terror in 1938. Aleksandr Cherviakov stayed on as chairman of the Belarusian TsIK until 1937, when he was driven to suicide after being denounced as an "enemy of the people." Saak Ter-Gabrielian served for a stint as head of the Armenian government, but he was eventually purged and died in prison in 1937.

As stated in the introduction, an analysis of territorialization always means examining asymmetries in power relations. The complex negotiations and renegotiations of the RSFSR-Ukrainian border after 1920 provide an illuminating example of how functionaries tried to manage the diversity of Soviet space and territorial disputes on the macro, meso, and micro levels. For all their disagreements, Soviet politicians and experts established a territorial order that did not create more problems than it solved for the greater part of the people on the ground. Cases such as Uspens'ka/Uspenskaia, Milove/Chertkovo, or Borisovka/Ohybne were exceptions, not the rule.

Initially, Moscow's institutionalization of korenizatsiia, the rise of the "centrist" faction in the KP(b)U, and the revisions of the border between the RSFSR and the BSSR in the spring of 1924 encouraged planning for a large-scale border revision in favor of Ukraine. However, in the Belarusian case, the territorial revisions were not primarily attempts to showcase affirmative nationality policies but rather an effort to create an economically and administratively sustainable entity in the west. The RSFSR-UkrSSR negotiations that followed soon after the revision of the Belarusian border had started were not open to public debate. Territorial experts such as Konstantin Yegorov had considerable agency during the search for solutions. Exigencies of governance were often left unspoken, but they played a decisive role. The two major setbacks experienced by the Ukrainians in 1924—the loss of the territories around Tahanrih and Shakhty as well as the RKP(b) Politburo's overruling of the Cherviakov Commission's decisions—were the most striking examples. The Piedmont Principle could be used as an argument during the negotiations, but it did not prove to be decisive for the outcome.

Later, Stalin's emergence as the country's uncontested leader ushered in the decline of national communism throughout the Soviet Union. This applied to the "centrist" faction of the KP(b)U in Kharkiv as well. After the Skrypnyk affair in 1932–1933, Ukrainian politicians understood that they were putting their lives at risk if they said anything that could be construed as too nationalist in content. This would have certainly included any further claims on the border with the RSFSR.

From the micro perspective, implementation of the Russian-Ukrainian border followed its own rationale. As Di Fiore, Haslinger, and Gibson have already shown, land property or land use were crucial for border making on the ground.[155] In the Soviet frame a prospective boundary was not supposed to separate a village from its fields, pastures, and forests. In cases where an intended republican border did cut off villages from their fields and forests, initiatives launched by aggrieved peasants stood a good chance of being heard by leading state institutions. But when the Russian and Ukrainian sides failed to reach a consensus in considering the merits of a local initiative, borders were left as they were, as was the case in Uspens'ka/Uspenskaia and in Milove/Chertkovo.

As they demarcated the Russian-Ukrainian border, the surveyor commissions in the field even tried to establish mechanisms to facilitate future land amelioration efforts: if a field passed between border villages, the result was expected to lead automatically to a revision of the border. The authorities, however, did not always follow this ideal. In the case of the Borki woods or the villages of Ohybne and Borisovka, the same patterns emerged as in Uspens'ka/Uspenskaia and Milove/Chertkovo, albeit at the micro level.

Delineating borders is never straightforward, as power asymmetries translate into geography. Taking border negotiations between the RSFSR and the UkrSSR as a starting point, we can see that korenizatsiia was to a certain extent a clever marketing trick to promote Soviet power in non-Russian regions. When it seemed that a potential large-scale border revision in favor of the UkrSSR might boost Ukraine's strength or rile Moscow's power base within the RSFSR, the party leadership retreated from commitments previously made. Party leaders were not going to allow the game to slip beyond their grasp. Even though Moscow tended to favor claims submitted by the RSFSR, the Ukrainian authorities were able to achieve at least some concessions as in the case of Miropol'e/Myropillia.

The bordering process offered Soviet activists plenty of opportunities to perform state power. They hence enabled the discussion and solution of local territorial conflicts within the scope of bureaucratic processes. At the end of the 1920s, the Soviet state had taken roots in the margins.

CHAPTER 4

Central Asia

How to Discuss a Common Border

> We will not organize a referendum, because men at the top are deciding on the delimitation, not men at the bottom.
>
> —Yusup Abdrakhmanov, 1924

Together with Ukraine and the South Caucasus, Central Asia was a cornerstone of the Soviet state. In 1926 about 13.8 million people lived in the region (including Kazakhstan, Kyrgyzstan, Uzbekistan, Tajikistan, and Turkmenistan), a little more than 9 percent of the entire population.[1] This region is dominated by large deserts in the south and west and by steppes in the north, but it also contains fertile regions such as the Fergana Valley, Zhetisu/Semirech'e, and the banks alongside the Amu Darya and Syr Darya rivers. They form larger oases in an arid region, ideal for growing cotton crops.[2] A nomadic herder culture dominated the steppe and desert areas, whereas an urban culture characterized the oases. Social movement between nomadic and settled communities was widespread.[3]

Due to seasonal droughts, control over the water supplies was key to economic prosperity throughout the region. Even though Turkic languages and Islamic culture were widespread, the herder societies in the northern steppe differed from the sedentary ones in the oases. Furthermore, the way of herding animals was distinct in mountainous and steppe areas. Tashkent, with its railway connection to the European part of Russia, served as the regional administrative hub for Russian imperial and later early Soviet rule. In a herculean task, Soviet politicians projected national borders onto this fractured terrain in 1924.[4]

The main goal here is to explore the decision-making process, the framing of national-territorial disputes, and the eminent agency of indigenous politicians. The results of national delimitation between 1924 and 1929 will not be the main focus of attention. Arne Haugen has already analyzed the decisions and results in detail.[5] Unlike the Russian-Ukrainian and the Armenian-Azerbaijani cases, the focus of debate was not only about the territories themselves but also about the ideas applied to national-ethnographic categories. Indigenous politicians struggled over different options of how to manage the region, between a federal and a strictly national one. The outcome of these struggles would change the Central Asian societies irreversibly, but it would also institutionalize Soviet power.

The Colonial Heritage of Central Asia

Russian expansion into the Kazakh steppe began in the eighteenth century. Step by step the empire extended its influence southward in the region. In the 1860s the imperial armies conquered the Emirate of Bukhara as well as the Khanates of Khiva and Kokand for good. Whereas Khiva and Bukhara remained semi-independent protectorates, the tsarist government installed the Governor-Generalship of Turkestan in 1867, which was administered from Tashkent. In 1886 it was renamed Turkestan Krai. In the north, the Governor-Generalship of the Steppes was created in 1882, with its administrative center in Omsk. Like some parts of the Caucasus these two regions were governed through military institutions. Until its last decade Russian officials directed their rule in a way aimed at avoiding open resistance. Military expeditions in this remote region were difficult to manage and cost-intensive. Locals kept some autonomy and were exempt from military conscription.[6]

Russian imperial expansion in Central Asia assumed a new quality in the second half of the nineteenth century. Other than in the South Caucasus and the steppe, local elites were no longer coopted into the imperial nobility. Additionally, at the end of the nineteenth century, Turkestan became a favorite destination for settlers from the European part of the empire. The latter often drove the nonsedentary part of the population from the most fertile grounds, for example in the Zhetisu/Semirech'e region. Hence the land and population of Central Asia became objects of colonial exploitation.[7]

In Central Asia, civil war had already broken out in 1916, when the indigenous population rebelled against government plans to introduce forced labor conscription to mobilize human resources for the war effort in Europe. The imperial government brutally crushed the rebellions, killing between a hundred thousand and two hundred thousand people. This also led to a lasting politicization of the native population. In the political field, the dichotomy between them and the settlers fully crystallized.[8] The collapse of the tsarist authority in February 1917 further inflamed an existing revolutionary situation. The chain of events between 1917 and 1920 are complex, but some background is required.[9]

Central Asia's first main political conflict revolved around the Russian and Ukrainian settlers, on one hand, and the indigenous population, on the other. From 1917 to late 1919 large parts of Central Asia were only nominally under Soviet control, because they were cut off from Soviet Russia by White armies stationed in Siberia. In Turkestan, soviets formed at the grassroots level in larger towns, but soldiers and railway workers of European descent dominated them to the detriment of Muslim inclusion. They deliberately repressed indigenous initiatives for statehood such as the Turkestan Autonomy with its center in Kokand in February 1918. Such colonialist repression would trigger what would eventually contribute to local insurgencies, led by those commonly labeled as Basmachi.[10]

In October 1919 the Red Army intervened. The party leadership in Moscow ordered an end to discrimination against the indigenous population.[11] With the help of Tatar intermediaries, Moscow began to visibly reverse Russian imperial colonialist practices.[12] It allowed local authorities to expel Russian and Ukrainian settlers from the lands that these colonists had appropriated from indigenous peoples. In doing so, however, the Bolsheviks had to manage a balancing act of political interests, as railway workers and soldiers (most of them European) still formed a key pillar of support for Soviet power in the region.[13] The party began to lobby for indigenous support and recruit progressive natives into its ranks. Certain strata of the native population were particularly open to joining the new state power.[14]

At the outset of the twentieth century, a movement of well-educated and progressively minded indigenous elites emerged in Turkestan, Bukhara, and Khiva. These were young Muslim reformers, mostly of urban, merchant background—known as Jadids—who tried to modernize Central Asia's colonialized societies. In their urban environments, they promoted a new method of education (*usul-i jadid*) to further cultural and social emancipation. They had maintained contacts with scholars far beyond Central Asia in Constantinople or Cairo.[15]

The rivalry between the Jadids and the *ulama*, the traditionally educated elite, fueled the second main political conflict in Central Asia. In and after 1917 this conflict divided native political spheres. It also gained a linguistic dimension as the *ulama* continued to use Farsi, the traditional court language, whereas the Jadids began to use only Chaghatay Turkic.[16] Thus the Jadids' progressive, emancipatory stance isolated them from both the settler communities and traditional institutions.

The steppe in the north and the desert in the southwest were barely urbanized and dominated by herder communities. The *ulama* and the Jadids formed much weaker social strata in those regions. There Russian-educated indigenous activists would gain much more influence. The imperial government had funded a few Russian-language schools. Their graduates formed a thin indigenous imperial elite in the region who could participate in the imperial political discourse. Alikhan Bukeikhanov gained particular prominence, as he was elected delegate for the Constitutional Democrats to the First Duma. He took a leading role in the movement that formed with the Alash Orda an indigenous statehood in the steppe from 1917 to 1920. Today this is considered a precursor of modern Kazakhstan. Even though the victory of the Red Army in the steppe led to its dissolution, the Bolsheviks soon after coopted progressively minded Alash activists. Some of them, like Ishenaly Arabaev, had also participated in Jadid circles.[17]

Until 1920 the traditional rulers could maintain their power in Bukhara and Khiva supported by the conservative *ulama* and merchants. The Red Army crushed them after it gained the upper hand in Turkestan. The Bolsheviks then helped the Jadids to take power, as they formed the core of the Young Khivan and the Young Bukharan parties. The most famous among the latter were the poet and journalist Aburauf Fitrat and the revolutionary Faizulla Khodzhaev. Khodzhaev himself was a descendant of a merchant family in Bukhara and made his stand as a dedicated opponent of the emir in and after 1917. As the Young Bukharans came to power, they immediately started a modernizing campaign, investing in education. They also switched the official language from Farsi to Uzbek—taking a stance against the old elites.[18]

The former Jadids' views and their social position made them viable allies for the Bolsheviks.[19] The latter thus began to include them in their ranks. For these newly coopted indigenous communists, the very meaning of *class*, *revolution*, or *socialism* seemed blurred. Despite the party's best efforts and ideological indulgence, the numbers of native communists remained low.[20] So it seems natural that the indigenous communists—like the Kara-Kirgiz activist Yusup Abdrakhmanov—shared with the Bolsheviks the idea of being a chosen avant-garde that would reshape their societies. Both were elitist.[21]

National perceptions of these indigenous progressive activists were in flux. Many of them had initially shared the idea of a Greater Turkestan that would include not only the former Turkestan Krai but also Bukhara, Khiva, and the steppe in the north. Being a "Turk" was not unambiguously tied to language or ethnicity. In the urban centers, inhabitants were often bilingual, in Turkic and in Farsi. People could easily identify with more than one category. The term *uzbek* gained more prominence, whereas *sart* as a designation for the sedentary population disappeared.[22]

In this period, the meaning of the term *uzbek* was ambiguous. An older meaning referred to the nomadic tribes who had defeated the Timurids at the end of the fifteenth century, whereas the newer "Chaghatayist" view referred to the sedentary population as well as to the legacy of Timur's empire and Chaghatay literature. During the revolutionary turmoil, the second meaning became dominant but also exclusive in relation to Farsi-speaking people. The persisting ambiguity would lead to confusion during the debates to come.[23]

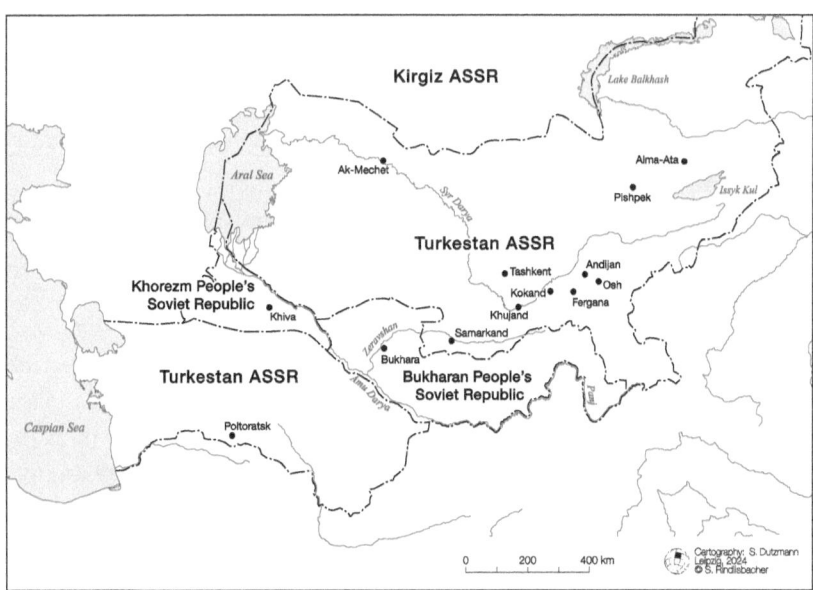

FIGURE 13. Political map of Central Asia, 1923.

Competing Ideas of Soviet Statehood in Central Asia

As soon as Central Asia came under Moscow's direct control, the Bolsheviks reintroduced the territorial frames of the *ancien régime* to bring some semblance of order to the chaotic political landscape. The Turkestan ASSR and the Kirgiz ASSR (or Kirrespublika) were successors to the prerevolutionary Governor-Generalship of the Steppes and Turkestan Krai. The Soviet People's Republics of Bukhara and Khorezm—where the Young Bukharans and Young Khivans seized power—were successors of the Emirate of Bukhara and Khanate of Khiva.[24]

Railway and telegraph connections between Central Asia and European Russia remained poor. New railway lines such as the Turksib, which was to link Siberia with the Fergana Valley, were still only in the planning stage.[25] Local insurgents, labeled as Basmachi, kept harassing the local Soviet government, then disappearing into the mountainous parts of the Fergana Valley or retreating to China and Afghanistan. Consequently, rural and mountainous areas were barely governable. In some areas, civil war continued well into the 1930s.[26]

The new Soviet order provided tantalizing opportunities for young activists. Among them was Turar Ryskulov. Born in 1894, he had studied in an imperial school in Pishpek (today Bishkek) and participated in the 1916 uprising. In 1918 he became commissar for health issues in Turkestan, in early 1920 then head of the TurkTsIK. Ryskulov took a visible stance against the settlers. Together with other top politicians, he advocated the transformation of Turkestan, Bukhara, and Khiva into a Turkic national entity. However, this idea was soon squashed, and Ryskulov was transferred to other assignments.[27]

In Tashkent, party representatives installed an intermediary body alongside the Turkkomissiia in late 1919. The Red Army commander Mikhail Frunze was among its leaders. When discussing the future Turkestan, they thought of a division along ethnonational lines to ease tensions among the newly recruited native communists.[28] This policy met with opposition in Moscow, when a commission of the Russian Communist Party's Central Committee—with Georgii Chicherin as its leader—sought to preserve Turkestan as a territorial unit. They argued that this was the best way to guarantee a functioning water supply as well as to maintain the railway and telegraph networks.[29] Chicherin and his colleagues were using arguments like the ones that would later play a role in the formation of the ZSFSR in 1922.

Whereas Lenin favored a federal solution in the South Caucasus, he preferred a national option for Central Asia. There his primary political goal was to weaken the influence of the European settlers and to strengthen the power base of the indigenous activists.[30] In the South Caucasus, in contrast, representatives of the local population, except for the Turks, were already well integrated into the party. Settler communities never played a political role similar to that in Central Asia. In 1920 and 1921 no final decisions had been made. Everything was set aside for consideration at some undetermined future time.

After the Civil War, ideas of a Greater Turkestan lost much of their appeal, particularly after anti-Bolshevik insurgents in Central Asia propagated "pan-Turkist" ideas. Most prominent among them were Akhmet-Zaki Validov and Enver Pasha, the former Ottoman minister of war. Both had once been Soviet allies but then turned against them and joined the Basmachi. The Red Army would eventually smash them. Enver was killed in the summer of 1922. Validov went into exile. After this, the idea of Greater Turkestan gained an anti-Soviet connotation.[31]

Moreover, in the years between 1920 and 1923, native communists fractured the party organizations along lines defined by "nationality." Although this effort started as an elite phenomenon, it had lasting effects on the functioning of institutions. State and party in Turkestan were split between networks that defined themselves as Turkmen, Uzbek, and Kirgiz. This division eventually forced indifferent native Bolsheviks to take sides, and the party had to find viable answers to these challenges. National delimitation was one option.[32]

The Turkkomissiia (1919-1920), with its successors the Turkbiuro (1920-1922) and the Sredazbiuro (1922-1934), became the agency for implementing and supervising party rule in Turkestan, Bukhara, and Khorezm. As in the later imperial period, the steppe, the Kirrespublika, was less likely to be seen as a part of Central Asia and was therefore supervised by other party institutions.[33] Experienced "European" party members were supposed to transmit political guidelines to regional party activists. In 1922 and at the beginning of 1923, the Sredazbiuro favored plans for a Central Asian Federation following the example of the ZSFSR. In addition, some activists were pushing for regional territorial reforms, such as the creation of an Autonomous Fergana Oblast or a Kara-Kirgiz Mountainous Oblast.[34]

In 1922 Ryskulov came back to the political stage of Central Asia as head of the Turkestan Sovnarkom. He had dropped his previous support for a Greater Turkestan. In his new position he lobbied for an inclusive Central Asian Federation. In an address to the Turkestan party leadership, he expressed his fear that economic disputes could inflame national conflicts. Nonetheless, the party should consider Central Asia as an interconnected whole. Its structure could only be federal, while the principles of raionirovanie would shape local structures.[35]

Other native activists, such as Abdulla Rakhimbaev, a distinguished member of the Communist Party of Turkestan, and Faizulla Khodzhaev, head of the Bukharan government, pushed for a national delimitation without any federal umbrella. To this end, they could rely on experts from Narkomnats such as Ivan Trainin, who argued that Soviet power should create national-territorial units to guarantee economic progress. In Trainin's view, the party would support such an approach even in cases where the population lacked awareness of itself as a nation.[36]

In 1924 Central Asia underwent a major territorial restructuring. Shortly after Lenin's death in January 1924, the territorial issue appeared at the top of the regional agenda. The Orgbiuro of the RKP(b) in Moscow sent Yan Rudzutak to discuss with Central Asian comrades the prospects of national delimitation into Kirgiz, Uzbek, and Turkmen parts.[37] This initiative then gained its own momentum among the native communists. The general mood within the party turned against a federal option. Turar Ryskulov lost his position as head of the Turkestan Sovnarkom; he was replaced by Sharustam Islamov, a fierce supporter of the delimitation.

Seeing that Moscow was not opposed to their plans, Abdulla Rakhimbaev and Faizulla Khodzhaev renewed their own efforts in this direction. They saw a window of opportunity to enlarge their own power base.[38] The Central Committee of the Bukharan Communist Party thus lobbied for the unification of all "Uzbeks," who had for centuries been divided among different khanates and empires. The Soviet rule would now ensure that "the peoples [*narodnosti*] of Central Asia assemble and merge on the basis of national unity, as soon as they have created separate Soviet republics: the Uzbeks, Turkmens, and Kirgiz in the existing Kirrespublika. The Tajik people [*narodnost'*] will form out of [the regions] Matcha, Karategin, and Garm an autonomous Tajik republic within Uzbekistan-Bukhara."[39]

This was the Bukharan party's maximal program—Samarkand would be the capital, Uzbekistan the fifth republic of the Soviet Union. Tashkent, the seat of the Sredazbiuro, would make up a part of the future Uzbekistan as well. In the eyes of the Bukharan party leaders and their allies from Turkestan, delimitation appeared to be an easy task, simply dividing Uzbek and Kirgiz territories. But the essential challenge was to gain even within the party an agreement on what or who was *Kirgiz* or *Uzbek*.[40]

Even though indigenous communists began to take a stance on behalf of a certain nationality, the meaning of this term had not yet crystallized. Ancestry, kinship, or tribal belonging, as well as the distinction between sedentary and nomadic predominated as means of self-identification. Terms were still fluid, and people could easily refer to more than one category.[41]

As mentioned above, the term *uzbek* was undergoing a reinterpretation. The Russian term *kirgiz* also saw a shift in meaning. Prior to 1925 the distinction between Kyrgyz and Kazakh as we understand them today was weak in Russian administrative language. Party and state institutions had been using the term *kirgiz* to designate both Kazakh (*kirgiz-kazak*) and Kyrgyz (*kara-kirgiz* or *dikokamennye kirgizy*). The two distinctive features between these categories were, first, the difference between horizontal nomadism in the steppe (Kazakh) and vertical nomadism in the mountains (Kyrgyz) and, second, their social hierarchies, culture, and language.[42] Hence for the debates in 1924, I use *kirgiz* in its ambiguous meaning. At the same time, the term *tajik* as we use it today had also not yet fully crystallized. It was applied to designate the sedentary Farsi-speaking population in remote eastern Bukhara. In 1924 it was associated with backwardness and had little political appeal. This would change significantly *after* the delimitation.[43]

To follow the course of the debate, it is also crucial to keep in mind the distinction between "European" and "indigenous" party activists. All of them were well aware of this difference, but they perceived each other as indispensable allies when opposing the settlers and the traditionalist elites. Together they formed the nexus of Soviet power in the region. In daily practice, their relation translated into not a coarse master-servant dependency but a situation akin to progressive social workers and teenagers. Ivan Mezhlauk, an activist at the Sredazbiuro in Tashkent, emphasized this in a letter to Stalin: "The Sredazbiuro has yet to make any decisions about these [territorial] issues. . . . We Europeans should refrain from taking part in these controversies and give the local [*mestnye*] comrades [the opportunity] to express their views as freely and as fully as possible."[44]

Sultanbek Khodzhanov, since 1921 Turkestan's people's commissar for education, kept promoting federalist approaches and therefore bitterly opposed any plans for national delimitation in Central Asia.[45]

CHAPTER 4

Born in 1894, Khodzhanov was also a young politician who had experienced a meteoric rise. He had been a teacher and in 1917 had gotten involved with the Alash movement. At first, he fought the Turkestani Soviets, who were dominated by Russian and Ukrainian settlers, but later he joined the Bolsheviks. Appointed to prominent political positions, he kept promoting the idea of a unified Turkestan.[46] Approaches like Khodzhanov's still had prominent supporters in Moscow. Grigorii Broido, previously the deputy head of Narkomnats, argued in an expert opinion for the Central Committee of the RKP(b) that even if national delimitation were inevitable, all of the republics would have to be coordinated by a Central Asian Federation.[47]

Despite such dissenting opinions, the Communist Party of Turkestan and the majority of members from the Sredazbiuro opted for national delimitation.[48] To be clear, the reason behind the national option was not to divide and conquer the local population, as many Western researchers have claimed.[49] The European and indigenous communists were well aware of the national factionalism within their organization. They feared it would spill over, and the cultural and economic differences within the Central Asian population would turn into national antagonisms. Sedentary people would dominate state and party, which might generate a secessionist movement among the nomads.[50] Moreover, with the experience of the Transcaucasian Federation in mind, the members of the Sredazbiuro also had to take into account the considerable amount of funding spent on an additional layer of federal administration.[51] In the end, even dedicated proponents of a federal solution such as Khodzhanov had to stick to the party line, but not without showing their displeasure whenever possible.[52]

The Sredazbiuro decided to launch the delimitation process on 10 May 1924. According to a first draft, Turkestan, Bukhara, and Khorezm would be dissolved. The prospective Uzbek and Turkmen republics were to have SSR status, while the Tajik, Kara-Kirgiz, and Karakalpak entities would become autonomous oblasti. Those areas of Turkestan inhabited by Kirgiz-Kazak, in particular the Zhetisu region, would be attached to the Kirrespublika.[53] Uzbekistan received the highest status as it was considered to have a functional economic base in cotton growing and in the urban centers, whereas the reasons for granting the same status to Turkmenistan seem much less clear. Adrienne Edgar identifies the republic's peripheral location as one such reason.[54]

The Politburo in Moscow adopted this draft on 12 June 1924, but a large number of details remained unclear. The party only issued guidelines. Bukhara and Turkestan were to be dissolved and their territories redistributed to national entities. Tashkent, the main administrative town in Central Asia and the seat of the Sredazbiuro, would be part of Uzbekistan. That seemed clear. But the Politburo left the fate of Khorezm open, as its government had initially objected to national delimitation. Khorezmian party activists had even proposed setting up national entities within their state but keeping Khorezm and leaving its borders as they stood. Notwithstanding Khorezm's fate, the Politburo invited indigenous party activists to discuss the details of this delimitation. The Sredazbiuro would set up a special Delimitation Commission.[55]

Considering the complexity of the task, this was a smart move by the Politburo. The party only established a general framework and left the politicians on the ground to find practical and "efficient" solutions. This enabled the Politburo to avoid any practical responsibility. Even so, as in the Russian-Ukrainian case, it reserved its right to approve or disapprove of the outcome.

National Delimitation and Moscow's Delegation of Responsibility

The politicians involved in delimitation discussed not only future borders but also the very words used to designate what was at stake. Hence, when they used words such as *uzbek*, they could be referring to a certain group of people but also to the words themselves and their pertinence to a debate. At first glance, the discussions may seem confusing, but these documents provide insight into a unique moment when categories and meanings were in flux before crystallizing into something that would then become commonly shared.

In the early summer of 1924, the stakes of this wager on national territory were already clear: Turkestan would be divided between the emerging national republics. The Tashkent region and the Fergana Valley were the economic and demographic icing on the Turkestani cake. As in the Russian-Ukrainian case, every side wanted to get as many assets—not necessarily territory—as possible.

The Delimitation Commission of the Sredazbiuro met in August and September 1924 to discuss and decide the new territorial structure. In advance, Uzbek, Turkmen, Kirgiz-Kazak, and Kara-Kirgiz subcommissions were set up to prepare proposals on how to delimit the region.[56] Their convening at the sessions of the Delimitation Commission foreshadowed a looming showdown for the competing factions of the soon-to-be dissolved Communist Party of Turkestan. On 16 August 1924 eighteen delegates first met under the chairmanship of Isaak Zelenskii.[57] Zelenskii was a respected, experienced Bolshevik. Born to a Jewish family in Saratov, he had been a member of the party since 1906. At this meeting, he had to play the roles of arbiter and adviser to indigenous Bolsheviks. First, he warned all of the participants to mind their manners, engage in cultured discussion, and avoid chauvinist utterances. The commission's members had to set an example for regular party members and for the common people.[58]

A close reading of the commission's minutes and shorthand notes offer intricate insights into the way key party activists dealt with a challenge that simultaneously involved political, economic, and national issues. All of the members of the Sredazbiuro as well as outside experts could join the commission and express advice.[59] Zelenskii—together with Iosif Vareikis and Oto Karklin, both respected European Bolsheviks—assumed an advisory role in most of the sessions that followed. They explained to their Central Asian comrades formal party procedures and the practical meaning of party directives. Representatives of the Russian and Ukrainian settlers in Central Asia were deliberately excluded from these discussions.

During the commission's meetings, the indigenous Bolsheviks split into two competing factions. They argued within Stalin's definition of nationality when linking aspects of language, culture, and economy with territory.[60] One faction encompassed those like Khodzhanov who had previously opposed the very idea of national delimitation. They were predominantly members of the Kirgiz-Kazak subcommission. In debate, they often referred to historical and cultural aspects. The other faction was made up of members of the Uzbek subcommission, who mostly focused on economic aspects. They rejected historical arguments and simply relied on what they considered the status quo: for example, that all sedentary people who were growing cotton were to be considered Uzbeks and would have to be part of a future Uzbekistan.

At the very start, Zelenskii warned all participants that the preliminary framework established by the Politburo was binding. No one could simply revise it.[61] Vareikis suggested that every subcommission would include at least one European for the sake of "balance."[62] Then Zelenskii exhorted all of the participants to keep in mind that they were now acting within the confines of the party line. In conclusion, he also mentioned that interpreters would have to be provided for those who did not understand Russian. During meetings, it would also happen that a member of the commission would say something in his native language. In such cases, the stenographer laconically noted "utterance in the Muslim language."⁶³

After addressing these preliminary organizational issues, the members of the commission turned to the question of which statistics would be considered for the delimitation process. The commission had census data from 1897, 1911, 1917, and 1920. Zelenskii voted in favor of the 1897 census as the most reliable one, but in a nine to eight vote, the commission decided against any particular preference.⁶⁴ After a notably short discussion about Turkmenistan's future borders, the commission began to take up increasingly controversial topics.⁶⁵

Sharustam Islamov, the head of the Turkestan Sovnarkom and of the Uzbek subcommission, was well aware of the subtle challenges. He would soon become a prominent advocate of the pro-delimitation faction, and unlike many of his adversaries he understood how to adapt his language to the party line. This, however, did not stop him from trying to make "his" prospective nation as large as possible. He therefore tried to argue that sedentary people identifying as Kurama and Kipchak would be counted as Uzbeks.⁶⁶

Islamov added that the case of the Karakalpak was similar because the people designated by this term were referring to other words to identify themselves. Using a map that stood in the middle of the room, he pointed out the volosti that should be added to the future Uzbek republic. His main argument was that the commission had to draw the border along the economic raiony, and all of those with a predominantly Uzbek population should become part of the Uzbek republic.⁶⁷

Islamov's presentation seemed to suggest that the task was easy, but he encountered fierce opposition. First, Sultan Segizbaev, a representative from the Tashkent region, criticized Islamov's view as too simplistic. Segizbaev was a young and dedicated Bolshevik who had been politicized during the 1916 uprising and joined the RKP(b) in 1918. He referred to the historical dimension to demonstrate the absurdity of national delimitation. He pointedly asked Islamov what the word *kurama* meant in his native language and how he used it in relation to the Uzbek and Karakalpak. Zelenskii interjected, saying that this would be debated later, but Segizbaev insisted. He emphasized that *uzbek* had an older, inclusive meaning because it was derived from Özbeg Khan, a fourteenth-century ruler under whom the Golden Horde had reached its apogee of power. His subjects began calling themselves *uzbek*.⁶⁸

Sandzhar Asfendiarov, who was ten years older than Segizbaev and one of the few indigenous graduates of the imperial school in Tashkent, assisted Segizbaev. In opposition to Islamov's economic interpretation, Asfendiarov underlined the historical and cultural dimensions. He referred to the fuzziness of the ethnographic terms *uzbek* and *sart* and noted that the 1920 census had often confused them. The same thing happened with *kurama*: "The word *kurama* means *rag rug*—a mixture. This group includes the most different of tribes [*plemena*] and so the question should be solved by a conference of the Kurama ... they should decide where they belong."[69] Asfendiarov went on to remind his comrades that, under tsarist rule, terms and changes from sedentary to nomadic lifestyle had been fluid: "*kirgiz* and *nomad* [*kochevnik*] were synonyms. The nomads had no right to own land. During statistical surveys, the Kirgiz declared themselves Uzbek or Kurama to acquire land or keep it. This fact is easy to prove by means of numerous examples in the *aul*s and *kishlak*s.[70] This means that the existing statistics need a corrective."[71]

Sultanbek Khodzhanov, a well-known opponent of national delimitation, loudly supported his two comrades. He went even deeper into the intricate challenges surrounding questions of belonging and highlighted again that in its historical meaning the term *uzbek* could also include Kirgiz tribes.[72] Like Asfendiarov and Segizbaev, Khodzhanov sought to question the legitimacy of Uzbek claims and of the delimitation as such. At this point, Zelenskii interrupted Khodzhanov's monologue, as he—a party activist with a long history of dialectical argumentation—was perplexed by the complexity of the terminology. The chairman asked the speaker: "So, a Kirgiz is also an Uzbek?" Khodzhanov's answer was even more challenging:

> Yes, he is also an Uzbek. The historical meaning of the tribes [*plemena*] is such that the Turkic peoples [*tiurkskie narody*] founded two big unions: the Kirgiz-Kazak and the Uzbek. However, *uzbek* is a random term and not an ethnographic one. It evolved because they were subjects of a certain Özbeg Khan. He was a Muslim, and he forced all his subjects to adopt Islam [*musul'manstvo*]. Thus all people of the [Kirgiz-Kazak] union that Özbeg Khan vanquished became Uzbeks as well as Muslims. . . .
>
> It has been historically confirmed that Uzbeks and Kirgiz represent the same old union that was formed at the same source by Turkic tribes [*tiurkskie plemena*]. This proves that there is no original Uzbek tribe [*uzbekskoe plemia*] as such.[73]

After these terminological and historical explanations, Khodzhanov went straight to the materialistic points of the ongoing delimitation. He insisted that the commission must address irrigation issues. In his view, the future Uzbek republic should not get all the water resources. The Kirgiz-Kazak republic needed access to water supplies as well, he said. He approached the map and urged the commission to avoid complicated, jagged boundaries. However, in doing so, he added, the commission would then have to find a means of compensating one republic or the other.[74] At this point, Zelenskii reminded his comrades once more that they were not members of a trade delegation and must draw the borders only for rational and justifiable reasons.[75] Hence the first session was concluded.

The next day, on 17 August, the commission met again, but this time more than forty people were sitting in the room, as every member had also brought his deputy.[76] Such a crowd did not make the resolution of controversial issues any easier. The participants began with a discussion of borders in the Fergana Valley. Urazliev, a representative of the Kara-Kirgiz, complained that the Uzbek side would not present good-faith

FIGURE 14. Picture of the Territorial Commission for Delimitation of the Central Asian Republics, 1924.

arguments. On one hand, they would freely claim tribes in the Fergana Valley to be Uzbek that could also be considered Kirgiz. On the other, they would offer Osh to the future Kara-Kirgiz republic on the basis of communist principles, but Osh, when compared with the well-connected town of Andijan, was little more than a market square without any railroad connection.[77]

Ishenaly Arabaev, representative of the Kara-Kirgiz, vigorously supported the idea of national delimitation and the creation of a distinct Kara-Kirgiz entity. Previously, he had supported the Alash party, but with the creation of the Kirrespublika in 1920, he turned into a proponent of Kara-Kirgiz autonomy.[78] While participating in the Delimitation Commission, Arabaev had longed to contribute to the debate for a long time but was unable do so in Russian. Therefore, he had to wait for an interpreter. Finally, he had his chance to demonstrate his own expertise on the historical evolution of the word *uzbek*.[79] Arabaev again referred to the old meaning of *uzbek* to challenge the claims of the Uzbek subcommission. He further argued against the tendency to define everybody who grew cotton as Uzbeks. These people would have to define themselves. Then he returned to the topic at hand and made a political statement. Referring to Stalin, Arabaev argued that the towns had to belong to the population in the hinterland. Thus Andijan should be part of the Kara-Kirgiz entity.[80]

This was too much for Abdurakhim Khodzhibaev, a member of the Fergana Oblast Executive Committee and delegate on the Uzbek subcommission. He defended the censuses of 1917 and 1920 and shouted at Arabaev: "You cannot provide for the pursuit of happiness for the Kara-Kirgiz at the expense of the Uzbeks."[81] Later, Khodzhibaev would distance himself from an Uzbek identity and adopt a Tajik one. But in the summer of 1924, that moment had not yet come.

While the faction around Khodzhanov kept reminding the audience that the focus on national differences among the population in Central Asia had only recently been introduced, Islamov and Khodzhibaev addressed these differences as if they already represented social reality.[82] Khodzhibaev tried repeatedly to explain to comrades such as Arabaev how one defines belonging: "Who produces cotton? The Uzbeks do that! Here your [Arabaev's] word is wrong. The word you want to use to blame [us] creates confusion. This is an unfriendly, this is a noncommunist action."[83]

The mood was so tense that Zelenskii had to intervene again. He ordered a break. The participants would have a moment to cool down.

After the break, Khodzhanov was introduced as the next speaker. As a supporter of a Central Asian Federation, he asked his comrades again whether divisions along national lines were necessary when the Fergana Valley itself constituted an economically functional unit. With that, he again called into question the entire enterprise: "Until 1920 we didn't have divisions between Kirgiz, Kara-Kirgiz, and Uzbek. At that time, there was only a Muslim population. Sometimes, someone talked about Turks as the politically most progressive part of the population [*narod*]. The population was mixed and differences among the tribes were moderate, and this is why the censuses from these years are highly erroneous.... I propose to call all Muslims *Turks*, *Uzbeks*, and so on, this means *Central Asian Turk* or *Central Asian Muslim* [*to ia predlagaiu vsekh musul'man nazvat' tiurkami, uzbekami i t. d. chto oznachaet sredne-aziatskii tiurk ili sredne-aziatskii musul'manin*]."[84]

In his reply to Khodzhanov, Islamov excluded such historical considerations, referring again to what he perceived as the status quo. Unlike Khodzhanov, he carefully framed his arguments and made his proposal appear as "efficient" as possible: "Now we are delineating the territories of the Turkestan Republic [based on] who lives [here] now. We are defining the borders starting from this point. The Uzbek territory is where Uzbeks live. The Kirgiz territory is where Kirgiz live."[85]

After a short break, the heated debate continued. Zelenskii tried to reach an agreement on the Fergana Valley. Khodzhanov once more intervened and called for a discussion of where to include the people identifying as Kipchak and Kashgari. Zelenskii rebuffed him. The chairman wanted results. However, the balloting that ensued turned into a nightmare. In Communist Party commissions, ballots with dissenting votes were rare, but now the votes were tied.[86] Zelenskii saw it as necessary to deliver a sermon on proper behavior: "We are communists.... We apply the principles of universal efficiency [*obshchaia tselesoobraznost'*]. Here, however, some comrades have yielded to a feeling that is based on narrow national interests [*uzko natsional'nye interessy*]. ... You are not representatives of a bourgeois state, and you are not preparing for a military expedition. If there were no ... Communist Party, then you would have declared war on each other."[87]

Zelenskii kindly reminded his comrades how to play the multilayered game of power. The balloting resumed. This time, the commission was able to make decisions. They distributed volost after volost in the Fergana Valley between the prospective Uzbek and Kara-Kirgiz entities. Among other things, they assigned Osh to the Kara-Kirgiz Oblast and

Andijan to Uzbekistan.[88] With that, the first big issues seemed to be solved.

Zelenskii then planned to discuss the Kirgiz-Kazak border. Vareikis reminded all of the participants to focus on what was at stake. Historical and tribal matters were to be avoided.[89] Seitkali Mendeshev, a Kirgiz-Kazak representative, started his presentation on borders in the Tashkent region. Once again ignoring the Politburo decision that Tashkent would form part of a future Uzbekistan, he argued that the Kirrespublika would need a worthy capital and that Tashkent would be the best choice. Mendeshev demonstratively ignored Vareikis's "advice" and emphasized that the Kurama were not at all an Uzbek tribe. Hence the discussion again deteriorated into a historical debate. Even though speakers started their opening remarks by stressing "we are all communists," the commission split repeatedly into two hostile factions. Compromise seemed impossible. The mood in the room grew tense again.[90] After a break, the commission reconvened at 9:00 p.m. Islamov spoke first: "there are some comrades here who do not know the uezdy, and this is why they lie, they lie until they swoon. . . . I repeat, if everyone counts with his own numbers, if it is not possible to agree on any defined numbers, we will have no order."[91]

Islamov's seemingly pragmatic approach quickly proved to be sleight of hand, as he referred to the 1920 census as the only reliable one. He took a map and presented his comrades with the prospective Uzbek territory. At the end, he postulated: "We say that this map is the true map. We will not retreat from this."[92] Islamov also proposed staffing the special regional subcommissions with two representatives from each side and one European. Khodzhanov protested loudly. Zelenskii was not able to contain his frustration any longer: "The work of our commission has turned into its own kind of chatter. It is an arena for . . . discussions held at the bazaar in the old town. . . . Do you really think that three Uzbeks, three Kirgiz, and I will just sit down together and start to make peace?! Excuse me, but I cannot accept this."[93]

Zelenskii reminded all of the participants one more time that they should prepare for the meetings. Most arguments sounded as if there had been no preparation at all. The commission continued to get hung up on matters of procedure. The same two factions once again crystallized around Islamov and Khodzhanov, respectively. Some participants began to make a scene. Karklin and Zelenskii shouted at the audience that further debate was futile. The chairman then closed the session.[94]

Three days later, on 20 August, the Sredazbiuro met in secret session. Zelenskii was absent, but Vareikis and Karklin were there to remind Khodzhanov and Islamov that they should watch their behavior at the sessions. Personal conflicts and resentments should not impede rational debate. The Sredazbiuro accepted this call to order with a vote of six to two.⁹⁵

On 21 August 1924 the commission convened for another meeting, but the Europeans' exhortations that participants behave "correctly" again fell on deaf ears. Zelenskii sought to continue the debate on the border between the Uzbek and Kara-Kirgiz entities. Islamov retreated from his "true map" and made an offer: the volosti of Aleksandrovsk, Ak-Dzhar, and Kosh-Kurgan would make up part of the "Kirgiz oblast," but then he argued that the river Chirchik should belong to the future Uzbek republic.⁹⁶

Khodzhanov responded to this potential compromise, pointing out that the proposal would divide irrigation between the prospective republics. The division would have to be economically viable: "As soon as we accept delimitation, we must then accept the practical consequences that logically follow from this step. We were not in favor of any delimitation. They have forced us to come here, but those who wanted delimitation should remain logical until the end."⁹⁷ Analyzing Islamov's new proposal, he consciously or unconsciously expressed the core rationale behind his rival's argument: "We are not dividing Turkestan along national lines but along the lines of sedentary and nonsedentary [populations]."⁹⁸ The dividing line between the prospective Uzbek and Kirgiz entities ran alongside perceived boundaries of sedentary and pastoralist economies.

After everyone had made his point, the next round of balloting produced a majority for the Uzbek plan. The volosti around Tashkent would join the future Uzbek republic. This was a red line for Khodzhanov and his supporters. They protested the result loudly. Once again, Khodzhanov and Islamov plunged into an argument, this time over which volosti precisely the proposal would include. When they could not agree on basic terms, they lost control. Islamov and Khodzhanov called each other liars. As Zelenskii intervened, Khodzhanov then accused the head of the commission of "pursuing Uzbekization."⁹⁹ Zelenskii ordered another break. Islamov and Khodzhanov were to cool down.

After an hour, they met again, only to go in circles once more. Zelenskii held another round of balloting addressing Islamov's and

Khodzhanov's proposals. The result turned out to be another tie: eight to eight. In the end, a subcommission was tasked with debating which entity would get the three volosti around Tashkent. Then the commission attached Chinaz Volost to the Kirrespublika and divided Mirzachul' Uezd between the Kirrespublika and Uzbekistan.[100]

After a second break, the commission reconvened at 12:40 a.m. The issue of the Kirgiz and Tajik populations within Bukhara awaited discussion. It soon turned out that the subcommission tasked with the Kirgiz issue was unable to present any comprehensive results. The estimated numbers of Kirgiz in Bukhara ran from 33,000 to 350,000 people. Zelenskii appointed another subcommission to study the issue.[101] The Sredazbiuro would have to decide on this matter later. The commission then moved on to discuss the prospective Tajik Autonomous Oblast.[102] Abdurakhim Khodzhibaev presented a plan based on Bukharan census data from 1913. Within Bukhara, there were about 1.2 million Tajiks. In the eastern parts, where Tajiks lived in compact settlements, an autonomous entity with about 600,000 inhabitants (some 400,000 of whom were Tajik) would be formed.[103]

The main lines of contention in 1924 revolved around the opposition of Kirgiz vs. Uzbek. From this perspective, the potential differences between Uzbeks and Tajiks seemed secondary. Both communities practiced a sedentary lifestyle and shared a similar culture; many were bilingual. As already mentioned, before 1924, the word *tajik* was often associated with people from the mountainous backwater of eastern Bukhara.[104] For this reason, some of the participants began to wonder whether the very existence of a Tajik nation was still up for debate, and no one complained why there was no Tajik subcommission. In the end, the proposal for a Tajik Autonomous Oblast was accepted.[105]

On 6 September 1924 the commission met for its final session. The participants continued to have problems playing by the rules. Zelenskii tried to call everyone to order in the hope of finding a quick solution for the three contested volosti near Tashkent.[106] But when the participants began to introduce petitions from the villages and auls concerned and requested an in-depth discussion of the new national borders, the Europeans hit the brakes. Vareikis indicated that the commission would be deciding only a rough framework for the future borders. The details would be discussed by the Sredazbiuro. Having listened to all of the petty details submitted, Zelenskii again reminded his audience: "if we decide such issues in the Delimitation Commission, then it will be as in the case of the Kara-Kirgiz [on 21 August] . . . we were sitting around for four hours; everything had been discussed, every aul, every settlement, and every *vershok* [inch] of territory. This does not have any essential meaning, but we can sit for a long time."[107]

Even though he had previously spoken out against any further detailed discussion in a small setting, this was what Zelenskii in fact did. After the meeting on 6 September, he called to his office the four heads of the subcommissions: Islamov (Uzbek), Khodzhanov (Kirgiz-Kazak), Abdrakhmanov (Kara-Kirgiz), and Kaigizys Atabaev (Turkmen). Zelenskii designated the group as the Editorial Commission (Redaktsionnaia komissiia). This small circle now had to find a solution for the messy outcome of the discussions at the meetings. The leaders of the different subcommissions set about editing the minutes and stenographs. In doing so, they tried to make amendments and delete some of their contributions to the sessions. In the end, a majority vote yielded agreement on the preliminary borders of Uzbekistan and Turkmenistan, as well as those of the Tajik, Kara-Kirgiz, and Karakalpak autonomous oblasti. The new borders of the Kirrespublika were defined only by their omission in relation to others.[108] There is no clear information about how the members of the Editorial Commission voted. But given the circumstances, we can presume that Zelenskii favored the Uzbek side, while the Kirgiz-Kazak representative openly opposed it.[109] One day later, the Sredazbiuro approved the Editorial Commission's decision.[110] At that point, national delimitation was transformed from concept to administrative reality.

The local population itself had no voice in this process. It was a party issue, and the minutes were marked "top secret" (*sovershenno sekretno*). Nonetheless, it was a decision-making process carried out by indigenous Bolsheviks. The Europeans on the Delimitation Commission saw themselves only as advisers. Zelenskii, Karklin, and Vareikis could have broken the series of tie votes in favor of one side or the other much earlier, but they viewed their role differently. They wanted to appear neutral and give their Central Asian comrades the right and responsibility to decide on "their" territories. The indigenous Bolsheviks had split in two factions. The representatives of the prospective Uzbek republic favored delimitation. Representatives of the prospective Kirgiz-Kazak republic favored a federal solution. Representatives of the Kara-Kirgiz like Arabaev supported delimitation to realize the Kara-Kirgiz entity that had failed in 1922. The underlying reason for these differences was the economic prospects of these territorial entities. The Uzbek republic would control most of the water supply and, with it, the region's cotton production. The Turkmen, Kara-Kirgiz, and Kirgiz-Kazak were left with poorly developed steppes and mountainous areas. Within a federal framework, the economic assets and liabilities would have been shared.

Only at the end and in a small setting did Zelenskii vote with the Uzbek faction. Their arguments, which tilted toward the present situation, fit the party line much better. Zelenskii, like his superiors in Moscow, was focused on future development. Consequently, the Bolsheviks' longing for "efficiency" often favored the Uzbek side, as the Uzbek republic was expected to coordinate and increase the production of cotton that was so desperately needed to accelerate industrialization in the European part of the Soviet Union.[111]

The decisions taken in the late summer of 1924 had far-reaching consequences for the population of Central Asia. Everyone had to cope with abstract national categories. This distinction now served as a crucial element in defining the relation between the state and its citizens. As a result, nomads within the territory of the prospective Uzbekistan were suddenly classified as a minority, like the Kara-Kirgiz in the Pamir Mountains.[112]

Even though the members of the Delimitation Commission could not agree on numerous details, the Soviet press announced the national delimitation of Central Asia in mid-September 1924.[113] On 14 September 1924 a joint commission of the TsK of the Communist Party of Turkestan and the Sredazbiuro confirmed the Editorial Commission's solution. It seemed to have been a compromise, because nobody was happy. According to Zelenskii, it was delimitation "done with an axe."[114] Two days later, on 16 September, the TurkTsIK issued an official proclamation on national delimitation that was disseminated throughout the union.[115] At that point, the Bukharan and Khorezmian party leaderships proclaimed their consent.[116] On 11 October, the Politburo in Moscow discussed the Central Asian issue and agreed to most of the Delimitation Commission's decisions, with one major exception: most of the contested territories around Tashkent (Chinaz, Krest'iansk, Spask, and Mirzachul'/Syr-Dar'insk) were to be attached to the future Uzbek republic.[117]

In his final report to the Central Committee, Yan Rudzutak, head of the Sredazbiuro, emphasized once again that there had been no alternative to national delimitation in Central Asia. Tensions between the Uzbek and the Kirgiz within the Turkestan party were putting Soviet rule at risk. Delimitation would guarantee the region's stability and progress.¹¹⁸ Rudzutak silently ignored the Kirgiz-Kazak representatives' desperate lobbying for an alternative, federal solution.

Konstantin Yegorov, the territorial expert from Moscow, was also involved in the huge task of delineating Central Asia. As always, he complained of the lack of statistical data and maps for the region. In his report to Ter-Gabrielian, the head of the All-Union Commission for Raionirovanie, he wrote: "after providing a description of the borders of the republics in Central Asia and receiving approval from the Presidium of the TsIK, we will need one or one and a half years to stabilize the republics' external borders, and we should focus our maximum attention on their interior arrangement without changing the external borders. [In the meantime,] we have to collect all of the claims of the republics against one another as material for further study."¹¹⁹

The case of Tajikistan would soon gain its own momentum. The renaming of the former eastern Bukhara and Turkestani Pamir into Tajikistan with its predominately rural Farsi-speaking population led to the institutionalization of Tajik autonomy within the newly established Uzbekistan. Until the national delimitation, language was not much considered as a focal point of nationalism. This changed as leading politicians in the newly formed Tajik ASSR saw linguistic

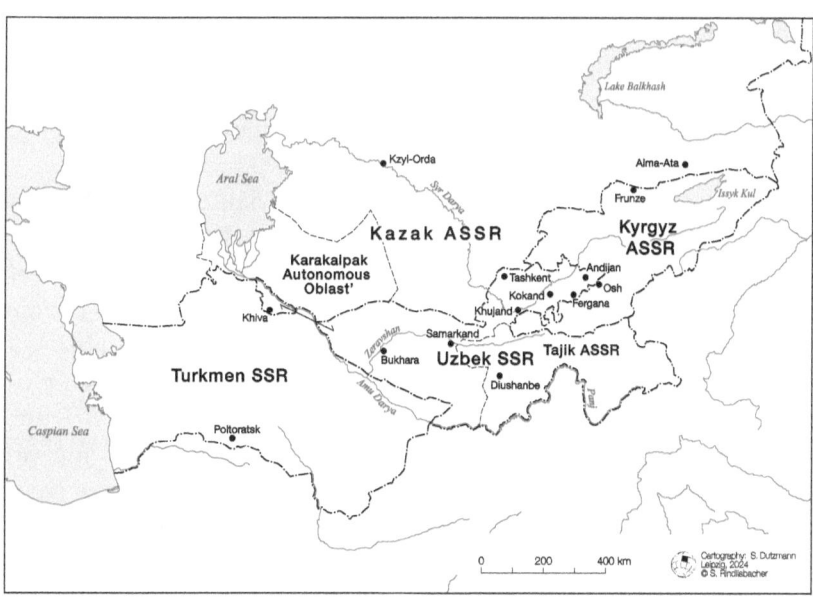

FIGURE 15. Political map of Central Asia, 1926.

opposition (Uzbek vs. Tajik) as an instrument to propel their own careers. Some former Bukharan cadres like Abdukadyr Mukhiddinov and Abdurakhim Khodzhibaev were able strengthen their political standing under the roof of Tajik autonomy. From there they would lobby to include "Tajik-speaking" towns such as Khujand, Samarkand, and even Bukhara into a Greater Tajikistan.[120]

Managing Implementation of Borders on the Ground

In October 1924 the Central Asian republics as we know them today began to take shape. However, their precise boundaries and status remained in flux for some time.[121] As foreseen, Turkmenistan and Uzbekistan immediately gained the status of Socialist Soviet Republics (SSRs), the highest possible status within the Soviet federal framework. The Uzbek republic included most of the towns, the most significant companies, and Central Asia's cotton production. Economically and politically, Uzbekistan was almost self-sustaining.[122] The other republics were far less developed economically and thus more dependent on Moscow. The Kirrespublika remained an Autonomous Socialist Soviet Republic (ASSR) within the RSFSR, while the Kara-Kirgiz and Karakalpak Autonomous Oblasti (AO) were initially subordinated to the Kirrespublika. In 1925 the difference between the Kazakh and Kyrgyz was legally established, and the Kirrespublika changed its name to the Kazakh ASSR or simply Kazakhstan. Subsequently, the Kara-Kirgiz AO was also renamed the Kyrgyz AO or simply Kyrgyzstan. One year later, it gained ASSR status, equal to that of the Kazakh entity.[123]

Territorial issues continued to create difficulties. The southwestern part of the Fergana Valley was especially coveted. Its fate provides an example of problem management in the region. As in other regions of Central Asia, experts and politicians often lacked suitable cartographic materials.[124] In October 1925 the TsIK in Moscow called into being a new territorial commission for the Fergana Valley. It was made up of a troika under Grigorii Petrovskii, a leading Ukrainian party figure, Mukhamedkhafii Mirza-Galiev from the RSFSR (as Kyrgyzstan and Kazakhstan were still part of the RSFSR), and Said Ali Khodzhaev from Uzbekistan.[125] Others, such as the territorial expert Iosif Magidovich, also participated in the meetings as advisers. There the Uzbek side tried to acquire the town of Osh from Kyrgyzstan, as Uzbek leaders considered its population to be Uzbek. For exigencies of governance, the Kyrgyz representative pointed to their need for an administrative center. The commission dismissed the Uzbek initiative without further discussion. Mirza-Galiev complained that save for Osh the Kyrgyz had received only the mountainous parts of the Fergana Valley. For this reason, Dublitskii, the top territorial expert in Kyrgyzstan's capital of Frunze (today Bishkek), proposed that the borders of the former Osh Volost be used as a starting point for revisions.[126] Petrovskii dispatched a technical commission under Magidovich to the valley in order to investigate current land use and irrigation canals.[127]

During the Petrovskii Commission's sessions, the Kyrgyz representatives also tried to change the status of Isfara and Sokh Volosti. The valleys and rivers belonged to Uzbekistan, while the steppe hills around them belonged to Kyrgyzstan. Due to this decision, two larger Uzbek languets had formed within Kyrgyzstan. Even though such a demarcation was complex even by Soviet standards, a Kyrgyz proposal to dissolve the languets was rebuffed. Petrovskii stressed the initial rationale for delimitation, as the national composition—mostly Tajik-speaking—and economic structure in these river valleys differed in comparison with the surrounding mountainous areas populated by herders.[128] As shown below, deliberations over how best to exploit the oilfields in Sokh also played a role.

At the next session on 25 March 1926, the commission nevertheless made some revisions in favor of the Kyrgyz side. For instance, it decided that Chap-Kuluk and Isfana Volosti would be attached to Kyrgyzstan since their population was predominantly Kyrgyz.[129] But for economic reasons, the commission made some exceptions, separating the coal mines of Suliukta from Isfana Volost and leaving them within Uzbekistan.[130]

Aleksandr Beloborodov, who had also taken part in revising the RSFSR-Ukrainian border, had to assess Petrovskii's recommendations for the TsIK. In his review, he argued against any division of the irrigation system in the Fergana Valley: "[as] it is important for the Soviet Union not to break up this very important cotton raion [large scale] of Central Asia, which is united by common sources of irrigation."[131] The republican borders thus had to follow the boundaries of agriculture and cattle breeding that seemingly conflated with the national-ethnographic distinction between Uzbek and Kyrgyz introduced above. The previous fluidity between the herder and settled communities was ignored. Subsequently, the VTsIK and the TsIK accepted most of the recommendations proposed by the Petrovskii Commission.[132]

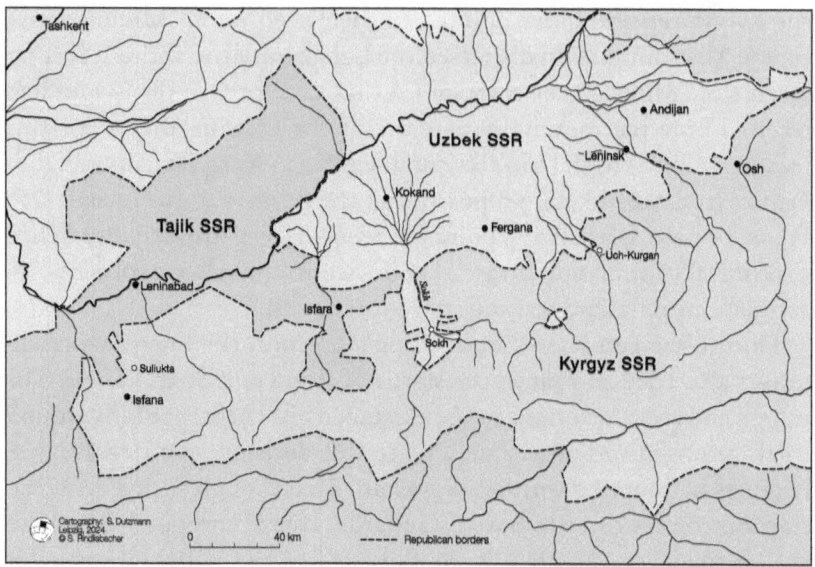

FIGURE 16. Political map of the Fergana Valley, 1940.

Although most border changes were in favor of the Kyrgyz side this time around, the Osh okrug administration was still not happy. In a memorandum a group of Osh officials argued to rectify the border in the southwestern Fergana Valley. As Uzbekistan had acquired all of the larger settlements and river valleys, the local Kyrgyz government found itself unable to install a functional administration in the remaining mountainous areas.[133] Moreover, Kyrgyz officials pointed to the fact that the Uzbek side had control over all of the arable fields and the irrigation system, especially the Sokh and Isfara rivers. The Kyrgyz herdsmen, who had been using these rivers to water their animals, were now excluded from their means of subsistence.[134] Mastering the territorial discourse as they marshaled their national, economic, and administrative arguments, the functionaries from Osh were adamant that the Uzbek-Kyrgyz border had to be revised again, if the Kyrgyz territory in the southwestern Fergana Valley was to be at all governable.

This appeal from Osh found support in Moscow as exigencies of governance were basic matters of concern for both party and state. The TsIK once again established a commission to settle the details. The chairman of this second commission for the Fergana Valley was the Turkmen party activist Biashim Kul'besherov. In January 1927 the panel's three members met on site. Seitkali Mendeshev—who had already been involved in the initial delimitation—served as the representative of the RSFSR. Said Ali Khodzhaev again represented Uzbekistan. Territorial experts such as Dublitskii and Magidovich joined the meetings as advisers.

Kul'besherov and his comrades began by deciding to study the national composition and economic dependencies of the region and to engage with the local population.[135] In the sessions that followed, they reopened older issues such as the Uch-Kurgan rail hub, even though the TsIK had already decided in September 1926 that it was to remain in Uzbekistan.[136] This hub was located about 50 kilometers southwest of Osh and played an important role as a regional crossroads. The surrounding town had a population of about 5,500 people, who were predominantly Tajik-speaking, but the hinterland was populated by about 20,000 Kyrgyz. It was expected the latter would be provided with better access to transportation opportunities and basic state administration. Moreover, Kul'besherov emphasized that attaching Uch-Kurgan to Kyrgyzstan would simplify the jagged border. Khodzhaev opposed the idea, mentioning that the lifestyle and culture of the Tajiks resembled that of the Uzbeks. Kul'besherov, however, relativized language as a distinctive element: "It is true that the difference between the languages does not prevent the Uzbeks and the Tajiks from understanding one another, but the same mutual understanding can be observed between the Tajiks and the Kyrgyz."[137] Despite distinctions, Kul'besherov indirectly referred to communalities among the Central Asian population.

In the end, Kul'besherov and Mendeshev outvoted Khodzhaev. Uch-Kurgan would move to Kyrgyzstan. Then Kul'besherov and his comrades revisited the issue of the mines in Suliukta and of Sokh Volost. The Kyrgyz side produced a new argument for the transfer of the mines: most of the workers in the coal mines were actually Kyrgyz.[138] Subsequently, the commission voted in their favor. For Sokh Volost, the commission found a solution that would be worthy of Solomon. Khodzhaev's protests notwithstanding, Kul'besherov and Mendeshev recommended attaching Sokh to Kyrgyzstan but leaving the water resources and newly discovered oil fields under Uzbek administration.[139] In his final report to the TsIK, Kul'besherov reminded his superiors that, despite protests from one side or the other, the commission had tried to find "efficient" solutions. Furthermore, he stressed that mutual interests and not narrow-minded national ones were critical in the decision to transfer the territory to Kyrgyzstan but to place the Sokh oil fields under Uzbek exterritorial administration. The Uzbek institutions simply seemed better suited to exploiting them.[140]

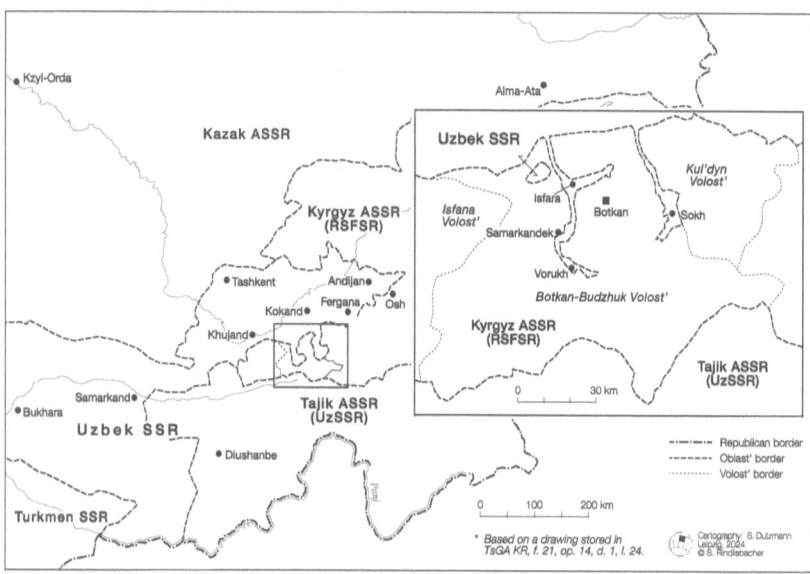

Figure 17. Adapted map of Kyrgyz Botkan-Budzhuk Volost and Uzbek Sokh and Vorukh Volosti, 1928.

The TsIK responded to Kul'besherov's recommendations in a way that could be called erratic at best. On 4 May 1927 it approved most of them, as in the case of Uch-Kurgan, but it made two significant changes: Sokh and the Suliukta mines were to stay in Uzbekistan.[141] Yet just one month later, the TsIK revised this decision. On 8 June 1927 it ordered Suliukta and its mines to be attached to Kyrgyzstan. This territorial transfer was enacted on the ground almost a year later, on 1 April 1928, as the mining company, its capital and real estate, along with the nearby schools, clubs, and hospital passed from Uzbek to Kyrgyz administration.[142]

Some historians have suggested that the Soviet state and party leadership made territorial decisions out of a preference for the Uzbek side.[143] The aforementioned re-revisions, however, provide us with a more differentiated picture. In the end, the Communist Party did not care about belonging or territories as such. They were only parts of a larger social machinery. The main task was to ensure governance over a certain region, meaning that the authorities could reach out to the communities on their territory for policing and taxation in due time. Last but not least, the party also could mobilize the local population for the socialist project.

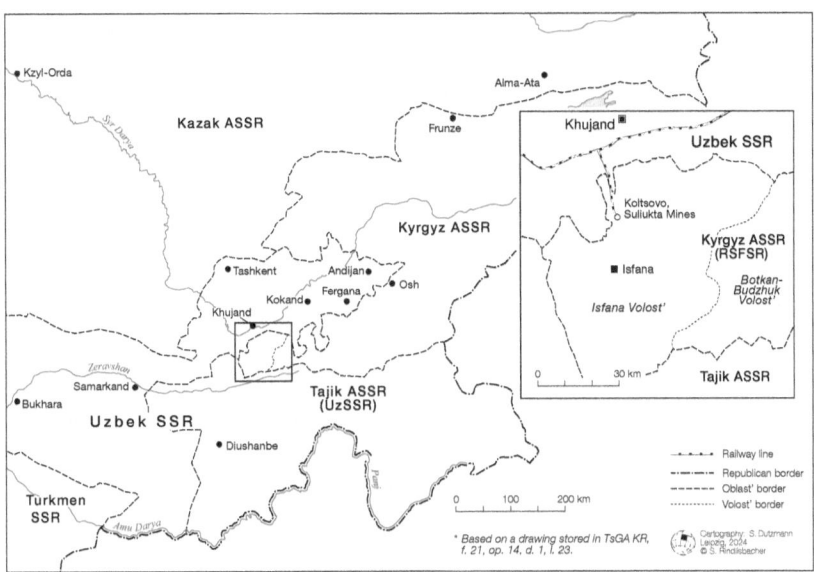

FIGURE 18. Adapted map of Kyrgyz Isfana Volost, 1928.

Despite the Kul'besherov Commission's work, the borders continued to create problems for the people of the Fergana Valley. For instance, in Isfana Volost the rural soviets of Chimkhan and Sumbula used a pasture called Yulduz-kak in the spring and fall. Their volost was transferred from Uzbekistan to Kyrgyzstan in February 1927, but the local Uzbek administration in Khujand still considered Yulduz-kak part of its territory.[144] In the spring of 1927 it dispatched police to detain the Kyrgyz herdsmen and extract a tax of twenty kopecks for every head of sheep on hand. The chairman of the local Kyrgyz administration in Isfana appealed to Frunze for help:

> The narrow-minded employees in the lower-level Soviet apparatus [on the Uzbek side] are not able to see what is at stake and imagine the harm they are doing to the population's economy. They won't provide the population of Kyrgyzstan a means of using these pastures freely....
>
> This is why I ask you to resolve this issue and to define the boundary correctly. The situation is very critical for the [Kyrgyz] population [*naselenie*], as the population of Uzbekistan continues with its mockery of the Kyrgyz.[145]

Border issues not only created problems for the local population but for the central authorities as well. The repeated territorial re-revisions created outright chaos within the TsIK. As mentioned previously, the TsIK had been rather erratic in its revisions. For this reason, in August 1927 the TsIK imposed, self-critically, a three-year moratorium on all border revisions throughout the union.[146] In February 1929 Stalin signaled to the party that the leadership was unwilling to discuss any more border issues between union republics. In his eyes, they were unnecessary obstacles to his industrialization project.[147]

Despite such signals from Moscow, things did not get any easier, particularly when Tajik politicians successfully lobbied for the status of union republic at the end of 1929. The major issue in this separation was the restructuring of the Uzbek-Tajik border. Whereas Tajik representatives laid claim to major towns like Bukhara and Samarkand, Uzbek representatives sharply dismissed such aspirations. In the end the region around Khujand was transferred from Uzbekistan to Tajikistan in 1930. The Uzbek nationality was now seen as distinct from Tajik. The state institutions would eventually demand that the population end its bilingualism. Someone could be Tajik or Uzbek, but not (anymore) both at the same time.[148]

In 1936 Kyrgyzstan and Kazakhstan also gained SSR status. Since then, the Fergana Valley has been divided in an overly complex arrangement among three national entities of equal rank. Minor border revisions in the valley were still possible. Surveying commissions repeatedly discovered "irregularities" on the ground. In such cases, interrepublican commissions had to step in and find a convenient solution. For example, surveyors reported in 1937 that Tajik kolkhozes from Proletarian Raion near Khujand (Leninabad between 1936 and 1991) were cultivating fields that nominally belonged to Kyrgyz Liailiak Raion. To avoid any further problems, the governments of both republics simply agreed to adapt the de jure as de facto. Hence in mid-1938 about seven square kilometers were transferred from Kyrgyzstan to Tajikistan.[149]

These kinds of bilateral border changes were common in the Fergana Valley. However, they often failed to satisfy formal legal requirements—that is, ratification by the All-Union Supreme Soviet. The jagged boundaries in the valley also led to conflicts between communities over access to fields and water supply. Some of these conflicts even led to deadly violence among the locals.[150] As was the case along the Russian-Ukrainian and Armenian-Azerbaijani borders, the republican border was expected to conform to land and field use between neighboring villages. Any

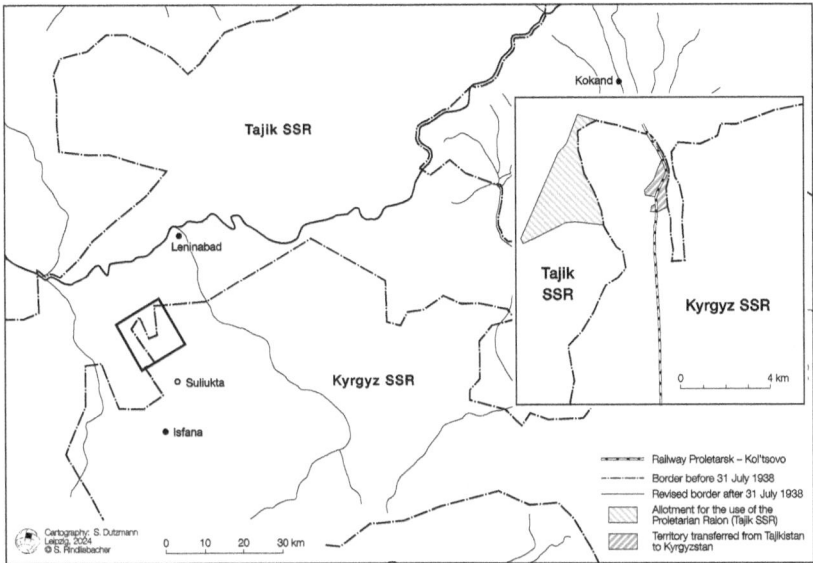

FIGURE 19. Adapted map of a border revision between Proletarian (Tajik) and Liailiak (Kyrgyz) Raiony, 1938.

exchanges in the use of fields, pastures, and forests were automatically considered changes to the republican borders. This was the ideal. Reality tended to differ. Local administrations did not always inform their superiors about such changes, and if they did, such notes sometimes disappeared in the vast machinery of the Soviet bureaucracy.[151]

Discussion of a Common Border

In the eyes of the party leadership, Isaak Zelenskii's mission in Central Asia was a smashing success. Soon he would replace Rudzutak as head of the Sredazbiuro, and he would hold this powerful position until 1931, when the party appointed him head of the Central Union of Consumer Cooperatives (Tsentrosoiuz). In August and September 1924 Zelenskii proved to be an able negotiator. He let the native communists discuss their concerns about national delimitation, but he also orchestrated at least some of the decisions made within a small, exclusive circle. Even though the indigenous communists fiercely fought for opposing projects, this process offered them an opportunity to form and eventually institutionalize Soviet structures in their societies. The European and the indigenous communists hence identified their main goal as modernizing a "backward" region. National structures seemed to be the best means to achieve this goal.

Most native communists had a progressive background and had been influenced by movements such as the Jadids or Alash Orda. During debates on national delimitation, they were all well aware of the stakes. Moscow had delegated the task specifically to indigenous representatives, deliberately excluding Ukrainian and Russian settlers. Discussions revolved around the difficulty of how to define a certain group and of how to distribute the economic and demographic assets of Central Asia among the new political entities.

In this debate, the native communists quickly split into two hostile factions. One was clearly in favor of a division along national lines. The other faction opposed such a strict division in favor of a federative concept. On one hand, representatives of the prospective Uzbek republic supported delimitation because they expected to gain control over cotton production, Central Asia's most important economic asset. On the other hand, representatives of the envisioned Kirgiz-Kazak republic favored a Central Asian Federation, which would guarantee the sharing of economic assets and liabilities. In this dispute, party leaders favored the former over the latter, as boosting cotton production was crucial for the development of the Soviet economy as a whole. In addition, Zelenskii and Vareikis hoped that national delimitation would bring an end to the factionalism that had paralyzed Turkestani institutions since 1920.

Whereas the delimitation in 1924 crystallized around the dichotomy between Kirgiz and Uzbek, its implementation led to the crystallization of two other dichotomies. On one hand, Uzbekistan experienced a polarization between Uzbek and Tajik. This led eventually to the formation of the Tajik SSR in 1929. On the other hand, the distinction between Kazakh and Kyrgyz as we use it today fully developed in the administrative sphere when the two distinct and separate ASSRs formed in 1926.[152]

Indigenous Bolsheviks who adopted national-ethnographic approaches—people such as Faizulla Khodzhaev, Yusup Abdrakhmanov, or Sharustam Islamov and their networks—were able to profit from the support of the party leadership and thus become Soviet "ethnonational entrepreneurs."[153] Faizulla Khodzhaev soon rose to head the Uzbek government in 1924, and Sharustam Islamov received high-ranking posts in the Uzbek party apparatus. The proponents of a federal solution such as Turar Ryskulov lost much of their prior political influence.

Sultanbek Khodzhanov and Sandzhar Asfendiarov received no major state and party assignments after 1924. However, most of the politicians involved in delimitation would fall victim to the Stalinist terror.

Compared to the revision of the Russian-Ukrainian border, experts played a much smaller role in the delimitation of Central Asia. Even though party and state functionaries were able to consult them, indigenous Bolshevik politicians made key decisions, relying on their own knowledge of the region. Comparison with the Russian-Ukrainian case points up another difference in Central Asia. In Eastern Europe, experts and politicians were debating which criteria would decide a future border: national-ethnographic or economic considerations. In other words, economy and ethnography appeared as two distinct categories that most often did not converge. In Central Asia, however, things seem to have been much less complicated from this perspective. According to the approach that prevailed in August and September 1924, socio-economic considerations were key in defining national belonging. This is why a set of intricately jagged borders with numerous enclaves could take shape in the Fergana Valley but not along the border between the RSFSR and Ukraine.

Chapter 5

Armenia and Azerbaijan
How to Search for a Common Border

> In the past, the first reason for misunderstandings was the century-old tradition of the nomad population.... The second reason was the small quantity of pastures.... The last reason was the lack of field surveyors.
>
> —Yakov Kochetkov, 1924

The southern part of the Caucasus region was the odd man out in the Soviet state. Here, in contrast to the Russian-Ukrainian borderland or Central Asia, Soviet power did not have to promote a national framework. Nationally and religiously perceived dichotomies already permeated everyday life. This was due in particular to the rise of industrialization and increasing urbanization during the late tsarist era. Moreover, conflicting religious faiths and economic structures contributed to the formation of differences perceived as national. The party and state leadership in Moscow was well aware of the tensions in the region, but they preferred not to be bothered and established an intermediary supervisory body—first the Kavbiuro and then the Zakkraikom.

The South Caucasus was dominated by three major national communities. According to the 1926 census, 5.9 million people or roughly 4 percent of the Soviet Union's population lived there in largely compact regions: 1.8 million Georgians, 1.3 million Armenians, and 1.7 million Turks. At the time, the term "Azerbaijan" referred only to a region and not to a certain nationality. Smaller communities like the Abkhaz, Ossetians, Lezgins, or Talysh made up a little more than half a million people. Russians and Ukrainians counted for about 400,000 people spread out over the region.[1]

To date, researchers have focused mainly on those issues of autonomy that have continued to trouble the region well into the twenty-first century. Nagorno-Karabakh and Abkhazia are the most prominent examples.[2] After all, the ZSFSR, like the RSFSR, embraced numerous autonomous oblasti and republics. Arsène Saparov has concluded that the formation of autonomous territories such as Abkhazia, Nagorno-Karabakh, and South Ossetia were a means of conflict resolution, while Svante Cornell argues that the very existence of autonomous entities within the South Caucasian republics facilitated the escalation of ethnic conflicts during the dissolution of the USSR.[3] Krista A. Goff and Jamil Hasanli have provided an in-depth analysis of the development of the national minorities in Soviet Azerbaijan, the intricate interplay of state promotion and discrimination, and the long-term effects of Soviet nationality policies.[4] However, this focus on the autonomous areas and national minorities in the South Caucasus narrows the scope too much, and the problematic institutionalization of the borders between the federal republics, particularly between Armenia and Azerbaijan, slip easily out of sight.

Republican territorialization in the South Caucasus can best be analyzed from two perspectives: that of border formation and that of border crossings. First, it is necessary to recapitulate the most important political and social developments within the region between 1918 and 1920. They shaped the mindsets and challenges that the Bolsheviks faced as they conquered the region in 1920-1921. After that, I give three different but interconnected examples of how border disputes between Armenia and Azerbaijan were managed in the 1920s. Finally, I analyze how the creation of national territories affected a space where a considerable part of the population was mobile.

An Oddity within the Soviet State

As a center of the global oil industry, Baku had been a vibrant hotbed of modernity since the late nineteenth century.[5] The town was multi-ethnic, and it was here that tensions between predominantly skilled Christian Armenian clerks and largely unskilled Turkish-speaking Muslim workers first began to mount.[6] From 1904 to 1906 the city was an epicenter of violence between the Armenian and Muslim communities. The urban masses were often politicized along national lines. The Social Democratic party Hummet (Endeavor) and later the nationalist party Musavat (Equality) found success among the Turkish-speaking

Muslim communities, while the Dashnaktsutiun (Revolutionary Federation) played a similar role among the Armenians. Transnationally oriented political factions like the Bolsheviks were marginal by comparison with their nationalist opponents.[7] The Georgian communities also developed a national movement, in which the Menshevik Social Democrats enjoyed particular influence after 1917. Its center was Tiflis, the capital of the viceroyalty (*namestnichestvo*), the imperial administrative center for the Caucasus region.[8] Reinforced by atrocities during the First World War and the Civil War and subsequent mass displacements and resettlements, national dichotomies had not only solidified in the urban centers but spread into the countryside as well.

After the collapse of the Russian Empire and the rise of the Bolsheviks in Petrograd, politicians in the South Caucasus had to find a practical answer to the new geopolitical situation. On 9 March 1917 (22 March 1917, New Style), the Provisional Government in Petrograd installed the Ozakom, the Special Transcaucasian Committee, which was intended to replace the imperial viceroyalty. In November, after the Bolshevik coup, this committee refused to recognize Russia's new rulers. Renaming itself the Transcaucasian Commissariat, officials in Tiflis established an independent government for the region. Then, on 22 April 1918, Georgian, Armenian, and Azerbaijani representatives agreed to form a Transcaucasian Federation. Under pressure from the Ottoman Empire and Germany—with whom the Transcaucasian Federation was still at war—this supranational state collapsed within a month, and the three republics declared their independence.[9] The Central Powers considered it more advantageous to sign separate peace treaties in Batum in June 1918 and therefore play the three against one another, particularly as they soon were entangled in territorial disputes. Armenia was in the worst position, as it found itself in a three-front conflict with Azerbaijan over the areas surrounding Nagorno-Karabakh, Kazakh, Zangezur, and Nakhichevan; with Turkish nationalists under Mustafa Kemal (later known as Atatürk) over Kars; and with Georgia over the Lori, Borchaly, and Akhalkalaki.[10]

The Bolsheviks briefly seized power in Baku in April 1918 but were cut off from the Azerbaijani hinterland. Even though the Bolsheviks strove to enlist the town's different communities in their cause, the Baku Commune under Stepan Shaumian was broadly seen as pro-Armenian among the Turkish-speaking population. After four months, the commune collapsed in the wake of simultaneous advances by Ottoman forces on one hand and British troops on the other. Most of the members of its government (the so-called twenty-six Baku commissars) were captured and shot by British troops. After a short interlude under the Centrocaspian Dictatorship, which benefited from British support and supervision, the Azerbaijani government, based primarily in Yelizavetpol' (today Gəncə), was able to take Baku with the help of Ottoman troops in late September 1918. The city's capture was followed by a major pogrom against the city's Armenian inhabitants.[11]

In Tiflis the Georgian Mensheviks succeeded in establishing a fairly stable democratic government after a general election.[12] Noe Zhordania, one of their leaders, took office as prime minister in June 1918. His government first tried to gain German support, then, once the Germans were defeated, recognition from the Allied powers. Surrounded by shattered empires, Georgia and Armenia in December 1918 plunged into a short war over territory that resulted in approximately one thousand casualties.[13] Under pressure from the British government, the parties agreed to a ceasefire and the establishment of a neutral zone in the Georgian-Armenian borderland.[14]

About two years after the debacle of the Baku Commune, the Red Army conquered the South Caucasian republics. Azerbaijan's oil fields were, of course, the primary objective behind this campaign. In early 1920 the Red Army was victorious in almost every theater of war, but the Soviet war economy required cheap oil. Baku's oil fields were easy to exploit, but they could be used efficiently only if the hinterland and the supply lines—such as the Baku-Batumi railway—were under Soviet control as well.[15] In April 1920 the Red Army thus attacked Azerbaijan and occupied Baku. In that same December the Bolsheviks seized the opportunity to take over the Armenian Republic, suffering under a Turkish invasion. In the first months of 1921 the Red Army then launched an invasion of Georgia and drove Zhordania's Menshevik government into exile. Even though Armenia, Azerbaijan, and Georgia remained formally independent Soviet republics, RSFSR people's commissariats were soon interfering with their railway administration, as well as the telegraph and the postal systems, to secure the transport of petroleum.[16] Most people in positions of responsibility were party members and adhered to the party line as dictated from Moscow. The Kavbiuro, led by Sergo Ordzhonikidze, fulfilled the role of intermediary, like the Turkbiuro.

The fate of the South Caucasus revealed the limits of the Paris Peace Conference. For example, during negotiations for the 1920 Treaty of Sèvres with the Ottoman Empire, representatives of the Entente foresaw eastern Anatolia as a future part of Armenia, which they called Wilsonian Armenia. However, even before the treaty could be signed, this future order was already being undermined by two developments: Red Army successes in the Russian Civil War and the rebellion of Turkish nationalist forces under Mustafa Kemal against Entente occupation. Having toppled the Ottoman government, these nationalist forces began to press deeper into Anatolia's east. The Soviet government and the Turkish nationalists both saw the terms of the Sèvres treaty as an existential threat. This shared interest found expression in two peace treaties, one signed in Moscow in March 1921 and the other in Kars in October 1921. Here the RSFSR and the three South Caucasian Soviet governments made far-reaching territorial concessions, particularly at the expense of Wilsonian Armenia.[17] The two treaties not only ignored the Entente's plan but even left the previously Russian imperial province of Kars to the new Turkish state. The three satellite republics in the South Caucasus had no choice but to accept the outcome.[18] Their communist leaders had to play by the rules.

To better coordinate the economy, reduce ethnic tensions, and consolidate power, the Bolsheviks pressured the three republics of the South Caucasus to form a federation.[19] The Georgian Soviet government, in particular, followed unilateral policies in foreign trade and on monetary issues. On learning that the Georgian government was still patrolling its inter-republican borders, Moscow intervened directly.[20] Such unilateral measures ran counter to Moscow's general line, as this intervention might be seen as a direct form of foreign rule and play into the nationalists' hands.[21] The three Soviet republics thus formed the Federative Union of Socialist Soviet Republics of Transcaucasia (FSSSRZ) on 12 March 1922, with Tiflis as its administrative seat.[22] When this structure proved to be dysfunctional, Ordzhonikidze lobbied for a more centralized federal project to facilitate the export of oil products. In this cause, he enlisted Lenin's support.[23] In October 1922 a majority of the Georgian party leadership resigned to protest this more centralized federation, fearing their republic would end up being marginalized.[24] This conflict later became known as the "Georgian affair," mentioned above. Despite the resignations, the more centralized Transcaucasian Socialist Federative Soviet Republic, the ZSFSR, took shape on 13 December 1922.[25] The scholar Stephen Blank sees in the ZSFSR the creation of a model of centralization that would later characterize Stalinist rule.[26] Tiflis allegedly became "an imperial center in its own right."[27] However, in daily practice centralization would often remain a paper tiger. Republican functionaries proved able to maintain their agency in everyday political affairs, as long as the party via the Zakkraikom did not intervene directly.

The three members of the ZSFSR jealously guarded their privileges. The constitution granted them the prerogative in areas such as education, justice, health care, and agriculture. The federation's main task was to coordinate the South Caucasian economy, keep Baku's oil flowing, and handle the all too many disputes among the republics. Moscow even made some concessions. Ultimately, it gave more in subsidies to the South Caucasus than to any other region. Such measures were to safeguard the political stability of this geopolitically sensitive region. The South Caucasus was thus one of the most privileged regions within the entire Soviet state, politically as well as financially.[28]

Despite these privileges, the region remained far from politically stable. In August 1924 an insurgent movement shook Georgia, in particular the regions of Guria, Imereti, and Kakheti. This uprising had the support of the Georgian government in exile. At the beginning, it seemed possible that this rebellion might overthrow Soviet power, but the Red Army rallied to crush the rebels with the utmost ferocity. Around ten thousand people died in battle and during the repressive measures that followed.[29] The Bolsheviks understood that the existing Soviet order could collapse at any moment. Rebellions seemed imminent in Armenia and Azerbaijan as well. Thus the party tried to consolidate its rule in the region through a policy of carrot and stick.[30]

The Armenian Bolsheviks faced particular challenges. Among the South Caucasian republics, Armenia was the smallest and economically the weakest. It also had the lowest number of inhabitants, a large part of whom had experienced repeated displacement and resettlement between 1915 and 1921.[31] Despite these disadvantages, it had to deal with thousands of refugees still arriving from the former Ottoman Empire and Greece. Some fifty thousand Armenian refugees settled in the Republic of Armenia between 1921 and 1927.[32] This number may not seem high in absolute terms, but it was a considerable challenge for a war-torn country with only 880,000 inhabitants in 1926. It would be wrong, however, to view Armenia and Armenians as marginalized within the Soviet framework. Relative to the size of their population, Armenians were overrepresented in federal institutions—for instance, in the ZakTsIK administration—while Turks were severely underrepresented.[33] In the eyes of some Bolsheviks, the Armenians came close to being an "oppressor nationality" like the Russians, a nationality the party did not need to promote as such.[34]

The Muslim Turks presented the party with a broad array of challenges. Illiteracy among this part of the South Caucasian population was extremely high, making it exceedingly difficult for socialist propaganda to reach them.[35] Furthermore, around a third of the population in Azerbaijan had a nonsedentary way of life. Due to climatic conditions, the nomadic population and its cattle had to wander from summer pastures to winter pastures and back again. This made the Muslim herdsmen appear particularly backward. As a result, the party dedicated special attention to their advancement. They did not want to repeat the mistakes committed by the Baku Commune, mistakes that had alienated the Muslim population.[36] As a backward and "oppressed" nationality, the Muslim Turks benefited in particular from the affirmative policies enacted in the South Caucasus.[37]

Puzzling Borders

All of the regional state functionaries had to play the game and follow the supervision of the intermediary party body. The Kavbiuro was initially the highest party organ for the entire Caucasus region. Sergo Ordzhonikidze served as its head from 1920 to 1922. Then, in March 1922, the party restructured its intermediary agency and formed a committee for the South Caucasus exclusively: the Zakkraikom, which Ordzhonikidze also chaired until 1926.[38] By virtue of this post, he was able to act as the party's regional strongman. Despite his undiplomatic manners, or because of them, he implemented and supervised Soviet power as Moscow required.

The party immediately found itself confronted with serious territorial conflicts. Immediately after their Sovietization, the three South Caucasian republics clearly lacked defined borders. Party organs had to make some tough decisions: the regions of Nakhichevan and Kazakh were attached to Azerbaijan, Zangezur and Lori to Armenia, as well as Borchaly and Akhalkalaki to Georgia.[39] The most contested region was Nagorno-Karabakh, which was largely populated by Armenians. Despite its demographic composition, the Kavbiuro attached it to Azerbaijan in July 1921. The exact reasons for this decision remain unclear, but economic considerations may have tilted the scales in Azerbaijan's favor. Nagorno-Karabakh simply had better connections with Baku than with Erivan' (from 1936, Yerevan). The Armenian representatives tried in vain to reverse this decision.[40]

FIGURE 20. Political map of the South Caucasus region at the end of 1921.

Provisional solutions were found for all of these border settlements, but they were simply drafted without any knowledge of the border territories.[41] Moreover, at the beginning of March 1923, Aleksandr Beloborodov, at the time head of the Administrative Commission at VTsIK in Moscow, noted—with some degree of horror—that by the terms of these provisional agreements some regions belonged to two republics and some to none. He urged the ZakTsIK and ZakSovnarkom to resolve these territorial issues immediately, but that never happened.[42]

Before the First World War, the region that would later become the Armenian-Azerbaijani borderland had contained almost no ethnically mixed settlements save for the larger towns.[43] During the war, many villages were burned down, forcing the inhabitants to leave. As a result, after 1921 numerous villages were deserted. Neighboring villages began to compete for deserted fields and pastures. Acts of violence became commonplace, such as burning fields or stealing cattle, particularly if the owners were from another community.[44] Even though party and state authorities organized several conferences on border questions between 1921 and 1923, they were forced to realize that it was one thing to find a solution to a given problem at the table in Tiflis and quite another to implement that solution on the ground. They had to deal with passive resistance and open hostility from regional administrators as well as local inhabitants.[45]

After Sovietization, ethnically charged or, to put it better, ethnically framed conflicts continued to cause problems for regional Bolshevik elites. The term "misunderstanding" (*nedorazumenie*) served in the Soviet bureaucracy as a euphemism for such unrest. Some of these misunderstandings degenerated into armed conflict between rival communities.[46] Federal actors had to step in, out of fear that local communist functionaries would side with "their" people. Thus commissions from Tiflis were to conduct missions to the disputed areas and look into the details of what was going on.[47] Local and regional experts, particularly field surveyors, did more than play key roles in the complex negotiations or provide expertise about issues that were important to officials in Tiflis. Locals could also perceive these lower-level experts as "neutral" mediators. Though the Transcaucasian administration enjoyed only limited funding, it nonetheless hired eight well-paid experts in the 1920s to collect data, arbitrate in border disputes, and survey pastures and the modes of their distribution.[48]

Federal commissions from Tiflis were the Bolshevik government's main tool for solving territorial conflicts on the ground. Politicians working together with surveyors would find workable settlements. The Territorial Commission of the ZakTsIK coordinated all such efforts and wielded enormous authority, at least in theory.[49] In contrast to territorial issues among republics of the USSR, where every republic involved had to consent to a border revision, the Territorial Commission of the ZSFSR had the authority, in principle, to resolve certain issues against the will of a member republic.[50] Several subcommissions were sent to border villages and pastures to acquaint themselves with the situation on site.[51]

Analysis of the conflicts and efforts to find solutions in the Armenian-Azerbaijani borderland reveal that federal institutions, the ZakTsIK in particular, usually did not favor one side or the other. Rather, they tried to find what they considered "efficient" (*tselesoobraznye*) solutions. Some parts of this border were easier to define than others. Particularly in the highland areas, boundaries were marked by mountain ridges.[52] The borders in the north and in the south were much more subject to dispute, as there was neither a single mountain range nor a river to provide a "natural" marker. This was where the unsettled borders that so bothered Beloborodov lay. In contrast to other regions of the Soviet state, the administrative borders of the imperial period did not serve as standards for the new republican ones.[53] Apart from the raw decisions by the Kavbiuro in 1921, the borders delineating the three republics were in an *uti possidetis* state, meaning that an area belonged to the republic that controlled it.[54] This led to challenges on the ground when neighboring communities struggled over pastures and fields. According to early Soviet law, it was the state and its Narkomzem that distributed such lands to communities. Hence everyone saw the necessity for a territorial fine-tuning among the republics, but the making of such agreements turned out to be very complicated, as the following case studies illustrate.

In Shinikh Airum, a mountainous area northeast of Lake Sevan, sedentary Christian Armenian and seminomadic Muslim Turk communities clashed over the right to use certain pastures and fields. After Sovietization, the area became part of Soviet Armenia, but soon discussions were underway to attach it to Azerbaijan, especially since it was economically more closely connected with the Azerbaijani side and populated by Turkic Muslim herdsmen. Bashkend, an Armenian village, served as a local center in the area. About three thousand people lived there, and they had no desire to change their republican affiliation. To understand the stakes better, we have to go back to the complex system of land distribution among local communities that existed before 1917.

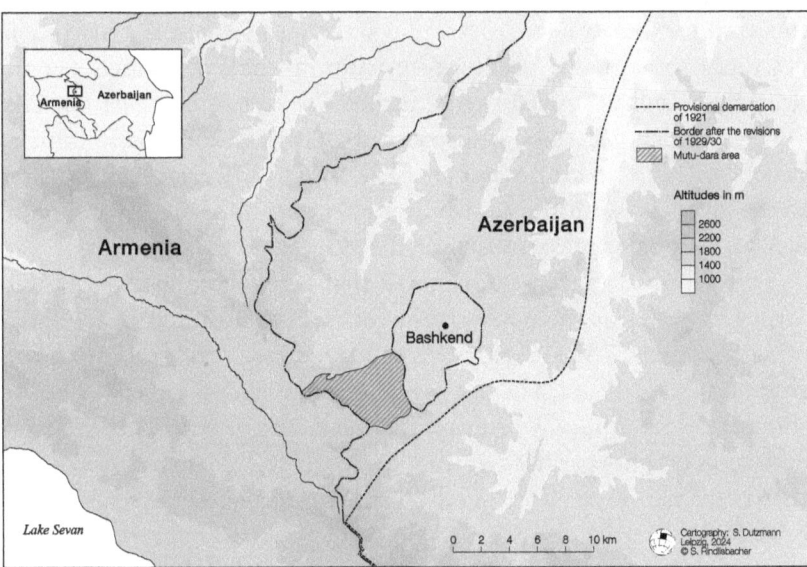

FIGURE 21. Delimitation of the republican borders in the region around Bashkend, 1930.

Under the old regime the peasants of Bashkend did not have enough land for subsistence. They would lease pastures and fields, mostly from local Muslim landowners (*bei* or *bek*). For instance, in 1901 four peasants from Bashkend leased 347 desiatinas (about 382 hectares) of arable land in an area called Mutu-dara from Asad-bek Sultanov. At a notary's office in Yelizavetpol', all of the parties signed a contract on an expensive sheet of paper that bore an official imperial stamp. Mutu-dara was a part of Sultanov's estate in the region. The contract was limited to nine years, but it could be extended by mutual agreement. Each year the peasants had to pay Sultanov three hundred rubles in advance. As both parties were satisfied with the deal, the contract was renewed twice.[55] The 347 desiatinas were too much land for the four peasants alone, so they sublet it to other peasants from Bashkend and herdsmen from neighboring Muslim communities. Among them was a man named Dzhafar Rassul-ogly and his family.[56] Dzhafar Rassul-ogly himself was the leader of a local group of herdsmen and had a criminal reputation going back to before the war. After the Sovietization of the South Caucasus, the fields in the region of Shinikh Airum remained a source of contention even though all private property in land had been abolished in theory.

In 1922 herdsmen under the leadership of Dzhafar Rassul-ogly took Mutu-dara from the Armenian peasants by force. Their argument was that Asad-bek Sultanov had been a Muslim and his land was now their land. The peasants from Bashkend argued that they had been working this land for over twenty years and it was theirs.[57] Then the herdsmen destroyed some of the peasants' agricultural tools. In return, people from Bashkend destroyed the herdsmen's winter huts (*zimoviki*). The Transcaucasian government dispatched an official commission under Yakubov, a high-ranking member of ZakTsIK's Territorial Commission, to the location. With the aid of three comrades and a surveyor named Sen'ko, Yakubov had to investigate the situation.[58]

The commission from Tiflis noted that arable land in the area was extremely scarce as there were many rocky areas ill-suited to any form of agriculture.[59] The surveyor Sen'ko also stressed the severity of the situation in Bashkend. The peasants had only 0.8 desiatinas (0.9 ha) of suitable land per head, whereas their Muslim neighbors had about 1.3 desiatinas (1.4 ha) per head at their disposal.[60] Sen'ko did not mention that herdsmen need more space to graze their cattle than sedentary peasants do to grow their crops.

Each side was able to state its claims before the commission. The Armenians pointed again to the fact that they had been leasing the land from the bei. Thus they should keep it. In response, Dzhafar Rassul-ogly said that the four Armenian tenants had been subletting some of the land to the inhabitants of Bashkend as well as to Muslim herdsmen in the region. Even though everyone in the region knew of his dubious past, Dzhafar Rassul-ogly tried to give his previous life a positive spin in front of the commission. He highlighted the fact that, under the old regime, he had fought the local bei and had even served two years in prison. In the end, everyone signed statements presenting all of their claims, but the commission proved unable to make any decision.[61]

During the interaction between the officials and the locals, the ideological framework was obvious. *Kulak* (rich peasant) and *bei/bek* (Muslim lord) were key terms for describing an enemy of the party in rural areas, much like *burzhui* (bourgeois) in the urban context.[62] These terms as such were mostly void of meaning, but in a dispute over land use they were often used by one side to diminish the standing of the other.

In the years that followed, the ZakTsIK delayed any decision concerning the region of Shinikh Airum. People from the region therefore kept sending petitions for a change of republican affiliation.[63] Relations between Bashkend and its neighboring communities deteriorated further. In September 1925 the chairman of the rural soviet wrote a desperate letter to Tiflis:

> The people from Shinikh are harassing us. We can't any longer graze our cattle on the pastures. When we graze our cattle, they steal it. When we ask the chairman of the *uchastka* administration, he holds up the case for several days. During this time, they sell the stolen cattle.
>
> Such things happened between 1921 and 1925. I ... have proof that from March to September 1925 fifty head of livestock were stolen: horses, oxen, and other horned cattle.[64]

In September 1925 armed skirmishes caused a panic among the inhabitants of Bashkend. They, too, sent a petition to Tiflis, begging the responsible organs to deport Dzhafar Rassul-ogly. He had threatened the people of Bashkend with a gun and had even injured one of them.[65]

Facing such alarming reports, a new commission was assigned the task of investigating and finding a solution for Shinikh Airum.[66] The utter failure of this commission was unique even by Transcaucasian standards, but the story reveals the wide array of challenges that typically confronted such commissions. Iosif Onanov, a secretary of the

ZakTsIK, was in charge. He was joined by Armenian and Azerbaijani representatives identified as Gritsenko and Ishkhanov respectively, as well as two surveyors, Sen'ko from Armenia, and Khaustov from Azerbaijan. The commission's goal was to find a workable solution for the disputed pastures and to submit a proposal for a revision of the Armenian-Azerbaijani border in this area.

Working conditions in Shinikh Airum were challenging at best. Maps had gone missing and local boundary stones had been destroyed or tampered with.[67] After one week, the surveyor Khaustov and Chairman Onanov got into a serious disagreement. This was partly because it was not clear whether the surveyors were to have a decisive say in the commission's work. Onanov tried to exclude them. Khaustov would not accept such an alleged degradation. Then Onanov complained about Khaustov's slow pace of work. Khaustov responded that this was due to bad equipment. Up to this point, the quarrel was more or less professional, but then it became political. Onanov later reported: "Khaustov began to scream in front of a peasant crowd and Armenian as well as Azeri policemen. He told them quite clearly that our commission was an extraordinary troika, that it was one-sided. Its aim was to expel the Muslim population from their ancestral grounds and give these territories to the Armenians."[68] As Onanov intended to discredit Khaustov, it is not clear what "really" happened in the village and what was actually said. Nonetheless, his report hints that the peasants and herdsmen could be mobilized by this issue. They saw demarcation as a question of who would have access to certain resources in the future.

The disagreement between Onanov and Khaustov intensified, and the mission failed completely. Khaustov claimed that Onanov was incompetent, favored the Armenian side, and was planning to draw the borders without visiting the areas in question.[69] In return, Onanov accused Khaustov of speaking with the dubious Dzhafar Rassul-ogly in Turkish.[70] Not only could personal antagonisms produce such failure, but so could protests by locals fearing that a solution would harm their economic interests.

The Shinikh Airum issue remained unresolved and therefore kept troubling the locals as well as the federal administration. The mood on the ground was tense. Only one month later, in October 1925, the inhabitants of Bashkend reported seeing surveyors from Azerbaijan in the area. Among them, Abgar Kharatian, a thirty-three-year-old peasant, said he and five other people from the village encountered an armed group of Azerbaijani officials accompanied by Dzhafar Rassul-ogly while collecting pears in a forest near the village:

> The forester Mamedov [from the Azerbaijani side] approached us and asked for whom we were harvesting the pears. I answered that he could prohibit the collection of pears in his forestry, but we are in Armenia here. Then he asked where the border was, and I answered that it was behind the mountain ridge of Sari-Bulag in Shnykh-su. The Azerbaijanis took half of the pears we had harvested, and we left the other half on the ground as we . . . left out of fear. I asked the former bandit Dzhafar Guly [Dzhafar Rassul-ogly] why these people were here, what they were doing. Dzhafar Guly answered that they were marking the new border as they had received a commission from the center. The fields and the forests were to be attached to Azerbaijan. . . . Then I asked why no Armenian representatives from our forestry were present. Dzhafar answered that the Azerbaijanis had informed the Armenian forester, but he did not show up. Thus the Azerbaijanis are now marking the new border by themselves. . . . The next day, they continued surveying, and I personally observed how they placed a marker [*kurgan*] in a part of the forest that we had leased from the Armenian forestry. . . .[71]

This quote reflects the full extent of the antagonism between Azerbaijani officials and Armenian residents. But it also shows that Abgar Kharatian was easily able to communicate with the representatives of the "others." For all the violence that had afflicted the region since the late nineteenth century, we should not forget that these communities had nonetheless been living together for a long time.

On learning of these events, Armenian officials protested loudly to Tiflis. The Territorial Commission under Sarkis Kas'ian condemned any kind of unilateral Azerbaijani activity on Armenian soil with a clarity rarely found in its minutes. It ordered an immediate stop. A special commission was tasked with investigating the incidents and calling those involved to account—in particular the head of the forestry in Azerbaijani Kazakh Province, Mamedov, and the "former bandit" Dzhafar Rassul-ogly—as their "activities were disturbing the good-neighborly relations between the two nationalities [*narodnosti*]."[72] At the same session, the Territorial Commission also discussed the failed Onanov Commission. It found the work of the surveyors Khaustov and Sen'ko satisfactory—contrary to Onanov's claims—and ordered further investigations into the incidents. The outcome of the investigation into this matter did not end favorably for Onanov. The ZakTsIK fired him.[73]

The following year, disturbances in the area were again exacerbated when Azerbaijani policemen arrested Armenian surveyors during their work. The Armenian Narkomzem had commissioned two surveyors, Kovalev and Troitskii, to inspect the region of Shinikh Airum. With them was a young assistant named Matevasian. On 20 October 1926 people from the Azerbaijani village of Gachiliar took notice of them and informed the local police. The policemen detained the three men and sent them to Tauz.[74] One week later, the authorities in Erivan' learned that their surveyors were in an Azerbaijani prison. An appeal was sent to Tiflis, urging intervention on the part of the ZakTsIK and demanding the immediate release of the three men. The ZakTsIK promptly asked the AzTsIK to resolve the matter.[75] After a week AzTsIK Secretary Kiazimov replied that the three had in fact been arrested, because the ZakTsIK had prohibited surveying in Shinikh Airum. He also added that the Azerbaijani police had released them after interrogation. In his reply, Kiazimov explicitly warned that the Armenian authorities should take care not to send any more surveyors to this territory without the consent of the ZakTsIK.[76] The affair was ultimately settled, but the surveyors' arrest and their delayed release were symptomatic of both the poor relations that persisted between the two republics and the federal institutions' lack of authority. It was only one of many obstructions during territorialization.

Despite resistance from regional officials on the ground, the federal administration continued to make efforts to resolve the Shinikh Airum issue. On 11 January 1927 the commissars for agriculture from Armenia and Azerbaijan, Aramais Yerzinkian and Dadash Buniat-Zade, respectively, joined the Territorial Commission in Tiflis. Invested with the authority of their offices, they were expected to settle the matter of Shinikh Airum once and for all. Initially, it looked as if they could reach an agreement. The area would form a part of Azerbaijan, and the village of Bashkend would remain a part of Armenia. To maintain a territorial link to Armenia, the village was to receive a small strip of land, the aforementioned area of Mutu-dara. But suddenly the talks soured. Yerzinkian, the Armenian commissar, had agreed to this transfer, as he was expecting something in return. The Azerbaijani summer pastures of Alagelliar, south of Lake Sevan, approximated an Azerbaijani enclave within Armenian territory. To rectify this border, Yerzinkian wanted

Alagelliar to be transferred to Armenia. On hearing this, his Azerbaijani counterpart, Buniat-Zade, informed his comrades that he had no mandate to negotiate over Alagelliar. Yerzinkian then withdrew his consent to the transfer of Shinikh Airum.[77] The ZakTsIK ordered them to find a solution within two weeks, but in fact, nothing happened at all.[78] The federal center again proved unable to assert its formal authority.

Only in February 1929, roughly eight years after the Sovietization of the South Caucasus, did the ZakTsIK manage to conclude and ratify a border agreement among all three republics. As this was a compromise among all of the parties concerned, no one was satisfied. With respect to Shinikh Airum, it was expected to be transferred to Azerbaijan, but the ZakTsIK stated explicitly that Bashkend, as a larger Armenian settlement, would remain part of the Armenian Republic. As had been discussed in 1927, Mutu-dara was expected to connect the village with the rest of Armenia.[79]

In response, the herdsmen of Shinikh Airum sent urgent petitions and telegrams to Tiflis and even to TsIK Chairman Mikhail Kalinin in Moscow.[80] They complained of economic hardship and a lack of land vis-à-vis the inhabitants of Bashkend in the "Ararat Republic": "How have we wronged Soviet power? For one peasant, Soviet power is like a mother, for another like a stepmother. In recent months, they have taken our houses and our buildings on the fields of Mutu-dara ... Bala, Cha-chikh, Katiuklu, Khanumtala, and others. They took them from the map of Azerbaijan and put them on the map of Armenia."[81]

Politicians in Moscow had no intention of getting involved in South Caucasian problems and sent the petitions back to Tiflis. The comrades there had to take care of the matter. The ZakTsIK now launched another investigation—and the surveyor Chkhenkeli again explained to his superiors that Mutu-dara was the strip of land expected to connect Bashkend with Armenia and that this strip of land was claimed by Dzhafar Rassul-ogly and his herdsmen as well as by the peasants of Bashkend.[82] In the end, the ZakTsIK ordered a redistribution of the land to the advantage of the Muslim herdsmen and attached the area of Mutu-dara de jure to Azerbaijan. With that, Bashkend and the surrounding territory became an Armenian enclave within Azerbaijan.[83]

Under Soviet rule, the existence of such an enclave did not pose any great challenge. The territorial division more or less reflected land use in the area. In 1978 Bashkend was even renamed Artsvashen to make it sound more Armenian. When the Soviet Union collapsed, however, Armenia and Azerbaijan plunged into war as a result of the

Nagorno-Karabakh conflict. Azerbaijani troops occupied Artsvashen and expelled its inhabitants in 1992. Most of the houses there were destroyed, and the area was abandoned.

The border area in the south between the regions of Megri and Kariagino (today Füzuli), right at the border with Persia, faced many of the same complex challenges as Shinikh Airum. In the mid-1920s several commissions were tasked with resolving border issues that had emerged there. In 1924 senior representatives from Armenia and Azerbaijan, in the persons of Aramais Yerzinkian and Mir Dzhafar Bagirov, met in Tiflis to search for a settlement acceptable to both sides. Surprisingly, they found a compromise and drew a new border on a map. However, as soon as the surveyors arrived on site to stake out the changes, they had to report back to Tiflis that the border established at the negotiating table was not feasible in practice.[84] The whole issue had to be reconsidered.

In 1925 territorial affiliations in the southern border region were vague at best. The south shared some characteristics with the north. Here, too, Armenian villages had previously leased land from a bei. However, there were also other factors at stake. Geologists had discovered copper ore in the Armenian-Azerbaijani border area near Megri. This suggested a potential for establishing a local mining industry.

In this regard, Azerbaijan's Niuvadi rural soviet was of particular interest. This rural soviet consisted of Niuvadi itself and its two small neighboring villages Einazur and Tugut. The rural soviet was rather small, with a population of about 650 Turkish-speaking people, but these people were vehemently opposed to joining Armenia.[85] In a petition to the ZakTsIK in October 1925, they stressed that their agricultural economies were closely linked to Azerbaijan, and they were afraid being marginalized under Armenian rule: "All the institutions in [Azerbaijani] Kariagino Uezd operate in our native language, but in [Armenian] Megri Uezd in Armenian. Most officials in Megri Uezd do not speak the Tatar language [i.e., Turkish] at all, and if we want to contact them, we have to find a translator."[86]

The Niuvadi representatives argued for using national and economic factors, completely in line with the official Soviet discourse of the day, but the Armenian authorities in Megri apparently found more convincing arguments to include this rural soviet in their uezd. First, the latter highlighted that the recently discovered copper ore could lead to a future mining industry. Local herdsmen and peasants would be able to find work in this new industry. This was something that would advance the region as a whole.⁸⁷ Then they stressed that Niuvadi was just 20 versta (21 kilometers) from Megri in Armenia, but 150 versta (160 kilometers) from Kariagino in Azerbaijan. Furthermore, they insisted that the local state institutions in Megri were fully able to function in the "Muslim language" as well as Armenian. They then went on to voice their suspicions that ulterior motivations were at play in the three villages. According to the Armenian representatives, some people in Niuvadi profited from living at such a remove from Kariagino. The distance allowed them to misappropriate state funds, graze cattle without paying pasture fees, and cut wood without a license: "this stratum of kulaks and wealthy peasants opposes a transfer of their villages to Megri Uezd. The poorest peasants remain under the economic and ideological influence of the kulaks and the former beks."⁸⁸

In addition, the Armenian side also seems to have stooped to forging petitions from Niuvadi to further its cause. In the months that followed, two letters reached Tiflis. The first was written in Armenian but signed with names in Arabic-Turkic script. Both pretended to represent the impoverished peasants of Niuvadi, ostensibly oppressed by wealthy kulaks. Inclusion in Megri Uezd would present new opportunities for them culturally and economically. Experts in Tiflis assessed the petitions as forgeries and ignored them.⁸⁹

The dispute over Niuvadi continued to create problems even at the highest levels of the state and party administration. In the summer of 1927 a new commission under the commissars of agriculture from Armenia and Azerbaijan, Yerzinkian and Buniat-Zade, as well as Georgii Sturua (from the Georgian TsKK), was tasked with finding a solution. It failed, because its representatives could not even manage to travel to the site in question. That November, Buniat-Zade openly rejected the transfer of the Niuvadi rural soviet to Armenia.⁹⁰

Overriding Azerbaijani objections, the ZakTsIK did go ahead and attach the Niuvadi rural soviet to Armenia as part of a larger package of revisions to the border in February 1929.⁹¹ This was, of course, not in response to the Armenians' anti-kulak propaganda but was done in the interest of local economic development. Copper mining was to bring industry to the region, and the locals would be able to find employment there.⁹² Thus, as in other parts of the Soviet Union, economic arguments involving something like a prospective copper mine could easily outstrip national arguments on a small, local level. Even though the vision of a mining company in Niuvadi was never realized, the area remains a part of Armenia to this day. Thus the ZakTsIK defined the republics' territory in terms of not only the status quo but also future development. However, these decisions were not bound by a condition that the envisioned development would ever be realized.

In the summer of 1926 surveyors from Tiflis set out to define the boundary between the villages of Sevakiar (today Sevakar, Armenia) and Zor (Azerbaijan) south to the town of Geriusy (today Goris). In this case, representatives of the two villages were unable to agree on who in fact owned the fields separating them. This encompassed an area of seventeen desiatinas, or about sixteen hectares. The representatives of Zor accused their Armenian neighbors of occupying certain fields during the First World War and holding on to them ever since. The representatives of Sevakiar countered that their people had built an orchard on the land, which they had leased from a bei thirty years before. The bei then suddenly took it back for his own use, and now one of his heirs was cultivating a part of it.[93] Thus a surveyor named Rukhiladze, a deputy from the Territorial Commission, decided to attach the orchard to Armenia but to grant its former owner in Zor the right to use parts of it.[94]

Living in one Soviet republic and farming land in a neighboring Soviet republic was not easy. Firid Memed Ali-ogly, the "owner" of the orchard in question, was soon complaining that Armenian officials were preventing him from harvesting his fruit. Moreover, he insisted that he had planted seventy-two of the trees in question himself.[95] The Territorial Commission again intervened and ordered the local Armenian administration in Zangezur to respect Firid Memed Ali-ogly's right to use the orchard.[96] Generously put, the reaction from the authorities in Zangezur was a display of peasant cunning at best. They denied any ill will and stressed that Firid Memed Ali-ogly was in fact allowed to use the orchard. But, they added, in the wake of a redistribution of land in the interim "a few pear trees" had ended up in the possession of the peasants from the village of Zeiv. As a result, they continued, there were now two orchards, and the Territorial Commission's ruling left only the latter one for Firid's use.[97]

Firid Memed Ali-ogly's orchard again demonstrates the general weakness of the federal government in Tiflis to enact its decisions. The Zangezur authorities continued to play games, thus denying Firid Memed Ali-ogly access to the trees until 1930. The secretary of the ZakTsIK in Tiflis was furious with the Armenian authorities, not only for refusing to enforce the legal framework but for justifying their actions on such dubious grounds.[98] In the spring of 1930 representatives of the Armenian and the Azerbaijani sides set up a new commission and visited the fields. There they once again recognized Firid Memed Ali-ogly's claims and reaffirmed his right to the orchard on Armenian territory. In the end, the whole issue was much ado about nothing, but Firid's orchard had created problems for the federal administration for more than four years. Worst of all, the size of the orchard added up to nothing more than a single hectare.[99]

The large-scale territorial revision enacted on 18 February 1929 aimed at resolving such territorial disputes, but it soon turned out to be unsatisfactory. Federal surveyors still encountered numerous difficulties in their daily work. The borders of all three republics in the ZSFSR totaled 1,800 kilometers. Yet at the end of 1930 eight hundred kilometers had yet to be surveyed or mapped. In a report to the chairman of the ZakTsIK, the surveyors Chkhenkeli and Yeganov explained that they had met with resistance from village representatives and peasants as well as republican officials. Nonetheless, they tried to do their jobs as best they could.[100] Around 1928–1929, federal support for the surveyors began to wane. The Territorial Commission was facing budget cuts and had to fire most of its employees, including its experts. By 1931 Yeganov and Chkhenkeli were the only federal employees still working on territorial issues.[101] State funds were flowing elsewhere, leaving large stretches of the borders separating the South Caucasian

FIGURE 22. Political map of the South Caucasus at the end of 1936.

republics inadequately surveyed. Although the surveyors marked some borders by erecting signs, many segments lacked signs as well. The federal commissions and their surveyors had managed to solve some issues between border communities, but plenty of others were left unsettled. The ZakTsIK had invested a great deal of time and effort in resolving territorial disputes during the 1920s, but the results could not meet expectations. When the ZSFSR was dissolved in 1936, the territories of the republics it had overseen were confirmed to a large extent, but many details remained unsolved. Even in the 1980s, maps of the Soviet military often depicted areas where the border between the Armenian and Azerbaijan SSR was not defined.[102]

A Fixed Border and a Mobile Population

Borders between Soviet republics are often considered a purely administrative matter that has little impact on daily life for the population.[103] This might be true for some parts of the population, indeed for the greater part, but for people who lived near such borders, like Firid Memed Ali-ogly, demarcation could have a very negative impact on their way of life, day in and day out.[104] The same situation affected people who led a nonsedentary way of life. As in Central Asia, nonsedentary forms of cattle breeding were an important part of the rural economy in the South Caucasus.[105] Every year, herdsmen—nomads (*kochevniki*), as they were officially called—along with their flocks and herds, roamed from winter pastures in the flatlands of the east to summer pastures in the highlands of the west and north. Officials even distinguished between "full" nomads (*kochevniki*), who moved between summer and winter pastures without a fixed place of residence, and seminomads (*polukochevniki*), who moved between their place of residence and summer pastures.[106]

During the nineteenth century relative peace under Russian imperial rule led to an increased number of herders and their livestock. This subsequently provoked conflicts over pastureland with the sedentary population. Constant competition over scarce resources among different communities was one factor that caused violent clashes to spread out from the urban to the rural areas during the troubles of 1905. This remained an important factor in the nationalized conflicts after the collapse of Russian imperial rule after 1917.[107]

In the mid-1920s the share of nomads was quite small, only about sixty thousand in a region with a population of about six million.[108]

Half of them were Muslim Turks wandering between Armenia and Azerbaijan.[109] Moreover, the Soviet administration considered around a third of the population in Azerbaijan—about 800,000 people—to be seminomads.[110] Traditionally, these Muslim households migrated from their villages in the summer: for example, from Azerbaijan's Kazakh Uezd to Armenia's Dilizhan Uezd, where Bashkend was located. Conflicts with the local sedentary population were simply an everyday occurrence, but so were other forms of social interaction such as trade.

Tsarist officials had not interfered much in the rural economy, aside from levying taxes and making sporadic attempts to propagate Orthodox Christianity. Nonetheless, the tsarist state had already devised a system of classification for the local population. This system saw Christians (such as the Georgians and Armenians) as civilized and progressive, while non-Christians were viewed as uncivilized and backward.[111] The nonsedentary Muslim population found itself at the bottom of this ethnographic hierarchy. The Bolsheviks and Soviet ethnographers later adopted this model in a much more rigid way, but without the religious normativity. Due to their long-standing cultural and political traditions, the Georgians and Armenians (unlike the Azerbaijani Turks) counted as advanced nations—much like Russians, Ukrainians, Jews, or Germans.[112] Nomads presented an obstacle to the state-sponsored project of an all-encompassing normalization of space and society— that is, the use of rational criteria to impose a new order on society and its understanding of economics, nationality, culture, and gender.[113] Yet at the outset, the Bolsheviks perceived the "backward" part of the population as a potential ally of the proletariat and thus worthy of the party's full political support.

The "pasture issue" (*pastbishchnyi vopros*) was the term that Soviet administrators applied to land-related disputes between sedentary Armenian peasants and nonsedentary Muslim herdsmen. Such disputes were linked to the general issue of territory, absorbed a great deal of federal resources, and continued to exacerbate relations between the Armenian and Azerbaijani authorities. In 1924 and 1925 nomads and seminomads from Azerbaijan used about four hundred square kilometers of summer pastures in Armenia.[114] Even though the federal administration tried in earnest to settle conflicts among different interest groups, the sheer number of conflicts and their complexity left functionaries in Tiflis overwhelmed. However, sedentary and nonsedentary parts of the population also shared a long tradition of coexistence. Peasants and nomads traded daily in commodities such as cheese or corn. As mentioned above, peasants and herdsmen used to lease pastures to and from one other.[115] But these practices fundamentally challenged the Soviet state's claim to regulating land distribution. During the NEP Soviet functionaries tolerated these traditions, but at the end of the 1920s they began to intervene more and more.[116] They criminalized not only trading but other traditional forms of interaction between sedentary peasants and nomads as well.

Throughout the 1920s the pasture issue continued to create problems for the Soviet administration.[117] With the support of the Zakkraikom and the ZakTsIK, peasants and nomads could use the nationalized fields and forests that they had been using since before the war. Starting in 1923, they had to pay a certain agricultural tax, but so did all of the other regions of the Soviet state.[118] However, this situation was untenable, because in the early years of the ZSFSR, agriculture was the domain of the republics.[119] The Armenian and the Azerbaijani Commissariat for Agriculture wrangled over a form of pasture distribution that was advantageous to their side, but the federal authorities could only arbitrate. Only in 1929 was a Transcaucasian Commissariat for Agriculture established, but its main purpose was to coordinate and promote collectivization. Meanwhile, the political power of federal institutions declined even more, while republican institutions gained in influence.[120]

On the ground, relations between the Muslim nomads and the sedentary Armenian peasants remained poor. Ottoman atrocities in Anatolia during the First World War and the constant influx of Armenian refugees exacerbated existing conflicts. The Communist Party was forced to intervene. In November 1922 the Zakkraikom introduced a party directive in favor of the herdsmen, stating that the latter should be allowed to use the pastures in Armenia, and that the Azerbaijani People's Commissariat for Agriculture, not the Armenian one, should take care of them.[121] With this step, the federal authorities attempted to institutionalize procedures for settling such cross-border matters, but they discovered that they simultaneously had to deal with the resistance of the authorities in both republics.

Seasonal migration from one pasture to another created numerous opportunities for conflict. For example, the nomadic way of life contributed to the rapid spread of a cattle plague that afflicted the region. During migration, the federal government in Tiflis had tried to enact measures against the plague, but they failed to contain it fully.[122] Another source of conflict was the fact that during migration the nomads

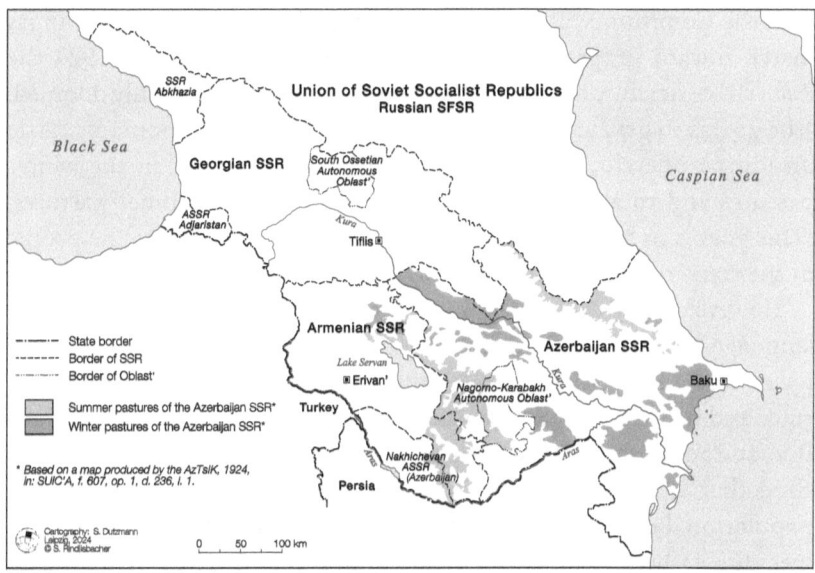

FIGURE 23. Adapted map of the winter and summer pastures of the Azerbaijan SSR, 1 June 1924.

also had to graze their flocks. Although the ZakTsIK introduced rules to govern changes of pasture, this did not improve the situation. Complaints poured in. Herdsmen did not always take the roads the administration provided them, and on their way, they continued to let their cattle graze on fields that belonged to nearby Armenian villages.[123]

Disputes related to summer pastures simply would not abate. Even when the people's commissariats for agriculture offered an alternative pasture, the nomads often did not much care for it. They kept using their "ancestral grounds."[124] Though the federal and republican authorities refused to recognize such arguments de jure, they had to de facto—especially since the party line favored the nomads. Of course, this then also led to conflicts with those who had just acquired the formal right to use these pastures from the same state authorities. In such cases, surveyors and emissaries from Tiflis were called in to arbitrate over and over again.[125]

Once the vision of world revolution receded, the Bolshevik leadership decided to accelerate the development of the Soviet economy to build the material basis for a future socialist society in one country. The pursuit of this grand undertaking for a better future ran up against a nomadic population bound to past practices. But this does not mean that the Communist Party simply ignored "backward" practices in its march toward progress. It took a long-term perspective. In 1924 the ZakTsIK officially proclaimed that nomadism was historically doomed: "the goal is to gradually change from nomadic and seminomadic cattle breeding to developed agriculture [*kul'turnoe zemledelie*] in the winter pastures and to an alpine form of economy in the summer pastures. [This goal is to be achieved] with the maximal assistance of the people in the transition to new forms of agriculture."[126]

However, the ZakTsIK was careful to couch its vision in acceptable language. The establishment of new agricultural forms was a project for a more distant future. Most functionaries within the state bureaucracy and the party apparatus understood this proclamation as Dadash Buniat-Zade, Azerbaijan's commissar for agriculture, had. He emphasized that this change would affect about a third of the Azerbaijani population, because most winter pastures were not arable in the summer due to heat and aridity. Many improvements (e.g., irrigation or campaigns against malaria) still had to be carried out.[127]

Party activists sought to agitate and mobilize the nomads and seminomads because they saw the *bedniaki* (poor peasants), *seredniaki* (middle peasants), and *batraki* (landless people) as possible allies of the proletariat.[128] By sending propagandists and activists to the pastures, they tried but ultimately failed to make inroads among this part of the population. Shota Palavandishvili, one of the party propagandists, expressed his deep disappointment in May 1928: "From a political perspective, the nomads as such are completely undeveloped and appear as an impenetrable mass. Most of them are illiterate. In personal conversations, I have assured myself that they are not interested in anything or anyone beyond their own affairs."[129]

At the end of the 1920s this kind of political indifference was seen as a direct threat to the party and its goal of modernizing the economy and society by means of the first five-year plan. The nomads seemed to provide an ideal social stratum onto which the communists could project their nightmares. Therefore, it is not surprising that Palavandishvili, after reporting these expressions of political indifference, openly attacked the nomads, as a "*kulak-dashnak* element."[130] Although the mostly Muslim, Turkish-speaking nomads were far from being kulaks or harboring sympathy for Armenian nationalists, accusations of this nature would soon prove very dangerous.

The Cultural Revolution crushed the idea of Soviet modernization evolving over the long term. Social and economic change had to be realized now and at any price. In the course of the first five-year plan, agriculture was supposed to deliver surpluses for export that would bring in revenue to finance industrialization. The party forced the peasants and nomads throughout the union to join the kolkhozes and sovkhozes in order to control their production and extract as many resources as possible.[131] The party was no longer willing to wait for the people to modernize the economy. They had to be pushed. In the South Caucasus this was the tipping point that allowed nationalist and social arguments against nomadism to descend into political violence. Nomads and seminomads quickly evolved from obstacles to enemies. Party activists such as Buniat-Zade, who had previously opposed plans for any kind of sweeping sedentarization, found themselves forced to stick to the shifting rules of the party game.[132]

In early 1930 anti-kulak repression reached an initial climax.[133] It proved to be a disastrous year for the nomadic economies, in the ZSFSR and throughout the union. Party activists now saw the nomads solely as under kulak domination and branded them as outlaws. In February the Azerbaijani branch of the secret police (OGPU) initiated a massive campaign against these kulaks. They arrested and deported more than a thousand people together with their families. After this wave of open repression, party activists once again "encouraged" the remaining *bedniaki* and *seredniaki* to join the collective farms.[134] At the same time, clashes between migrating nomads and newly formed Armenian collective farms broke out. Soviet Armenia had claimed the summer pastures for Armenian collective farms. But the Azerbaijani authorities and the nomads did not respect such unilateral decisions. This, together with a rejection of collectivization, led to upheaval in the rural areas. In the spring of 1930 the collectivization campaign brought some regions of the Soviet Union to the brink of civil war. In the villages of the South Caucasus, numerous communist propagandists were murdered. The regime's response was brutal.[135] It was at this point that Stalin intervened to slow the collectivization campaign. The situation seemed perilously close to slipping beyond the party's control. Some party activists, he warned, were "dizzy with success."[136]

In the South Caucasus this change of tone in Moscow toward collectivization had no immediate positive effect on the nomads and peasants. On the contrary, the anti-nomad policy even intensified under the pretext of collectivization. In 1931 the ZakTsIK tripled the tax on use of summer and winter pastures for people who had yet to join a collective farm. The goal was, of course, to coerce them to do exactly that.[137] As the republican administrations still controlled land distribution, the newly established Armenian collective farms insisted on their claims to all of the summer pastures in Armenia, and in 1930 and 1931 the Armenian government decisively threw their support behind such initiatives.[138] The Azerbaijani government in turn tried to mobilize the ZakTsIK to protect "their" nomads. In the end, the ZakTsIK allowed the nomads to use the summer pastures in Armenia "for one last time" in 1932.[139] Despite such concessions, the Zakkraikom had already resolved to liquidate nomadism as such.[140] Unlike the barely literate nomads and seminomads, Armenian activists had used state and party institutions to gain control over Armenia's summer pastures. At this time, the already weak federal institutions, such as the ZakTsIK, that could articulate a common Transcaucasian policy and address competing interests began to fade from view.[141] Hence, with the support of the Zakkraikom, Armenian representatives were able to force the Transcaucasian Commissariat for Agriculture to sharply reduce the nomads' access to summer pastures in favor of Armenian collectives.[142]

As in other parts of the union, forced collectivization proved a disaster for cattle breeding. Nomads and seminomads preferred to slaughter or sell their cattle or flocks before joining a kolkhoz or sovkhoz.[143] When some of them did enter a collective with their cattle and flocks, officials and activists on site faced other kinds of severe challenges. They were unable to provide enough fodder, stables, or veterinary treatment despite the diminished numbers of animals arriving.[144] Managing collectivized pastures presented another problem for collective farms, as many of them went unused amid the administrative chaos.[145] In the Azerbaijani regions of Kazakh and Tauz, the party and state authorities restructured the entire rural economy from the ground up. The nomads and seminomads were expected to work on newly established cotton farms and provide Soviet industry with cheap resources.[146] Yet there was also a huge problem with housing, as the state could barely manage to provide construction materials.[147]

Compared to Central Asia, however, the number of casualties among the nomads and seminomads was much lower in the South Caucasus. It appears to be just as complex to analyze why people died as it is to understand how they survived.[148] In 1934 famines broke out in the Armenian-Azerbaijani borderlands. According to reports from the Zakkraikom, several hundred people—but not thousands or millions—died.[149] There were at least three specifically regional factors that played a role in keeping the number of victims comparatively low. First, people had a means of escaping. In the Armenian-Azerbaijani border region, more than twelve thousand rural households were abandoned between 1930 and 1934.[150] Unlike in Kazakhstan, the borders between republics were not sealed off to refugees.[151] Herdsmen and peasants were thus able to flee the appalling conditions in the countryside for boom towns such as Baku or Erivan'.[152] Turkish-speaking people even tried to cross into Turkey.[153] Second, the share of "full" nomads was comparably low. In stark contrast to the nomads of Kazakhstan or the resettlement campaigns in Tajikistan, the seminomads of the South Caucasus could better manage forced settlement, as they were already familiar with the regional climate and sedentary economy.[154] Finally, unlike the situation in Ukraine, the Kuban, or Kazakhstan, there was no rigid confiscation policy in the South Caucasus. From Moscow's perspective, the region was already fulfilling its primary economic purpose as a supplier of oil and gas.[155] Advancing the rural economy and boosting cotton production were secondary, and the absolute and relative numbers of nomads and seminomads seemed insignificant in the grand scheme of things.

Stalin's warning that some comrades were "dizzy with success" corresponded roughly with the rise of Lavrentii Beriia as the dominant figure in the ZSFSR. Already first secretary of the Georgian party since 1931, Beriia would serve simultaneously as head of the Zakkraikom from 1932 to 1937. He hewed closely to Stalin's new line of decelerating collectivization and was quick to see to its enforcement throughout the region. In a report to Stalin in November 1934, Beriia stressed that collectivization in Transcaucasia would take longer due to factors such as climate and geography. Although himself a reckless careerist, Beriia blamed predecessors, such as Buniat-Zade and Yerzinkian, for introducing destructive measures during collectivization and producing catastrophic results: "Mistakes committed in 1930–1931 led to a deterioration of the political situation in the village. Kulaks and anti-Soviet elements exploited this, and in the end, all of the Transcaucasian republics were forced to face a sharp decline in cultivated fields and a selling-off of cattle in the private sector."[156]

It is hardly surprising that Buniat-Zade and Yerzinkian fell victim to the Great Terror in the South Caucasus three years later. For Beriia collectivization was a long-term goal. Consequently, he resorted to positions shared by his predecessors in the 1920s. Within the framework of what appeared to be a more tolerant policy, people from Azerbaijan were able to lease summer pastures in Armenia again, but they had to follow specific bureaucratic procedures. As a result, the number of seminomads and especially nomads declined significantly.[157] Nonetheless, seasonal movement of cattle led to repeated clashes in the border area that contributed to the mutual distrust between Armenian and Azerbaijani communities.[158]

Throughout the rest of the Soviet era, nomadic forms of life and agriculture endured, but it was only a marginal part of the rural economy in the South Caucasus. The party and state deliberately neglected nomadic life, which they still considered archaic and fated to slip into oblivion, but they did not take any more repressive actions against it.[159] The number of uncontrolled border crossings and interregional contacts beyond the official realm of economic activity dropped considerably. Even though forced Soviet modernization had not led to the deaths of millions as in Ukraine or Central Asia, it nevertheless had a fatal impact on South Caucasian societies, making them increasingly homogeneous in spatial terms.

The Failure to Find a Mutually Accepted Border

In the South Caucasus, functionaries and experts made numerous attempts to determine and implement a common border regime for the three Soviet republics, but they ultimately failed to establish a coherent territorial order.[160] Due to a lack of support and the eagerness of republican elites to have a direct line to Moscow, the ZSFSR was dissolved in 1936.[161] Many pending border issues had yet to be resolved, and the republican governments kept trying to revise the territorial configuration.[162] In comparison with the Russian-Ukrainian border and the Fergana Valley, the party and state leadership in Moscow and the Zakkraikom in Tiflis shied away from any detailed decision making. Fearing to alienate one community while promoting another, the party leadership deliberately refrained from solving these territorial disputes by command. In contrast to the Ukrainian and Central Asian cases where authoritative commissions under Cherviakov and Zelenskii were installed, lower-ranking Transcaucasian communists had to micromanage these issues on their own, without any kind of brief from the party. Even though a lot of effort and resources were dedicated to these territorial issues, no comprehensive resolution could be found, as every side could obstruct the process as much as the game allowed. Thus large parts of the border between Armenia and Azerbaijan lingered in a permanent state of limbo without resolution.[163]

National dichotomies among the population were much more crystallized in the South Caucasus than in the previously discussed cases. Ideas from the raionirovanie debate that aimed to overcome territorialization based on a national-ethnographic frame fell on particularly deaf ears here. There was no resistance worth mentioning within the party and state apparatus against the formation of Soviet nation-states. For many it appeared to be the only possible path for the region.

Despite their differences of opinion and occasional clashes, sedentary and nonsedentary communities were used to daily interaction in trading activity or leasing land. First, the party promoted the "backward" nonsedentary herdsmen (Turks) and protected them from claims made by the more "developed" sedentary population (Armenians). But during collectivization, the herdsman became an "enemy of the people." When the party criminalized certain traditional economic activities, the Armenian authorities used the momentum to expel the Turkish Muslim nomads from "their" summer pastures.

Chapter 6

How to Contextualize "Khrushchev's Gift"?

> In 1954 Khrushchev took Crimea away from Russia for some reason and gave it to Ukraine.
>
> —Vladimir Putin, 2022

In early 2014 Russia invaded and then annexed Crimea, at the time an autonomous republic within Ukraine. Since then, it has been practically impossible to discuss the creation of the Soviet Union's internal borders without addressing the 1954 transfer of Crimea. It was as a result of this transfer that Crimea belonged to Ukraine in 1991. Ukraine's territorial integrity was predicated on these 1991 borders. For the international community and Ukrainians, Russia's actions were a violation of international law. The Russian side has countered by trying to undermine the legitimacy of the 1954 transfer. In pursuit of this line, the trope of Crimea as "Khrushchev's gift" seeks to accomplish a good deal: convince the international community that something presented as a gift from an erratic leader can easily be reclaimed.[1]

This 1954 transfer was anything but singular. It therefore seems like a worthy endeavor to revisit the Crimean issue in light of the Soviet Union's historical experience with changes to its internal borders. Even though Stalin did not like territorial revisions between the union republics, they nonetheless occurred after 1929. The territorial thinking established in the 1920s—national considerations, economic dependencies, and exigencies of governance—persisted well into the 1970s. The following overview puts this kind of reasoning in a diachronic perspective. Beginning with the transfer of Putivl' Volost from the RSFSR to Ukraine in 1926, I go on to examine border changes during and after the Second World War, ending with those that took place under Nikita Khrushchev and Leonid Brezhnev.

The Transfer of Putivl' Volost and the Missing Bronze Bells

In the 1920s it may sound like something of a tautology to say that administrative transfers of territory entailed bureaucratic activity. In the course of revising the territory between the RSFSR and Ukraine, the markedly uneven border in the region around the small town of Putivl' was "rectified." The former Putivl' Uezd was part of Kursk Guberniia and consisted of fifteen volosti, the old regime's smallest territorial entity. In its initial decision the Cherviakov Commission sought to transfer nine of these volosti from the RSFSR to Ukraine.[2] This, however, turned out to be but a preliminary ruling because—as previously mentioned—the Politburo interfered and determined that all of Putivl' Uezd should be attached to Ukraine.[3] Neither the RSFSR nor the Ukrainian side was happy with this, especially because the eastern part of Putivl' Uezd was predominantly Russian-speaking and cut off from the rest of the uezd by the Seim River. From an administrative point of view, it made more sense to leave this part in the RSFSR. Even though the RSFSR and Ukrainian representatives were unable to agree on many other territorial issues, they did manage to revise the Politburo's decision somewhat in this instance. This serves as a key example that the party leadership could not simply enforce a solution that both republics involved opposed. For much of 1925 the fate of Putivl' Uezd remained in limbo, but on 16 October 1925 the TsIK decided to transfer fourteen of the fifteen volosti from the RSFSR to Ukraine, including Putivl' Volost itself.[4]

Thus Putivl' Volost, an area of 161 square kilometers, became part of the territorial restructuring implemented in early March 1926. According to the latest available census data, from 1920, about 22,600 people—7,700 in the town and 14,900 in the countryside—lived in the volost. Local authorities estimated that the population had grown in the interim to about 37,000 by early 1926. Party structures in the Putivl' area were rather weak. According to the 1920 census, around 130,000 people lived in the fourteen volosti at issue, but there were only 170 party members and 159 candidate members—that is, about three per mille of the population.[5]

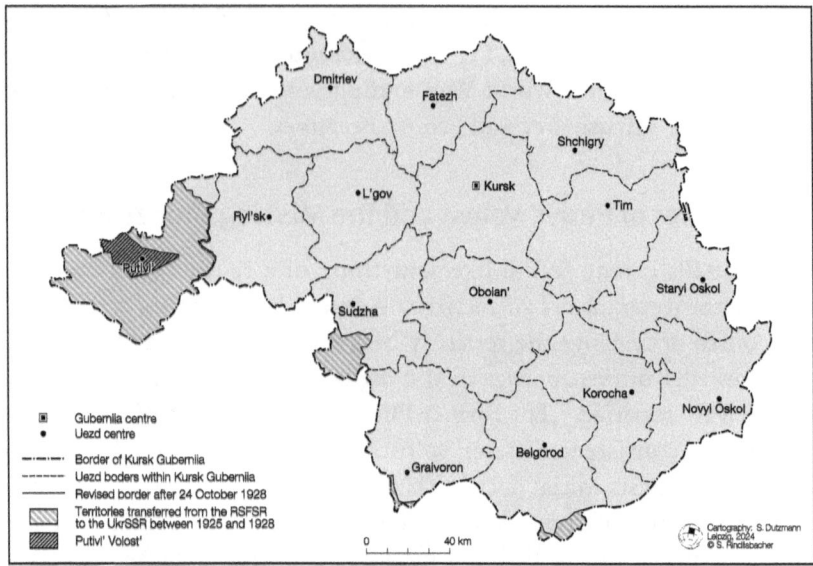

FIGURE 24. Location of Putivl' Volost within Kursk Guberniia, 1925.

Documents collected during the transfer of Putivl' Volost provide a snapshot of this small provincial shire. Putivl' and the surrounding area had no particular industry to speak of other than forestry.[6] In the Middle Ages Putivl' had been an important fortress with a monastery. It even provides the setting for a part of the medieval epic poem *The Tale of Igor's Campaign*, an essential part of the East Slavic canon. The Molchansk (also Molchensk) monastery was one of the few local attractions. In the early twentieth century Putivl' Volost, together with its moderately urban center, was of average importance. The clearest indication of its mediocrity is that the RSFSR was not worried about "losing" it, and the Ukrainian administration was not eager to "gain" it. Unlike the region around Milove/Chertkovo, there was no major company, railway hub, or marketplace at stake. It was just an agricultural region with a small, almost insignificant urban center. Less than 20 percent of the population in the volost spoke Ukrainian, but this played no role in the decision. Although it was mostly Russian-speaking, Putivl' Volost was transferred because, from Moscow's perspective, it simply seemed more "efficient" with respect to regional governance. It was easier to administer Putivl' from a Ukrainian regional center such as Hlukhiv than from the more distant town of Kursk in the RSFSR.[7]

The removal of the monastery's bells during the transfer to Ukraine was a clear sign of mutual distrust. This action also served as a major source of consternation for the VUTsVK vis-à-vis the TsIK and provides a further example of the overlapping interests of the all-union and the RSFSR governments. On learning of the bells' removal, VUTsVK Secretary Panas Butsenko sent an alarmed letter to TsIK Secretary Avel' Yenukidze on 24 February 1926, complaining that the former monastery's bronze bells were being removed on orders from Ryl'sk Uezd. He emphasized that this was clearly "anti-party behavior" and noted that, during the transfer of the Taganrog and Shakhty regions, the Ukrainian side had followed the instructions laid out by the Sovnarkom and VTsIK to the letter.[8] Yenukidze promised to look into the matter. On 15 March 1926, after the transfer of the fourteen volosti had been completed, the VTsIK issued an order that no movable property could be taken from territories during a transfer.[9] Although the instructions had been explicitly clear with regard to this issue, the chairman of the UIK in Ryl'sk seized the moment to write an impertinent letter to the Ukrainian authorities. He admitted that on 25 November 1925 he had ordered the removal of all of the bells, which had totaled 490 poods or 8,016 kilograms of bronze. He argued that he had done this in accordance with Soviet law and promised to send all of the necessary documentation to the Ukrainian authorities.[10] Although the Ukrainian side kept up its protests, it does not appear that the Ryl'sk UIK ever returned the bells or provided compensation. The RSFSR administration took not only material assets before the transfer but also important personnel.[11] Panas Butsenko complained in another letter to Yenukidze that the comrades from the Kursk party organization had reallocated the best party activists away from the territories that would be transferred to Ukraine.[12]

With relatively few resources, the Putivl' Volost was more a burden than an asset for the Ukrainian administration. Today the Ukrainian town of Putyvl' remains a backwater without strategic value. Other than in Crimea or in the Donbas, no one is interested in revisiting the 1926 transfer.

From Plenty to Scarcity

The era of open-ended debates over border management within the Soviet state ended with the dawn of the Cultural Revolution in 1929–1930. After Stalin's unambiguous sign during the meeting with the

Ukrainian writers in February 1929, border changes became more and more difficult to accomplish within the state apparatus. However, there are precious few rules without an exception.

In the eastern border region between Ukraine and the RSFSR, a territorial problem troubled the local administrations. The rural soviet of Dar'ino-Yermakovka, belonging to the RSFSR, was largely surrounded by Ukrainian territory. In the 1930s several initiatives were undertaken to transfer this rural soviet to Ukraine, but Stalin himself rejected any further changes in this case.[13] Then, in 1944, with the Second World War still raging, the Supreme Soviets of the republics concerned revisited the case and voted unanimously to transfer Dar'ino-Yermakovka to the UkrSSR.[14] This small area of about forty-five square kilometers with eight hundred inhabitants was finally able to change its republican affiliation in September 1945.[15] Aside from the transfer of Crimea, Dar'ino-Yermakovka was the last noteworthy revision of the border between Ukraine and the RSFSR.

Other border revisions resulted from Stalin's repressive policies. For instance, during the Second World War some national-territorial units were dissolved as means of collectively punishing a certain nationality. The Checheno-Ingush and the Kabardino-Balkarian ASSR in the North Caucasus are prominent cases of such dissolution. There is virtually no literature on the fate of the territories other than the deportation of their population. Archival documents are scarce. As a matter of fact, the population was deported and the territory divided among the neighboring ASSRs and Georgia. In 1957 the Soviet leadership under Nikita Khrushchev revised this collective punishment and restored the territories of these autonomous republics in the North Caucasus. This means that in 1944 half of their lands, about 6,500 square kilometers, were transferred from the RSFSR to Georgia. In 1957 they were reattached to the RSFSR.[16]

The border revisions with Latvia and Estonia in favor of the RSFSR in January 1947 were based on considerations of nationality. The Supreme Soviet accepted the transfer of territories around Narva and the region of Petseri (today Pechory) from Estonia to the RSFSR. In the same session the formal head of the Soviet Union also acclaimed the reallocation of the Abrene area (today Pytalovo) from Latvia to the RSFSR. Both decisions were officially grounded in the predominantly Russian nationality of the local population.[17]

In contrast to the case of Putivl' with its missing bronze bell episode, there are only a few official documents that allow us to reconstruct the decision-making processes and implementation of the transfers after 1929. This pattern did not change with Stalin's death, as we can see from the case of Crimea in 1954. The folder about the Crimean issue in the documents of the All-Union Supreme Soviet contains only three sheets.[18] The same is true for similar territorial transfers between Kazakhstan and Uzbekistan in this period.[19]

Changes in the mode of documentation mirrored a general shift in Soviet decision making. Starting in the early years of Stalin's dictatorship, a move to informal, verbal decisions took place. The supreme leader often used ambiguous signs to rule party and state, and local functionaries tried to respond appropriately.[20] The resulting lack of documentation leaves considerable room for interpretation. When historians cannot find documents, they tend to fill in the gaps by relying on memoirs by the politicians involved. However, such documents are intrinsically biased, as they are written post factum and repurposed for and from a particular point of view.[21] Nonetheless, they help us to discuss two cases: the transfer of Crimea in 1954, and the border revisions between Uzbekistan and Kazakhstan between 1956 and 1971.

Building a Canal Efficiently

Sometimes, historians have the opportunity to participate in some small way in the events that they are trying to study and understand. In November 2016, when I was still collecting material for this book in Moscow, I had the chance to visit an exhibition that had been set up on Manezh Square, next to the Kremlin. Under the title "Russia—My History" (*Rossiia moia istoriia*), the curators had employed the full array of modern tools and techniques available to cast Russia's history since 1945 in the most positive and patriotic light. Of course, after the Russian occupation and annexation of Crimea in 2014, the curators had to address the transfer from the RSFSR to Ukraine in 1954 as well. They naturally opted for the most patriotic interpretation and described this transfer as nothing more than a "gift" that Nikita Khrushchev had given Ukraine on the occasion of the three hundredth anniversary of the Treaty of Pereiaslav. Moreover, the curators stressed that the transfer of Crimea to Ukraine took place in violation of Soviet law. Thus the 1954 transfer to Ukraine should itself be considered "illegal." It is the kind of argument that representatives of the Russian state have put forward on numerous other occasions. Their aim is to imply that when

Russia seized and annexed Crimea in 2014, it was effectively restoring the "legal" order.[22]

Now, it is true that 1954 marked the three hundredth anniversary of the Treaty of Pereiaslav. The event in question was the signing of an agreement between the Cossack Hetmanate under Bohdan Khmel'nyts'kyi and Tsar Aleksei Mikhailovich in the town of Pereiaslav on the Dnieper River. This agreement has long been interpreted by the Russian side as the start of a union between Ukrainians and Russians. Therefore, throughout the first half of 1954, parades, banquets, concerts, and ceremonies were held throughout the RSFSR and the UkrSSR to celebrate this momentous occasion with tremendous fanfare.[23] One of the main political motivations for the celebration was to soothe tensions between the two republics. A full-blown propaganda campaign centered around brotherly relations was to help heal the wounds inflicted by local resistance to Soviet rule after the Second World War, especially in western Ukraine.[24]

The 2016 exhibition in Moscow was itself a well-executed display of propaganda aimed at influencing public opinion. But there are no specific archival documents to support the idea that Crimea was a "gift" on the occasion of the anniversary of the Pereiaslav agreement. The historian Gwendolyn Sasse in fact deconstructed this assumption in her 2007 study. According to Sasse, the reasons for the transfer lay primarily in a desire to facilitate the peninsula's economic development.[25] Oleh Bazhan and his colleagues have confirmed her conclusion in their document collection. Despite extensive archival research, they have not been able to find a shred of evidence to lend credence to the narrative presented in 2016 in Moscow. Their book shows clearly that economic considerations lay behind the transfer.[26] "Sources" that infer Nikita Khrushchev was the *spiritus rector* of the transfer of Crimea to Ukraine were written and published much later. For example, a man named Knyshevskii argued in an article published in 1994 that Khrushchev had told him in 1944 that he, as first secretary of Ukraine, had talked with Stalin about the possibility of transferring Crimea from the RSFSR to the UkrSSR.[27] In the end, this is secondhand information and hearsay.

I consider the idea of Crimea being "Khrushchev's gift" as a trope in the sense presented by Hayden White. As a figure of speech it is useful for understanding past experience that "resist description in unambiguous prose."[28] Applied to the matter under discussion here, "Khrushchev's gift" provides a meaning for the transfer of Crimea, even if this does not match up with archival documentation.

The trope of "Khrushchev's gift" is not restricted to Russian revisionist circles; it can also be found in western handbooks as well as in journalistic reports. I do not want to engage in finger pointing, but the use of the trope has to be addressed. The historian Robert Magocsi employed this trope in his well-received monograph on Ukrainian history. There the events of 1954 are a marginal note, but Magocsi explains the transfer of Crimea as a "gift" from the "Soviet authorities" to Ukraine. William Taubman does the same in his contribution to the *Cambridge History of Russia*.[29] In German, the trope can be found in Kerstin S. Jobst's popular book on Ukrainian history.[30] Of course, in all three cases the transfer of Crimea in 1954 is a sidenote. Jeremy Smith does something similar in his article on the nationality question in the early Khrushchev era, and even Ronald Suny suspects Khrushchev of not having taken "the borders between Soviet republics seriously."[31]

In the interwar period Crimea's territorial affiliation had not featured in the debates between Russia and Ukraine over their shared borders, as had, say, the Kuban region.[32] Crimea's population had been diverse, with a history of conflicts. After the Russian conquest in the late eighteenth century, the peninsula saw an influx of Russian, Ukrainian, and German settlers in the nineteenth, while the imperial government deprived the Crimean Tatars of their land and forced many to leave.[33] According to the 1926 census, the largest population groups were Russians (53 percent), Crimean Tatars (26 percent), Germans (6 percent), Ukrainians (5 percent), and Jews (3 percent). Mixed into all of this were smaller communities of Armenians, Greeks, and Bulgarians, to name but a few.[34] The Second World War devastated the peninsula's infrastructure as well as its population. The Soviets deported the ethnic Germans during the Wehrmacht's advance in 1941. The German police and SS forces murdered Crimea's Jews, along with the Roma and Krymchak populations. After the Wehrmacht evacuated the peninsula in 1944, the Soviets then deported the remaining Crimean Tatars. Consequently, from 1945 to 1991 Russians and Ukrainians made up over 90 percent of the population on the peninsula.[35]

Confronted with such massive destruction and human losses, the Soviet authorities in Crimea encountered tremendous difficulties during postwar reconstruction. Among these difficulties was the development of agriculture, as was so often the case in the Soviet Union. In turn, one of the chief obstacles to agricultural development on the peninsula was seasonal drought. To remedy this situation, Gosplan developed an enormous irrigation project. The solution would be a canal of four hundred kilometers that would bring fresh water from the Dnieper to irrigate Crimea's arid fields.[36] For the realization of this project, it seemed "efficient" to have Crimea and Ukraine in the same union republic. It is also worth noting that planning for this project got underway at least two years before Stalin's death. This, of course, raises the question if the supreme leader might have found himself deciding whether to implement Crimea's transfer to Ukraine had he lived another year.

On 19 February 1954 the presidium of the Supreme Soviet adopted a resolution on the transfer of Crimea from the RSFSR to Ukraine. During this session numerous leading political functionaries delivered speeches for later publication. In their remarks they highlighted the friendship between the two great nations but also mentioned some of the original reasons for the transfer. Kliment Voroshilov, the chairman of the presidium of the Supreme Soviet, noted that "only conditions unique to the Soviet Union allow for a fair resolution of territorial issues, a resolution based on economic efficiency [*khoziaistvenno-ekonomicheskaia tselesoobraznost'*] with the full consent and brotherly cooperation of the peoples."[37] As can be seen, Voroshilov invoked the Soviet buzzword "efficiency" in his speech, but in doing so he established a causal link between the transfer and economic considerations. Even though the term "efficiency" was itself as fuzzy as the notion "the friendship of peoples," this reference was rooted in the North Crimean Canal project.

During the same session of the Supreme Soviet, party and state functionaries could not help but dwell on "the friendship of peoples," but it was not used to justify the transfer as such. Sharaf Rashidov, then chairman of the Uzbek Supreme Soviet, contributed a largely vacuous speech, but he did mention the anniversary of the Pereiaslav agreement—and did so in a way that is revealing: "The transfer of Crimean Oblast to the Ukrainian SSR is happening in heady days, when the entire Soviet people is celebrating the three hundredth anniversary of Ukraine joining Russia. [This] is another clear manifestation of the wise national policy of the Communist Party [*iavliaetsia novym iarkim proiavleniem mudroi natsional'noi politiki Kommunisticheskoi partii*], which aims to develop the working and intellectual forces of our country equally."[38] Even if Rashidov was drawing heavily on the full array of hackneyed phrases available to him, we see in his statement that the anniversary and the timing of Crimea's transfer are coincidental. His wording suggests nothing else. Moreover, he identifies the Communist Party and its "wise" policies as the driving forces behind the transfer. Since Stalin's death, politics in the Soviet Union had become less rigid. As the new "collective leadership" decentralized economic planning, territorial changes between union republics were beginning to make their way back onto the political agenda.[39] Rashidov would remain an influential regional power broker for the next twenty-five years. In 1959 he was appointed first party secretary in Uzbekistan. He stayed in this position until the so-called Cotton affair allegedly drove him to suicide in 1983.[40]

By the time of the transfer in February 1954, Nikita Khrushchev had been the party's first secretary for almost six months. The following year, he would force Prime Minister Georgii Malenkov, his chief rival, from power.[41] The memoirs of people close to Khrushchev at the time offer further evidence to support the assumption that the reason behind the transfer of Crimea to Ukraine was "efficiency" in economic development. Khrushchev's son Sergei wrote that his father had indeed initiated the transfer of Crimea but had done so because of the North Crimean Canal.[42] Relying on such accounts, Mark Kramer has argued that the transfer of Crimea may have played an important role in Khrushchev's efforts to consolidate power. In his view, Khrushchev secured the peninsula's transfer to win support among the Ukrainian party leadership under Oleksii Kyrychenko. He also suggests that Khrushchev was using the transfer to boost the number of Russians in the UkrSSR, so as to strengthen the "brotherly relationship" between the two republics. However, their approach fails to explain why the transfer of such an economically desolate region with a largely non-Ukrainian population would have helped Khrushchev win the support of the Ukrainian party leadership. In 1954 Crimea was not an asset but a liability.[43]

Later, public perception would place the transfer in a causal relation within a convenient trope. Khrushchev gave Crimea to the Ukrainian republic on the occasion of the anniversary of the Treaty of Pereiaslav to secure Ukrainian party support for his rise to power. The chain of events sounds conclusive. It suggests an easy answer to a complex political question and brings separate historical events together to form a meaningful whole. Thus historians, journalists, and, of course, politicians are easily able to absorb this trope even though it lacks historical substance.

The curators of the 2016 exhibition in Moscow found an easy solution by relying on publicly shared tropes. If visitors already believed that Crimea was transferred to Ukraine as one of those episodes of Khrushchev's erratic behavior, then they would have been open to an interpretation of events that suggests such an act was "illegal" even under

Soviet rule. Hence the exhibition confirmed what was already known. "Khrushchev's gift" thus easily feeds into revisionist arguments.

After the transfer, Crimea's infrastructure became even more closely linked to that of the UkrSSR mainland. Pipelines, canals, and electric power lines came to provide the peninsula with fresh water and electricity. Only after the completion of the North Crimean Canal in 1976 did it become possible to develop Crimean agriculture as Gosplan had imagined decades earlier. All sides were able to benefit.[44]

In the wake of the turmoil of 2014, highly emotional, patriotic orations in Ukraine and in Russia drowned out the narrative that Crimea's transfer to Ukraine took place for reasons of economic development. Since the annexation, the canal and pipelines had fallen into disuse and disrepair. After the Russian invasion of Ukraine in February 2022, one of the first goals of the Russian troops was to secure the canal's access to the Dnieper River and again pump water to the drought-ridden peninsula.[45] However, this effort came to naught when the Kakhovka dam that had supplied the canal was destroyed in June 2023.[46]

Cultivating "Virgin Lands": Contested Borders between Kazakhstan and Uzbekistan

The transfer of Crimea to Ukraine in 1954 can appear singular in the Soviet context only if we ignore all the smaller and larger territorial revisions that took place in other regions of the Union. Compared to Crimea, the negotiations over territory between Kazakhstan and Uzbekistan offer a much better glimpse into how Soviet institutions worked and how the successors of the once allegedly naïve indigenous comrades had learned to master power plays within the party and once-assumed asymmetries of power became more fluid.

After the delimitation of the Central Asian republics in the 1920s, the border in the steppes near Tashkent remained a matter of contention between Kazakhstan and Uzbekistan. But once the first five-year plan was launched, Stalin refused to consider any territorial changes save for a few rare cases. One of those cases was Karakalpak Autonomous Oblast, a sparsely populated steppe area, which was detached from the RSFSR and turned over to the Uzbek republic in 1936. Also at that time, Kazakhstan and Kyrgyzstan were raised to the status of union republics.[47]

From 1956 to 1971 Kazakhstan and Uzbekistan "adjusted" their borders on several occasions—and not without some political wrangling

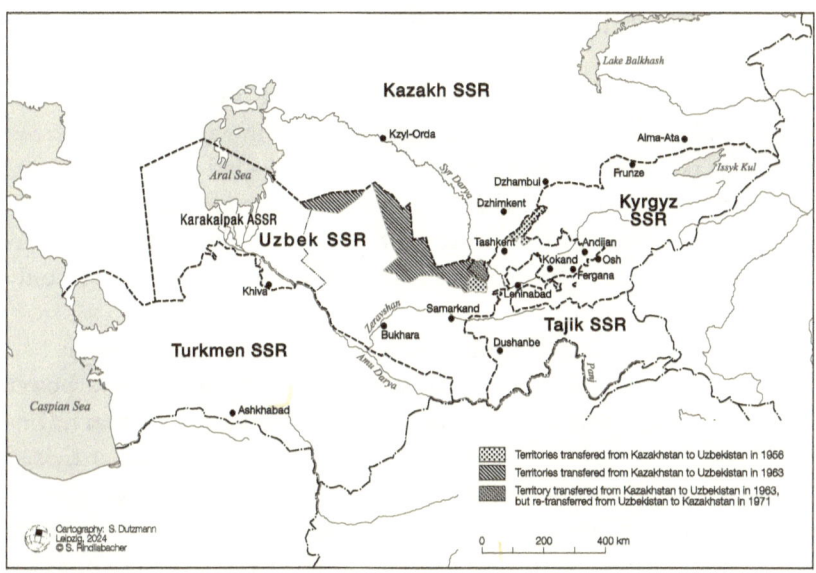

FIGURE 25. Political map of Central Asia, 1975.

behind the scenes. The first of these revisions came in 1956 and involved Bostandyk Raion near Tashkent and part of the Hungry Steppe. Altogether, five thousand square kilometers were transferred from Kazakhstan to Uzbekistan.[48] Zhumabek Tashenev, chairman of the Kazakh Supreme Soviet, summarized the reasons behind this move in a speech in Alma-Ata on the occasion of the transfer. First, Uzbek kolkhozes and sovkhozes had already been using land that nominally belonged to Kazakhstan. Second, Uzbek irrigation projects were better suited to promoting the expansion of cotton cultivation into the Hungry Steppe (Mirzachul'). While the Kazakh economy was focusing increasingly on coal, metallurgy, and oil, the Uzbek economy was specializing in cotton. It therefore seemed "efficient" to transfer Kazakhstan's cotton-growing areas to Uzbekistan. Finally, Bostandyk Raion was home to a power plant and enterprises that supplied Tashkent, so that here, too, it seemed more efficient to let the Uzbek republic run such vital infrastructure.[49]

This transfer, however, did not put an end to the border revisions. Uzbekistan's leaders continued to press for more territory. This was primarily because "their" collective farms were still leasing extensive amounts of Kazakh land along the border area west of Tashkent. The Uzbek politicians again argued that it would be easier to administer this land directly from Tashkent. In 1963 they were rewarded for their persistence. About thirty-seven thousand square kilometers from Chimkent and Kzyl-Orda Oblasti—a territory a little larger than Belgium (and more than 25 percent larger than Crimea)—was transferred from Kazakhstan to Uzbekistan. Soviet media hailed the revision, noting that this would enable the Uzbek sovkhozes and kolkhozes to boost cotton production in the Hungry Steppe. They also praised the territorial transfer as a "brotherly act" that could have been realized only under Soviet conditions.[50]

Despite the fanfare of propaganda in the media at the time, it had been possible to pull off this transfer of territory only after a power struggle behind the scenes. Months before the transfer took place, Dinmukhammed Kunaev, first secretary of the Kazakh party, had criticized Moscow several times for interfering in matters concerning Kazakh territory. He would later say that he was convinced that he "knew more than [Khrushchev] about the real situation in the republic, but also about the mood and feelings of the people and relations between the nationalities [*mezhnatsional'nye otnosheniia*]."[51] Since Stalin's death, the Soviet Union had been caught up in an enormous land reclamation project known as the Virgin Lands campaign. The aim of this campaign was to use allegedly uncultivated soil to increase productivity in agriculture. One of the target areas was Central Asia. Large irrigation projects were to provide water to boost cotton production. Khrushchev fully committed himself to the project.[52] His rationale was based on ideas to increase productivity, not the promotion of one nationality at the expense of another. Nonetheless, Kunaev saw Khrushchev's decision as an attempt to play the republican leaders against one another.

Among the Kazakh political elites, Ismail Yusupov, the first secretary of the party in Kazakhstan's Chimkent Oblast, saw the transfer of Kazakh territory to Uzbekistan as a means of advancing his own career. He sent Khrushchev a memorandum in which he argued for the transfer of Kazakhstan's cotton-growing areas to Uzbekistan, as it would be more efficient for the all-union economy. Much later, Yusupov would justify his actions, saying, "I informed Kunaev about the decline of cotton production in the respective raiony. But while workers from other Kazakh regions, even from throughout the union, had previously come for the cotton harvest, the entire workforce was now being directed to reclaiming virgin and long-uncultivated soil."[53] The diversion of workers from cotton to land reclamation posed a threat to cotton yields. This was bound to grab Khrushchev's attention. The ambitious Yusupov sought to find an "efficient" solution for the labor shortage in cotton production.

In December 1962 Kunaev and his colleagues from the Kazakh Central Committee traveled to Moscow for a visit to promote Kazakh culture in the Soviet capital. During a personal meeting, the Soviet leader informed Kunaev that he was going to transfer the raiony in question to Uzbekistan. The latter was shocked. In his memoirs, Kunaev would later claim that he openly warned Khrushchev of what was at stake: "I won't be able to prove the 'efficiency' [*tselesoobraznost'*] of this plan to my people. First, we have better experience in reclaiming Virgin Lands [than the Uzbeks do]. Second, we have begun to reclaim the Hungry Steppe. . . . Give us the equipment and the money, and we will do everything to increase the production of cotton. Last of all, [Chimkent] Oblast is the most densely populated part of the republic with a Kazakh population. We are playing with fire, as relations between the republics could become more difficult."[54] Despite Kunaev's protest, Khrushchev insisted on the transfer. As Kunaev had refused to play the game as required, he lost his position as the Kazakh party's first secretary. Khrushchev replaced him with a loyal follower: Yusupov. Kunaev did not fall too far, however, as he became chairman of the Council of Ministers—that is, the premier of the Kazakh government.

Two years later, the party leadership replaced Khrushchev because of, among other things, his failures in the Virgin Lands campaign and his seemingly erratic leadership.[55] With Leonid Brezhnev in power, Kunaev had a chance of regaining his previous office. Not long after Khrushchev's dismissal, Yusupov "lost control" over the Kazakh party apparatus, thus enabling Brezhnev to recall Kunaev to the office of first secretary.[56] For the next twenty-two years, until 1986, Kunaev remained the leading political figure in Kazakhstan. He became a symbol of stability but also of stagnation.[57] During his tenure he used his connections to lobby for a reversal of the territorial transfer that had precipitated his fall in late 1962.

Accordingly, in 1971 the three most densely populated raiony (Dzhetysai, Kirov, and Pakhtaaral') that Kazakhstan "lost" in 1963 were indeed returned.[58] This time, unlike after other territorial transfers, there was no accompanying propaganda campaign. The official media made no mention of it. There were no lengthy speeches praising "conditions unique to Soviet power" or "brotherly friendship." Kunaev and his Kazakh comrades had been able to make their point and reclaim some territory.

The numerous conflicts that arose in Central Asia in 1963 in the wake of these transfers revealed challenges when politicians tampered with the borders between Soviet republics. Not only national pride but also access to certain resources, professional careers, and regional development were at stake. The state and party leadership in Moscow may have undertaken transfers of territory with economic efficiency in mind, but republican authorities saw such moves as a measure of national standing, in terms of preferential or discriminatory treatment. Despite their official commitment to the "friendship of peoples," regional rulers, such as Kunaev in Kazakhstan, had to make political calculations with local national sentiment in mind. The national forms that the Bolsheviks had created were now developing a will of their own. Moscow came to understand the broader implications of territorial transfers and refrained from additional territorial revisions among the union republics. The stakes seemed too high and possible economic gains too uncertain. This is yet another reason why all the initiatives of the Armenian authorities to address the status of Nagorno-Karabakh failed.[59]

Three Elements of Soviet Territorial Thinking

Gifts were no category of Soviet spatial thinking; efficiency was, both synchronically and diachronically. This efficiency could be understood in an economic way by easing administration, boosting cotton production, improving irrigation, or reclaiming Virgin Lands. It could also be understood in the sense of administering a national majority within a certain territory or in the form of exigencies of governance in remote regions. Sentimental appeals to the "friendship of peoples" provided form but never content when it came to territorial transfers.

This "troika" of Soviet territorial thinking, developed in the 1920s, would remain crucial for border revisions between union republics until the 1970s. However, each case was unique, and depending on the politicians involved, one of the factors could gain preeminence and the other two could slip into the background. In the border revisions between Kazakhstan and Uzbekistan economic considerations, mainly the goal to increase cotton production, provided the key arguments. In the case of Petsery/Pechory or Abrene/Pytalovo the national composition of the population provided the decisive argument. In the cases of Putivl'/Putyvl' or Dar'ino-Yermakovka/Darïno-Yermakivka neither economic considerations nor national composition played a decisive role, which instead went to exigencies of governance in the form of border rectification.

Party leaders played a crucial role within the power structure, but the extent of their input into specific decisions can be exaggerated. There is ample evidence showing that Khrushchev did indeed play a key role in the transfer of Kazakh territory to Uzbekistan in 1963: Kunaev's demotion is but one example. But Khrushchev's involvement in Crimea in 1954 is far harder to detect. The trope of "Khrushchev's gift" seems to fill an epistemological void. Even though no "smoking gun" document supports this notion, the trope has come to be broadly accepted as an easy explanation for a complex issue. By diverting people's attention to Khrushchev and his allegedly erratic behavior, it has paved the way for revisionist arguments. In 2014 the Russian government simply picked a low-hanging fruit.

Conclusion

In November 1917 it was far from settled that the Soviet state would adopt a nationalized federal structure. In the years that followed, the Bolshevik government created different tools for governing party and state. In the margins, particularly in Ukraine, the South Caucasus, and Central Asia, the revolutionary government had to deal with a nationally mobilized, non-Russian-speaking population. Together they made up almost half of Soviet citizens. Thus the Bolsheviks had to find pragmatic solutions for including these politicized masses.

The Austromarxist raionirovanie concept lost much of its initial support, whereas national forms of administrative-territorial structuring provided a valuable nexus for korenizatsiia—namely, cadre promotion and popular mobilization. Raionirovanie lacked this mobilizing effect; even worse, from Moscow's perspective, its implementation created an administrative mess. As a result, in practice, the national approach turned out to be the most convenient way of managing diversity. In a subliminal process, most of the party and state functionaries—Gosplan expert Konstantin Yegorov is but one example—adapted to this pragmatism.

National-ethnographic structures became the foundation of the new federative state. This created not only a plethora of challenges but also opportunities. Studying these territorialization processes offers a standpoint to understand the USSR's place in global history.[1] The Bolsheviks identified the structural problems of nationalist movements, minority representation, and detachment of the margins from the center. Most of them soon realized that the nationality question would not miraculously fade away. Their vanguard party had to manage it thoroughly. Beginning with day-to-day improvisations, they then transformed their growing experience into a pragmatic tool to govern their supranational realm. This was a unique contribution of the Bolshevik revolution to global history. It served as example for ethnographically heterogeneous, modernizing states like China, Ethiopia, India, Indonesia, or Yugoslavia.

The creation of borders—the delineation of who and what should be inside or outside—reveals asymmetries of power at work. The Soviet realization of national self-determination was to be based on territory and linked with a set of privileges, such as additional funding and direct access to Moscow. In the early 1920s an ethno-territorial hierarchy developed, starting with the rural soviets and moving up the ladder of territorial entities to raiony, oblasti, autonomous republics, and the virtually sovereign union republics. Questions of drawing borders, border revision, and maintenance were the subject of heated debates as issues of resource distribution, careers, and privileges increasingly came to be seen as interconnected.

Even though the status of autonomous entities within the RSFSR and the structure of the USSR changed over time, the basic framework of Soviet territorial thinking that developed in the 1920s would last until 1991. Numerous autonomous oblasti and republics continue to exist in the Russian Federation, the successor state of the RSFSR, to this day. Even though smaller national entities, such as the national raiony and national rural soviets, were abolished in the late 1930s, larger national entities managed to survive this shift. On Stalin's orders the more than two hundred Soviet nationalities (*narodnosti*) of the 1920s were replaced with a set of "about sixty nations" (*natsii*). The minor national entities lost institutional support, the remaining major ones could profit from this Stalinist logic, as each of them had the privilege of a distinct territory and administration within the USSR.[2] These national entities were even able to enhance and strengthen their institutional standing over time. The union republics would eventually possess all the attributes of independent states.[3] The Bolshevik government would dismantle larger national entities only under extraordinary circumstances, as happened with the Volga German ASSR in 1941 or the Checheno-Ingush ASSR in 1944. Their dissolution was part of a wave of collective repression directed against nationalities suspected of collaboration with the German enemy during the Second World War.

Up until the constitutional reform of 1936, the hierarchy of national entities within the Soviet framework appeared to be in flux. In the South Caucasus, opposition to the very existence of the ZSFSR never ended. The Georgian party and to a certain extent its Azerbaijani counterpart were never happy with the Transcaucasian Federation, which they saw as dominated by Armenians.[4] The reform provided them with a window of opportunity to dissolve the ZSFSR.

Then, on 6 December 1936, the new Stalinist constitution went into effect. In it the Soviet leadership not only promised equal rights for all of its citizens (including previously ostracized priests or kulaks), but it also enlarged the number of union republics. Kyrgyzstan, Kazakhstan, Armenia, Azerbaijan, and Georgia obtained this most privileged status with its extra funding and direct access to Moscow. The basic framework that would endure until 1991 had been established. Stalin, the *spiritus rector* behind the new constitution, also provided three conditions for achieving union republic status. First, he stressed that the titular nationality must have a compact majority within its territory. Second, the republic must have a population of more than one million people in order to create a proper state administration. Third, Stalin insisted that a union republic had to border on non-Soviet territory. This final point appeared peculiar, but Stalin explained:

> Of course, we do not have any republics that want to leave the USSR, but as any union republic has the right to leave the USSR, we must make sure that this right does not become a dead letter. Let us take, for example, the Bashkir or the Tatar republics. Can we allow these autonomous republics to gain union republic status? Could they logically and virtually claim to leave the USSR? No, they cannot. Why? Because they are surrounded on all sides by Soviet republics and oblasti. In fact, they have nowhere to go. . . . This is why such republics cannot join the ranks of the union republics.[5]

Stalin was extremely sensitive about formalities as they were a power tool in themselves. As we have seen, Lenin viewed the slogan for national self-determination as a necessary antidote to the emergence of "real" secessionist movements. In 1936 Stalin laid out his three criteria post factum. Between 1922 and 1936 the status of a union republic was

CONCLUSION 175

granted to polities such as Belarus or Azerbaijan that had had experience with formal independence during the Civil War—no matter how short—or existed on the periphery of the Soviet state, such as Turkmenistan, Tajikistan, or Kyrgyzstan. Mongolia, though de facto part of the Soviet empire, remained formally independent as a people's republic.

In the 1920s not only the hierarchies but also the very shapes of the national entities under Bolshevik rule were in flux. Even when the party formally prioritized national-ethnographic criteria over economic ones in 1922, the outcome was far from finalized. Between 1923 and 1930 the party leadership delegated national-territorial issues to numerous commissions and subcommittees. Regional party activists, political leaders, and experts had to convene and find workable solutions. The All-Union Politburo did not want to get involved in the details, but it did reserve for itself the right to approve or reject solutions. In Eastern Europe and Central Asia almost all of the territories experienced some kind of large-scale revision. Everywhere the Soviet government looked, it faced problems similar to those at the Paris Peace Conference when two sides claimed the same territory. For the Bolsheviks the task was even more challenging, as they could neither distinguish between winner and loser nations, nor could they accept plebiscites. Even if the Bolsheviks relied on mass support in a rhetorical sense, they refrained from any larger mobilization of the public in this sensitive matter. A mobilized public could easily slip beyond their control. Thus cadres who had to follow the party discipline were tasked with revising and implementing new borders.

Drawing on imperial Russian expertise, the Bolshevik government was able to develop a set of powerful tools for describing and prescribing Soviet space. Building on the GOELRO project for the electrification of the European territories, Gosplan's proposal for raionirovanie spread throughout the Soviet state and underwent regional adaptations. Initially, considerations of energy efficiency provided a rough framework, but soon other factors came into play: regional geography, chains of production, and exigencies of governance. As a concept, raionirovanie would have offered an alternative to national-ethnographic structuring. This failed due to resistance from the margins and its lack of any mobilizing effect.

Although raionirovanie was not realized as originally conceived, Gosplan did establish viable concepts for analyzing and discussing Soviet space. The formation of ethnonational territories combined with korenizatsiia provided a power tool that proved efficient in mobilizing the population. Taken together, raionirovanie and korenizatsiia offered a set of seemingly scientific answers to overcome challenges of a "backward" population. As Cherviakov wrote in his report to the Politburo in 1924, the resulting outcomes could provide a showcase for the Soviet Union's affirmative nationality policies.[6] However, such showcasing alone was no decisive argument in the debate and was openly neglected when the party leadership considered other factors more important. For state and party leaders, the Piedmont Principle may have sounded nice on paper, but it had negligible impact on practical decisions.

During the 1920s Gosplan was particularly involved in collecting information on the Soviet space. At the same time, its experts were debating a comprehensive reform and drafting plans to promote economic growth. Gosplan, its expertise, and its five-year plans would prove very effective tools in Stalin's hands after 1929. Experts such as Konstantin Yegorov, who had been remarkably active in Gosplan's first years, were fired or reassigned in the early 1930s. Moreover, the regional solutions for raionirovanie, which had involved so many different voices, were scrapped in 1930. From Moscow's perspective, the different adaptations of raionirovanie led to administrative chaos.

The three regional case studies examined here reveal that Soviet leaders and experts discussed each case individually. In practice we can observe three ways in which the Bolsheviks dealt with national-territorial disputes. The first was quite simple and thus the one commissions resorted to most often: giving preference to one side and discriminating against the other. For the most part, this is what happened during the revision of the Russian-Ukrainian border. However, commissions also practiced two other ways of regulating national-territorial issues. The second way was much more intricate. A commission could take seemingly complex economic and cultural boundaries and declare them to be national borders, as was done in parts of the Fergana Valley. The third way was to not make any in-depth decision at all. This was the most unsatisfying solution, leaving a national-territorial issue in limbo. This was the approach taken in Milove/Chertkovo, in Ohybne/Borisovka, in the Sokh Valley, and with a large part of the border between Armenia and Azerbaijan.

The agency of the officials tasked with solving national-territorial issues differed from region to region. In the South Caucasus and Central Asia, they enjoyed considerable freedom in their search for feasible solutions, but not so in the case between the RSFSR and Ukraine. The mood within the Cherviakov Commission was tense, and the split between the RSFSR and the Ukrainian delegation was quickly exposed. The commission's recommendations were then rejected by the Politburo. Most Ukrainian territorial claims were dismissed in favor of the RSFSR. The representatives of the regions of the RSFSR, in this case the North Caucasus Krai, had particular influence on the decision making in Moscow. Nonetheless, the party and state functionaries were able to find a common border.

In Central Asia the delimitation process served as a means to teach regional party cadres how to act within the party hierarchy. Even though the negotiations were turbulent and confusing for the European party activists, they also saw these sessions as an educational tool. The Europeans gave their indigenous comrades the opportunity to voice their views and explained how the decision-making process would operate and what it meant to adhere to the party line. Nationalism was certainly not "artificially" introduced into Central Asia. Some indigenous Bolsheviks had already adopted these ideas and saw national delimitation as an opportunity to increase their own powerbase. But among them also emerged a faction that fiercely opposed national delimitation in favor of a federal structuring combined with raionirovanie. Delimitation and the discussion of it by indigenous communists appear to have been crucial tools for institutionalizing Soviet power in Central Asia.

Whereas the Sredazbiuro and the Cherviakov Commission succeeded in paving the path for an encompassing territorial revision, the Territorial Commission at the ZakTsIK failed to do the same. It did not have the backing necessary to produce a coherent plan and lost itself in a plethora of patchwork solutions. Leading party members, such as Ordzhonikidze or later Mamiia Orakhelashvili, refused to get directly involved. Even though representatives of the republics participated in negotiations, the implementation of the agreements reached often came to naught due to opposition from one side that saw its interests at risk—for example, the 1927 Armenian-Azerbaijani agreement on Bashkend and Alagelliar.

The Zakkraikom did not prevent local actors from undermining a coherent revision. It hoped to remain above the fray in a region steeped in national antagonisms. The price of this restraint was the failure to establish a clearly defined territorial order. Nonetheless, the interaction between state and party functionaries and the population on an everyday basis—that is, the very process of searching for a border—provided opportunities to perform state authority in the margins, as happened, for instance, in Shinikh Airum or in the case of Firid Memed Ali-Ogly's orchard.

Experts enjoyed considerable influence in the Russian-Ukrainian border revision but somewhat less in the South Caucasus. In Central Asia experts served as mere consultants, while indigenous communists, who were believed to know "their" region better, made the fundamental decisions. In the case of the RSFSR and Ukraine, as well as Central Asia, regional politicians and experts were able to reach and implement agreements, tense quarrels notwithstanding. Even though most of the politicians, activists, and experts involved were not happy with these results, they nonetheless accepted the compromises reached.

The party favored certain sides in deciding border issues such as the RSFSR vis-à-vis Ukraine in Eastern Europe and Uzbekistan in Central Asia. Moscow's preferences mostly emphasized economic reasons or exigencies of governance. However, one should not simply assume that "less favored republics" regularly fell victim to deliberate discrimination or that the Bolshevik leaders always sided with their "favorites." Despite its tendency to support the RSFSR or Uzbekistan, Moscow could promote the interests of others on minor issues, as it did with the UkrSSR in Miropol'e/Myropillia or Kyrgyzstan in Suliukta or Uch-Kurgan. In Eastern Europe and Central Asia poorly solved disputes, such as those over Milove/Chertkovo, were the exception, not the rule. Moreover, if both republics opposed a certain directive by the Politburo, as happened with Putivl' Uezd, the party leadership could be convinced to revise its decision.

The example of Putivl' Volost indicates that not every border area was contested. As this volost was an economically underdeveloped entity with high deficit spending, the RSFSR was not eager to "keep" it, and the Ukrainian side was not eager to "obtain" it. Republican representatives were looking not simply to enlarge "their" territory but to gain more valuable economic assets, as the North Caucasus Krai did with the areas around Tahanrih/Taganrog and Shakhty.

Problems often arose when the exact separating lines had to be defined. Field commissions were tasked with marking the borders on the ground. On a local scale the newly established boundaries were expected to conform to patterns of local land use. Exchanges of land between border villages would ideally result in a corresponding adjustment of the republican border in question. People otherwise considered indifferent to nationality began to use such concepts as a strategy for defending daily interests.⁷ In several cases such as Znob' or Shinikh Airum, local interest groups could successfully reverse projected borders from above.

Challenges with field surveying and local struggles over fields, pastures, and woods were ubiquitous in the early Soviet state. We can track them in the border region between Ukraine and the RSFSR, in Central Asia as well as in the South Caucasus. However, in no other region did such struggles overlap with cultural, religious, and economic dichotomies as they did between Armenia and Azerbaijan. Nonetheless, there, too, functionaries and experts helped to integrate (and separate) the population into state structures.

For the first thirteen years or so of Soviet rule, we have plenty of documents that allow detailed insights into territorialization processes such as the bronze bell episode in Putivl'. After the Cultural Revolution, decision making most often happened orally rather than on paper. Nonetheless, archival documents together with various sources such as memoirs and contemporary press reports allow us to reconstruct the decision making that led to the rare border revisions after 1929. Localizing the transfer of Crimea in 1954 in a larger context of territorial revisions reveals that the factors of Soviet territorial thinking remained the same. "Gifts" provided no category for decision making, whereas economic efficiency, national affiliation, and exigencies of governance did. These three categories were not well defined, and they could contradict each other. Between 1917 and 1991 they competed for supremacy. Party leaders and experts could shift emphasis, but together these categories defined what was seen as politically possible. As border revisions were closely tied to changes in the local power structure and privileges, resistance against such plans grew over time. This was one of the key reasons why only a few borders were revised after 1953 and why subsequent initiatives like the one in Nagorno-Karabakh kept running up against a brick wall in Moscow.

In the South Caucasus politicians and experts were far from solving national-territorial disputes. These would become liabilities after 1991. Today the de facto border between Armenia and Azerbaijan consists literally of minefields.⁸ If both sides are ever to make peace, they will have to reach an agreement on a common border, but in doing so, they will be unable to rely on a coherent Soviet-era precursor. Hence there is de jure no clearly defined border between them. This absence, however, is not a trap that Stalin, Ordzhonikidze, or Beriia put in place to keep the republics of the South Caucasus in check or to haunt later generations. Researchers such as Alexander Morrison and Madeleine Reeves have complained that such myths surrounding the Soviet borders are nonetheless "remarkably persistent."[9]

The Soviet Union is gone for good, but its federal skeleton is still present in the current international order. At first, post-Soviet governments were reluctant to touch its bones. Even though Armenia de facto controlled parts of Nagorno-Karabakh, it had refrained from annexing it and insisted on the fiction of a separate Artsakh state. Even though there were populist initiatives to alter the existing borders in the 1990s in Crimea, in northern Kazakhstan, in the Georgian Akhalkali Province, or in the Fergana Valley, they were explicitly not adopted by the incumbent governments. The statesmen opted to respect the status quo. In the case of Crimea, Gwendolyn Sasse concluded in 2007 that such revisionist claims were "confined to the political margins."[10]

Some of the original motivations that lay behind the creation of certain borders have, of course, ceased to exist. For example, the nonsedentary share of the population in the South Caucasus and Central Asia is now close to zero. As the creators of these borders paid attention to formalities as well as regional economic and social dependencies, the borders of the member republics functioned in the post-Soviet context rather well. In this respect, the countries that emerged from the collapse of the Soviet Union at first had much in common with the countries of Africa. There the postcolonial political elites (apart from Morocco) recognized the states and borders as staked out by the European powers.

Then, in 2008, Russia widened the existing cracks when it recognized Abkhazia and South Ossetia as independent states. In Central Asia all five nation-states still formally adhere to the Soviet framework—skirmishes and small wars notwithstanding. Uzbekistan, Tajikistan, and Kyrgyzstan do not call into question the numerous complex enclaves of the Fergana Valley. All post-Soviet governments, Russia included, thought that doing so would be far too risky.

Over the last decade the post-Soviet order has increasingly resembled Europe in the interwar period, when revisionist powers allowed the Versailles order to collapse. In 2014 Russia deliberately opened Pandora's Box when it annexed Crimea. Now, new aspiring imperial powers are trying to revise the existing order, creating an extremely dangerous and volatile situation in international politics. The structure itself is at stake. All fifteen successor republics might formulate reasonable territorial claims, be it Kyrgyzstan in the Sokh Valley, Armenia in Nagorno-Karabakh, or Russia and Ukraine alongside the intricate border dividing Milove/Chertkovo. But is it worth risking long-term stability for such short-term gains?

Glossary

AK Rus. administrativnaia komissiia (administrative commission)

AMSSR Rus. Avtonomnaia Moldavskaia sotsialisticheskaia sovetskaia respublika (Autonomous Moldavian Socialist Soviet Republic)

AO Autonomous oblast

ASSR Autonomous socialist soviet republic

ATK Rus. administrativno-territorial'naia komissiia (administrative-territorial commission)

aul Small mobile community of herders

AzSSR Rus. Azerbaidzhanskaia sotsialisticheskaia sovetskaia respublika (Socialist Soviet Republic of Azerbaijan, 1920–1991)

bedniak Poor peasant

bei/bek Member of a wealthy stratum of (Muslim) society; often used in a derogatory sense

desiatina Russian imperial unit to measure area; one desiatina equals 1.09 hectares

dompredzak Rus. dom predvaritel'nogo zakliucheniia (prison for pre-trial detention and short sentences)

GOELRO Rus. Gosudarstvennaia komissiia po elektrifikatsii Rossii (State Commission for Electrification of Russia, 1920–?)

Gosplan Rus. Gosudarstvennaia obshcheplanovaia komissiia pri Sovete truda i oborony RSFSR (State Planning Commission at the Council of Labor and Defense of the RSFSR, 1921–1923); Gosudarstvennaia planovaia komissiia pri Sovete truda i oborony SSSR (State Planning Commission at the Council of Labor and Defense of the USSR, 1923–1937)

GPU Rus. Gosudarstvennoe politicheskoe upravlenie pri TsIK SSSR (State Political Administration at the TsIK SSSR, 1922–1923), see also OGPU

guberniia (Rus.) Administrative-territorial unit, the same as Ukr. huberniia; comparable to a province

gubispolkom Rus. gubernskii ispolnitel'nyi komitet (guberniia executive committee)

gubkom Rus. gubernskii partiinyi komitet (guberniia party committee)

huberniia (Ukr.) Administrative-territorial unit, the same as Rus. guberniia; comparable to a province

Kavbiuro Rus. Kavkazskoe biuro TsK RKP(b) (Caucasian Bureau of the Central Committee of the Russian Communist Party [Bolshevik]), 1920–1922

GLOSSARY

KEPS Rus. Komissiia po izucheniiu estestvennykh proizvoditel'nykh sil strany Akademii nauk (Commission for the Study of the Country's Natural Productive Forces at the Academy of Science, 1915-1930)

Kirrespublika Rus. Kirgizskaia avtonomnaia sotsialisticheskaia sovetskaia respublika (Kirgiz Autonomous Socialist Soviet Republic, 1920-1925)

kishlak Wintering place for herdsmen

korenizatsiia Literally *indigenization*, a Bolshevik party policy to recruit cadres among national minorities to popularize Soviet power

KP(b)U Ukr. Komunistychna Partiia (bil'shovykiv) Ukraïny (Communist Party [Bolshevik] of Ukraine)

kulak Derogatory word for a rich peasant

Narkomnats Rus. Narodnyi komissariat po delam natsional'nostei RSFSR (People's Commissariat of Nationality Affairs of the RSFSR, 1917-1924)

Narkomzem Rus. Narodnyi komissariat zemledeliia (People's Commissariat for Agriculture)

NEP Rus. Novaia ekonomicheskaia politika (New Economic Policy)

OGPU Rus. Ob"edinënnoe gosudarstvennoe politicheskoe upravlenie pri TsIK SSSR (Unified State Political Administration at the TsIK USSR, 1923-1934)

OIK, okrispolkom Rus. okruzhnoi ispolnitel'nyi komitet (okrug executive committee)

okrug (Rus.) Administrative-territorial unit, comparable to a county (post-reform)

okruha (Ukr.) Ukr. administrative-territorial unit, the same as Rus. okrug

okrvykonkom Ukr. Okruzhyi vykonavchyi komitet (okruha executive committee)

Ozakom Rus. Osobyi zakavkazskii komitet (Special Transcaucasian Committee, 1917-1918)

povit (Ukr.) Administrative-territorial unit, the same as Rus. uezd; comparable to a county (pre-reform)

raion (Rus./Ukr.) Administrative-territorial unit; comparable to a district

raionirovanie Literally *regionalization*, an all-encompassing plan to reform the administrative-territorial structure of the Soviet state between 1920 and 1930

Revkom Rus. Revoliutsionnyi komitet (Revolutionary Committee)

RIK, raiispolkom Rus. raionnyi ispolnitel'nyi komitet (raion executive committee)

RKP(b) Rus. Rossiiskaia kommunisticheskaia partiia (bol'shevikov) (Russian Communist Party [Bolshevik], 1918-1925)

RSDRP Rus. Rossiiskaia sotsial-demokraticheskaia rabochaia partiia (Russian Social-Democratic Workers' Party, 1898-1918)

RSFSR Russian Socialist Federative Soviet Republic, 1918-1991

SNK, Sovnarkom Rus. Sovet narodnykh komissarov (Soviet of People's Commissars)

GLOSSARY

Sredazbiuro Rus. Sredneaziatskoe biuro TsK RKP(b)/VKP(b) (Central Asian Bureau of the TsK RKP[b[/VKP[b], 1922-1936)

SSR Rus. Sotsialisticheskaia sovetskaia respublika, 1918-1936; Sovetskaia sotsialisticheskaia respublika, 1936-1991 (Socialist Soviet Republic, i.e., union republic, the highest rank in the Soviet federal order)[1]

SSRA Rus. Sotsialisticheskaia sovetskaia respublika Armenii (Socialist Soviet Republic of Armenia, 1920-1991)

STO Rus. Soviet truda i oborony pri SNK RSFSR, 1920-1923 (Council of Labor and Defense at the Soviet of People's Commissars RSFSR, 1920-1923); Sovet truda i oborony pri SNK SSSR (Council of Labor and Defense at the Soviet of People's Commissars of the USSR, 1923-1937)

TASSR Rus. Turkestanskaia avtonomnaia sotsialisticheskaia sovetskaia respublika (Autonomous Socialist Soviet Republic of Turkestan, 1918-1924)

TsIK Rus. Tsentral'nyi ispolnitel'nyi komitet SSSR (Central Executive Committee of the USSR, 1923-1937)

TsK Rus./Ukr. Tsentral'nyi komitet (Central Committee of the Communist Party)

TsKK Rus. Tsentral'naia kontrol'naia komissiia (Central Control Commission)

TsSU Rus. Tsentral'noe statisticheskoe upravlenie (Central Statistical Administration)

Turkbiuro Rus. Turkestanskoe biuro TsK RKP(b) (Turkestan Bureau of the Central Committee of the Russian Communist Party [Bolshevik], 1920-1922)

Turkkomissiia Rus. Osobaia vremennaia komissiia VTsIK i SNK RSFSR po delam Turkestana (Special Provisional Commission of the VTsIK and SNK RSFSR for Turkestan Affairs, 1919-1920)

uezd (Rus.) Administrative-territorial unit; the same as Ukr. *povit*; comparable to a county (pre-reform)

UIK Rus. uezdnyi ispolnitel'nyi komitet (uezd executive committee)

UkrDerzhplan Ukr. Derzhavnyi planovyi komitet USRR (State Planning Committee of the UkrSSR)

UkrSSR Ukrainian Socialist Soviet Republic, 1919-1991, see also USRR

USRR Ukr. Ukraïns'ka sotsialystychna radians'ka respublika (Ukrainian Socialist Soviet Republic)

USSR Union of Soviet Socialist Republics, 1922-1991

UzSSR Rus. Uzbekskaia sotsialisticheskaia sovetskaia respublika (Uzbek Socialist Soviet Republic, 1924-1991)

VIK Rus. volostnoi ispolnitel'nyi komitet (volost executive committee)

VKP(b) Rus. Vsesoiuznaia kommunisticheskaia partiia (bol'shevikov) (All-Union Communist Party [Bolshevik], 1925-1952)

volost' (Rus./Ukr.) Administrative-territorial unit; comparable to a shire

VSNKh Rus. Vysshii sovet narodnogo khoziaistva (Supreme Soviet of the National Economy)

GLOSSARY

VTsIK Rus. Vserossiiskii tsentral'nyi ispolnitel'nyi komitet (All-Russian Central Executive Committee, 1917–1937)

VUTsVK Ukr. Vseukraïns'kyi tsentral'nyi vykonavchyi komitet (All-Ukrainian Central Executive Committee, 1919–1937)

ZakGosplan Rus. Zakavkazskaia planovaia komissia (Transcaucasian Planning Commission, 1923–1937)

Zakkraikom Rus. Zakavkazskii kraevoi komitet TsK RKP(b)/VKP(b) (Transcaucasian Regional Committee of the TsK RKP[b]/VKP[b], 1922–1937)

ZakSNK Rus. Zakavkazskii sovet narodnykh komissarov (Transcaucasian Soviet of People's Commissars, 1922–1937)

ZakTsIK Rus. Zakavkazskii tsentral'nyi ispolnitel'nyi komitet (Transcaucasian Central Executive Committee, 1922–1936)

ZSFSR Rus. Zakavkazskaia sotsialisticheskaia federativnaia sovetskaia respublika (Transcaucasian Socialist Federative Soviet Republic, 1922–1936)

Notes

Note on Terminology, Abbreviation, Transliteration, Calendar, and Maps

1. With the introduction of the 1936 constitution the adjectives "Socialist" and "Soviet" switched places in all the designations of the federal entities of the Soviet state.

Introduction

1. Letter from D. Kozachkov to Lazar' Kaganovich, 26 October 1926, Gosudarstvennyi arkhiv Rossiiskoi Federatsii (GA RF), fond (f.) 3316, opis' (op.) 17, delo (d.) 721, listy (ll.) 49–50.
2. Lewis H. Siegelbaum and Leslie P. Moch, "Transnationalism in One Country? Seeing and Not Seeing Cross-Border Migration within the Soviet Union," *Slavic Review* 75, no. 4 (2016): 970–86.
3. Kate Brown, *A Biography of No Place: From Ethnic Borderland to Soviet Heartland* (Cambridge, MA: Harvard University Press, 2003), 40.
4. Vladimir Putin, "Address by the President of the Russian Federation," 21 February 2022, http://en.kremlin.ru/events/president/transcripts/67828.
5. Vladimir Lenin [Ul'ianov], "Address to the First All-Russian Congress of the Navy, 22 November/5 December 1917," in his *Polnoe sobranie sochinenii* (hereafter *PSS*), 5th ed., 55 vols. (Moscow: Izdatel'stvo politicheskoi literatury, 1974), 35:115.
6. Benedict Anderson sees the map alongside the census and the museum as the main tools of exercising imperial power over the margins. See his *Imagined Communities: Reflections on the Origin and Spread of Nationalism*, 3rd ed. (New York: Verso, 2003), 56–65.
7. Michael David-Fox, *Crossing Borders: Modernity, Ideology, and Culture in Russia and the Soviet Union* (Pittsburgh: University of Pittsburgh Press, 2015), 48–71; Adeeb Khalid, "Backwardness and the Quest for Civilization: Early Soviet Central Asia in Comparative Perspective," *Slavic Review* 56, no. 2 (2006): 232–35.
8. James M. Peterson and Jacek Lubecki, *Globalization, Nationalism, and Imperialism: A New History of Eastern Europe* (Budapest: Central European University Press, 2023), 2–3.
9. Dominic Lieven, *Empire: The Russian Empire and Its Rivals* (New Haven: Yale University Press, 2001), 302–9.
10. Anderson, *Imagined Communities*, 110–11; Josep M. Colomer, *Great Empires, Small Nations: The Uncertain Future of the Sovereign State* (New York:

Routledge, 2007), 3–17; Ulrike von Hirschhausen and Jörn Leonhard, *Empires: Eine globale Geschichte, 1780–1920* (Munich: C. H. Beck, 2023), 14–18.

11. On "new imperial history," see Ronald G. Suny, "Dialektika imperii: Rossiia i Sovetskii soiuz," in *Novaia imperskaia istoriia postsovetskogo prostranstva*, ed. Ilya Gerasimov et al. (Kazan: Tsentr issledovanii natsionalizma i imperii, 2004), 163–96; Mark R. Beissinger, "Soviet Empire as 'Family Resemblance,'" *Slavic Review* 65, no. 2 (2006): 294–303; Juliette Cadiot, *Le laboratoire impérial: Russie-URSS, 1860–1940* (Paris: Éditions CNRS, 2007), 213; Ilya Gerasimov, Jan Kusber, and Alexander Semyonov, introduction to their *Empire Speaks Out: Languages of Rationalization and Self-Description in the Russian Empire* (Leiden: Brill, 2009), 23–25; Valerie A. Kivelson and Ronald G. Suny, *Russia's Empires* (New York: Oxford University Press, 2017), 1–16; Lewis Siegelbaum and Krista Goff, introduction to their *Empire and Belonging in the Eurasian Borderlands* (Ithaca, NY: Cornell University Press, 2019), 3–4; Ilya Gerasimov, "Narrating Russian History after the Imperial Turn," *Ab Imperio*, no. 4 (2020): 55–56; Shoshana Keller, *Russia and Central Asia: Coexistence, Conquest, Convergence* (Toronto: University of Toronto Press, 2020), 15; Ilya Gerasimov, Alexander Semyonov, and Marina Mogilner, "Toward a Postnational History of Eurasia: Deconstructing Empires and, Denationalizing Groupness," *Ab Imperio*, no. 1 (2023): 9–15; F. Benjamin Schenk, "'A Sixth Part of the World': The Career of a Spatial Metaphor in Russia and the Soviet Union, 1837–2021," *Kritika: Explorations in Russian and Eurasian History* 24, no. 2 (2023): 352–53.

12. See, e.g., Siegelbaum and Goff, *Empire and Belonging*.

13. Lenin, "Chto delat'? Nabolevshie voprosy nashego dvizheniia," in *PSS*, 6:117–20.

14. Francine Hirsch, *Empire of Nations: Ethnographic Knowledge and the Making of the Soviet Union* (Ithaca, NY: Cornell University Press, 2005), 7–8.

15. Jürgen Osterhammel and Jan C. Jansen, *Kolonialismus: Geschichte, Formen, Folgen*, 9th ed. (Munich: C. H. Beck, 2021), 73–80.

16. Paul Werth, "Russia's Borders in the East and West," *Kritika: Explorations in Russian and Eurasian History* 22, no. 3 (2021): 644.

17. Lynne Viola, "The Aesthetic of Stalinist Planning and the World of the Special Villages," *Kritika: Explorations in Russian and Eurasian History* 4, no. 1 (2003): 103.

18. Nick Baron, "Nature, Nationalism and Revolutionary Regionalism: Constructing Soviet Karelia, 1920–1923," *Journal of Historical Geography* 33 (2007): 573, 593.

19. Osterhammel and Jansen, *Kolonialismus*, 28–30, 73–77.

20. Camille Lefebvre, *Frontières de sable, frontières de papier: Histoire de territoires et de frontières, du jihad de Sokoto à la colonisation française du Niger, XIXe–XXe siècles* (Paris: Publications de la Sorbonne, 2015), 413–20; Hélène Blais, "An Intra-Imperial Conflict: The Mapping of the Border between Algeria and Tunisia, 1881–1914," *Journal of Historical Geography* 37 (2011): 178–90.

21. From a legal—and, as we will see, from a practical—point of view, William Partlett's and Herbert Küpper's fundamental assumption that indigenous populations in Soviet Central Asia or in the Caucasus were not an equal part of the Soviet demos is inappropriate. See, for example, Partlett and Küpper,

The Post-Soviet as Post-Colonial: A New Paradigm for Understanding Constitutional Dynamics in the Former Soviet Empire (Cheltenham, UK: Edward Elgar, 2022), 8. Despite equality before the law, instances of othering occurred in cultural practices. See Eric R. Scott, *Familiar Strangers: The Georgian Diaspora and the Evolution of Soviet Empire* (Oxford: Oxford University Press, 2016), 20–22.

22. Keller, *Russia and Central Asia*, 14. Problematizing Soviet rule in Central Asia as "colonial" is also one major topic of Gero Fedtke, *Roter Orient: Muslimkommunisten und Bolschewiki in Turkestan, 1917–1924* (Cologne: Böhlau, 2020), 18. However, Botakoz Kassymbekova, Marlène Laruelle, Aminat Chokobaeva, and David Chioni Moore point to the potential of studying the history of Soviet Central Asia from a post-colonial perspective: Botakoz Kassymbekova, *Despite Cultures: Early Soviet Rule in Tajikistan* (Pittsburgh, PA: University of Pittsburgh Press, 2016), 199–204; Marlène Laruelle, *Central Peripheries: Nationhood in Central Asia* (London: UCL Press, 2021), 210–12; Botakoz Kassymbekova and Aminat Chokobaeva, "On Writing Soviet History of Central Asia: Frameworks, Challenges, Prospects," *Central Asian Survey* 40, no. 4 (2021): 483–503; Botakoz Kassymbekova, "On Decentering Soviet Studies and Launching New Conversations," *Ab Imperio*, no. 1 (2022): 115–20; and David Chioni Moore, "East, West, and South: Complex Asymmetries in Postcolonial/Post-Soviet Debates since 2001," *Ab Imperio*, no. 1 (2024): 37. Chioni Moore's "transhistorical" and "transgeographic" conception of "colonialism" is problematic for historic analysis as it turns into a timeless category.

23. Benedict Anderson made this a core argument of his study (*Imagined Communities*, 56–65).

24. Tereza Hendl et al., "(En)Countering Epistemic Imperialism: A Critique of 'Westsplaining' and Coloniality in Dominant Debates on Russia's Invasion of Ukraine," in *Contemporary Security Policy*, 4 December 2023, http://doi.org/10.1080/13523260.2023.2288468.

25. Marc Ferro, *Colonization: A Global History* (New York: Routledge, 1997), 15–17; Andrew Porter, *European Imperialism, 1860–1914* (New York: Palgrave Macmillan, 1994), 1–2; Osterhammel and Jansen, *Kolonialismus*, 19–24.

26. Terry Martin argues that "affirmative action" remained a Soviet core policy until 1991 (*The Affirmative Action Empire: Nations and Nationalism in the Soviet Union, 1923–1939* [Ithaca, NY: Cornell University Press, 2001], 461). On the challenge of "decolonization," see also Alexander Herbert and Bryan Gigantino, "The Poverty of Cultural History: Decolonization, Race, and Politics in Post-Socialist Studies," *LeftEast*, 1 January 2024, https://lefteast.org/the-poverty-of-cultural-history-decolonization-race-and-politics-in-post-socialist-studies/.

27. On the Paris Peace Conference and its global impact, see Manela Erez, *The Wilsonian Moment: Self-Determination and the International Origins of Anticolonial Nationalism* (Oxford: Oxford University Press, 2007); Leonard V. Smith, *Sovereignty at the Paris Peace Conference of 1919* (Oxford: Oxford University Press, 2018); Maciej Górny, *Vaterlandszeichner: Geografen und Grenzen im Zwischenkriegseuropa* (Osnabrück: fibre, 2019); Elżbieta Kwiecińska, "Poland's 'Civilising Mission' and Ukrainian Statehood at the Paris Peace Conference," in *Making Ukraine: Negotiating, Contesting and Drawing the Borders in the Twentieth Century*, ed.

Constantin Ardeleanu and Olena Palko (Montreal: McGill-Queen's University Press, 2022), 91-96.

28. The often-used bureaucratic terms *tselesoobrazno* and *tselesoobraznost'* are hard to translate. They appear in this book as "efficiently" and "efficiency."

29. Report from Aleksandr Cherviakov to the Politburo RKP(b), 30 November 1924, Tsentral'nyi derzhavnyi arkhiv vyshchykh orhaniv vlady ta upravlinnia Ukraïny (TsDAVO), f. 1, opys (op.) 2, sprava (spr.) 1808, arkush (ark.) 10-14.

30. Martin, *Affirmative Action Empire*, 274-82.

31. Francine Hirsch, "The Soviet Union as a Work-in-Progress: Ethnographers and the Category Nationality in the 1926, 1937, and 1939 Censuses," *Slavic Review* 56, no. 2 (1997): 251-78; Ulla Connor, *Territoriale Grenzen als Praxis: Zur Erfindung der Grenzregion in grenzüberschreitender Kartographie* (Baden-Baden: Nomos, 2023), 94.

32. Robert Conquest, *The Last Empire* (London: Ampersand, 1962), 28-31; Olaf Caroe, *Soviet Empire: The Turks of Central Asia and Stalinism* (London: MacMillan, 1967), 145-49; Hélène Carrère d'Encausse, *The Great Challenge: Nationalities and the Bolshevik State, 1917–1930* (New York: Holmes and Meier, 1992), 179; Rakhim Masov, *Istoriia topornogo razdeleniia* (Dushanbe: Irfon, 1991), 113-14; Arslan Koichiev, *Natsional'no-territorial'noe razmezhevanie v ferganskoi doline, 1924–1927 gg.* (Bishkek: self-pub., 2001), 48-55.

33. Brown, *Biography of No Place*, 20.

34. Martin, *Affirmative Action Empire*, 10-12; Jeremy Smith, *Red Nations: The Nationalities Experience in and after the USSR* (Cambridge: Cambridge University Press, 2013); Jeremy Smith, *The Bolsheviks and the National Question, 1917–1923* (London: St. Martin's Press, 1999); Ronald G. Suny, *The Revenge of the Past: Nationalism, Revolution, and the Collapse of the Soviet Union* (Stanford, CA: Stanford University Press, 1993), 84-126; Gerhard Simon, *Nationalismus und Nationalitätenpolitik in der Sowjetunion: Von der totalitären Diktatur zur nachstalinistischen Gesellschaft* (Baden-Baden: Nomos, 1986), 34-82.

35. Hirsch, *Empire of Nations*; Martin, *Affirmative Action Empire*; Juliette Cadiot, "Kak uporiadochivali raznoobrazie: Spiski i klassifikatsii natsional'nostei v Rossiiskoi imperii i v Sovetskom soiuze, 1897-1939 gg.," *Ab Imperio*, no. 4 (2001): 177-206.

36. Hirsch, *Empire of Nations*, 14.

37. Anssi Paasi, *Territories, Boundaries and Consciousness: The Changing Geographies of the Finnish-Russian Border* (Chichester, UK: John Wiley and Sons, 1996); Mathijs Pelkmans, *Defending the Border: Identity, Religion, and Modernity in the Republic of Georgia* (Ithaca, NY: Cornell University Press, 2006); Sabine Dullin, *La frontière épaisse: Aux origines des politiques soviétique, 1920–1940* (Paris: EHESS, 2014); Aleksandr Rupasov and Aleksandr Chistikov, *Sovetsko-finliandskaia granitsa, 1918–1938 gg: Ocherki istorii* (St. Petersburg: Avrora, 2016); Sören Urbansky, *Beyond the Steppe Frontier: A History of the Sino-Russian Border* (Princeton, NJ: Princeton University Press, 2020).

38. Arne Haugen, *The Establishment of National Republics in Soviet Central Asia* (New York: Palgrave Macmillan, 2003), 235-37; Adrienne Lynn Edgar, *Tribal Nation: The Making of Soviet Turkmenistan* (Princeton, NJ: Princeton University Press, 2004), 46-47; Adeeb Khalid, *Making Uzbekistan: Nation, Empire, and*

Revolution in the Early USSR (Ithaca, NY: Cornell University Press, 2015), 369; Arsène Saparov, *From Conflict to Autonomy in the Caucasus: The Soviet Union and the Making of Abkhazia, South Ossetia and Nagorno Karabakh* (London: Routledge, 2015), 137; Nick Baron, *Soviet Karelia: Politics, Planning, and Terror in Stalin's Russia, 1920–1939* (New York: Routledge, 2004), 48; Alexandr Voronovici, "Overlapping Spaces: Negotiating and Delineating the Ukrainian-Moldovan Border during the Interwar and Wartime Years," in *Making Ukraine*, 210-37.

39. For Ukraine, see Hennadii Yefimenko, "Vyznachennia kordonu mizh USRR ta RSFRR," *Problemy istoriï Ukraïny* 20 (2011): 135-76; Vasyl' Boyechko, Oksana Hanzha, and Borys Zacharchuk, *Kordony Ukraïny: Istorychna retrospektyva ta suchasnyi stan* (Kiev: Osnovy, 1994); and Vasyl' Boyechko, Oksana Hanzha, and Borys Zacharchuk, *Formuvannia derzhavnykh kordoniv Ukraïny, 1917–1940 rr.* (Kiev: AN USRR, 1991). For Belarus, see Sergei Khomich, *Territoriia i gosudarstvennye granitsy Belarusi v XX veke: Ot nezavershennoi etnicheskoi samoidentifikatsii i vneshnepoliticheskogo proizvola k sovremennomu "status quo"* (Minsk: Ekonompress, 2011). For Georgia, see Nat'ela Mirianašvili, *sak'art'velos teritoriuli c'vlilebani amierkavkasiis respublikebt'an, 1918–1938 cc.* (Tbilisi: universali, 2012). For Armenia, see Karen Xač'atryan, Hamo Suk'iasyan, and Gegam Badalyan, *Xorhrdayan Hayastani ev lġin-i tarack'ayin korustnerë 1920–1930-akan t'vakannerin* (Yerevan: HHGAA, 2015).

40. Haugen, *Central Asia*, 209.

41. Hirsch, *Empire of Nations*, 7; Cadiot, *Laboratoire impérial*, 209-10; Khalid, *Making Uzbekistan*, 270.

42. Christian Teichmann, *Macht der Unordnung: Stalins Herrschaft in Zentralasien, 1920–1950* (Hamburg: Hamburger Edition, 2016), 243; Fedtke, *Roter Orient*, 417; Adeeb Khalid, "Nationalizing the Revolution in Central Asia: The Transformation of Jadidism, 1917–1920," in *A State of Nations: Empire and Nation-Making in the Age of Lenin and Stalin*, ed. Ronald G. Suny and Terry Martin (Oxford: Oxford University Press, 2001), 156-59.

43. Konstantin Egorov, "Printsip federatsii, samoopredeleniie narodnosti i ekonomicheskoe raionirovanie" (The principle of federation, self-determination, and economic raionirovanie), 22 May 1922, GA RF, f. 5677, op. 4, d. 15, l. 92; Vladimir Dosov's comment on Yegorov's presentation, 15 May 1926, Arkhiv Rossiiskoi akademii nauk (ARAN), f. 350, op. 2, d. 74, l. 67.

44. Yurii Andropov reminded his audience on the occasion of the USSR's sixtieth anniversary that the nationality question was of utmost importance for the functioning of the state ("Shest'desiat let SSSR," in *Izbrannye rechi i stat'ia* [Moscow: Izdatel'stvo politicheskoi literatury, 1983], 5–19).

45. This is my suggestion for operationalizing these terms. See also Leif Jerram, "Space: A Useless Category of Historical Analysis," *History and Theory* 52, no. 3 (2013): 419.

46. For further reading on space, territory, and territorialization, see Charles S. Maier, "Consigning the Twentieth Century to History: Alternative Narratives for the Modern Era," *American Historical Review* 105, no. 3 (2000): 808; Henri Lefebvre, *La production de l'espace*, 4th ed. (Paris: Anthropos, 2000), 35-57; Karl Schlögel, *Im Raume lesen wir die Zeit: Über Zivilisationsgeschichte und Geopolitik* (Munich: Carl Hanser, 2003), 393; David Delaney, *Territory: A Short Introduction*

(Malden, MA: Blackwell, 2005), 10–16; Nick Baron, "New Spatial Histories of 20th-Century Russia and the Soviet Union: Exploring the Terrain," *Kritika: Explorations in Russian and Eurasian History* 9, no. 2 (2008): 433–47; Charles S. Maier, *Once within Borders: Territories of Power, Wealth, and Belonging since 1500* (Cambridge, MA: Harvard University Press, 2015), 6–8; Agnes Laba, *Die Grenze im Blick: Der Ostgrenzendiskurs der Weimarer Republik* (Marburg: Verlag Herder-Institut, 2019), 19–27; Goetz Herrmann and Andreas Vasilache, "Grenze, Staat und Staatlichkeit," in *Grenzforschung: Handbuch für Wissenschaft und Studium*, ed. Dominik Gerst, Maria Klessmann, and Hannes Krämer (Baden-Baden: Nomos, 2021), 68–88.

47. On the notion of USSR as a façade federation see, e.g., Claire Mouradian, *L'Arménie*, 5th ed. (Paris: Presses universitaires de France, 2013), 71; Richard Pipes, *The Formation of the Soviet Union: Communism and Nationalism 1917–1923*, 3rd ed. (Cambridge, MA: Harvard University Press, 1997), vii; and Suny and Kivelson, *Russia's Empires*, 396.

48. David Newman, "Boundaries," in *A Companion to Political Geography*, ed. John Agnew et al. (Malden, MA: Blackwell, 2008), 126; Dominik Gerst and Hannes Krämer, "Methodologie der Grenzforschung," in *Grenzforschung*, 124–25. On the older "essentialist" ideas, see Friedrich Ratzel, *Politische Geographie* (Munich: Oldenbourg, 1897), 9–14, 471–95.

49. Stephan Rindlisbacher, "From Space to Territory: Negotiating the Russo-Ukrainian Border, 1919–1928," *Revolutionary Russia* 31, no. 1 (2018): 99–100.

50. Laura Di Fiore, "The Production of Borders in Nineteenth-Century Europe: Between Institutional Boundaries and Transnational Practices of Space," *European Review of History* 24, no. 1 (2017): 41. See also Nick Baron, Luminita Gatejel, and Stephan Rindlisbacher, "'Drawing the Line': Border Commissions in Eastern Europe," *Journal of Modern European History* 22, no. 1 (2024): 3–5.

51. Peter Haslinger, "Dilemmas of Security: The State, Local Agency, and the Czechoslovak-Hungarian Boundary Commission, 1921–25," *Austrian History Yearbook* 46 (2018): 193–200; Catherine Gibson, *Geographies of Nationhood: Cartography, Science, and Society in the Russian Imperial Baltic* (Oxford: Oxford University Press, 2022), 176–216.

52. Jacobo García-Álvarez and Paloma Puente-Lozano, "Recent Geohistorical Research on Boundarymaking: Challenging Conventional Narratives on Borders and Modern State-Building," *Geography Compass* 16, no. 1 (2022): 3.

53. Krista A. Goff, *Nested Nationalism: Making and Unmaking Nations in the South Caucasus* (Ithaca, NY: Cornell University Press, 2020), 161–66.

1. The Leninian Moment

1. Sergei Vvedenskii, "Ob izmenenii granitsy Kurskoi gubernii s Ukrainy," 1924, GA RF, f. 5677, op. 5, d. 29, l. 101.

2. The regions of Julian March and Dalmatia are only one example. See Marina Cattaruzza, *Italy and Its Eastern Border, 1866–2016* (New York: Routledge, 2016).

3. Mark E. Blum and William Smaldone, introduction to *Austro-Marxism: The Ideology of Unity* (Leiden: Brill, 2016), 1:10–12; Börries Kuzmany, Matthias Battis, and Oskar Mulej, "Accommodating National Diversity within States: Territorial and Non-Territorial Approaches since the Late 19th Century," *Nationality Papers* 50, no. 5 (2022): 851–52.

4. Otto Bauer, *Die Nationalitätenfrage und die Sozialdemokratie* (Vienna: Ignaz Brand, 1907), 510–19.

5. Iosif Stalin [Dzhugashvili], "Marksizm i natsional'nyi vopros," in his *Sochineniia* (Moscow: Gosudarstvennoe izdatel'stvo politicheskoi literatury, 1954), 2:296, 362–67. In proposing such an essentialist idea, Stalin excluded, for instance, the Jews from being a nationality, as they did not represent a majority of the population anywhere (except in the shtetl) and thus had no "territory."

6. Roni Gechtman, "A 'Museum of Bad Taste'? The Jewish Labour Bund and the Bolshevik Position Regarding the National Question, 1903–14," *Canadian Journal of History* 43, no. 1 (2008): 49–50.

7. Bauer, *Nationalitätenfrage*, 22–23.

8. Stephen J. Blank, *The Sorcerer as Apprentice: Stalin as Commissar of Nationalities, 1917–1924* (Westport, CT: Greenwood, 1994), 8.

9. Lenin, "Tezisy po natsional'nomu voprosu," in *PSS*, 23:314–21; Lenin, "O prave natsii na samoopredelenie," in *PSS*, 25:255–320; Lenin, "Revoliutsionnyi proletariat i parvo natsii o samoopredelenii," in *PSS*, 27:61–68; Lenin, "Chto delat'?," in *PSS*, 6:117–20.

10. Lenin, "Nuzhen li obiazatel'nyi gosudarstvennyi iazyk?," in *PSS*, 24:295.

11. Lenin, "K voprosu o natsional'nostiakh ili ob 'avtonomizatsii,'" in *PSS*, 45:356–62.

12. Jesse Kauffman, *Elusive Alliance: The German Occupation of Poland in World War I* (Cambridge, MA: Harvard University Press, 2015), 106–40.

13. Woodrow Wilson, *Essential Writings and Speeches of the Scholar-President*, ed. Mario R. DiNunzio (New York: New York University Press, 2006), 403–7; Xosé M. Núñez Seixas, "Wilson's Unexpected Friends: The Transnational Impact of the First World War on Western European Nationalist Movements," in *The First World War and the Nationality Question in Europe: Global Impact and Local Dynamics*, ed. Xosé M. Núñez Seixas (Leiden: Brill, 2021), 37–64.

14. Erez, *Wilsonian Moment*, 6; Larry Wolff, *Woodrow Wilson and the Reimagining of Eastern Europe* (Stanford, CA: Stanford University Press, 2020), 5–6, 238–39; Smith, *Sovereignty*, 10; Núñez Seixas, introduction to *First World War*, 1.

15. Suny, *Red Flag Unfurled*, 86–87.

16. Adeeb Khalid underlines this synchronicity in *Central Asia: A New History from the Imperial Conquests to the Present* (Princeton, NJ: Princeton University Press, 2021), 168.

17. Omer Bartov and Eric D. Weitz, eds., *Shatterzone of Empires: Coexistence and Violence in the German, Habsburg, Russian, and Ottoman Borderlands* (Bloomington: Indiana University Press, 2015).

18. Erez, *Wilsonian Moment*, 56–61; Wolff, *Woodrow Wilson*, 168–227; Smith, *Sovereignty*, 102–42. John Connelly highlights the agency of the East Europeans

in these bordering processes: *From Peoples into Nations: A History of Eastern Europe* (Princeton, NJ: Princeton University Press, 2020), 360-61.

19. Górny, *Vaterlandszeichner*, 97-129.

20. Carole Fink, *Defending the Rights of Others: The Great Powers, the Jews, and International Minority Protection, 1878-1938* (Cambridge: Cambridge University Press, 2004), 133-61.

21. Róbert Keményfi, "Grenzen-Karten-Ethnien: Kartenartige Konstituierungsmittel im Dienst des ungarischen nationalen Raumes," in *Osteuropa kartiert: Mapping Eastern Europe*, ed. Jörn Happel and Christophe von Werdt (Berlin: Lit, 2010), 210-11; Górny, *Vaterlandszeichner*, 125-26.

22. Brendan Karch, "Plebiscites and Postwar Legitimacy," in *Beyond Versailles: Sovereignty, Legitimacy, and the Formation of New Polities after the Great War*, ed. Marcus M. Payk and Roberta Pergher (Bloomington: Indiana University Press, 2019), 16-37; Thomas Mack Barker and Andreas Moritsch, *The Slovene Minority of Carinthia* (New York: Columbia University Press, 1984), 146-71; Nina Jebsen and Martin Klatt, "The Negotiation of National and Regional Identity during the Schleswig-Plebiscite Following the First World War," *First World War Studies* 5, no. 2 (2014): 181-211.

23. Alan Sharp, *The Versailles Settlement: Peacemaking after the First World War, 1919-1923*, 3rd ed. (London: Palgrave MacMillan 2018), 160-63.

24. Marina Cattaruzza, "The Making and Remaking of a Boundary: The Redrafting of the Eastern Border of Italy after the Two World Wars," *Journal of Modern European History* 9, no. 1 (2011): 67-75; Peter Haslinger, *Der ungarische Revisionismus und das Burgenland, 1922-1932* (Frankfurt am Main: Peter Lang, 1994), 37-43, 193; Isabelle Davion, "Teschen and Its Impossible Plebiscite: Can the Genie Be Put Back in the Bottle?," in Payk and Pergher, *Beyond Versailles*, 38-58.

25. Smith, *National Question*, 2-3; Per Anders Rudling, *The Rise and Fall of Belarusian Nationalism, 1906-1931* (Pittsburgh: University of Pittsburgh Press, 2015), 73-76; Fabian Baumann, *Dynasty Divided: A Family History of Russian and Ukrainian Nationalism* (Ithaca, NY: Cornell University Press, 2023), 162-204; Etienne Peyrat, *Histoire du Caucase au XXe siècle* (Paris: Fayard, 2020), 77-82; Richard G. Hovannisian, *The Republic of Armenia* (Berkeley: University of California Press, 1971), 1:70-78; Tomohiko Uyama, "The Alash Orda's Relations with Siberia, the Urals, and Turkestan: The Kazakh National Movement and the Russian Imperial Legacy," in *Asiatic Russia: Imperial Power in Regional and International Contexts*, ed. Tomohiko Uyama (London: Routledge, 2012), 271-87; Khalid, *Making Uzbekistan*, 57-65.

26. Declaration of the Rights of the Peoples in Russia (signed by Stalin and Lenin), 2 November 1917 (15 November 1917, New Style), Rossiiskii gosudarstvennyi arkhiv sotsial'no-politicheskoi istorii (RGASPI), f. 2, op. 1, d. 24219, ll. 1-2.

27. Yuri Slezkine, "The USSR as a Communal Apartment, or How a Socialist State Promoted Ethnic Particularism," *Slavic Review* 53, no. 2 (1994): 420-21.

28. Timothy K. Blauvelt, "Ideology Meets Practice in the Struggle for the Transcaucasus: Stepan Shaumyan and the Evolution of Bolshevik Nationality Policy," *Caucasus Survey* 8, no. 1 (2020): 90.

29. Jon Smele, *The "Russian" Civil Wars, 1916–1926: Ten Years That Shook the World* (London: Hurst and Co., 2015).
30. Hirsch, *Empire of Nations*, 6–7.
31. Lesley Chamberlain, *Lenin's Private War: The Voyage of the Philosophy Steamer and the Exile of the Intelligentsia* (New York: St. Martin's, 2007), 100–130.
32. Institut Marksizma-Leninizma pri TsK KPSS, ed., *Vtoroi s"ezd RSDRP, iiul'–avgust 1903 goda: Protokoly* (Moscow: Gosizdat, 1959), 421.
33. Stalin, "Kontrrevoliutsiia i narody Rossii," *Proletarii*, 13 August 1917 (26 August 1917, New Style), reprinted in *Revoliutsionnoe dvizhenie v Rossii v avguste 1917 g.: Razgrom kornilovskogo miatezha*, ed. D. Chugaev, P. Avvakumov, and S. Gaponenko (Moscow: AN SSSR, 1959), 345–47.
34. Paul Werth, *How Russia Got Big: A Territorial History* (London: Bloomsbury, 2025).
35. Slezkine, "Communal Apartment," 434–35.
36. Iosif Vareikis, "Novyi etap natsional'nogo stroitel'stva v Srednei Azii," in *Natsional'no-gosudarstvennoe razmezhevanie Srednei Azii*, ed. Isaak Zelenskii and Iosif Vareikis (Tashkent: Sredniaia Aziia, 1924), 59; Slezkine, "Communal Apartment," 415.
37. Declaration on the Rights of the Working and Exploited People, 13 January 1918 (26 January 1918, New Style), in Upravlenie delami Sovnarkoma SSSR, *Sobranie uzakonenii i razporiazhenii pravitel'stva za 1917–1918 gg.* (Moscow, 1942), 234.
38. Lenin, "O nashei revoliutsii: Po povodu zapisok N. Sukhanova," in *PSS*, 45:381.
39. Lara Douds, *Inside Lenin's Government: Ideology, Power and Practice in the Early Soviet State* (London: Bloomsbury, 2018), 169.
40. Douds, *Inside Lenin's Government*, 96, 149–50.
41. Section 8 of the 1918 RSFSR constitution, in *Ocherk istorii sovetskoi konstitutsii*, ed. Yu. Kukushkin and O. Chistiakov (Moscow: Politizdat, 1987), 242.
42. Institut Marksizma-Leninizma pri TsK KPSS, *Vos'moi s"ezd RKP(b), mart 1919 goda: Protokoly* (Moscow: Gosudarstvennoe izdatel'stvo politicheskoi literatury, 1959), 46–47.
43. Smith, *National Question*, 31–34; Blank, *Sorcerer as Apprentice*, 99–100; Slezkine, "Communal Apartment," 422.
44. Cadiot, *Laboratoire impérial*, 128–29.
45. On the idea of a census as tool of governance, see David W. Darrow, "Census as a Technology of Empire," *Ab Imperio*, no. 4 (2002): 145–47.
46. Khalid, *Central Asia*, 161–62.
47. Marko [Marco] Buttino, *Revoliutsiia naoborot: Sredniaia Aziia mezhdu padeniem tsarskoi imperii i obrazovaniem SSSR* (Moscow: Zven'ia, 2007), 271–80; Khalid, "Nationalizing the Revolution," 146–47; Fedtke, *Roter Orient*, 276–83, 311–12.
48. Smith, *Bolsheviks and the National Question*, 47.
49. Daniel E. Schafer, "Local Politics and the Birth of the Republic of Bashkortostan, 1919–1920," in Suny and Martin, *State of Nations*, 165–90; Smele, *"Russian" Civil Wars*, 49–50; Smith, *Bolsheviks and the National Question*, 47–48,

94–98; Norihiro Naganawa, "Tatars and Imperialist Wars: From the Tsar's Servitors to the Red Warriors," *Ab Imperio*, no. 1 (2020): 191–95.

50. "Protokol no. 25 ob"edinënnogo zasedaniia Kraikoma, Kraimusbiuro i Komiteta inostrannykh kommunistov KPT i predstavitelei Turkkomissii po voprosu ob avtonomii Turkestana," 17 January 1920, in *Rossiia i Tsentral'naia Aziia: Konets XIX–nachalo XX veka. Sbornik dokumentov i materialov*, ed. Dina Amanzholova, T. Dalaeva, and G. Sultangalieva (Moscow: Novyi khronograf, 2017), 322.

51. Jörg Baberowski, *Der Feind ist überall: Stalinismus im Kaukasus* (Munich: Deutsche Verlags-Anstalt, 2003), 250–52; Khalid, *Central Asia*, 172–74; Iurii Demin, "The Bolsheviks and the Soviet Socialist Republic of Iran, 1920–21: Moscow's Politics and the Ambitions of Regional and Local Political Actors," *Kritika: Explorations in Russian and Eurasian History* 25, no. 2 (2024): 273–98.

52. Fedtke, *Roter Orient*, 16; Khalid, "Nationalizing the Revolution," 156.

53. A. Adigamov, "Zaiavlenie Bashrevkoma po voprosu o Tatarskoi Respublike," *Zhizn' natsional'nostei*, no. 5/61 (1920): 2.

54. Smith, *Bolsheviks and the National Question*, 93–94; Marina Cattaruzza, "Das nationale Problem der Sozialdemokratie und der internationalen kommunistischen Bewegung, 1889–1953," in *Die Moderne und ihre Krisen: Studien von Marina Cattaruzza zur europäischen Geschichte des 19. und 20. Jahrhunderts*, ed. Sacha Zala (Göttingen: V&R unipress, 2012), 249–50; Blank, *Sorcerer as Apprentice*, 22–29; for an example, see G. Skalov, "Ekonomicheskoe ob"edinenie sr.-aziatskikh respublik kak faktor natsional'noi politiki," *Zhizn' natsional'nostei*, no. 5 (1923): 40–45.

55. Mikhail Vladimirskii, *Organizatsiia Sovetskoi vlasti na mestakh* (Moscow: Gosizdat, 1919), 7–9, 52–54.

56. Konstantin Egorov, *Raionirovanie SSSR: Sbornik materialov po raionirovaniiu s 1917 po 1925 god* (Moscow: Planovoe khoziaistvo, 1926), 50–52; Vladimir Kruglov, *Organizatsiia territorii Rossii v 1917–2007 gg.: Idei, praktika, rezul'taty* (Moscow: IRI RAN, 2020), 57–58.

57. Smith, *Bolsheviks and the National Question*, 51–52; Stalin, "Politika sovetskoi vlasti po natsional'nomu voprosu v Rossii," in *Sochineniia*, 4:351–63.

58. Institut Marksizma-Leninizma pri TsK KPSS, *Voz'moi s"ezd RKP(b)*, 425.

59. Blank, *Sorcerer as Apprentice*, 52–53, 208–9.

60. On the Turkbiuro and its successor institution, the Sredazbiuro, see Shoshana Keller, "The Central Asian Bureau, an Essential Tool in Governing Soviet Turkestan," *Central Asian Survey* 22, no. 2/3 (2003): 281–97; and Fedtke, *Roter Orient*, 294–312.

61. Smith, *Bolsheviks and the National Question*, 184; Khalid, *Central Asia*, 177.

62. Manuïl's'kyi, Letter to Stalin, 2 September 1922, in *TsK RKP(b)-VKP(b) i natsional'nyi vopros*, ed. L. Gatagova, L. Kosheleva, and L. Rogovaia (Moscow: Rosspen, 2005), 1:76–77.

63. Stalin, Letter to Lenin, 22 September 1922, in *TsK RKP(b)-VKP(b)*, 1:78.

64. Stalin, Letter to Lenin, 22 September 1922, in *TsK RKP(b)-VKP(b)*, 1:78.

65. Lenin, Letter to Lev Kamenev, 26 September 1922, in *PSS*, 45:212, italics in the original.

66. Stephen J. Blank, "The Transcaucasian Federation and the Origins of the Soviet Union, 1921-1922," *Central Asian Survey* 9, no. 4 (1990): 36-37.

67. Blank, "Transcaucasian Federation," 48.

68. Jeremy Smith, "The Georgian Affair of 1922: Policy Failure, Personality Clash or Power Struggle?," *Europe-Asia Studies* 50, no. 3 (1998): 519-44; Segvard Kharmandarian, *Lenin i stanovlenie Zakavkazskoi Federatsii, 1921-1923* (Yerevan: Aiastan, 1969), 347-71; Stephen F. Jones, "The Establishment of Soviet Power in Transcaucasia: The Case of Georgia, 1921-1928," *Soviet Studies* 40, no. 4 (1988): 631-32; Stephen Kotkin, *Stalin*, 3 vols. (London: Allen Lane, 2014), 1:477-81.

69. Smith, *Bolsheviks and the National Question*, 202-5; Pipes, *Formation of the Soviet Union*, 269-81; Simon, *Nationalismus*, 37; Blank, "Transcaucasian Federation," 51-52.

70. Lenin, "K voprosu o natsional'nostiakh," in *PSS*, 45:356-62.

71. Smith, *Bolsheviks and the National Question*, 187-88.

72. Smith, *Bolsheviks and the National Question*, 237; this distinction became even more striking after Stalin's ascent to power (Martin, *Affirmative Action Empire*, 356-62).

73. Institut Marksizma-Leninizma pri TsK KPSS, *Dvenadtsatyi s"ezd RKP(b), 17-25 aprelia 1923: Stenograficheskii otchet* (Moscow: Politizdat, 1968), 691-97; Martin, *Affirmative Action Empire*, 19-20, 75, 274-76; Hirsch, *Empire of Nations*, 94-98.

74. George Liber, "Korenizatsiia: Restructuring Soviet Nationality Policy in the 1920s," *Ethnic and Racial Studies* 14, no. 1 (1991): 15-23; Cadiot, *Laboratoire imperial*, 134-38; Baberowski, *Feind ist überall*, 316-19.

75. B. F. Sultanbekov, ed., *Tainy natsional'noi politiki TsK RKP: Chetvertoe soveshchanie TsK RKP s otvetstvennymi rabotnikami natsional'nykh respublik i oblastei v g. Moskve 9-12 iiunia 1923 g. Stenograficheskii otchet* (Moscow: Insan, 1992), 4-9; Blank, *Sorcerer as Apprentice*, 188-89.

76. Kotkin, *Stalin*, 1:497.

77. Stalin, Concluding address at the Fourth Convention of the TsK RKP(b) with distinguished party activists from the national republics and oblasti, 12 June 1923, in Sultanbekov, *Tainy natsional'noi politiki*, 260.

78. Sultanbekov, *Tainy natsional'noi politiki*, 265.

79. Sultanbekov, *Tainy natsional'noi politiki*, 262.

80. Khalid, *Central Asia*, 177.

81. Shorthand notes of the enlarged commission of the TsIK SSSR to draft the constitution for the USSR, 14 April 1923, in *TsK RKP(b)-VKP(b)*, 1:120-24; sections 1b and 6 of the 1924 constitution, in *Ocherk istorii*, 266-68.

82. Kruglov, *Organizatsiia territorii*, 114.

83. Martin, *Affirmative Action Empire*, 33-41; Cadiot, "Kak uporiadochivali raznoobrazie," 186-87; Stephan Rindlisbacher and Frank Grelka, introduction to *"Our Work with the Masses Is Not Worth a Kopeck . . .": A Document Collection on German and Polish Rural Soviets in Ukraine during the NEP, 1923-1929* (Wiesbaden: Harrassowitz, 2021), 26.

84. Tsentral'ne statystychne upravlinnia USRR, *Natsional'nyi sklad sil's'koho naselennia Ukraïny* (Kharkiv: TsSU USRR, 1927), 198; Cadiot, *Laboratoire impérial*, 132-34.

85. "Protokol zasedaniia TsK RKP(b) po voprosu o vydelenii Chechni iz sostava Gorskoi Respubliki, 22 October 1922," in *TsK RKP(b)-VKP(b)*, 1:88–89; Jeronim Perović, *Der Nordkaukasus unter russischer Herrschaft: Geschichte einer Vielvölkerregion zwischen Rebellion und Anpassung* (Cologne: Böhlau, 2015), 242–52.

86. Liudmyla Hutsalo, "Reformuvannia ta likvidatsiia natsional'nykh administratyvnykh odynyts'," *Visnyk Akedemii pratsi i sotsial'nykh vidnosyn Federatsii profsilok Ukrainy*, no. 5 (2005): 148–49.

87. Malte Rolf, "Nationalizing an Empire: The Bolsheviks, the Nationality Question, and Policies of Indigenization in the Soviet Union, 1917-1927," in Núñez Seixas, *First World War*, 78–79.

88. Blank, *Sorcerer as Apprentice*, 86–87.

89. Martin, *Affirmative Action Empire*, 356–57; Slezkine, "Communal Apartment," 434; Lieven, *Empire*, 290.

90. For further discussion on this metaphor, see Schenk, "'Sixth Part of the World.'"

2. Gosplan

1. Minutes of the ninety-first meeting of the Section for Raionirovanie, 1 June 1922, Rossiiskii gosudarstvennyi arkhiv ekonomiki (RGAE), f. 4372, op. 15, d. 63, l. 87. The State General Planning Commission was founded in 1921 as a temporary adjunct to the Council of Labor and Defense (STO) but was soon institutionalized. Two years later, its name was shortened to State Planning Commission. Though the emergence of Gosplan is crucial to understanding the early Soviet state, there have been only a few monographs on the subject—most of which are now rather old: see Mark R. Beissinger, *Scientific Management, Socialist Discipline and Soviet Power* (London: Tauris, 1988); Michael Ellman, *Socialist Planning*, 3rd ed. (Cambridge: Cambridge University Press, 2014); Heiko Haumann, *Beginn der Planwirtschaft: Elektrifizierung, Wirtschaftsplanung und gesellschaftliche Entwicklung Sowjetrusslands, 1917–1921* (Düsseldorf: Bertelsmann, 1974); Alec Nove, *An Economic History of the USSR, 1917–1991* (London: Penguin, 1992); and Eugène Zaleski and Marie-Christine MacAndrew, *Planning for Economic Growth in the Soviet Union, 1918–1932* (Chapel Hill: University of North Carolina Press, 1971).

2. Ol'ga Sukhova and Ol'ga Filenkova, "Natsional'nyi vopros i raionirovanie v RSFSR v 1920-e–nachale 1930-kh godov: Upravlencheskie strategii i ikh realizatsiia. Po materialam Povolzh'ia," *Noveishaia istoriia Rossii*, no. 1 (2017): 66.

3. Blank, *Sorcerer as Apprentice*, 160–62; Perović, *Nordkaukasus*, 344–45; Stephen Velychenko, *Painting Imperialism and Nationalism Red: The Ukrainian Marxist Critique of Russian Communist Rule in Ukraine, 1918–1925* (Toronto: University of Toronto Press, 2015), 13–14.

4. Simon, *Nationalismus*, 34–40; Pipes, *Formation of the Soviet Union*, 269–81.

5. Hirsch, *Empire of Nations*, 82. Hirsch dedicated the second chapter of her book (62–98) to the debate on regionalization (*raionirovanie*) between Narkomnats and Gosplan; see also Slezkine, "Communal Apartment," 427; and Blank, *Sorcerer as Apprentice*, 82–85.

6. Section for Raionirovanie, Minutes of the sixth session, 24 January 1923, RGAE, f. 4372, op. 15, d. 137b, l. 7.

7. Konstantin Egorov, "Avtobiograficheskie materialy" (Autobiographical materials), 15 November 1954, RGAE, f. 634, op. 1, d. 41, l. 1.

8. Alun Thomas, *Nomads and Soviet Rule: Central Asia under Lenin and Stalin* (London: Tauris, 2018), 43.

9. On experts in the West, see Górny, *Vaterlandszeichner*, 113.

10. "Regionalization" (regional scale) or "districtization" (district scale) are the literal translations of the Russian term *raionirovanie*, however "territorialization" would combine both aspects.

11. Shorthand notes of the first session of the Commission for Raionirovanie (Komissiia po raionirovaniu SSSR) at the TsIK, 14 November 1925, GA RF, f. 6892, op. 1, d. 40, ll. 10–11; Boris Knipovich, *Metodologiia raionirovaniia* (Moscow: Gosizdat, 1921), 5–8.

12. Mikhail Vladimirskii, "Osnovnye momenty ekonomicheskogo raionirovaniia" (Considerations on economic raionirovanie), 13 February 1928, ARAN, f. 350, op. 2, d. 250, ll. 14–15.

13. Nailya Tagirova, "Mapping the Empire's Economic Regions from the Nineteenth to the Early Twentieth Century," in *Russian Empire: Space, People, Power, 1700–1930*, ed. Jane Burbank, Mark von Hagen, and Anatolyi Remnev (Bloomington: Indiana University Press, 2007), 128–31; Marina Loskutova, "Regionalisation, Imperial Legacy, and the Soviet Geographical Tradition," in *Empire De/Centered: New Spatial Histories of Russia and the Soviet Union*, ed. Sanna Turoma and Maxim Waldstein (Farnham, UK: Ashgate, 2013), 136–37.

14. Nick Baron, "The Mapping of Illiberal Modernity: Spatial Science, Ideology and the State in Early Twentieth-Century Russia," in *Empire De/Centered*, 111–13; Tagirova, "Mapping," 131–32.

15. Tagirova, "Mapping," 131.

16. Tagirova, "Mapping," 133.

17. Loskutova, "Regionalisation," 140.

18. See also the compilation of the most influential prerevolutionary concepts on raionirovanie in Knipovich, *Metodologiia raionirovaniia*, maps 1–17.

19. Ol'ga Shul'gina, "Administrativno-territorial'noe delenie Rossii v XX veke: Istoriko-geograficheskii aspekt" (diss., MGPU, Moscow, 2005), abstract, 20–21; Boris Knipovich, Presentation on methods to organize agricultural raiony, 26 March 1921, RGAE, f. 4372, op. 15, d. 2, ll. 14–17; Lenin, "Tezisy po natsional'nomu voprosu," 23:317.

20. Baron, "Mapping of Illiberal Modernity," 116–19.

21. Walter Christaller, "Wie ich zu der Theorie der zentralen Orte gekommen bin: Ein Bericht, wie eine Theorie entstehen kann, und in meinem Fall entstanden ist," *Geographische Zeitschrift* 56, no. 2 (1968): 93; on the reception of Christaller's model, see Karl R. Kegler, *Deutsche Raumplanung: Das Modell der 'zentralen Orte' zwischen NS-Staat und Bundesrepublik* (Paderborn: Schöningh, 2015).

22. Walter Christaller, *Die zentralen Orte in Süddeutschland: Eine ökonomisch-geographische Untersuchung über die Gesetzmässigkeit der Verbreitung und Entwicklung der Siedlungen mit städtischen Funktionen* (Jena: Fischer, 1933).

23. Sovnarkom, decree of 18 January 1918, GA RF, f. 5677, op. 4, d. 1, l. 2.

24. Commentary on Sovnarkom's decree of 18 January 1918, GA RF, f. 5677, op. 4, d. 1, l. 8.

25. Circulars of the AK VTsIK, 1920-1921, GA RF, f. 5677, op. 4, d. 1, ll. 36, 41, 50, 61, 121, 132.

26. Nikolai Bukharin and Yevgenii Preobrazhenskii, *Azbuka kommunizma* (Petrograd: Gosizdat, 1920), § 47.

27. Lenin, "O 'levom' rebiachestve i o melkoburzhuaznosti," in *PSS*, 36:300-301; Friedrich Asschenfeldt and Max Trecker, "From Ludendorff to Lenin? World War I and the Origins of Soviet Economic Planning," *Europe-Asia Studies* 76, no. 1 (2024): 10-28.

28. On spatial legibility and illegibility, see James C. Scott, *Seeing Like a State: How Certain Schemes to Improve the Human Condition Have Failed* (New Haven: Yale University Press, 1998), 11-52; William Rankin, *After the Map: Cartography, Navigation, and the Transformation of Territory in the Twentieth Century* (Chicago: University of Chicago Press, 2016), 15; and Martin Jeske, *Ein Imperium wird vermessen: Kartographie, Kulturtransfer und Raumerschließung im Zarenreich, 1797-1919* (Berlin: De Gruyter, 2023), 45. See also Darrow, "Census as a Technology," 145-47; and Konstantin Egorov, "V. I. Lenin o sotsialisticheskom raionirovanii" (V. I. Lenin on socialist raionirovanie), around 1954, RGAE, f. 634, op. 1, d. 2, ll. 2-4.

29. Circular of the AK VTsIK, 12 January 1921, GA RF, f. 5677, op. 4, d. 1, ll. 52-60.

30. Hirsch, *Empire of Nations*, 21-24.

31. Manfred Hildermeier, *Geschichte der Sowjetunion, 1917-1991: Entstehung und Niedergang des ersten sozialistischen Staates* (Munich: C. H. Beck, 1998), 236; Nove, *Economic History*, 82-83, 93-95.

32. Douds, *Inside Lenin's Government*, 129-31.

33. GOELRO stands for Gosudarstvennaia komissiia po elektrifikatsii Rossii (State Commission for the Electrification of Russia).

34. On the GOELRO project, see G. Krzhizhanovskii, *Ob elektrifikatsii* (Moscow: Gosizdat, 1921); and Gosudarstvennaia komissiia po elektrifikatsii Rossii, *Plan elektrifikatsii RSFSR: Vvedenie k dokladu 8-mu s"ezdu sovetov* (Moscow: Gosudarstvennoe tekhnicheskoe izdatel'stvo, 1920).

35. Karl Schlögel, *Petersburg: Das Laboratorium der Moderne, 1909-1921* (Frankfurt am Main: Fischer, 2009), 370-73.

36. Ivan Aleksandrov, *Ekonomicheskoe raionirovanie Rossii* (Moscow: Tipografiia III Internatsional, 1921), 11-15; Konstantin Egorov, "Razvitie teorii sovetskogo ekonomicheskogo raionirovaniia v trudakh Gosplana" (The theoretical development of Soviet economic raionirovanie in Gosplan's studies), no date, RGAE, f. 634, op. 1, d. 5, ll. 133-34; Konstantin Egorov, "Razvitie teorii sovetskogo ekonomicheskogo raionirovaniia v trudakh prof. A. G. Aleksandrova" (The theoretical development of Soviet economic raionirovanie in Prof. A. G. Aleksandrov's studies)," no date, RGAE, f. 634, op. 1, d. 5, ll. 140-41; Minutes of the fifth session of the Section for Raionirovanie at Gosplan, 10 June 1921, RGAE, f. 4372, op. 15, d. 2, l. 42.

37. Konstantin Egorov, "Ekonomicheskoe raionirovanie i administrativnaia reforma RSFSR," *Vlast' sovetov*, no. 4-6 (1922): 25; I. Vechelovskii, On raionirovanie, 1922, RGAE, f. 4372, op. 15, d. 63, ll. 99-102.

38. E. P. Malysheva, "Administrativno-territorial'noe ustroistvo Svetskogo gosudarstva," in *Administrativno-territorial'noe ustroistvo Rossii*, 218; Circular from the VTsIK Administrative Territorial Commission, 24 January 1921, GA RF, f. 5677, op. 4, d. 1, l. 61.

39. Alan Ball, "Building a New State and Society: NEP, 1921-1928," in *The Cambridge History of Russia*, ed. Ronald G. Suny (New York, Cambridge University Press, 2006), 3:168-69; Lewis H. Siegelbaum, *Soviet State and Society between Revolutions, 1918-1929* (New York: Cambridge University Press, 1992), 83-84.

40. Nove, *Economic History*, 78-81.

41. Haumann, *Beginn der Planwirtschaft*, 109.

42. Even in 1924, members of the party leadership complained about the inconclusiveness of the existing demographic data; see Yan Rudzutak, Report on national delimitation of Central Asia to the TsK RKP(b), 26 October 1924, in *TsK RKP(b)-VKP(b)*, 1:246.

43. Map on the GOELRO plan, undated, RGAE, f. 634, op. 1, d. 7, l. 17; Ivan Aleksandrov, *Elektrifikatsiia i transport* (Rostov-na-Donu: Gosizdat, 1921), 4.

44. Vladimirskii, *Osnovnye polozheniia*, 8; Section for Raionirovanie, Minutes of the twelfth session, 22 July 1921, RGAE, f. 4372, op. 15, d. 2, ll. 65-70; Konstantin Egorov, "Natsional'noe razmezhevanie i ekonomicheskoe raionirovanie" (National delimitation and economic raionirovanie), 15 May 1926, ARAN, f. 350, op. 2, d. 74, l. 14; Vladimirskii, "Osnovnye momenty ekonomicheskogo raionirovaniia," ARAN, f. 350, op. 2, d. 250, l. 15; Afanasii [Panas] Butsenko, Report on raionirovanie in Ukraine, 1924, TsDAVO, f. 1, op. 2, spr. 1807, ark. 2-3.

45. Minutes of the Section for Raionirovanie, RGAE, f. 4372, op. 15, dd. 2, 63, 137b, 138b, 323.

46. Egorov, "Avtobiograficheskie materialy," RGAE, f. 634, op. 1, d. 41, l. 1.

47. Hirsch, *Empire of Nations*, 69; Sukhova and Filenkova, "Natsional'nyi vopros," 64.

48. Egorov, "Ekonomicheskoe raionirovanie," 25-26.

49. Section for Raionirovanie, Minutes of the twenty-eighth session, 10 April 1922, RGAE, f. 4372, op. 15, d. 63, ll. 140-38.

50. Gleb Krzhizhanovskii, introduction to *Voprosy ekonomicheskogo raionirovaniia SSSR: Sbornik materialov i statei, 1917-1929 gg.* (Moscow: Gosizdat, 1957), 6-7.

51. Map of the territorial units proposed by Gosplan, 6 January 1925, GA RF, f. 6892, op. 1, d. 49, ll. 5-6.

52. L. Hamilton Rhinelander, "The Creation of the Caucasian Vicegerency," *Slavonic and East European Review* 59, no.1 (1981): 15-40.

53. Mikhail Vladimirskii's address to the Section for Raionirovanie, 26 May 1921, RGAE, f. 4372, op. 15, d. 2, l. 1.

54. Vladimirskii's address to the Section for Raionirovanie, RGAE, f. 4372, op. 15, d. 2, l. 1.

55. Section for Raionirovanie, Minutes of the second session, 31 May 1921, RGAE, f. 4372, op. 15, d. 2, ll. 29–34. For further discussion on "mental maps," see F. Benjamin Schenk, "Mental Maps: Die Konstruktion von geographischen Räumen in Europa seit der Aufklärung," *Geschichte und Gesellschaft* 28, no. 3 (2002): 493–514.

56. Egorov, "Printsip federatsii," GA RF, f. 5677, op. 4, d. 15, ll. 94–95; Smith, *National Question*, 15.

57. Presidium of the Section for Raionirovanie, Minutes of the first session, 20 October 1921, RGAE, f. 4372, op. 15, d. 3, l. 3.

58. S. Korichev, "K voprosu ob ekonomicheskom raionirovanii RSFSR," *Zhizn' natsional'nostei*, no. 12/147 (1922): 4–5.

59. Hirsch, *Empire of Nations*, 78–79.

60. Egorov, "Ekonomicheskoe raionirovanie," 25–26; Egorov, *Raionirovanie SSSR*, 10–11; Egorov, "Printsip federatsii," GA RF, f. 5677, op. 4, d. 15, ll. 92–94.

61. Section for Raionirovanie, Minutes of the fourth session, 7 June 1921, RGAE, f. 4372, op. 15, d. 2, l. 41.

62. Egorov, *Raionirovanie SSSR*, 42–47; Pëtr Alampiev, *Ekonomicheskoe raionirovanie SSSR* (Moscow: Izdatel'stvo ekonomicheskoi literatury, 1959), 1:108–21.

63. Quoted according to Konstantin Egorov, "M. I. Kalinin o problemakh ekonomicheskogo raionirovaniia" (M. I. Kalinin on the problems of economic raionirovanie), 20 November 1958, RGAE, f. 634, op. 1, d. 2, l. 26.

64. Alampiev, *Ekonomicheskoe raionirovanie*, 1:129–30.

65. Institut Marksizma-Leninizma pri TsK KPSS, *Dvenadtsatyi s"ezd RKP(b)*, 697. See also Malysheva, "Administrativno-territorial'noe ustroistvo," 219–20.

66. Comments made by Tsagurian at the conference of the All-Union Commission for Raionirovanie, 14 November 1925, GA RF, f. 6892, op. 1, d. 40, ll. 15, 21.

67. Konstantin Egorov, *Ekonomika raionov SSSR: Po materialam raionnykh kontrol'nykh tsifr na 1927–1928 god* (Moscow: Gosizdat, 1928), 53.

68. Section for Raionirovanie, Minutes of the sixty-ninth session, 5 October 1922, RGAE, f. 4372, op. 15, d. 63, ll. 24–23; Section for Raionirovanie, Minutes of the seventieth session, 9 October 1922, RGAE, f. 4372, op. 15, d. 63, ll. 22–20; Egorov, *Raionirovanie SSSR*, 116–19; Konstantin Egorov, "Istoriia raionirovaniia" (History of raionirovanie), 1959, RGAE, f. 634, op. 1, d. 5, l. 425; Resolution of the All-Union Commission for Raionirovanie, 5 January 1926, GA RF, f. 6892, op. 1, d. 41, ll. 20–21; Ivan Aleksandrov, *Osnovy khoziaistvennogo raionirovaniia SSSR* (Moscow: Ekonomicheskaia zhizn', 1924), 63–64.

69. Egorov, *Ekonomika raionov SSSR*, 46–47.

70. Etienne Peyrat, "Soviet Federalism at Work: Lessons from the History of the Transcaucasian Federation," *Jahrbücher für Geschichte Osteuropas* 65, no. 4 (2017): 534–35.

71. Section for Raionirovanie, Minutes of the seventy-third session, 23 October 1922, RGAE, f. 4372, op. 15, d. 63, l. 13.

72. Malysheva, "Administrativno-territorial'noe ustroistvo," 219.

73. Perović, *Nordkaukasus*, 344–45.

74. Kruglov, *Organizatsiia territorii*, 122–23.

75. On the significance of the volost court system, see Jane Burbank, "Thinking Like an Empire: Estate, Law, and Rights in the Early Twentieth Century," in *Russian Empire*, 200-201.

76. A. Kamenskii, "Tsentral'noe i mestnoe upravlenie i territorial'noe ustroistvo v kontekste reform XVIII veka," in *Administrativno-territorial'noe ustroistvo*, 88-90; Afanasii [Panas] Butsenko, *K voprosu raionirovaniia Ukrainy* (Kharkiv: Gosizdat Ukrainy, 1925), 6-11; Konstantin Egorov, "Osnovnye printsipy organizatsii novykh sovetskikh territorial'nykh obrazovanii" (The basic organizational principles of the new territorial formations), no date, RGAE, f. 634, op. 1, d. 5, ll. 144-45; Baron, "Nature, Nationalism," 568; Jeske, *Imperium wird vermessen*, 45.

77. Tagirova, "Mapping," 127; Ekaterina Pravilova, *Finansy imperii: Den'gi i vlast' v politike Rossii na natsional'nykh okrainakh, 1801-1917* (Moscow: Novoe izdatel'stvo, 2006), 33-40.

78. Vladimirskii, *Osnovnye polozheniia*, 6-7; I. Murugov, "Teoriia i praktika raionirovaniia" (Theory and practice of raionirovanie), 28 March 1927, ARAN, f. 350, op. 2, d. 191, ll. 2-6; Krasnovskii, "Administrativno-khoziaistvennoe raionirovanie Turkestanskoi SSR" (The administrative-economic raionirovanie of Turkestan), 1923, GA RF, f. 6892, op. 1, d. 34, l. 54; Egorov, *Raionirovanie SSSR*, 8; Konstantin Egorov, "Osnovy raionirovaniia RSFSR," in *Voprosy ekonomicheskogo raionirovaniia*, 182-83. Tracy McDonald chose this slogan as the title for her book on Soviet policies in rural areas during the 1920s: *Face to the Village: The Riazan Countryside under Soviet Rule, 1921-1930* (Toronto: University of Toronto Press, 2011).

79. Section for Raionirovanie, Minutes of the seventy-fourth session, 30 October 1922, RGAE, f. 4372, op. 15, d. 63, ll. 11-19; Joint meeting of Gosplan's Section for Raionirovanie and UkrDerzhplan's Section for Raionirovanie, 5 January 1924, TsDAVO, f. 1, op. 2, spr. 1801, ark. 2-4.

80. Ivan Cherliunchakevych, Address to Commission for Raionirovanie at the TsIK, 18 June 1925, GA RF, f. 6892, op. 1, d. 7, l. 2.

81. Narodnyi komissariat vnutrennikh del RSFSR, *Territorial'noe i administrativnoe delenie Soiuza SSR* (Moscow: NKVD, 1928), 21; Tsentral'ne statystychne upravlinnia USRR, *Natsional'nyi sklad*, v. The Moldovan Autonomous Socialist Soviet Republic counted as equal to an okrug. Note that between 1919 and 1928 the total territory of the UkrSSR changed several times.

82. Butsenko, *K voprosu*, 11-13; I. Yaroshevich, Presentation on raionirovanie in Ukraine, 6 November 1923, RGAE, f. 4372, op. 15, d. 137b, ll. 41-48; Cherliunchakevych, Address to the Commission for Raionirovanie, GA RF, f. 6892, op. 1, d. 7, l. 2.

83. Yaroslava Vermenych and Oleksandr Androshchuk, *Zminy administratyvno-terytorial'noho ustroiu Ukraïny XX-XXI. st.* (Kiev: NAN Ukraïny, 2014), 78-85; Oksana Sahach, "Zminy v administratyvno-terrytorial'nomu podili USRR na pochatku 20-kh rr. XX st.," *Regional'na istoriia Ukraïny*, no. 4 (2010): 167-76.

84. Filipp Makharadze, "O raionirovanii ZSFSR" (On the raionirovanie of the ZSFSR), 5 June 1925, sak'art'velos šinagan sak'meta saministros ark'ivi—partiuli ark'ivi (SŠSSA-PA), f. 13, op. 3, d. 78, l. 3.

85. Most archival documents of the Section for Raionirovanie at Zak-Gosplan concern the wages of its members and applications for leave. See sak'art'velos uaxlesi istoriis c'entraluri ark'ivi (SUIC'A), f. 631, op. 1, d. 457; and Gregor'ian, Remarks at the Conference of the All-Union Commission for Raionirovanie, 17 May 1926, GA RF, f. 6892, op. 1, d. 42, l. 28.

86. "Itogi soveshchaniia po raionirovaniiu pri Komissii raionirovaniia Gosplana ZSFSR" (Results of the Convention on Raionirovanie held by the Commission of Raionirovanie at Gosplan ZSFSR), no date, RGAE, f. 4372, op. 15, d. 376, l. 10. Plans for raionirovanie were hotly debated in official Transcaucasian periodicals such as *Zaria vostoka* (Dawn of the East) but without any practical impact. See, for example, "K raionirovaniiu Zakavkaz'ia," *Zaria vostoka*, no. 798, 7 February 1925, 1; "Eshche o raionirovanii Zakavkaz'ia," *Zaria vostoka*, no. 800, 10 February 1925, 1; "K voprosu o raionirovanii Zakavkaz'ia," *Zaria vostoka*, no. 804, 14 February 1925, 1; "K voprosu o raionirovanii Gruzii," *Zaria vostoka*, no. 805, 15 February 1925, 1; "Opiat' o raionirovanii Zakavkaz'ia," *Zaria vostoka*, no. 809, 20 February 1925, 1; and "Eshche o raionirovanii Zakavkaz'ia," *Zaria vostoka*, 27 February 1925, 1.

87. A. Gegechkori, Report on raionirovanie in Georgia, 8 October 1924, GA RF, f. 5677, op. 5, d. 487, l. 30.

88. The Georgian SSR had in addition three autonomous subunits—Abkhazia, Ossetia, and Ajara.

89. V. Ordzhonikidze, *Temi SSR Gruzii: Ikh ekonomicheskie i finansovye vozmozhnosti* (Tiflis: GruzGosplan, 1926), viii–ix.

90. Ordzhonikidze, *Temi SSR Gruzii*, 4–7.

91. Report of the Armenian Commission for Raionirovanie, 14 November 1925, GA RF, f. 6892, op. 1, d. 40, l. 107.

92. Raionirovanie Commission for Central Asia at Sredazbiuro TsK VKP(b), Shorthand notes, 2 September 1926, Tsentral'nyi gosudarstvennyi arkhiv Kyrgyzskoi Respubliki (TsGA KR), f. 949, op. 2, d. 11, l. 101.

93. Raionirovanie Commission for Central Asia, TsGA KR, f. 949, op. 2, d. 11, ll. 98–99.

94. Raionirovanie Commission for Central Asia, TsGA KR, f. 949, op. 2, d. 11, l. 100.

95. Raionirovanie Commission for Central Asia, TsGA KR, f. 949, op. 2, d. 11, ll. 104, 128.

96. Raionirovanie Commission for Central Asia, TsGA KR, f. 949, op. 2, d. 11, l. 98.

97. Raionirovanie Commission for Central Asia, TsGA KR, f. 949, op. 2, d. 11, l. 104.

98. Raionirovanie Commission for Central Asia, TsGA KR, f. 949, op. 2, d. 11, l. 115.

99. Raionirovanie Commission for Central Asia, TsGA KR, f. 949, op. 2, d. 11, ll. 128, 143.

100. Z. Mieczkowski, "The Economic Regionalization of the Soviet Union in the Lenin and Stalin Period," *Canadian Slavonic Papers* 8, no. 1 (1966): 111–12.

101. Coordinating Commission at Gosplan, Minutes of the twenty-fourth session, 23 October 1923, RGAE, f. 4372, op. 15, d. 138b, ll. 37–38.

102. Minutes of the directory board of IuVPlan, 29 March 1923, Gosudarstvennyi arkhiv Rostovskoi oblasti (GARO), f. R-98, op. 1, d. 115, l. 18.
103. Nikolai Eizmont to the NKVD RSFSR, 14 April 1923, GA RF, f. 5677, op. 4, d. 393, l. 1.
104. Rudling, *Rise and Fall*, 136.
105. Letter from the Belarusian Sovnarkom to the RSFSR Council of Labor and Defense (STO), 17 August 1921, in *Gosudarstvennye granitsy Belarusi: Sbornik dokumentov i materialov v dvukh tomakh*, ed. V. Snapkovskii et al., 2 vols. (Minsk: BGU, 2012-2013), 1:170-72; Decision of the Politburo TsK RKP(b), 12 July 1923, in *Gosudarstvennye granitsy Belarusi*, 1:195.
106. Minutes of the commission to transfer parts of Vitebsk Guberniia to the BSSR, 2-14 April 1924, in *Gosudarstvennye granitsy Belarusi*, 1:282-83; decision of Politburo TsK VKP(b), 18 November 1926, in *Gosudarstvennye granitsy Belarusi*, 2:10-11; Hirsch, *Empire of Nations*, 149-55; Rudling, *Rise and Fall*, 209-21; Khomich, *Territoriia*, 223; Evgenii Karelin, "Zapadnaia oblast' Gosplana: Iz istorii ekonomicheskogo raionirovaniia strany 1920-e gody," *Rossiiskaia istoriia*, no. 2 (2010): 15-18.
107. Section for Raionirovanie at UkrDerzhplan, Minutes, 29 July 1923, TsDAVO, f. 337, op. 1, spr. 2128, ark. 8.
108. Section for Raionirovanie at UkrDerzhplan, Minutes, 19 May 1923, TsDAVO, f. 337, op. 1, spr. 2128, ark. 5.
109. Industrial Section at Gosplan SSSR, Minutes, 23 February 1924, TsDAVO, f. 337, op. 1, d. 2128, ark. 35; Map of sugar production in the RSFSR-UkrSSR borderland, no date, TsDAVO, f. 337, op. 1, d. 2128, ark. 42.
110. Commission for Raionirovanie at UkrDerzhplan, "Vopros o vneshnikh granitsakh Ukrainy," 28 March 1924, TsDAVO, f. 337, op. 1, spr. 2128, ark. 47.
111. Vvedenskii, "Ob izmenenii granitsy Kurskoi gubernii s Ukrainy" (On the border revision between Kursk Guberniia and Ukraine), 1924, GA RF, f. 5677, op. 5, d. 29, ll. 101-3.
112. Kruglov, *Organizatsiia territorii*, 124-25.
113. Gleb Krzhizhanovskii, "Tezisy po raionirovaniiu" (Theses on raionirovanie), 1925, GA RF, f. 6892, op. 1, d. 50, l. 11.
114. Questionnaire signed by Konstantin Egorov, 1926, TsDAVO, f. 1, op. 3, spr. 600, ark. 3; Ukrainian translation of Egorov's questionnaire, 1926, Derzhavnyi arkhiv Kharkivs'koï oblasti Ukraïny (DAKhO), f. 845, op. 3, spr. 678, ark. 364-66.
115. Questionnaire signed by Konstantin Egorov, 1926, TsDAVO, f. 1, op. 3, spr. 600, ark. 3-4.
116. Materials of the Territorial Commission of Kharkiv Okruha, DAKhO, f. 845, op. 3, spr. 679-80.
117. Report from the Lozovskii Raion, 1926, DAKhO, f. 845, op. 3, spr. 679, ark. 148-51; Report from the Belodukhovskii Raion, 1926, DAKhO, f. 845, op. 3, spr. 680, ark. 103; Report from Belo-Kolodetskii Raion, 1926, DAKhO, f. 845, op. 3, spr. 680, ark. 124. The reports and the designation of the raiony are in Russian.
118. Shorthand notes of the All-Union Commission for Raionirovanie, 21 May 1926, GA RF, f. 6892, op. 1, d. 40, l. 74; S. Lepskii, On the financial

aspects of raionirovanie, 1925, GA RF, f. 6892, op. 1, d. 50, ll. 51–52; discussion of presentation by I. Mugurov at the Institute for Soviet Construction, 28 March 1927, ARAN, f. 350, op. 2, d. 191, ll. 37–38.

119. Reply to questionnaire from the Bol'she-Pisarevskii RIK, 1 October 1926, DAKhO, f. 845, op. 3, spr. 680, ark. 134. The report and the designation of the raion are in Russian.

120. Paper delivered by Konstantin Egorov to the All-Union Commission for Raionirovanie, 5 January 1926, GA RF, f. 6892, op. 1, d. 41, ll. 4–5.

121. Egorov, "Natsional'noe razmezhevanie," ARAN, f. 350, op. 2, d. 74, l. 31; Alampiev, *Ekonomicheskoe raionirovanie*, 1:148.

122. Comments regarding Konstantin Egorov's paper at the convention of the All-Union Commission for Raionirovanie, 5 January 1926, GA RF, f. 6892, op. 1, d. 41, ll. 40–51.

123. All-Union Commission for Raionirovanie, Invitation to a conference on the state of raionirovanie on 17 May 1926 in Moscow, 27 February 1926, TsDAVO, f. 1, op. 2, spr. 3158, ark. 84–85.

124. Iosif Magidovich, Report on Central Asia at the conference of the All-Union Commission for Raionirovanie, 17 May 1926, GA RF, f. 6892, op. 1, d. 42, l. 3.

125. Magidovich, Report on Central Asia, GA RF, f. 6892, op. 1, d. 42, l. 12. Before 1917 rivalries and alliances among local elites led to the division or merger of volosti. See Mirlan Bektursunov, "The Rise of the 'Lineage Proletariat': The Soviet State's Class Policy and Kyrgyz Lineage Society in the 1920s," *Ab Imperio*, no. 1 (2024): 110–13.

126. Magidovich, Report on Central Asia, GA RF, f. 6892, op. 1, d. 42, l. 18.

127. In these shorthand notes, he is named Gregor'ian, whereas in the Transcaucasian documents he appears as Grigorian: SUIC'A, f. 607, op. 1, d. 219, ll. 116–17, 118–23.

128. Presentation of the Transcaucasian delegation at the conference of the All-Union Commission for Raionirovanie, 17 May 1926, GA RF, f. 6892, op. 1, d. 42, ll. 28–31.

129. These designations *t'emi* (in Georgian) and *gavaṙak* (in Armenian) referred to the old imperial unit of *politseiskii uchastok* (police sectors). Within the Caucasian Viceroyalty the administrative tier of *politseiskie uchastki* corresponded to the volost level in most other parts of the Russian Empire.

130. Presentation of the Transcaucasian delegation, GA RF, f. 6892, op. 1, d. 42, l. 37.

131. Comments made by Ingorokva at the conference of the All-Union Commission for Raionirovanie, 17 May 1926, GA RF, f. 6892, op. 1, d. 42, l. 52; report of the Armenian delegation at the conference of the All-Union Commission for Raionirovanie, 21 May 1926, GA RF, f. 6892, op. 1, d. 40, ll. 106–7.

132. Ingorokva, Report on raionirovanie in Georgia at the All-Union Commission for Raionirovanie, 17 May 1926, GA RF, f. 6892, op. 1, d. 42, l. 68.

133. Comments made by Egorov at the conference of the All-Union Commission for Raionirovanie, 17 May 1926, GA RF, f. 6892, op. 1, d. 42, ll. 55–57.

134. Komissiia TsIK UzSSR po raionirovaniiu, *Materialy po raionirovaniiu Uzbekistana* (Samarkand: UzTsIK, 1926), vi.

135. Saak Ter-Gabrielian, Report on raionirovanie in Uzbekistan to the TsK VKP(b), not later than 27 September 1926, in *TsK RKP(b)-VKP(b)*, 1:432–36.

136. Jones, "Establishment of Soviet Power," 619–20.

137. Anonymous, "O prichinakh nesootvetstviia provedeniia raionirovaniia s setkoi Gosplana" (On the reasons why raionirovanie was not conducted according to the standards of Gosplan), 1928, GA RF, f. 6892, op. 1, d. 47, ll. 1–10.

138. Anonymous, "O prichinakh nesootvetstviia," GA RF, f. 6892, op. 1, d. 47, ll. 18, italics added.

139. Chugunov, Comments on I. Mugurov's presentation at the Institute of Soviet Construction, 28 March 1927, ARAN, f. 350, op. 2, d. 191, ll. 44–49.

140. Sheila Fitzpatrick, introduction to *Cultural Revolution in Russia, 1928–1931* (Bloomington: Indiana University Press, 1978), 8–40. Matthew Payne broadened Fitzpatrick's concept for the cultural realm, extending it to different fields of the economy, in *Stalin's Railroad: Turksib and the Building of Socialism* (Pittsburgh: University of Pittsburgh Press, 2001), 4–5. Michael David-Fox criticizes this use of "Cultural Revolution" and has proposed "Great Break" instead (*Crossing Borders*, 108–32); see also Siegelbaum, *Soviet State and Society*, 224–26. Here I prefer the term "Cultural Revolution" as it emphasizes the qualitative change that took place in 1928–1929. Concepts discussed in the 1920s that were expected to be implemented with the consent of the local population were decreed after 1929 without consideration of particular needs in different regions. Changes in these years produced new concepts not on how to best manage the Soviet state but on how to implement the existing concepts by force.

141. Egorov, "Natsional'noe razmezhevanie," ARAN, f. 350, op. 2, d. 74, l. 7.

142. Dosov, Comments on Egorov's presentation, 15 May 1926, ARAN, f. 350, op. 2, d. 74, l. 67.

143. Vladimirskii, "Osnovnye momenty raionirovaniia," ARAN, f. 350, op. 2, d. 250, l. 25.

144. Vladimirskii, "Osnovnye momenty raionirovaniia," ARAN, f. 350, op. 2, d. 250, ll. 20–21. On Gosplan's role in the first five-year plan, see Nove, *Economic History*, 142–43.

145. Stalin, "O zadachakh khoziaistvennikov," in *Sochineniia*, 13:39.

146. Gosplan SSSR, *Problemy rekonstruktsii narodnogo khoziaistva SSSR na piatiletie: Piatiletnii perspektivnyi plan na 5 s"ezde gosplanov* (Moscow: Planovoe khoziaistvo, 1929); Grigorii Fel'dman, "Analiticheskii metod postroeniia perspektivnykh planov," *Planovoe khoziaistvo*, no. 12 (1929): 97–127.

147. Ellman, *Socialist Planning*, 9–10.

148. Stalin, "Politicheskii otchet Tsentral'nogo Komiteta XVI s"ezdu VKP(b)," in *XVI s"ezd Vsesoiuznoi Kommunisticheskoi Partii (b): Stenograficheskii otchet* (Moscow: Gosizdat, 1930), 45.

149. Hiroaki Kuromiya, *Stalin's Industrial Revolution: Politics and Workers, 1928–1932* (Cambridge: Cambridge University Press, 1990), 162–70; Hiroaki Kuromiya, *Freedom and Terror in the Donbas: A Ukrainian-Russian Borderland, 1870–1990s* (Cambridge: Cambridge University Press, 1998), 151–61.

150. "O likvidatsii okrugov: Postanovlenie TsIK i SNK SSSR," *Zaria vostoka*, no. 2466, 26 July 1930, 1; Shul'gina, "Administrativno-territorial'noe delenie

Rossii v XX veke," 226–34; P. Zaitsev, "Pochemu uprazdniaetsia okruzhnoe zveno v sisteme sovetskogo apparata," in *Ot okruga k raionu: Sbornik statei i offitsial'nykh materialov* (Moscow: Vlast' sovetov, 1930), 35–36.

151. To concentrate on the bigger picture, I must neglect certain episodes of territorial reform. For example, the Ukrainian Soviet government dissolved the okruhy (okruga) in 1930 and introduced oblasti only in early 1932. For over a year, there was no intermediary level between the center in Kharkiv and the small-scale raiony: Tsentral'nyi ispolnitel'nyi komitet SSSR, *Administrativno-territorial'noe delenie Soiuza SSR: Izmeneniia, proizshedshie s 1 noiabria 1931 g. po 1 iuliia 1932 g.* (Moscow: Vlast' sovetov, 1932), 10–11.

152. Kruglov, *Organizatsiia territorii*, 127–29.

153. Decree on the administrative division of the Armenian SSR, 20 July 1921, Hayastani azgayin arkhiv (HAA), f. 123, op. 1, d. 6, l. 66.

154. Convention for Raionirovanie ZSFSR at Zakkraikom, mid-1930, SŠSSA-PA, f. 13, op. 8, d. 64, ll. 1–9.

155. Report to the Zakkraikom on the results of raionirovanie, 12 February 1931, SŠSSA-PA, f. 13, op. 9, d. 89, ll. 1–34; Stalin, "Politicheskii otchet Tsentral'nogo Komiteta XVI s"ezdu," 45.

156. Egorov, "Avtobiograficheskie materialy," RGAE, f. 634, op. 1, d. 41, l. 2.

157. Boris Shtoulberg et al., "Soviet Regional Policy," in *Regional Development in Russia: Past Policies and Future Prospects*, ed. Hans Westlund et al. (Cheltenham: Elgar, 2000), 53–54. In Armenia, for example, a certain Professor A. Z. Tamashev published a leaflet on cattle breeding that explained how crossbreeding should be carried out in each raion depending on climate and fertility: *Porodnoe raionirovanie i osnovnye printsipy metizatsii krupnogo rogatogo skota v SSR Armenii* (Erivan': IRSKh, 1933), 31–34.

158. Niccolò Pianciola, "Stalinist Spatial Hierarchies: Placing the Kazakhs and Kyrgyz in Soviet Economic Regionalization," *Central Asian Survey* 63, no. 1 (2017): 84–85; Gosplan SSSR, *Piatiletnii plan narodno-khoziaiztvennogo stroitel'stva SSSR*, 3rd ed. (Moscow: Planovoe khoziaistvo 1930), 3:302–60.

159. Sarah I. Cameron, *The Hungry Steppe: Famine, Violence, and the Making of Soviet Kazakhstan* (Ithaca, NY: Cornell University Press, 2018); Robert Kindler, *Stalins Nomaden: Herrschaft und Hunger in Kasachstan* (Hamburg: Hamburger Edition, 2014); Niccolò Pianciola, "The Benefits of Marginality: The Great Famine around the Aral Sea, 1930–1934," *Nationalities Papers* 48, no. 3 (2020): 513–29.

160. Martin, *Affirmative Action Empire*, 291–302, 345–56; search warrants of the Zakkraikom, 13 February 1936, SŠSSA-PA, f. 13, op. 14, d. 7, l. 1.

161. Shul'gina, "Administrativno-territorial'noe delenie," 226–39.

162. For example, Pëtr Alampiev considered the intellectual achievements of the 1920s (despite some minor adjustments) a model of emulation for the Soviet state's future territorial policy (*Ekonomicheskoe raionirovanie SSSR*, 1:223–24).

163. Hirsch, *Empire of Nations*, 293–302; Martin, *Affirmative Action Empire*, 442–51.

164. Malysheva, "Administrativno-territorial'noe ustroistvo," 226–31; Kruglov, *Organizatsiia territorii*, 231–34.

3. Ukraine and the RSFSR

1. Stefan Rudnyckyj, *Ukraina und Ukrainer*, 2nd ed. (Berlin: Kroll, 1915); Yefim Karskii, *Etnograficheskaia karta belorusskogo pelmeni* (St. Petersburg: n.p., 1903); Guido Hausmann, "Das Territorium der Ukraine: Stepan Rudnyc'kyjs Beitrag zur Geschichte räumlich-territorialen Denkens über die Ukraine," in *Die Ukraine: Prozesse der Nationsbildung*, ed. Andreas Kappeler (Cologne: Böhlau, 2011), 145–57; Vytautas Petronis, *Constructing Lithuania: Ethnic Mapping in Tsarist Russia ca. 1800–1914* (Stockholm: Stockholm University, 2007), 138–73; Dorota Michaluk, "Emerging States and Border-Making in Times of War: Negotiating the Ukrainian-Belarusian Borders in 1918," in *Making Ukraine*, 164–69; Volodymyr Kravchenko, *The Ukrainian-Russian Borderland: History versus Geography* (Montreal: McGill-Queen's University Press, 2022), 15–46.

2. Darius Staliūnas, "The Identification of Subjects according to Nationality: In the Western Region of the Russian Empire in 1905–1915," *Ab Imperio*, no. 3 (2020): 66–67.

3. Thomas Chopart, "Identifier, légitimer, stigmatiser: Les matériaux de la Délégation ukrainienne à la Conférence de la Paix de Paris, 1918–1920," *Matériaux pour l'histoire de notre temps*, 113–14, no. 1 (2014): 180–85; Borislav Chernev, "Ukraine's Borders at the Brest-Litovsk Peace Conference, 1917–18," in *Making Ukraine*, 78–81.

4. On the western border, see Jan Jacek Bruski, "The Path to the Treaty of Riga: The Establishment of the Polish-Ukrainian Border, 1918–21," in *Making Ukraine*, 124–26.

5. Tsentral'noe statisticheskoe upravlenie, *Vsesoiuznaia perepis' naseleniia 1926 goda* (Moscow: TsSU, 1928), 11:10.

6. Agreement between the Provisional Government and the Central Rada, 4 July 1917 (17 July 1917, New Style), in *Revoliutsiia i natsional'nyi vopros: Dokumenty i materialy po istorii natsional'nogo voprosa Rossii i SSSR v XX veke*, ed. Semën Dimanshtein (Moscow: Kommunisticheskaia akademiia, 1930), 3:62–63; Provisional instructions of the Provisional Government to the General Secretary in Ukraine, 4 August 1917 (17 August 1917, New Style), in Dimanshtein, *Revoliutsiia i natsional'nyi vopros*, 3:63–64; Blank, *Sorcerer as Apprentice*, 3–4; Hennadii Yefimenko, "Die Grenzziehung zwischen der Sowjetukraine und Russland: Kriterien, Verlauf, Ergebnisse," *Nordost-Archiv* 27 (2018): 171–73.

7. Third Universal of the Central Rada, 7 November 1917 (20 November 1917, New Style), TsDAVO, f. 1115, op. 1, spr. 4, ark. 9.

8. Immo Rebitschek, "State Building under Occupation: Pavlo Skoropadsky's Hetmanate in 1918," *Revolutionary Russia* 32, no. 2 (2019): 226–50.

9. Konstantin Drozdov, "Belogorodchina v sostave Ukrainskoi derzhavy getmana P. P. Skoropadskogo: Okkupatsiia ili prisoedinenie?," *Belgorodskii kraevedcheskii vestnik*, no. 6 (2006): 11–35.

10. Stephen Velychenko, *State Building in Revolutionary Ukraine: A Comparative Study of Governments and Bureaucrats, 1917–1922* (Toronto: Toronto University Press, 2011), 208–23; Smele, *'Russian' Civil Wars*, 91–103.

11. Torsten Wehrhahn, *Die Westukrainische Volksrepublik: Zu den polnisch-ukrainischen Beziehungen und dem Problem der ukrainischen Staatlichkeit in den Jahren*

1918 bis 1923 (Berlin: Weissensee, 2004), 223–27; Benjamin Conrad, *Umkämpfte Grenzen, umkämpfte Bevölkerung: Die Entstehung der Staatsgrenzen der Zweiten Polnischen Republik, 1918–1923* (Stuttgart: Steiner, 2014), 99–102, 204–9.

12. Decision of the Ukrainian Sovnarkom, 6 January 1919, TsDAVO, f. 2, op. 1, spr. 14, ark. 11.

13. Minutes of the Ukrainian Sovnarkom, 28 November 1918-31 January 1919, TsDAVO, f. 2, op. 1, spr. 14.

14. Meeting of representatives from the RSFSR and the UkrSSR, 25 February 1919, TsDAVO, f. 2, op. 1, spr. 47, ark. 93; note on the partition of Chernigov Guberniia, 2 May 1919, TsDAVO, f. 2, op. 1, spr. 47, ark. 75. See also Boyechko, Hanzha, and Zacharchuk, *Kordony Ukraïny*, 51.

15. Letter from the VUTsVK to the VTsIK, 17 March 1920, GA RF, f. 5677, op. 1, d. 170, ll. 3–6; correspondence between the Administrative Commission of the VTsIK and the NKID RSFSR, December 1921/January 1922, GA RF, f. 5677, op. 1, d. 168, ll. 5, 11, 12, 14; minority report of the Ukrainian delegation with the Cherviakov Commission, 28 November 1924, GA RF, f. 6892, op. 1, d. 5, l. 18.

16. The chairman of the Donetsk gubrevkom to the VTsIK, 14 March 1920, GA RF, f. 5677, op. 1, d. 83, l. 19; Semën Sul'kevich, *Administrativno-politicheskoe stroenie SSSR*, part 1: *Izmeneniia administrativno-territorial'nykh deleniia SSSR za period s 1917 goda po 1924 god* (Leningrad: Izvestiia TsIK SSSR i VTsIK, 1924), 215.

17. Correspondence between the Ukrainian and the Russian Soviet governments, TsDAVO, f. 2, op. 1, spr. 47, ark. 1–51; correspondence between the NKVD RSFSR and the Donetsk ispolkom, October/November 1920, GA RF, f. 5677, op. 1, d. 83, ll. 49, 51; decision of the VTsIK, 26 April 1920, GA RF, f. 5677, op. 1, d. 83, l. 29; Konstantin Egorov, Report on the claims of the RSFSR on territories of the UkrSSR in the region of the River Derkul, 5 April 1927, GA RF, f. 1235, op. 27, d. 222, l. 4; Yefimenko, "Vyznachennya kordonu," 159–60, 166; Yurii Galkin, introduction to *Sbornik dokumentov o pogranichnom spore mezhdu Rossiei i Ukrainoi v 1920–1925 gg. za Taganrogsko-Shakhtinskuiu territoriiu Donskoi oblasti* (Moscow: Shcherbinskaia tipografiia, 2007), 7–15.

18. Conrad, *Umkämpfte Grenzen*, 245–51.

19. Voronovici, "Overlapping Spaces," 210–37.

20. Hirsch, *Empire of Nations*, 70–79.

21. In the 1930s, a stricter official distinction between these terms was established: *narodnost'* referred to ethnicity, *natsional'nost'* to nationality. See Hirsch, *Empire of Nations*, 37–42; Cadiot, *Laboratoire impérial*, 189; and Laruelle, *Central Peripheries*, 20–22.

22. Shorthand notes of the Commission to Revise the Borders between the RSFSR, the UkrSSR, and the BSSR at the Presidium of the TsIK SSSR (hereafter Cherviakov Commission), 1 July 1924: GA RF, f. 3316, op. 17, d. 322, ll. 56–72; Hirsch, *Empire of Nations*, 104–8, 120–21; Cadiot, *Laboratoire impérial*, 13–14, 157–58; Adeeb Khalid, "National Consolidation as Soviet Work: The Origins of Uzbekistan," *Ab Imperio*, no. 4 (2016): 191.

23. Rogers Brubaker, *Nationalism Reframed: Nationhood and the National Question in the New Europe* (Cambridge: Cambridge University Press 1996), 7.

24. The term "centrist" is taken from Panas Butsenko, who used it to describe his network or "faction" within the KP(b)U. See Butsenko, "Otdel'nye vpechatleniia o pervom s"ezde KP(b)U" (Some impressions from the first congress of the KP[b]U), 1927, TsDAVO, f. 1, op. 3, spr. 2504, ark. 167.

25. Elena Borisënok, *Fenomen sovetskoi ukrainizatsii, 1920–1930-e gody* (Moscow: Evropa, 2006), 40, 52-54; Smith, *National Question*, 123-25; Velychenko, *Painting Imperialism*, 158-59; Jurij Borys, *The Russian Communist Party and the Sovietization of Ukraine: A Study in the Communist Doctrine of the Self-Determination of Nations* (Stockholm: P.A. Norstedt, 1960), 258-66; James E. Mace, *Communism and the Dilemmas of National Liberation: National Communism in Soviet Ukraine, 1918–1933* (Cambridge, MA: Harvard University Press, 1983), 49-62; Butsenko, "Otdel'nye vpechatleniia," TsDAVO, f. 1, op. 3, spr. 2504, ark. 167-70.

26. Elena Borisënok, *Stalinskii prokonsul Lazar' Kaganovich na Ukraine: Apogei sovetskoi ukrainizatsii, 1925–1928* (Moscow: Rodina, 2021), 108-47.

27. Institut Marksizma-Leninizma pri TsK KPSS, *Dvenadtsatyi s"ezd RKP(b)*, 691-96.

28. Afanasii Butsenko, "K uregulirovaniiu granits USSR s RSFSR," *Pravda*, no. 179/3111, 9 August 1925, 5.

29. Nikolai Eizmont to the Administrative Commission of the NKVD RSFSR, 14 April 1923, GA RF, f. 5677, op. 4, d. 393, l. 1; map showing border revisions between the North Caucasus Region and Ukraine, 1924, GARO, f. R-4185, op. 1, d. 143, l. 7.

30. Minutes of the IuVPlan directory board, 29 May 1923, GARO, f. R-98, op. 1, d. 115, l. 18; report by Vasilii Khronin published in *Sovetskii iug* on 11 March 1924, TsDAVO, f. 1, op. 2, spr. 1872, ark. 3; minutes of the Extraordinary Commission of the Politbuto KP(b)U on the Issue of the Taganrog and Shakhty Regions, 19 April 1924, TsDAVO, f. 337, op. 1, spr. 2128, l. 77.

31. Vasilii Khronin, ed., *Materialy po voprosu o prisoedinenii k iugo-vostochnoi oblasti Taganrogskogo, Aleksandro-Grushevskogo i Kamensko-Ekaterininskogo raionov Ukrainy* (Rostov-na-Donu: Tipografiia Shtaba TsKVO, 1924).

32. *Sovetskii iug*, no. 166/1164, 27 July 1924, 3.

33. Tahanrih okrvynkonkom to the VUTsVK, 14 March 1924, TsDAVO, f. 1, op. 2, spr. 1872, ark. 2.

34. Minutes of the UkrDerzhplan presidium, 22 May 1923, GA RF, f. 5677, op. 4, d. 393, l. 18; report of Tahanrih okrvynkonkom, 28 April 1924, TsDAVO, f. 1, op. 2, spr. 1872, ark. 15-25; Letavin, "Administrativnoe raionirovanie Donoblasti" (Administrative raionirovanie of Donets'k Oblast), 1924, TsDAVO, f. 337, op. 1, d. 2128, ll. 87-102; minutes of the South Industrial Section at Gosplan, 1 June 1923, RGAE, f. 4327, op. 15, d. 204, l. 35.

35. UkrDerzhplan, Report to the VUTsVK, 22 May 1923, GA RF, f. 5677, op. 4, d. 393, ll. 18-19; UkrDerzhplan, Draft to revise the borders in the north and the east of the UkrSSR, 3 August 1923, RGAE, f. 4372, op. 15, d. 327, l. 25.

36. Commission for Raionirovanie at UkrDerzhplan, "Vopros o vneshnikh granitsakh Ukrainy" (The question of the external borders of Ukraine), 28-29 March 1924, TsDAVO, f. 337, op. 1, spr. 2128, ark. 46-72.

37. B. Sukhov, Memorandum on the sugar industry (including a map), 1924, TsDAVO, f. 337, op. 1, spr. 2128, ark. 36-41.

38. Mykhailo Hrushevs'kyi, "K voprosu o vostochnykh granitsakh Ukrainy" (On the question of the eastern border of Ukraine), 1924, GA RF, f. 5677, op. 5, d. 28, ll. 23-30. On Hrushevs'kyi and his complex relationship with Soviet power, see Christopher Gilley, *The 'Change of Signposts' in the Ukrainian Emigration: A Contribution to the History of Sovietophilism in the 1920s* (Stuttgart: ibidem, 2009), 200-218; Expert opinions of the VUTsVK on the border revision with the RSFSR, 15 September 1924, Natsianal'ny arkhiŭ Respubliki Belarus' (NARB), f. 6, op. 1, d. 349, ll. 30-57.

39. Decision of the TsIK to install the Cherviakov Commission, 11 April 1924, GA RF, f. 3316, op. 17, d. 322, l. 87.

40. Avel' Enukidze to Avram Zolotarevskii, July 1924, GA RF, f. 6892, op. 1, d. 5, l. 32.

41. Decision of the TsIK to install the Cherviakov Commission, GA RF, f. 3316, op. 17, d. 32, l. 87.

42. Afanasii [Panas] Butsenko, "K voprosu uregulirovaniia gosudarstvennoi granitsy USSR, RSFSR i BSSR" (To the question of regulating the state borders of the UkrSSR, RSFSR, and BSSR), undated, TsDAVO, f. 1, op. 2, spr. 1807, ark. 29; A. Korobov, "Konspekt materialov po regulirovaniiu granits mezhdu USSR i RSFSR" (Summary of documents on regulating the borders between the UkrSSR and the RSFSR), 30 July 1924, GA RF, f. 5677, op. 5, d. 25, ll. 17-22.

43. Afanasii Butsenko, "K voprosu ob uregulirovanii gosudarstvennoi granitsy USSR s RSFSR i BSSR," *Izvestiia*, no. 239/2274, 18 October 1924, 3; Arsenii Khomenko, "Glavneishie statisticheskye dannye o chislennosti ukraintsev v prilegaiushchikh k Ukraine uezdakh Kurskoi i Voronezhskoi gub. i Donskoi oblasti" (The main statistical data on the numbers of Ukrainians in the border uezdy of Kursk and Voronezh Gubernii and Donets'k Oblast), 1924, TsDAVO, f. 1, op. 2, spr. 1807, ark. 59-63.

44. Minutes of the Politburo TsK KP(b)U, 27 July 1924, Tsentral'nyi derzhavnyi arkhiv hromads'kykh obiedan' (TsDAHO), f. 1, op. 6, spr. 48, ark. 95.

45. Martin Latsis, "Krasnyi terror," *Krasnyi terror: Ezhenedel'nik Chrezvychainoi komissii po bor'be s kontr-revoliutsiei na Chekho-Slovatskom fronte*, no. 1 (1 November 1918): 1-2.

46. Slezkine, "Communal Apartment," 420-21.

47. Shorthand notes of the Cherviakov Commission, 1 July 1924, GA RF, f. 3316, op. 17, d. 322, ll. 63-64.

48. Elena Borisënok, "Ukraina i Rossiia: Spor o granitsakh v 1920-e gody," in *Regiony i granitsy Ukrainy v istoricheskoi perspekive*, ed. Leonid Gorizontov (Moscow: Strategiia, 2005), 225.

49. Egorov, *Raionirovanie SSSR*, 8-12; see also the Shorthand notes of the Cherviakov Commission, July-November 1924: GA RF, f. 3316, op. 17, d. 322, ll. 55-73; GA RF, f. 5677, op. 5, d. 26, ll. 33-65; GA RF, f. 6892, op. 1, d. 19, ll. 21-35; and GA RF, f. 6892, op. 1, d. 20, ll. 3-30.

50. Minutes of the Politburo RKP(b), 12 July 1924, RGASPI, f. 17, op. 3, d. 448, l. 5.

51. Galkin, *Sbornik dokumentov*, 60.

52. Their absence was not the result of a misunderstanding, because they had been invited well in advance to join the meeting on 13 October in Moscow.

See Aleksandr Cherviakov's telegram to all members of the commission, 29 September 1924, NARB, f. 6, op. 1, d. 349, ll. 102-3.

53. Minutes of the Cherviakov Commission, 13 October 1924, GA RF, f. 5677, op. 5, d. 26, l. 15; Afanasii [Panas] Butsenko, Report to the TsK KP(b)U, between 23 October and 26 November 1924, TsDAVO, f. 1, op. 2, spr. 1807, ark. 67.

54. Minutes of the Cherviakov Commission, 21 October 1924, GA RF, f. 5677, op. 5, d. 26, ll. 20-21.

55. Minutes of the Bilateral Commission for Border Revision between Donets'k Huberniia and North Caucasus Krai, 8 September 1924, TsDAVO, f. 1, op. 2, spr. 1871, ark. 11; minutes of the Bilateral Commission for Border Revision between Donets'k Huberniia and North Caucasus Krai, 22 September 1924, GA RF, f. 6892, op. 1, d. 14, ll. 4-5; "Prisoedinenie k iugo-vostoku Taganrogskogo i Shakhtinskogo raionov," *Sovetskii iug*, no. 225/1228, 3 October 1924, 3.

56. Butsenko, "K voprosu ob uregulirovanii gosudarstvennoi granitsy," 3.

57. Shorthand notes of the Cherviakov Commission, 1 July 1924, GA RF, f. 3316, op. 17, f. 322, l. 56.

58. Poloz and Cherliunchakevych, "O vneshnikh granitsakh USSR," (On the external borders of the UkrSSR), undated, GA RF, f. 3316, op. 17, d. 322, ll. 42-46; Butsenko often referred to the Twelfth Party Congress in his reports; see "K voprosu uregulirovaniia gosudarstvennoi granitsy," TsDAVO, f. 1, op. 2, spr. 1807, ark. 31.

59. Minutes of the Cherviakov Commission, 23 October 1924, GA RF, f. 5677, op. 5, d. 26, ll. 23-24; Minutes of the Cherviakov Commission, 27 November 1924, GA RF, f. 5677, op. 5, d. 26, ll. 28-29; Minutes of the Cherviakov Commission, 28 November 1924, GA RF, f. 5677, op. 5, d. 26, ll. 30-31.

60. Minutes of the Cherviakov Commission, 23 October 1924, GA RF, f. 5677, op. 5, d. 26, ll. 23-24.

61. Section for Raionirovanie, Minutes of the forty-first session, 1 June 1922, RGAE, f. 4372, op. 15, d. 63, l. 87; Egorov, "Printsip federatsii," GA RF, f. 5677, op. 4, d. 15, ll. 94-95.

62. Afanasii [Panas] Butsenko, Report to the TsK KP(b)U, TsDAVO, f. 1, op. 2, spr. 1807, ark. 67. Butsenko's original letter is in Russian. Therefore the geographic names appear in Russian transcription.

63. Report of the Briansk gubispolkom, 10 September 1924, GA RF, f. 5677, op. 5, d. 23, ll. 1-2; Kursk Gubplan, "Ob izmenenii granitsy Kurskoi gubernii s Ukrainoi" (On the border revision between Kursk Guberniia and Ukraine), undated, GA RF, f. 5677, op. 5, d. 29, ll. 66-67.

64. Butsenko, Report to the TsK KP(b)U, TsDAVO, f. 1, op. 2, spr. 1807, ark. 68-69.

65. Letter from Butsenko to UkrDerzhplan, 25 October 1924, TsDAVO, f. 337, op. 1, spr. 2129, ark. 11.

66. Yegorov Subcommission, Minutes of the first session, 23 October 1924, RGAE, f. 4372, op. 15, d. 328, l. 28.

67. Letter of the TsSU to Avel' Enukidze, 10 October 1924, RGAE, f. 4372, op. 15, d. 327, l. 225; Yegorov Subcommission, Minutes of the third session, 12 November 1924, GA RF, f. 5677, op. 4, d. 389, l. 10.

68. D'iakonov, "Zakliuchenie po voprosu o prisoedinenii iuzhnykh uezdov Voronezhskoi gub. smezhnykh s Kharkovskoi gub. k USSR" (Summary of the question of the transfer of the southern uezdy of the Voronezh Guberniia to the UkrSSR), not later than 13 November 1924, GA RF, f. 6892, op. 1, d. 17, ll. 1–2; Górny, *Vaterlandszeichner*, 207–27.
69. D'iakonov, "Zakliuchenie po voprosu," GA RF, f. 6892, op. 1, d. 17, l. 22.
70. Rashin (chairman of the HATK) and Sliusarev (HubStatbiuro), Report to the Donets'k HATK, 14 November 1924, TsDAVO, f. 1, op. 2, spr. 1825, ark. 8.
71. Rashin and Sliusarev, Report to the Donets'k HATK, TsDAVO, f. 1, op. 2, spr. 1825, ark. 7. Rashin and Sliusarev erroneously speak about *raionirovanie* in Central Asia instead of "delimitation" (*razmezhevanie*).
72. Minutes of the Voronezh gubispolkom, 15–18 November 1924, GA RF, f. 6892, op. 1, d. 17, l. 25–27.
73. Minutes of the Voronezh gubispolkom, GA RF, f. 6892, op. 1, d. 17, l. 25.
74. Report of the Yegorov Subcommission to the Cherviakov Commission, 26 November 1924, GA RF, f. 3316, op. 17, d. 322, l. 17; Shorthand notes of the Cherviakov Commission, 27 November 1924, GA RF, f. 5677, op. 5, d. 26, l. 47.
75. Shorthand notes of the Commission Tasked with Constructing the Okruga and Raiony, 21 March 1925, GA RF, f. 6892, op. 1, d. 27, l. 68; Butsenko, *K voprosu raionirovaniia Ukrainy*, 6–8.
76. Shorthand notes of the Cherviakov Commission, 28 November 1924, GA RF, f. 6892, op. 1, d. 20, l. 17.
77. Shorthand notes of the Cherviakov Commission, 27 November 1924, GA RF, f. 5677, op. 5, d. 26, l. 45.
78. Shorthand notes of the Cherviakov Commission, 28 November 1924, GA RF, f. 6892, op. 1, d. 20, l. 21.
79. Minutes of the Cherviakov Commission, 27 November 1924, GA RF, f. 5677, op. 5, d. 26, ll. 28–29.
80. Shorthand notes of the Cherviakov Commission, 28 November 1924, GA RF, f. 6892, op. 1, d. 20, l. 3.
81. Martin, *Affirmative Action Empire*, 274–82.
82. Minutes of the Cherviakov Commission, 27 November 1924, GA RF, f. 5677, op. 5, d. 26, ll. 28–29.
83. Minutes of the Cherviakov Commission, 28 November 1924, GA RF, f. 5677, op. 5, d. 26, ll. 30–31.
84. Borisënok, "Ukraina i Rossiia," 229.
85. Shorthand notes of the Cherviakov Commission, 28 November 1924, GA RF, f. 6892, op. 1, d. 20, ll. 20, 27.
86. Minutes of the Cherviakov Commission, 28 November 1924, GA RF, f. 3316, op. 17, d. 322, l. 6.
87. Minority opinion of the RSFSR representatives, 29 November 1924, GA RF, f. 3316, op. 17, d. 322, l. 5.
88. Minutes of the VTsIK, 17 November 1924, GA RF, f. 3316, op. 17, d. 718, l. 41.
89. Minutes of the Cherviakov Commission, 27 November 1924, GA RF, f. 3316, op. 17, d. 322, l. 8.

90. Shorthand notes of the Commission for Raionirovanie RSFSR, 14 November 1924, GA RF, f. 6892, op. 1, d. 19, l. 17.
91. Report from Cherviakov to the Politburo RKP(b), 30 November 1924, TsDAVO, f. 1, op. 2, spr. 1808, ark. 11.
92. Minutes of the Politburo RKP(b), 11 December 1924, RGASPI, f. 17, op. 3, d. 480, 10, l. 3.
93. Letter from Cherviakov to Butsenko, 8 January 1925, TsDAVO, f. 1, op. 2, spr. 3143, ark. 3.
94. Minutes of the Cherviakov Commission, 23 January 1925, GA RF, f. 3316, op. 17, d. 718, ll. 70–71.
95. Afanasii [Panas] Butsenko, "Dokladnaia zapiska po voprosu ob uregulirovanii gosudarstvennykh granits USSR, RSFSR i BSSR" (Report on the question of regulating the state borders of the UkrSSR, RSFSR, and BSSR), May 1927, TsDAVO, f. 1, op. 3, spr. 2524, ark. 11-12.
96. UkrDerzhplan, Note on Shakhty and Taganrog, 1924, TsDAVO, f. 1, op. 2, spr. 1871, ark. 51-52; Vasylenko, "Pro derzhavni mezhi pomizh USRR ta RSFRR" (On the state borders between the UkrSSR and the RSFSR), 14 August 192[8], TsDAVO, f. 1, op. 3, spr. 2523, ark. 12.
97. Afanasii [Panas] Butsenko, Report on border revisions to the VUTsVK and to the Politburo KP(b)U, after December 10, 1924, TsDAVO, f. 1, op. 2, spr. 1808, ark. 61; Afanasii [Panas] Butsenko, Reply to Cherviakov's proposal from 8 January 1925, undated, NARB, f. 6, op. 1, d. 349, l. 118.
98. Letter from Cherviakov to Kviring, 8 January 1925, NARB, f. 6, op. 1, d. 349, l. 121.
99. Afanasii Butsenko, "K uregulirovaniiu granits USSR s RSFSR," *Pravda*, no. 179/3111, 9 August 1925, 5.
100. Douds, *Inside Lenin's Government*, 73-81.
101. Shorthand notes of the Cherviakov Commission, 27 November 1924, GA RF, f. 5677, op. 5, d. 26, l. 51.
102. Minutes of the Bilateral Commission for the Implementation of Changes to the Borders between the RSFSR, the UkrSSR, and the BSSR (hereafter Ter-Gabrielian Commission), 17 July 1926, GA RF, f. 6892, op. 1, d. 24, ll. 1-2.
103. Petitions from citizens of Gomel' Guberniia requesting the transfer of their villages to Ukraine, 1925-1928, TsDAVO, f. 1, op. 2, spr. 3277, 368 ark.
104. Petition from the village of Eremino, Starodub Volost, to the VUTsVK, 25 May 1925, TsDAVO, f. 1, op. 2, spr. 3277, ark. 12. The petitions from the villages of Novosel'ka, Pestrikovo, Nestruevo, Savenki (all of them part of Starodub Volost, RSFSR) used the exact same wording. See TsDAVO, f. 1, op. 2, spr. 3277, ark. 13, 15, 16, 17.
105. Afanasii [Panas] Butsenko, Table showing the areas requested for transfer from the RSFSR to the UkrSSR, 1924, GA RF, f. 3316, op. 17, d. 322, l. 81; Cherliunchakevych, "O vneshnikh granitsakh USSR," GA RF, f. 6892, op. 1, d. 13, l. 4.
106. Petition from P. Danechkin to the VTsIK, 15 March 1926, GA RF, f. 3316, op. 17, d. 720, l. 12.

107. Shorthand notes of the Ter-Gabrielian Commission, 17 July 1926, GA RF, f. 6892, op. 1, d. 24, l. 14.

108. Petition from Nikon Seroshtan to the VTsIK, 20 August 1926, GA RF, f. 3316, op. 17, d. 720, l. 9.

109. Petition from Nikon Seroshtan to the Territorial Commission of Sumy Okruha, 15 March 1926, Derzhavnyi arkhiv Sums'koï oblasti Ukraïny (DASO), f. 32, op. 1, spr. 72, ark. 139–40.

110. Shorthand notes of the Ter-Gabrielian Commission, GA RF, f. 6892, op. 1, d. 24, ll. 29-31.

111. VUTsVK to Sumy Okruha ATK, DASO, f. 32, op. 1, spr. 398, ark. 1.

112. Act of transfer for a part of Miropol'e Volost from the RSFSR to the UkrSSR, 2 September 1927, DASO, f. 32, op. 1, spr. 389, ark. 69; explanatory note to the VUTsVK minutes (table with all the settlements at stake), 1 April 1927, TsDAVO, f. 1, op. 3, spr. 604, ark. 1.

113. Petition from 433 citizens from the village (*sloboda*) of Zaoleshenka, Sudzha Volost, Kursk Guberniia, 22 February 1925, TsDAVO, f. 1, op. 2, spr. 1841, ark. 37, capitalization according to the original.

114. For further discussion of this problem, see Stephen Kotkin, *Magnetic Mountain: Stalinism as a Civilization* (Berkeley: University of California Press, 1997), 198–237.

115. Panas Butsenko, Note on a document from the Commission for National Minority Affairs in Sudzha Volost, TsDAVO, f. 1, op. 2, spr. 1841, ark. 65.

116. Petition from sixty citizens in the village of Uspens'ka to join the RSFSR, 20 November 1924, GA RF, f. 6892, op. 1, d. 14, l. 28; petition from a rally of citizens in the village of Uspens'ka, 29 November 1924, GA RF, f. 6892, op. 1, d. 14, l. 31.

117. Shorthand notes of the Second Bilateral Russian-Ukrainian Subcommission for the Implementation of Border Changes in the Taganrog and Shakhty Regions, 2–3 December 1925, TsDAVO, f. 1, op. 2, spr. 3143, ark. 169–73.

118. Petition from P. S. Vertelo to VTsIK and TsIK, 11 March 1927, TsDAVO, f. 1, op. 3, spr. 2562, ark. 15–16.

119. Afanasii [Panas] Butsenko to the TsK KP(b)U, 29 July 1927, TsDAVO, f. 1, op. 3, spr. 2524, ark. 1–3.

120. Minutes of the VKP(b) faction at TsIK, 25 May 1927, GA RF, f. 3316, op. 64, d. 412 b, l. 1.

121. Shorthand notes of the Second Bilateral Russian-Ukrainian Subcommission for Taganrog and Shakhty, TsDAVO, f. 1, op. 2, spr. 3143, ark. 176.

122. Report by Slepnev, head of the railway administration in Chertkovo, 15 November 1926, GA RF, f. 3316, op. 17, d. 721, l. 17.

123. Report by director of the Chertkovo slaughterhouse, August 1926, GA RF, f. 406, op. 13, d. 380, l. 22.

124. Senior Inspector Mikhailov to the People's Commissariat of Internal Trade (NarkomVnutorg) of North Caucasus Krai, 24 April 1925, GA RF, f. 406, op. 13, d. 380, l. 259.

125. Report by the former (Dmitrev) and current (Yevdokimov) directors of the Chertkovo slaughterhouse, 15 February 1926, GA RF, f. 406, op. 13, d.

380, ll. 154–55; report from NarkomVnutorg to the Council for the Economy (EKOSO) RSFSR, 16 March 1927, GA RF, f. A-259, op. 11b, d. 3279, l. 6.

126. NarkomVnutorg RSFSR to the NarkomVnutorg UkrSSR, 22 June 1926, GA RF, 5677, op. 5, d. 20, l. 42.

127. Report from Starobil's'k Okruha to the VUTsVK, undated, TsDAVO, f. 1, op. 2, spr. 1809, ark. 52–53.

128. Panas Butsenko, "Dokladnaia zapiska ob ispravlenii gosudarstvennykh granits USSR i Severo-Kavkazskogo Kraia v raione st. Chertkovo" (Report on correcting the state borders of the UkrSSR and North Caucasus Krai in the raion of the stanitsa Chertkovo), 6 December 1926, TsDAVO, f. 1, op. 2, spr. 1809, ark. 23–30.

129. Kozachkov to Kaganovich, GA RF, f. 3316, op. 17, d. 721, ll. 49–50.

130. The border between North Caucasus Krai and the UkrSSR was deliberately excluded from the discussions by the Cherviakov Commission. See Minutes of the Cherviakov Commission, 1 July 1924, GA RF, f. 5677, op. 5, d. 26, l. 7.

131. Shorthand notes of the Ter-Gabrielian Commission, 17 July 1926, GA RF, f. 6892, op. 1, d. 24, ll. 43–47; Butsenko, "Dokladnaia zapiska ob ispravlenii gosudarstvennykh granits USSR i Severo-Kavkazskogo Kraia v raione st. Chertkovo," f. 1, op. 2, spr. 1809, ark. 23–28; map showing the territorial claims of the Russian side, 1926, TsDAVO, f. 1, op. 2, spr. 1809, ark. 70.

132. S. Il'in, "Zakliuchenie po voprosu o raione stanitsii Chertkovo" (Summary on the question about the stanitsa Chertkovo), undated, GA RF, f. 3316, op. 17, d. 721, ll. 36–33.

133. Minutes of the TsIK, 8 March 1927, GA RF, f. 3316, op. 17, d. 721, l. 77; minutes of the TsIK, 26 November 1927, GA RF, f. 3316, op. 17, d. 721, l. 98.

134. Minutes of the Bilateral Russian-Ukrainian Subcommission for the Implementation of Border Changes in the Region of Graivoron, 2 April 1926, TsDAVO, f. 1, op. 3, spr. 630, ark. 14; shorthand notes of the Second Bilateral Russian-Ukrainian Subcommission for Taganrog and Shakhty, TsDAVO, f. 1, op. 2, spr. 3143, ark. 183; minutes of the Bilateral Commission Formed in Accordance with TsIK Decision of 11 February 1928, 28 February 1928, TsDAVO, f. 1, op. 2, spr. 3274, ark. 2–3.

135. P. Ia. Lizhnev-Fin'kovskii, "Uchastie zemleustroitelei v kul'turno-prosvetitel'noi rabote," *Zemleustroitel'* 1, no. 1 (1924): 6–8.

136. Minutes of the Bilateral Russian-Ukrainian Subcommission for Graivoron, TsDAVO, f. 1, op. 3, spr. 2546, ark. 52; minutes of the second meeting of the Bilateral Commission for Border Revisions between Donets'k Huberniia and North Caucasus Krai, 8 September 1924, TsDAVO, f. 1, op. 2, spr. 1871, ark. 8; map of land use between Stalino Okruha and Taganrog Okrug, 1927, TsDAVO, f. 1, op. 2, spr. 3274, l. 77.

137. Minutes of the VUTsVK, 10 July 1928, TsDAVO, f. 1, op. 4, spr. 1199, ark. 1.

138. VTsIK to the VUTsVK, 13 August 1928, TsDAVO, f. 1, op. 3, spr. 2563, ark. 15.

139. Forest Administration of the UkrSSR to the Briansk gubispolkom, 22 October 1927, TsDAVO, f. 1, op. 3, spr. 2563, ark. 14.

140. VUTsVK to the TsIK and the VTsIK, 31 July 1928, TsDAVO, f. 1, op. 4, spr. 1199, ark. 2.

141. TsIK to the VUTsVK, 12 October 1928, TsDAVO, f. 1, op. 4, spr. 1199, ark. 3.

142. Minutes of the VTsIK, 25 March 1929, TsDAVO, f. 1, op. 4, spr. 1199, ark. 8.

143. Citizens of Ohybne to the VUTsVK, signed by 149 households, 20 January 1927, TsDAVO, f. 1, op. 3, spr. 623, ark. 4.

144. Voronezh gubispolkom to the VUTsVK, 28 December 1926, TsDAVO, f. 1, op. 3, spr. 623, ark. 28.

145. Kupians'k Okruha Land Administration to the newspaper *Bednota* (Poverty), 13 December 1926, TsDAVO, f. 1, op. 3, spr. 623, ark. 25.

146. Valuiki UIK to the Kupians'k okrvykonkom, 21 January 1927, TsDAVO, f. 1, op. 3, spr. 623, ark. 18.

147. Article in *Bednota*, 22 October 1926, TsDAVO, f. 1, op. 3, spr. 623, ark. 13-17.

148. TsIK to the VUTsVK, 4 February 1927, TsDAVO, f. 1, op. 3, spr. 623, ark. 20.

149. Citizens of Ohybne to the VUTsVK, TsDAVO, f. 1, op. 3, spr. 623, ark. 5.

150. Afanasii [Panas] Butsenko, "Dokladnaia zapiska po voprosu ob uregulirovanii gosudarstvennykh granits mezhdu USSR i RSFSR" (Report on the question about the regulation of the state borders between the UkrSSR and the RSFSR), 9 July 1927, TsDAVO, f. 1, op. 3, spr. 2504, ark. 200.

151. Shorthand notes of Stalin's meeting with Ukrainian writers, 12 February 1929, RGASPI, f. 558, op. 1, d. 4490, l. 19. See also Leonid Maximenkov, "Stalin's Meeting with a Delegation of Ukrainian Writers on 12 February 1929," *Harvard Ukrainian Studies* 16, no. 3-4 (1992): 361-431.

152. Martin, *Affirmative Action Empire*, 291-302.

153. Mace, *Communism*, 100-111.

154. Martin, *Affirmative Action Empire*, 345-56; Mace, *Communism*, 296-98.

155. Di Fiore, "Production of Borders," 41-43; Haslinger, "Dilemmas of Security," 193-200; Catherine Gibson, "Attuning to Emotions in the History of Border-Making: The Estonian-Latvian Boundary Commission in 1920," *Journal of Modern European History* 22, no. 1 (2024), 44-45.

4. Central Asia

1. In 1926 only Uzbekistan and Turkmenistan had the status of union republics. Kyrgyzstan and Kazakhstan were autonomous republics within the RSFSR, Tajikistan an autonomous republic within Uzbekistan. Karakalpakstan was at the time an autonomous oblast within the Kazakh ASSR.

2. Julia Obertreis, *Imperial Desert Dreams: Cotton Growing and Irrigation in Central Asia, 1860-1991* (Göttingen: V&R unipress, 2017), 60-64.

3. Stefan Kirmse, "Raumkonzepte von Zentralasien: Ein historischer Überblick," in *Die politischen Systeme Zentralasiens: Interner Wandel, externe*

Akteure, regionale Kooperation, ed. Jakob Lempp, Sebastian Mayer, and Alexander Brandt (Wiesbaden: Springer, 2020), 27.

4. Maya Peterson, *Pipe Dreams: Water and Empire in Central Asia's Aral Sea Basin* (Cambridge: Cambridge University Press, 2019), 11-17; Hirschhausen and Leonhard, *Empires*, 416-25.

5. Haugen, *Central Asia*.

6. Alexander Morrison, *The Russian Conquest of Central Asia: A Study in Imperial Expansion, 1814-1914* (Cambridge: Cambridge University Press, 2021), 537-38; Keller, *Russia and Central Asia*, 112-13; Isabelle Ohayon and Tomohiko Uyama, "Mediators of the Empire in Central Asia, 1820-1928," *Cahiers du monde russe* 56, no. 4 (2015): 617-20; Tetsu Akiyama, *The Qïrghïz Baatïr and the Russian Empire: A Portrait of a Local Intermediary in Russian Central Asia* (Leiden: Brill, 2021), 1-11.

7. Daniel R. Brower, *Turkestan and the Fate of the Russian Empire* (London: Routledge, 2003), 20-25; Jennifer Keating, *On Arid Ground: Political Ecologies of Empire in Russian Central Asia* (Oxford: Oxford University Press, 2022), 210-12; Fedtke, *Roter Orient*, 55-56; Morrison, *Russian Conquest*, 4.

8. Jörn Happel, *Nomadische Lebenswelten und zarische Politik: Der Aufstand in Zentralasien 1916* (Stuttgart: Steiner, 2010), 15; Keller, *Russia and Central Asia*, 141-42; Ian W. Campbell, "Nationalizing Violence in a Collapsing Empire: A View from the Steppe," *Ab Imperio*, no. 3 (2020): 112-13; Alexander Morrison, Cloé Drieu, and Aminat Chokobaeva, introduction to *The Central Asian Revolt of 1916: A Collapsing Empire in the Age of War and Revolution* (Manchester: Manchester University Press, 2020), 19-20; Alexander Morrison, "Bab'i Bunty in Semirech'e: Gender, Class, and Ethnicity in Central Asia during the First World War," *Revolutionary Russia* 36, no. 1 (2023): 46-48.

9. For further discussion, see Khalid, *Central Asia*, 147-98; Svetlana Gorshenina, *Asie centrale: L'invention des frontières et l'héritage russo-soviétique* (Paris: Éditions CNRS, 2012), 189-300; and Fedtke, *Roter Orient*.

10. Khalid, *Central Asia*, 157-62; Reinhard Eisener, *Buchara im Strudel der Russischen Revolution: Auftakt und revolutionäres Umfeld, 1917-1919* (Potsdam: Thetis, 2023), 252-67.

11. Buttino, *Revoliutsiia naoborot*, 339-48; Fedtke, *Roter Orient*, 299-300.

12. Norihiro Naganawa, "Officious Aliens: Tatars' Involvement in the Central Asian Revolution, 1919-21," *Kritika: Explorations in Russian and Eurasian History* 24, no. 1 (2023): 81-90.

13. P. Lepeshinskii, Letter to Lenin, 19 May 1920, in *Rossiia i Tsentral'naia Aziia*, 344-47.

14. Smith, *National Question*, 99-101; Niccolò Pianciola, "Décoloniser l'Asie centrale? Bolcheviks et colons au Semireč'e, 1920-1922," *Cahiers du monde russe* 49, no. 1 (2008): 107-14; Happel, *Nomadische Lebenswelten*, 314-15.

15. Shoshana Keller, *To Moscow, Not Mecca: The Soviet Campaign against Islam in Central Asia, 1917-1941* (Westport, CT: Praeger, 2001), 44-47; Khalid, "Backwardness," 239-41; Cameron, *Hungry Steppe*, 77-79; Fedtke, *Roter Orient*, 179; Adeeb Khalid, *The Politics of Muslim Cultural Reform: Jadidism in Central Asia* (Berkeley: University of California Press, 1998), 80-82; Eisener, *Buchara*, 26-43.

16. Khalid, *Making Uzbekistan*, 295-96.

17. Keller, *Russia and Central Asia*, 139; Fedtke, *Roter Orient*, 379-81, 455; Uyama, "Alash Orda," 271-87; Xavier Hallez, "Le ralliement des Kazakhs au povoir soviétique, 1917-1920: Convictions politiques, système tribal et contexte russe," *Cahiers du monde russe* 56, no. 4 (2015) 746-47; Jipar Duishembieva, "'The Kara Kirghiz Must Develop Separately': Ishenaaly Arabaev, 1881-1933, and His Project of the Kyrgyz Nation," in *Creating Culture in (Post) Socialist Central Asia*, ed. Ananda Breed, Eva-Marie Dubuisson, and Ali Iğmen (Cham: Palgrave, 2020), 18-35; Anton Ikhsanov, "Aleksandr Nikolaevich Samoilovich (1880-1938) i ego polevye informanty: Konstruirovanie turkmenskoi kul'turnoi identichnosti" (PhD diss., Higher School of Economics, Moscow, 2023).

18. Khalid, *Muslim Cultural Reform*, 288-89; Khalid, *Making of Uzbekistan*, 53-54; Sergei Abashin, *Natsionalizmy v Srednei Azii: V poiskakh identichnosti* (St. Petersburg: Aleteiia, 2007), 183-84; Gorshenina, *Asie centrale*, 206.

19. Keller, *Russia and Central Asia*, 152; Khalid, *Making Uzbekistan*, 123-24.

20. The Communist Party of Turkestan had 23,810 members, while the Communist Party of Bukhara had 2,216 and the Communist Party of Khorezm had 774 members: Report on party members in the Central Asian republics, 1 March 1924, RGASPI, f. 62, op. 2, d. 91, l. 40. Concerning the role of European Bolsheviks in Central Asia, see Botakoz Kassymbekova and Christian Teichmann, "The Red Man's Burden: Soviet Officials in Central Asia in the 1920s and 1930s," in *Helpless Imperialists: Imperial Failure, Fear and Radicalization*, ed. Maurus Reinkowski (Göttingen: Vandenhoeck & Ruprecht, 2013), 163-86; and Hirsch, *Empire of Nations*, 164.

21. Stenograph of the Territorial Commission for Delimitation of the Central Asian Republics (hereafter Delimitation Commission), 17 August 1924, RGASPI, f. 62, op. 2, d. 104, l. 134.

22. The intricate evolution of the term *sart* cannot be discussed here. For a comprehensive analysis, see Abashin, *Natsionalizmy*, 95-176; Hirsch, *Empire of Nations*, 112-13; and Sergei Abashin, "Empire and Demography in Turkestan: Numbers and the Politics of Counting," in *Asiatic Russia*, 129-49.

23. Khalid, *Making Uzbekistan*, 14-16; Abashin, *Natsionalizmy*, 180-81; Khalid, "Nationalizing the Revolution," 155-58.

24. Until 1925 the people now known as Kazakh and the state known as Kazakhstan were referred to in Russian administrative language as Kirgiz and the Kirrespublika, respectively. On the Kirrespublika, see Dina Amanzholova, "Ispytanie vlast'iu: Iz istorii formirovaniia biurokratii Kazakhskoi ASSR, 1920-e gg.," *Cahiers du monde russe* 56, no. 4 (2015): 753-91. Some parts of Astrakhan Guberniia and the Magyshalk Peninsula of Turkestan were attached to the Kirrespublika. On the details of border making between the Kirrepublika and the Turkestan ASSR, see Alun Thomas, "The Caspian Disputes: Nationalism and Nomadism in Early Soviet Central Asia," *Russian Review* 76, no. 3 (2017): 502-25; and Gorshenina, *Asie centrale*, 206-7.

25. Buttino, *Revoliutsiia naoborot*, 21-27; Matthew J. Payne, *Stalin's Railroad: Turksib and the Building of Socialism* (Pittsburgh: University of Pittsburgh Press, 2001), 68, 134.

26. Marco Buttino, "Central Asia, 1916-1920: A Kaleidoscope of Local Revolutions and the Building of the Bolshevik Order," in *The Empire and Nationalism at War*, ed. Eric Lohr et al. (Bloomington, IN: Slavica Publishers, 2014), 109-35; Sergei Abashin et al., "Soviet Rule and the Delimitation of Borders in the Ferghana Valley, 1917-1930," in *Ferghana Valley: The Heart of Central Asia*, ed. S. Frederick Starr (Armonk, NY: M. E. Sharpe, 2011), 99. For instance, Iosif Magidovich, a leading Soviet geographer in Central Asia, was unable to visit certain parts of the region even in the mid-1920s due to Basmachi guerrilla activity (Report on Central Asia, 17 May 1925, GA RF, f. 6892, op. 1, d. 42, l. 3).

27. "Protokol No. 25 ob"edenënnogo zasedaniia Kraikoma, Kraimusbiuro i Komiteta inostrannykh kommunistov KPT i predstavitelei Turkkomissii," in *Rossiia i Tsentral'naia Aziia*, 314-18; Abashin, *Natsional'izmy*, 182-84; Naganawa, "Officious Aliens," 82; Eisener, *Buchara*, 428-30; Buttino, *Revoliutsiia naoborot*, 349-51.

28. "Doklad dopolnitel'nyi Turkdelegatsii (po delam Turkestana) lichno tov. Leninu, 16 June 1920," in *Rossiia i Tsentral'naia Aziia*, 369.

29. Mirzohid Rahimov and Galina Urazaeva, "Central Asian Nations and Border Issues," *Conflict Studies Research Centre* 10, no. 5 (2005): 2-3; Gorshenina, *Asie centrale*, 199-200; Abashin, *Natsionalizmy*, 183; Eisener, *Buchara*, 348-52.

30. Lenin, Letter to Stalin, 28 November 1921, in *PSS*, 44:255; Lenin, "Zamechaniia o proekte resheniia TsK o zadachakh RKP(b) v Turkestane," in *PSS*, 41:435.

31. Abashin, *Natsionalizmy*, 182-84.

32. Fedtke, *Roter Orient*, 400-410; Abashin, *Natsionalizmy*, 187; Gorshenina, *Asie centrale*, 202.

33. Keller, "Central Asian Bureau," 281-97; Gorshenina, *Asie centrale*, 203-4; Fedtke, *Roter Orient*, 310.

34. Abashin et al., "Soviet Rule," 105-6; Mirlan Bektursunov, "'Two Parts— One Whole?' Kazakh-Kyrgyz Relations in the Making of Soviet Kyrgyzstan, 1917-24," *Central Asian Survey* 42, no. 1 (2022): 109-26.

35. Ryskulov, Letter to Stalin, 20 February 1922, in *Rossiia i Tsentral'naia Aziia*, 465-66; Turar Ryskolov, Address to the plenum of TsK KPT, 28 July 1923, RGASPI, f. 62, op. 3, d. 9, ll. 14-16; see also Gorshenina, *Asie centrale*, 218-21.

36. Chika Obiya, "When Faizulla Khojaev Decided to Be an Uzbek," in *Islam in Politics in Russia and Central Asia: Early Eighteenth to Late Twentieth Centuries*, ed. Stéphane A. Dudoignon and Hisao Komatsu (London: Kegan Paul, 2001), 111-13; Ivan Trainin, "O plemennoi avtonomii," *Zhizn' natsional'nostei*, no. 2 (1923): 19-25.

37. "Vypiska iz postanovleniia Orgbiuro TsK RKP(b) po Turkestanskim voprosam," 31 January 1924, in *Rossiia i Tsentral'naia Aziia*, 524.

38. Gero Fedtke, "Wie aus Bucharern Usbeken und Tadschiken warden: Sowjetische Nationalitätenpolitik im Lichte einer persönlichen Rivalität," *Zeitschrift für Geschichtswissenschaft* 54, no. 3 (2006): 214-31; Iosif Vareikis to Stalin, 27 March 1924, in *TsK RKP(b)-VKP(b)*, 1:189-91.

39. Theses of the TsK of the Bukharan Communist Party, 10 March 1924, RGASPI, f. 62, op. 2, d. 101, l. 3. This document was edited and commented

on by Adeeb Khalid in "National Consolidation as Soviet Work: The Origins of Uzbekistan," *Ab Imperio*, no. 4 (2016): 185-200.

40. Ingeborg Baldauf, "Some Thoughts on the Making of the Uzbek Nation," *Cahiers du monde russe et soviétique* 32, no. 1 (1991): 79-96.

41. Haugen, *Central Asia*, 115-37; Thomas, *Nomads*, 45, 49; Victoria Clement, *Learning to Become Turkmen: Literacy, Language, and Power, 1914-2014* (Pittsburgh: University of Pittsburgh Press, 2018), 5; Hirsch, *Empire of Nations*, 112-13; Abashin, "Empire and Demography," 129-49.

42. Tetsu Akiyama, "Why Was Russian Direct Rule over Kyrgyz Nomads Dependent on Tribal Chieftains 'Manaps'?," *Cahiers du monde russe* 56, no. 4 (2015): 627-28; Nathan Light, "Kyrgyz Genealogies and Lineages: Histories, Everyday Life, and Patriarchal Institutions in Northwestern Kyrgyzstan," *Genealogy* 53, no. 2 (2018): 5-6; Duishembieva, "Kara Kirghiz," 15-16; Bektursunov, "Lineage Proletariat," 101-3.

43. Thomas, *Nomads*, 25; Cadiot, *Laboratoire impérial*, 167; Fedtke, *Roter Orient*, 30-31; Fedtke, "Wie aus Bucharern," 219-20; Abashin, *Natsionalizmy*, 188-90.

44. Mezhlauk to Stalin, 28 March 1924, RGASPI, f. 62, op. 2, d. 101, l. 53.

45. Sultanbek Khodzhanov, Minority opinion, 29 May 1924, RGASPI, f. 62, op. 2, d. 101, ll. 133.

46. D. R. Ashimbaev, *Kto est' kto v Kazakhstane: Entsiklopedicheskii slovar'*, 12th ed. (Almaty: Credo, 2012), 1189.

47. Grigorii Broido, note to the TsK RKP(b), prior to 4 June 1924, in *TsK RKP(b)-VKP(b)*, 1:216-20.

48. Decision of the KPT to dissolve Turkestan in favor of national entities, 23 March 1924, RGASPI, f. 62, op. 2, d. 101, l. 67; Mochanov, Report on Central Asia, May-June 1924, RGASPI, f. 62, op. 2, d. 91, l. 27.

49. Conquest, *Last Empire*, 28-31; Caroe, *Soviet Empire*, 145-49; Philip Shishkin, *Restless Valley: Revolution, Murder, and Intrigue in the Heart of Central Asia* (New Haven: Yale University Press, 2014), 238.

50. The Soviet ambassador to Bukhara, Znamenskii, to Karklin, 16 February 1924, RGASPI, f. 62, op. 2, d. 88, ll. 12-13; Znamenskii to Karklin, 15 March 1924, RGASPI, f. 62, op. 2, d. 88, ll. 23-24; minutes of the Uzbekistan Commission within the Sredazbiuro, 10 May 1924, RGASPI, f. 62, op. 2, d. 101, ll. 12-14; Karklin to the TsK RKP(b), 2 June 1924, in *TsK RKP(b)-VKP(b)*, 1:207-8; Zelenskii and Vareikis, introduction to *Natsional'no-gosudarstvennoe razmezhevanie*, 8-9; Fedtke, *Roter Orient*, 402-10.

51. Minutes of the Uzbekistan Commission, RGASPI, f. 62, op. 2, d. 101, ll. 14; Peyrat, "Soviet Federalism," 548-49.

52. Shorthand notes of the Sredazbiuro, 10 May 1924, RGASPI, f. 62, op. 2, d. 100, l. 10.

53. Minutes of the Sredazbiuro, 11 May 1924, RGASPI, f. 62, op. 1, d. 20, ll. 240-41. For a short time in mid-1924, it was not clear whether the Kirgiz-Kazak part of Turkestan was to form a separate, small Kirrespublika to counterbalance the larger entity of the same name in the north. For more information on this topic, see Gorshenina, *Asie centrale*, 230-31.

54. Edgar, *Tribal Nation*, 50-51.

55. Memorandum of a Khorezmian delegation to the Sredazbiuro, undated, RGASPI, f. 62, op. 2, d. 101, l. 64; minutes of the Politburo RKP (b), 12 June 1924, RGASPI, f. 17, op. 3, d. 443, ll. 17–18.
56. However, there were no Karakalpak or Tajik subcommissions. See Minutes of the Delimitation Commission, 16 August 1924, RGASPI, f. 62, op. 2, d. 110, ll. 19–20; and Gorshenina, *Asie centrale*, 221–25.
57. Shorthand notes of the Delimitation Commission, 16 August 1924, RGASPI, f. 62, op. 1, d. 104, l. 1.
58. Shorthand notes of the Delimitation Commission, 16 August 1924, RGASPI, f. 62, op. 1, d. 104, l. 2.
59. Shorthand notes of the Delimitation Commission, 16 August 1924, RGASPI, f. 62, op. 1, d. 104, l. 3.
60. Stalin, "Marksizm i natsional'nyi vopros," in *Sochineniia*, 2:296.
61. Shorthand notes of the Delimitation Commission, 16 August 1924, RGASPI, f. 62, op. 1, d. 104, l. 9.
62. Shorthand notes of the Delimitation Commission, 16 August 1924, RGASPI, f. 62, op. 1, d. 104, l. 13.
63. Shorthand notes of the Delimitation Commission, 16 August 1924, RGASPI, f. 62, op. 1, d. 104, l. 23. In this era, "Muslim" could still be used as an ethnographic signifier.
64. Shorthand notes of the Delimitation Commission, 16 August 1924, RGASPI, f. 62, op. 1, d. 104, l. 20.
65. Edgar, *Tribal Nation*, 62–66; Haugen, *Central Asia*, 185–88.
66. Shorthand notes of the Delimitation Commission, 16 August 1924, RGASPI, f. 62, op. 1, d. 104, ll. 30–31. As mentioned above, before 1917 people could easily identify with more than one category. "Kipchak" or "Kurama" could denote linguistic or kinship affiliations; see Hirsch, *Empire of Nations*, 112–13; Abashin, "Empire and Demography," 129–49; and Haugen, *Central Asia*, 139–45.
67. Shorthand notes of the Delimitation Commission, 16 August 1924, RGASPI, f. 62, op. 1, d. 104, ll. 35–37.
68. Shorthand notes of the Delimitation Commission, 16 August 1924, RGASPI, f. 62, op. 1, d. 104, l. 66.
69. Shorthand notes of the Delimitation Commission, 16 August 1924, RGASPI, f. 62, op. 1, d. 104, l. 68, italics added.
70. *Aul*: mobile settlement of yurts. *Kishlak*: wintering place for nomads.
71. Shorthand notes of the Delimitation Commission, 16 August 1924, RGASPI, f. 62, op. 1, d. 104, l. 69, italics added.
72. Shorthand notes of the Delimitation Commission, 16 August 1924, RGASPI, f. 62, op. 1, d. 104, l. 79.
73. Shorthand notes of the Delimitation Commission, 16 August 1924, RGASPI, f. 62, op. 1, d. 104, ll. 79–80, italics added.
74. Shorthand notes of the Delimitation Commission, 16 August 1924, RGASPI, f. 62, op. 1, d. 104, ll. 82–84.
75. Shorthand notes of the Delimitation Commission, 16 August 1924, RGASPI, f. 62, op. 1, d. 104, l. 90.
76. Minutes of the Delimitation Commission, 17 August 1924, RGASPI, f. 62, op. 2, d. 103, l. 9.

77. Shorthand notes of the Delimitation Commission, 17 August 1924, RGASPI, f. 62, op. 2, d. 104, ll. 107-10.
78. Minutes of the Uzbekistan Commission, 10 May 1924, RGASPI, f. 62, op. 2, d. 101, ll. 40-41; Duishembieva, "Kara Kirghiz," 35-36.
79. Shorthand notes of the Delimitation Commission, 17 August 1924, RGASPI, f. 62, op. 2, d. 104, ll. 112-13.
80. Shorthand notes of the Delimitation Commission, 17 August 1924, RGASPI, f. 62, op. 2, d. 104, ll. 113-14.
81. Shorthand notes of the Delimitation Commission, 17 August 1924, RGASPI, f. 62, op. 2, d. 104, l. 115.
82. In doing so, they were acting as "ethnonational entrepreneurs" before the ethnic community was even constituted; see Rogers Brubaker, *Ethnicity without Groups* (Cambridge, MA: Harvard University Press, 2004), 10-12.
83. Shorthand notes of the Delimitation Commission, 17 August 1924, RGASPI, f. 62, op. 2, d. 104, l. 117.
84. Shorthand notes of the Delimitation Commission, 17 August 1924, RGASPI, f. 62, op. 2, d. 104, l. 119, italics added.
85. Shorthand notes of the Delimitation Commission, 17 August 1924, RGASPI, f. 62, op. 2, d. 104, l. 128.
86. Shorthand notes of the Delimitation Commission, 17 August 1924, RGASPI, f. 62, op. 2, d. 104, l. 135.
87. Shorthand notes of the Delimitation Commission, 17 August 1924, RGASPI, f. 62, op. 2, d. 104, ll. 136-38.
88. Shorthand notes of the Delimitation Commission, 17 August 1924, RGASPI, f. 62, op. 2, d. 104, ll. 137-44.
89. Shorthand notes of the Delimitation Commission, 17 August 1924, RGASPI, f. 62, op. 2, d. 104, ll. 145-47.
90. Shorthand notes of the Delimitation Commission, 17 August 1924, RGASPI, f. 62, op. 2, d. 104, ll. 157-64.
91. Shorthand notes of the Delimitation Commission, 17 August 1924, RGASPI, f. 62, op. 2, d. 104, ll. 178.
92. Shorthand notes of the Delimitation Commission, 17 August 1924, RGASPI, f. 62, op. 2, d. 104, l. 182.
93. Shorthand notes of the Delimitation Commission, 17 August 1924, RGASPI, f. 62, op. 2, d. 104, ll. 184-85.
94. Shorthand notes of the Delimitation Commission, 17 August 1924, RGASPI, f. 62, op. 2, d. 104, ll. 185-87.
95. Minutes of the secret session of the Sredazbiuro, 20 August 1924, RGASPI, f. 62, op. 1, d. 21, l. 194.
96. Shorthand notes of the Delimitation Commission, 21 August 1924, RGASPI, f. 62, op. 2, d. 104, ll. 188-89. The Uzbek subcommission did not indicate whether these volosti would be part of the Kirgiz-Kazak or the Kara-Kirgiz entity.
97. Shorthand notes of the Delimitation Commission, 21 August 1924, RGASPI, f. 62, op. 2, d. 104, l. 190.
98. Shorthand notes of the Delimitation Commission, 21 August 1924, RGASPI, f. 62, op. 2, d. 104, l. 192.

99. Shorthand notes of the Delimitation Commission, 21 August 1924, RGASPI, f. 62, op. 2, d. 104, l. 196.
100. Shorthand notes of the Delimitation Commission, 21 August 1924, RGASPI, f. 62, op. 2, d. 104, ll. 204-7.
101. Shorthand notes of the Delimitation Commission, 21 August 1924, RGASPI, f. 62, op. 2, d. 104, ll. 227-33.
102. The Tajik entity would eventually gain ASSR status within Uzbekistan.
103. Shorthand notes of the Delimitation Commission, 21 August 1924, RGASPI, f. 62, op. 2, d. 104, ll. 233-34.
104. Fedtke, "Wie aus Bucharern," 219-20.
105. Minutes of the session of the Sredazbiuro, 31 August 1924, RGASPI, f. 62, op. 1, d. 22, ll. 39-46.
106. These were later attached to Uzbekistan; see Gorshenina, *Asie centrale*, 268-69.
107. Shorthand notes of the Delimitation Commission, 6 September 1924, RGASPI, f. 62, op. 2, d. 104, l. 263.
108. Minutes of the Editorial Commission, 6 September 1924, RGASPI, f. 62, op. 2, d. 110, l. 18.
109. Sultanbek Khodzhanov, Note of protest, undated, RGASPI, f. 62, op. 2, d. 110, ll. 11-12.
110. Minutes of the Sredazbiuro, 7 September 1924, RGASPI, f. 62, op. 2, d. 110, ll. 4-12.
111. Haugen, *Central Asia*, 206-10.
112. "Iz dokladnoi zapiski chlenov BukhTsIK," 7 October 1924, in *Rossiia i Tsentral'naia Aziia*, 530-32; VTsIK minutes, 29 December 1924, TsGA KR, f. 20, op. 1s, d. 108, l. 2.
113. Only after the issue had been settled did the all-union edition of *Izvestiia* launch a campaign about delimitation in Central Asia starting with B. Maiberg, "Natsional'no-gosudarstvennoe razmezhevanie respublik Srednei Azii," *Izvestiia*, no. 207/2242, 11 September 1924, 2.
114. RGASPI, f. 62, op. 2, d. 177, l. 41, quoted according to Rahimov and Urazaeva, "Central Asian Nations," 13. Masov later borrowed Zelenskii's expression for his book title: *Istoriia topornogo razdeleniia* (History of a division done with an axe).
115. "Sredne-aziatskoe razmezhevanie," *Izvestiia*, no. 214/2249, 19 September 1924, 2; "Natsional'noe razmezhevanie Srednei Azii i Khorezmskaia Respublika," *Izvestiia*, no. 215/2250, 20 September 1924, 3.
116. In Khorezm, the proponents for independence had been purged in the interim. The Khorezmian Communist Party now favored participation in delimitation; see Gorshenina, *Asie centrale*, 225.
117. Minutes of the Politburo TsK RKP (b), 13 October 1924, RGASPI, f. 17, op. 3, d. 468, l. 2.
118. Yan Rudzutak, report on the national delimitation of Central Asia to the TsK RKP(b), 26 October 1924, in *TsK RKP(b)-VKP(b)*, 1:242-47.
119. Egorov to Ter-Gabrielian, October 1925, GA RF, f. 6892, op. 1, d. 29, l. 24.
120. Abashin, *Natsionalizmy*, 189-94; Khalid, *Central Asia*, 207-9; Fedtke, "Wie aus Bucharern," 225-28.

121. Gorshenina, *Asie centrale*, 284; Aidarbekov's address to the Constitutive Assembly of the Kara-Kirgiz AO, 27 March 1925, TsGA KR, f. 20, op. 1, d. 11, l. 1k.

122. Haugen, *Central Asia*, 208-9.

123. Between 1925 and 1936 the term *kazak* was used in Russian. After 1936 it was replaced with *kazakh*. On the renaming of the Kirgiz Autonomous Socialist Soviet Republic into Kazak Autonomous Socialist Soviet Republic, see the VTsIK decree, 15 June 1925, in *Sobranie uzakonenii i rasporiazhenii rabochego i krest'ianskogo pravitel'stva RSFSR*, no. 43 (1925): 321; and David Gullette, *The Genealogical Construction of the Kyrgyz Republic: Kinship, State and 'Tribalism'* (Leiden: Global Oriental, 2010), 162-65.

124. Minutes of the Commission for Raionirovanie in the Kirgiz AO, 5 November 1925, GA RF, f. 6892, op. 1, d. 26, l. 5; Martin Jeske, "Ein Imperium wird vermessen: Kartographie, Kulturtransfer und Raumerschließung im Zarenreich (1797-1919)" (PhD diss., University of Basel, 2019), 360-61.

125. Minutes of the VTsIK, 6 October 1925, TsGA KR, f. 21, op. 1, d. 114, l. 71.

126. Dublitskii to Petrovskii, undated, TsGA KR, f. 21, op. 2, d. 76, l. 31.

127. Minutes of the Border Revision Commission for Central Asia at the TsIK, 20 March 1926, TsGA KR, f. 21, op. 14, d. 11, ll. 3-8.

128. Minutes of the Raionirovanie Commission for the Kara-Kirgiz AO, 5 March 1925, TsGA KR, f. 20, op. 1, d. 118, ll. 25-27; Minutes of the Border Revision Commission for Central Asia at the TsIK, 21 March 1926, TsGA KR, f. 21, op. 14, d. 11, l. 10.

129. Not to be confused with Isfara Volost, mentioned previously. In other documents Chai-Kuluk Volost is called "Chap-Kuluk."

130. Minutes of the Border Revision Commission for Central Asia at the TsIK, 25 March 1926, TsGA KR, f. 21, op. 14, d. 11, ll. 11-16; Komissiia TsIK UzSSR po raionirovaniiu, *Materialy*, 107-8.

131. Aleksandr Beloborodov, "Doklad o rabote komissii po uregulirovaniiu pogranichnykh sporov mezhdu RSFSR, UzSSR, TrkSSR" (Report on the work of the commission tasked with regulating border troubles between the RSFSR, Uzbekistan, and Turkmenistan), 25 May 1926, GA RF, f. 6892, op. 1, d. 26, ll. 18-19.

132. Minutes of the VTsIK, 30 August 1926, TsGA KR, f. 21, op. 3, d. 156, l. 11; minutes of the TsIK, 10 September 1926, GA RF, f. 6892, op. 1, d. 26, l. 24.

133. Report of the Osh okrispolkom, 30 August 1926, TsGA KR, f. 21, op. 1, d. 418, l. 48.

134. Report of the Osh okrispolkom, 30 August 1926, TsGA KR, f. 21, op. 1, d. 418, l. 49.

135. Biashim Kul'besherov, Report to the TsIK SSSR, undated, GA RF, f. 6892, op. 1, d. 45, l. 8.

136. Minutes of the TsIK, 10 September 1926, GA RF, f. 6892, op. 1, d. 26, l. 24. Here they had in mind the Uch-Kurgan rail hub in the southeast of the town of Fergana in Kokand Okrug, not the town (and rail hub) of the same name to the northwest of Andijan.

137. Biashim Kul'besherov, Report to the TsIK, GA RF, f. 6892, op. 1, d. 45, l. 17.

138. Minutes of the Border Revision Commission between the RSFSR and the UzSSR, 24 January 1927, GA RF, f. 6892, op. 1, d. 45, l. 5.

139. Minutes of the Border Revision Commission between the RSFSR and the UzSSR, 25 January 1927, GA RF, f. 6892, op. 1, d. 45, l. 6; Act of the local border commission, 14 February 1927, TsGA KR, f. 21, op. 14, d. 1, l. 6.

140. Biashim Kul'besherov, Report to the TsIK, GA RF, f. 6892, op. 1, d. 45, ll. 23-28.

141. Minutes of the TsIK, 4 May 1927, TsGA KR, f. 21, op. 2, d. 45, l. 133. On the present-day impact of these borders, see Rashid Gabdulhakov, "The Highly Securitized Insecurities of State Borders in the Fergana Valley," *Central Asia Fellowship Papers* 9 (2015): 7-9.

142. Act of the bilateral Uzbek-Kyrgyz Border Revision Commission, 28 March 1928, TsGA KR, f. 21, op. 14, d. 1, ll. 8-9.

143. Masov, *National Catastrophe*, 76; Koichiev, *Razmezhevanie*, 48, 54-55.

144. Act between the Osh (Kyrgyzstan) and Khujand (Uzbekistan) okrispolkomy, 14 February 1927, TsGA KR, f. 21, op. 14, d. 1, l. 6.

145. Isfana VIK to the TsIK of the KASSR, 3 April 1928, TsGA KR, f. 21, op. 14, d. 1, l. 57.

146. Minutes of the TsIK, 20 August 1927, GA RF, f. 3316, op. 64, d. 412, l. 6. This decision did not affect the South Caucasus. There the ZakTsIK was exclusively responsible for administrative-territorial issues.

147. Shorthand notes of the discussion between Stalin and Ukrainian writers, 12 February 1929, RGASPI, f. 558, op. 1, d. 4490, l. 19.

148. Hirsch, *Empire of Nations*, 176-86; Kassymbekova, *Despite Cultures*, 65.

149. Agreement of the bilateral Tajik-Kyrgyz commission, 8 July 1938, TsGA KR, f. 21, op. 14, d. 25, ll. 18-19.

150. Christine Bichsel, *Conflict Transformation in Central Asia: Irrigation Disputes in the Ferghana Valley* (London: Routledge, 2009), 106-12; Madeleine Reeves, *Border Work: Spatial Lives of the State in Rural Central Asia* (Ithaca, NY: Cornell University Press, 2014), 205-40; Muzaffar Olimov and Saodat Olimova, "Integration vs Disintegration: State Borders and Border Conflicts in the Isfara Valley," in *Post-Soviet Borders: A Kaleidoscope of Shifting Lives and Lands*, ed. Sabine von Löwis and Beate Eschment (New York: Routledge, 2023), 196-97; Anna Matveeva, "Divided We Fall . . . or Rise? Tajikistan-Kyrgyzstan Border Dilemma," *Cambridge Journal of Eurasian Studies*, no. 1 (2017): 4.

151. Reeves, *Border Work*, 85; Smith, "Nationality Policy," 987; Olimov and Olimova, "Integration," 193-94.

152. Haugen, *Central Asia*, 167-69; Alfrid K. Bustanov, *Soviet Orientalism and the Creation of Central Asian Nations* (New York: Routledge, 2015), 136.

153. Brubaker, *Ethnicity without Groups*, 10-12. On clientelism, see Timothy K. Blauvelt, *Clientelism and Nationality in an Early Soviet Fiefdom: The Trials of Nestor Lakoba* (London: Routledge, 2021), 232-34.

5. Armenia and Azerbaijan

1. Tsentral'noe statisticheskoe upravlenie, *Vsesoiuznaia perepis' naseleniia 1926 goda*, 14:6-10; Daniel Müller, *Sowjetische Nationalitätenpolitik in*

Transkaukasien, 1920–1953 (Berlin: Köster, 2008), 77–90; Laurence Broers, *Armenia and Azerbaijan: Anatomy of a Rivalry* (Edinburgh: Edinburgh University Press, 2019), 51–55; Goff, *Nested Nationalism*, 21.

2. Georgi Derluguian, *Bourdieu's Secret Admirer in the Caucasus: A World-System Biography* (Chicago: University of Chicago Press, 2005), 185–97; Jeremy Smith, "Nagorno Karabakh under Soviet Rule," in *The South Caucasus beyond Borders, Boundaries and Division Lines: Conflicts, Cooperation and Development*, ed. Mikko Palonkorpi (Turku: Juvenes, 2015), 9–25; Timothy K. Blauvelt, "'From Words to Action!' Nationality Policy in Soviet Abkhazia, 1921–1938," in *The Making of Modern Georgia, 1918–2012: The First Georgian Republic and Its Successors*, ed. Stephen F. Jones (London: Routledge, 2014), 232–62.

3. Saparov, *From Conflict to Autonomy*, 137, 176–77; Svante E. Cornell, "Autonomy as a Source of Conflict: Caucasian Conflicts in Theoretical Perspective," *World Politics* 54, no. 2 (2002): 275.

4. Goff, *Nested Nationalism*, 218–20; Jamil Hasanli, *Sovetskii Azerbaidzhan: Ot ottepeli k zamorozkam, 1959–1969* (Moscow: Rosspen, 2020), 388–424.

5. Sara Brinegar, "The Oil Deal: Nariman Narimanov and the Sovietization of Azerbaijan," *Slavic Review* 76, no. 2 (2017): 372–73; Audrey L. Altstadt, "The Baku City Duma: Arena for Elite Conflict," *Central Asian Survey* 5, no. 3–4 (1986): 61–63; Ronald G. Suny, *The Baku Commune, 1917–1918: Class and Nationality in the Russian Revolution* (Princeton, NJ: Princeton University Press, 1972), 5–8.

6. Christopher Rice, "Party Rivalry in the Caucasus: SRs, Armenians, and the Baku Union of Oil Workers, 1907–08," *Slavonic and East European Review* 67, no. 2 (1989): 228–43; Baberowski, *Feind ist überall*, 63–70.

7. Suny, *Baku Commune*, 13–27; Soli Shahvar and Anatoly Mishaev, "The Re-Radicalization of Baku Provincial Workers in 1916," *Revolutionary Russia* 36, no. 1 (2023): 60–63.

8. Reinelander, "Caucasian Vicegerency," 15–40.

9. Hovannisian, *Republic of Armenia*, 1:28–33; Peyrat, *Histoire du Caucase*, 77–86; Timothy K. Blauvelt and Adrian Briscu, "Who Wanted the TDFR? The Making and the Breaking of the Transcaucasian Democratic Federative Republic," *Caucasus Survey* 8, no. 1 (2020): 1–8.

10. Hovannisian, *Republic of Armenia*, 1:93–249; Peyrat, *Histoire du Caucase*, 87–88; Mouradian, *L'Arménie*, 62–64; Arsène Saparov, "Nagorno-Karabakh Conflict: What's Next?," *Ab Imperio*, no. 3 (2023): 187–88.

11. Suny, *Baku Commune*, 336–37; Blauvelt, "Ideology Meets Practice," 90; Alun Thomas, "Revisiting the 'Transcaspian Episode': British Intervention and Turkmen Statehood, 1918–1919," *Europe-Asia Studies* 75, no. 1 (2023): 138–40.

12. Eric Lee, *The Experiment: Georgia's Forgotten Revolution, 1918–1921* (London: Zed, 2017).

13. For apologetic document editions from the Georgian side, see *Iz istorii armiansko-gruzinskikh otnoshenii: 1918 god. Pogranychnye konflikty, peregovory, voina, soglashenie* (Tiflis: n.p., 1919); and *Dokumenty i materialy po vneshnei politike Zakavkaz'ia i Gruzii* (Tiflis: n.p., 1919).

14. Agreement between the Armenian and Georgian plenipotentiaries on the establishment of a neutral zone, 7–15 January 1919, HAA, f. 113, op. 3, d. 1, l. 22.

15. Brinegar, "Oil Deal," 375-76.

16. Peyrat, *Histoire du Caucase*, 103-4; Agreement between the three Transcaucasian republics and the RSFSR on railway, telegraph, and postal services, 24 May 1922, SUIC'A, f. 612, op. 1, d. 93, l. 5.

17. Stephan Rindlisbacher, "Between Proclamations of Friendship and Concealed Distrust: The Turkish-Soviet Border Commission, 1925-1926," *Journal of Modern European History* 22, no. 1 (2024): 56-57.

18. Shorthand notes of the Moscow conference between the RSFSR and the Grand National Assembly of Turkey, March 1921, HAA, f. 113, op. 3, d. 23, ll. 102-27; Treaty of Kars between three Transcaucasian republics and the Grand National Assembly of Turkey, 13 October 1921, HAA, f. 113, op. 3, d. 54, ll. 15-19; Jones, "Establishment of Soviet Power," 627; Peyrat, *Histoire du Caucase*, 102-5.

19. Decision of the TsK RKP(b) signed by Stalin, 5 April 1922, RGASPI, f. 64, op. 1, d. 61, l. 9; Baberowski, *Feind ist überall*, 253-55.

20. Smith, *National Question*, 196; Blank, "Transcaucasian Federation," 41.

21. Lenin to Lev Kamenev, 26 September 1922, in *PSS*, 45:212.

22. Kharmandarian, *Lenin i stanovlenie zakavkazskoi federatsii*, 240.

23. Peyrat, "Soviet Federalism," 533-34; Brinegar, "Oil Deal," 384-85.

24. Jones, "Establishment of Soviet Power," 631; Kharmandarian, *Lenin i stanovlenie Zakavkazskoi Federatsii*, 347-71.

25. "Pervyi Zakavkazskii s"ezd sovetov," *Zaria vostoka*, no. 149, 13 December 1922, 1.

26. Blank, "Transcaucasian Federation," 51-53.

27. Claire P. Kaiser, *Georgian and Soviet: Entitled Nationhood and the Specter of Stalin in the Caucasus* (Ithaca, NY: Cornell University Press, 2023), 24.

28. "Constitution (Fundamental Law) of the Transcaucasian Socialist Federative Soviet Republic," *Zaria vostoka*, no. 197, 11 February 1923, 5; Peyrat, "Soviet Federalism at Work," 536-38.

29. Jones, "Establishment of Soviet Power," 632-34; Georges Mamoulia, *Les combats indépendantistes des Caucasiens entre URSS et puissances occidentales: Le cas de la Géorgie, 1921-1945* (Paris: L'Harmattan, 2009); Kaiser, *Georgian and Soviet*, 90-91.

30. For further discussion of this problem, see Bruce Grant, "An Average Azerbaijani Village, 1930: Remembering Rebellion in the Caucasus Mountains," *Slavic Review* 63, no. 4 (2004): 703-31; and response of the TsK RKP(b) to the Georgian uprising, 27 October 1924, in *TsK RKP(b)-VKP(b)*, 1:248-51.

31. Claire Mouradian, *De Staline à Gorbachev: Histoire d'une république soviétique. L'Arménie* (Paris: Éditions Ramsay, 1990), 26-34. This book cannot discuss the "Armenian genocide" in depth; see, e.g., Thomas De Waal, *Great Catastrophe: Armenians and Turks in the Shadow of Genocide* (Oxford: Oxford University Press, 2015).

32. This number is based on an internal report of the Transcaucasian government from 11 November 1927 to fund suitable accommodation for these refugees, SUIC'A, f. 617, op. 1, d. 1800, l. 34. On the refugee issue, see Jo Laycock, "Developing a Soviet Armenian Nation: Refugees and Resettlement in the Early Soviet South Caucasus," in *Empire and Belonging*, 97-111; and Nick

Baron and Peter Gatrell, "Population Displacement, State-Building, and Social Identity in the Lands of the Former Russian Empire, 1917-23," *Kritika: Explorations in Russian and Eurasian History*, 4, no. 1 (2003): 51-100.

33. On 1 February 1928 there were 5,096 people working in Transcaucasian institutions: 1,224 Georgians, 1,175 Armenians, 134 Turks, 1,885 Russians, and 678 others (table, SŠSSA-PA, f. 13, op. 6, d. 250, l. 30).

34. Smith, *National Question*, 63-64.

35. Tsentral'noe statisticheskoe upravlenie, ed., *Vsesoiuznaia perepis' naseleniia 1926 goda*, 14:6-10.

36. Brinegar, "Oil Deal," 375-80; Suny, *Baku Commune*, 350; Jones, "Establishment of Soviet Power," 622.

37. Cadiot, *Laboratoire impérial*, 138.

38. Peyrat, "Soviet Federalism," 535-36; Scott, *Familiar Strangers*, 37-41.

39. Smith, *National Question*, 69-70; Mouradian, *De Staline à Gorbatchev*, 32-36.

40. Saparov, *From Conflict to Autonomy*, 117-23; Minutes of the Kavbiuro, 4 and 5 July 1921, RGASPI, f. 85, op. 18, d. 58, ll. 17-18. For one of many assumed intrigues behind this decision of the Kavbiuro in 1921, see Derluguian, *Bourdieu's Secret Admirer*, 185-87.

41. Decision on the provisional border between Armenia and Georgia, 6 November 1921, NAA, f. 113, op. 3, d. 1, l. 66; see also Mirianašvili, *sak'art'velos teritoriuli*, 105; and Xač'atryan, Suk'iasyan, and Badalyan, *Xorhrdayan Hayastani*, 145-46.

42. Aleksandr Beloborodov to the ZakTsIK, 3 March 1923, SUIC'A, f. 607, op. 1, d. 69, l. 91; Mikhail Skibitskii's report to the ZakTsIK, 1923, SUIC'A, f. 607, op. 1, d. 71, ll. 14-15. On the ill-defined borders, see Daniel Müller, "Die Armenier in den Kreisen Džebaril', Šuša und Dževanšir des Gouvernements Elizavetpol' nach den amtlichen 'Familienlisten' von 1886," in *Osmanismus, Nationalismus und der Kaukasus: Muslime und Christen, Türken und Armenier im 19. und 20. Jahrhundert*, ed. Fikret Adanir and Bernd Bonwetsch (Wiesbaden: Reichert, 2005), 69.

43. Müller, "Armenier in den Kreisen," 65-83.

44. Commission of the Zakkraikom tasked with solving the misunderstandings in the border regions, 6 November 1922, SUIC'A, f. 612, op. 1, d. 39, l. 32.

45. Chkhenkeli, Report on the history of the ZakTsIK Territorial Commission, 3 September 1927, SUIC'A, f. 607, op. 1, d. 1148, l. 14; Baberowski, *Feind ist überall*, 366-67.

46. Plan to transform the rural economy of the ZSFSR, November 1927, SUIC'A, f. 607, op. 1, d. 541, l. 37.

47. S. Voshchinskii, Report to the Zakkraikom on border issues in Borchaly Uezd, after 24 September 1924, SŠSSA-PA, f. 13, op. 3, d. 42, l. 29.

48. Yakov Kochetkov, Report to the ZakTsIK on the pastures in the Delizhan region of Armenia, 4 July 1924, SUIC'A, f. 607, op. 1, d. 218, l. 21; Budget of the Transcaucasian Land and Forest Commission, 1928/29, SUIC'A, f. 607, op. 1, d. 2270, l. 46.

49. The Territorial Commission of the ZakTsIK had different designations: Commission for the Establishment of Uezd Borders (Komissiia po

ustanovleniiu granits uezdov, 10 February 1923-30 January 1924); Commission to Resolve Issues of Land, Forest, and Water Use among the Republics of the ZSFSR (Komissiia po razresheniiu sporov po zemle-leso-vodopol'sovaniiu mezhdu respublikami, vkhodiashchimi v sostav ZSFSR, 30 January 1924-20 July 1927); Commission to Resolve Land and Forest Issues among the Republics of the Transcaucasian Federation (Komissiia po razresheniiu zemel'nykh sporov mezhdu respublikami Zakfederatsii, 20 July 1927-?). Their minutes are kept in SUIC'A, f. 607, op. 1, d. 68; SUIC'A, f. 607, op. 1, d. 78; and SUIC'A, f. 607, op. 1, d. 197. I could not find any documented activity for this commission after 14 March 1929.

50. Authorization of the ZakTsIK Territorial Commission, 20 July 1927, SUIC'A, f. 607, op. 1, d. 1148, ll. 8-9.

51. Chkhenkeli, The history of the ZakTsIK Territorial Commission, SUIC'A, f. 607, op. 1, d. 1148, l. 14.

52. Map of the economic administrative border between the SSRA and AzSSR, 15 June 1935, SUIC'A, f. 607, op. 1, d. 3720, l. 8.

53. Mountain ridges separating the Erivan' from Yelizavetpol' Guberniia in the east and southeast from Lake Sevan pose an exception.

54. Saparov, "Nagorno-Karabakh Conflict," 188. For further discussion of this problem, see Steven R. Ratner, "Drawing a Better Line: Uti Possidetis and the Borders of New States," *American Journal of International Law* 90, no. 4 (1996): 590-624.

55. Contract between Asad-bek Sultanov and four inhabitants of Bashkend, 22 March 1911 (4 April 1911, New Style), SUIC'A, f. 607, op. 1, d. 92, ll. 62-63.

56. Chkhenkeli, "Spravka po povodu upolnomochennykh Shinykh-Airumskogo obshchestva" (Inquiry on the occasion of the representatives of the Shinykh-Airum community), 13 September 1929, SUIC'A, f. 607, op. 1, d. 2543, l. 18. In related documents, the individual Dzhafar Rassul-ogly also appears as Dzhafar Kuli and Dzhafar Guly Khasan-ogly.

57. Note by Sen'ko, 6 August 1923, SUIC'A, f. 607, op. 1, d. 92, l. 42.

58. Act between the representatives of Shinikh Airum and Bashkend, 25 August 1923, SUIC'A, f. 607, op. 1, d. 92, l. 60.

59. Act between Shinikh Airum and Bashkend, SUIC'A, f. 607, op. 1, d. 92, l. 60.

60. Note by Sen'ko, SUIC'A, f. 607, op. 1, d. 92, l. 42.

61. Act between Shinikh Airum and Bashkend, SUIC'A, f. 607, op. 1, d. 92, l. 60.

62. On the term *kulak*, see Sheila Fitzpatrick, *Stalin's Peasants: Resistance and Survival in the Russian Village after Collectivization* (New York: Oxford University Press, 1994), 28-31.

63. Petition from the peasants in Krasnoe Mikhailovka, 12 September 1925, SUIC'A, f. op. 1, d. 3735, l. 8. The people in the Russian settlement of Krasnoe Mikhailovka expected their village to be more prosperous under Azerbaijani rule. They also argued that taxes were too high in Armenia.

64. Chairman of the Bashkend rural soviet to the ZakTsIK, September 1925, SUIC'A, f. 607, op. 1, d. 539, l. 65.

65. Minutes of the Bashkend village assembly, 17 September 1925, SUIC'A, f. 607, op. 1, d. 539, l. 72.
66. Folder of the local commission for Shinikh Airum, September–December 1925, SUIC'A, f. 607, op. 1, d. 539.
67. Report of the surveyor for Dilizhan Uezd (SSRA) to Onanov, 18 September 1925, SUIC'A, f. 607, op. 1, d. 3735, l. 7.
68. Onanov, Report to the ZakTsIK, 18 September 1925, SUIC'A, f. 607, op. 1, d. 539, l. 6.
69. Khaustov and Sen'ko, Report on incidents in Shinikh Airum, 16 September 1925, SUIC'A, f. 607, op. 1, d. 539, l. 26.
70. Report by Zardanian, senior forester, 25 September 1925, SUIC'A, f. 607, op. 1, d. 3735, l. 17.
71. Statement by Abgar Kharatian in the report of the Shamshad forestry on the unlawful action of Azerbaijani representatives within the territory of Armenia, 25 October 1925, SUIC'A, f. 607, op. 1, d. 3735, l. 27.
72. Minutes of the ZakTsIK Territorial Commission, 2 November 1925, SUIC'A, f. 607, op. 1, d. 197, l. 44.
73. Decision of the ZakTsIK, 8 February 1926, SUIC'A, f. 607, op. 1, d. 574, l. 4–5.
74. Kovalev, Report to the ZakTsIK, 22 October 1926, SUIC'A, f. 607, op. 2, d. 4119, l. 3.
75. Telegram from the ArmNarkomzem to the ZakTsIK with handwritten note regarding the urgency of the issue, 27 October 1926, SUIC'A, f. 607, op. 2, d. 4119, l. 2.
76. Kiazimov, secretary of the AzTsIK, to the ZakTsIK, 4 November 1926, SUIC'A, f. 607, op. 2, d. 4119, l. 10.
77. Minutes of the ZakTsIK Territorial Commission, 11 January 1927, SUIC'A, f. 607, op. 1, d. 197, l. 74.
78. Decision of the ZakTsIK, after 11 January 1927, SUIC'A, f. 607, op. 1, d. 1136, l. 19.
79. Decisions of the ZakTsIK, 18 February 1929, SUIC'A, f. 607, op. 1, d. 1150, ll. 93–96.
80. Telegram from representatives of Shinikh Airum to Mikhail Kalinin, 7 May 1929, SUIC'A, f. 607, op. 1, d. 2543, l. 16.
81. Petition from the community of Shinikh Airum, 22 June 1929, SUIC'A, f. 607, op. 1, d. 2543, l. 9.
82. Chkhenkeli, "Po povodu zhaloby upolnomochennykh," SUIC'A, f. 607, op. 1, d. 2543, l. 18.
83. Minutes of the ZakTsIK, 29 October 1929, SUIC'A, f. 607, op. 1, d. 2543, l. 29.
84. Skibitskii, "O zemel'nykh sporakh" (On land issues), 9 March 1927, SUIC'A, f. 607, op. 1, d. 557, l. 38.
85. Demographic composition of the Niuvadi rural soviet, without date, SUIC'A, f. 607, op. 1, d. 1149, l. 10.
86. Petition from the villages of Niuvadi, Tugut, and Einazur, 16 October 1925, SUIC'A, f. 607, op. 1, d. 1149, l. 11.

87. Skibitskii, "O zemel'nykh sporakh," SUIC'A, f. 607, op. 1, d. 557, l. 38.

88. Megri Uezd ispolkom to the ZakTsIK Territorial Commission, 20 October 1926, SUIC'A, f. 607, op. 1, d. 1149, l. 14.

89. Petition from the poor peasants in Niuvadi, 10 February 1927, SUIC'A, f. 607, op. 1, d. 1765, l. 16; Petition from the poor peasants in Niuvadi, 11 April 1927, SUIC'A, f. 607, op. 1, d. 1765, l. 44.

90. Report to the ZakTsIK Territorial Commission, 25 October 1928, SUIC'A, f. 607, op. 1, d. 1148, l. 60.

91. Decisions of the ZakTsIK, 18 February 1929, SUIC'A, f. 607, op. 1, d. 1150, ll. 93-96.

92. Skibitskii, "O zemel'nykh sporakh," SUIC'A, f. 607, op. 1, d. 557, l. 38.

93. Act issued by Rukhiladze on the border between the villages of Zor and Sevakiar, 26 August 1926, SUIC'A, f. 607, op. 1, d. 1156, ll. 6-7.

94. Act on the border between Zor and Sevakiar, SUIC'A, f. 607, op. 1, d. 1156, l. 13.

95. Firid Memed Ali-ogly, Petition, undated, SUIC'A, f. 607, op. 1, d. 1156, l. 17.

96. ZakTsIK Territorial Commission to the ispolkom in Zangezur, 8 July 1927, SUIC'A, f. 607, op. 1, d. 1156, l. 18.

97. Zangezur ispolkom to the ZakTsIK Territorial Commission, 6 October 1927, SUIC'A, f. 607, op. 1, d. 1156, l. 21.

98. Information bulletin at the ZakTsIK, undated, SUIC'A, f. 607, op. 1, d. 2281, l. 29.

99. Minutes of the local territorial commission (Zangezur/Karabakh), 29 April 1930, SUIC'A, f. 607, op. 1, d. 2281, l. 41.

100. Chkhenkeli and Eganov, Report to the presidium of the ZakTsIK, 31 October 1929, SUIC'A, f. 607, op. 1, d. 2270, l. 58 and 61; Chkhenkeli, Report on the activities of the Territorial Commission, 10 January 1931, SUIC'A, f. 607, op. 1, d. 2270, ll. 68-71.

101. Budget for field surveying in 1931, SUIC'A, f. 607, op. 1, d. 2270, l. 71.

102. Glavnoe upravlenie geodezii i kartografii pri Sovete ministrov SSSR, *Armianskaia SSR*, 1:50,000 (Moscow: General'nyi shtab, 1973-1990). See, e.g., the sheets K-38-128-A (Bashkend, 1973) or K-38-116-A (Tauz, 1976); and Hasanli, *Sovetskii Azerbaidzhan*, 420-24.

103. Siegelbaum and Moch, "Transnationalism in One Country?," 984-86.

104. Christine Bichsel highlighted the everyday significance of demarcation based on examples from the Fergana Valley (*Conflict Transformation*, 106-12).

105. Similar developments can be observed in Central Asia. See Stephan Rindlisbacher and Alun Thomas. "Paths Not Taken: How Did Nomadism Affect Border-Making during National Delimitation in Central Asia?" *Ab Imperio*, no. 2 (2023): 117-41.

106. This is how the surveyor Mikhail Skibitskii defined these forms of nonsedentary cattle breeding (SUIC'A, f. 607, op. 1, d. 541, l. 14). I use these terms as they were used in the Transcaucasian political discourse during the 1920s and 1930s. On the problematic term *kochevnik* in early Soviet debate, see Thomas, *Nomads*, 30-37; and Cameron, *Hungry Steppe*, 23, 56-57.

107. Saparov, "Nagorno-Karabakh Conflict," 186.

108. Minutes of the Transcaucasian conference on the pasture issue, 5 April 1931, SUIC'A, f. 607, op. 1, d. 3113, l. 29. There were about thirty thousand nomads in Georgia and thirty-thousand nomads in Azerbaijan. By contrast, nomads made up a clear majority in the Kyrgyz and Kazakh Autonomous Republics in the 1920s.

109. Mikhail Skibitskii, "Kochevoi vopros" (The nomad issue), November 1927, SUIC'A, f. 607, op. 1, d. 541, l. 37. Nomads and seminomads also wandered between Georgia and Armenia and between Azerbaijan and Georgia, but compared to the extent of movement between the Armenian and Azerbaijani republics, they were fewer in number and produced much less paperwork for federal state and party administrators.

110. Tsentral'noe statisticheskoe upravlenie, *Vsesoiuznaia perepis' naseleniia 1926 goda: Kratkie svodki. Narodnost' i rodnoi iazyk naseleniia SSSR* (Moscow: TsSU, 1928), 124; Tsentral'noe statisticheskoe upravlenie, *Vsesoiuznaia perepis' naseleniia 1926 goda*, 14:10; Dadash Buniat-Zade, Report to the ZakTsIK, 2 September 1924, SUIC'A, f. 607, op. 1, d. 1146, ll. 72–73; Report of the ZakSNK Pasture Commission, 1930, SUIC'A, f. 607, op. 1, d. 219, l. 116.

111. Baberowski, *Feind ist überall*, 82–83.

112. Martin, *Affirmative Action Empire*, 23–24.

113. Yanni Kotsonis and David Hoffmann, introduction to *Russian Modernity: Politics, Knowledge, Practices* (London: MacMillan, 2000), 9; David-Fox, *Crossing Borders*, 51–52; Thomas, *Nomads*, 18.

114. For the period between 1924 and 1925, 39,105 desiatinas (1 desiatina = 0.011 square kilometers) in Armenia were leased to nomads from Azerbaijan. See Report of the ZakSNK Pasture Commission, no date, SUIC'A, f. 607, op. 1, d. 219, l. 82.

115. Grigorian, "Tezisy po voprosu o zemleustroistve i raspredelenii v pol'zovanie razlichnykh ugodii (pastbishch i t. d.) i likvidatsii sporov na etoi pochve" (Theses on the question of land amelioration and the distribution of different lands [pastures, etc.] and the liquidation of such troubles), 1929, SUIC'A, f. 607, op. 1, d. 219, ll. 118–19.

116. Shota Palavandishvili, Report to the Zakkraikom on the pasture issue, 1927, SŠSSA-PA, f. 13, op. 5, d. 109, l. 2; Note by the Zakkraikom, 5 May 1928, SŠSSA-PA, f. 13, op. 6, d. 290, l. 98.

117. Report by the ZakSNK Pasture Commission, SUIC'A, f. 607, op. 1, d. 219, ll. 82–83.

118. Decision of the ZakTsIK to introduce a unified agricultural tax, 23 April 1923, SUIC'A, f. 607, op. 1, d. 38, l. 69.

119. "Konstitutsiia," *Zaria vostoka*, no. 197, 11 February 1923, 5 (chapter v, paragraph zh).

120. Payrat, "Soviet Federalism," 546–50.

121. Minutes of the Zakkraikom, 6 November 1922, SUIC'A, f. 612, op. 1, d. 66, l. 95.

122. Reports on the cattle plague appeared in the state and party newspaper *Zaria vostoka*: "Chumnaia epizootiia," no. 57, 25 August 1922, 2; "Epizootiia," no. 350, 14 August 1923, 2; "Bor'ba s chumoi na skote," no. 1136, 28 March 1926, 3; "Chuma likvidirovana," no. 1150, 14 April 1926, 2; "Chuma

vnov' poiavilas'," no. 1166, 5 May 1926, 2; Skibitskii, "Kochevoi vopros," SUIC'A, f. 607, op. 1, d. 541, l. 35.

123. NKVD SSRA to the ispolkom in Dilizhan, 19 May 1924, HAA, f. 113, op. 3, d. 120, l. 108.

124. Khimiashvili and Mamikoian, Report on Turkish communities in Borchaly, Dilizhan, and Kazakh, 3 May 1925, SŠSSA-PA, f. 13, op. 3, d. 314, ll. 7-8; shorthand notes of the Transcaucasian Convention on the Pasture Issue, SUIC'A, f. 607, op. 1, d. 3113, ll. 39-40.

125. Grigorian, "Tezisy po voprosu o zemleustroistve," SUIC'A, f. 607, op. 1, d. 219, l. 121.

126. Decision of the ZakTsIK, 4 September 1924, SUIC'A, f. 607, op. 1, d. 541, l. 1a. At the same time, Soviet experts were still debating whether Soviet modernization would be compatible with nomadism. For further discussion, see Cameron, *Hungry Steppe*, 46-47.

127. Buniat-Zade, Report to the ZakTsIK, SUIC'A, f. 607, op. 1, d. 1146, ll. 72-73.

128. Mikhail Miasnikov (aka Miasnikian), "Bor'ba partii s izvrazheniem leninizma" (The party's struggle with deviations from Leninism), 9 January 1925, SŠSSA-PA, f. 13, op. 3, d. 40, ll. 10-11.

129. Shota Palavandishvili, Report to the Zakkraikom, 5 May 1928, SŠSSA-PA, f. 13, op. 6, d. 290, l. 19. In Kazakhstan, party functionaries such as Filipp Goloshchëkin came to similar conclusions (Cameron, *Hungry Steppe*, 54-55, 59).

130. Palavandishvili, Report to the Zakkraikom, SŠSSA-PA, f. 13, op. 6, d. 290, l. 20.

131. Fitzpatrick, *Stalin's Peasants*, 49-53; Scott, *Seeing Like a State*, 217-18; Baberowski, *Feind ist überall*, 687-91; Paul R. Gregory, *The Political Economy of Stalinism: Evidence from the Soviet Secret Archives* (Cambridge: Cambridge University Press, 2003), 40-44.

132. Rally of TsK AKP(b), 31 January-1 February 1930, SŠSSA-PA, f. 13, op. 8, d. 84, ll. 10-13; ZakGPU, Report on incidents during the collectivization campaign in February and March 1930, SŠSSA-PA, f. 13, op. 8, d. 84, l. 24; Peyrat, *Histoire du Caucase*, 147-49.

133. Nicolas Werth, "Un état contre son peuple: Violences, répressions, terreurs en Union soviétique," in *Le livre noir du communisme: Crimes, terreur et répression*, ed. Stéphane Courtois et al. (Paris: Robert Laffont, 1997), 164-77.

134. Minutes of the TsK AKP(b), 15 February 1930, SŠSSA-PA, f. 13, op. 8, d. 193, l. 10.

135. ZakGPU, Report on incidents during the collectivization campaign in the spring of 1930, SŠSSA-PA, f. 13, op. 8, d. 84, ll. 14-24. See also Timothy K. Blauvelt, "Resistance and Accommodation in the Stalinist Periphery: A Peasant Uprising in Abkhazia," *Ab Imperio*, no. 3 (2012): 80; and Lynne Viola, *Peasant Rebels under Stalin: Collectivization and the Culture of Peasant Resistance* (New York: Oxford University Press, 1999), 132-45.

136. Stalin, "Golovokruzhenie ot uspekhov: K voprosam kolkhoznogo dvizhenia," *Pravda*, no. 60/4505, 2 March 1930, 1.

137. Minutes of the ZakTsIK presidium, 29 April 1931, SUIC'A, f. 660, op. 1, d. 1487, l. 2.

138. Petition from the executive board of the sovkhoz Ovtsevod to the Armenian Narkomzem, 24 August 1931, SUIC'A, f. 660, op. 1, d. 1482, ll. 3; decision of the Armenian Narkomzem, 15–16 October 1931, SUIC'A, f. 660, op. 1, d. 1482, ll. 4–7a.

139. Minutes of the ZakTsIK presidium, 28 March 1932, SUIC'A, f. 660, op. 1, d. 2447, l. 23.

140. Report on cattle breeding in the ZSFSR, 1931, SŠSSA-PA, f. 13, op. 9, d. 186, l. 84.

141. Peyrat, "Soviet Federalism," 546.

142. Conference at the ZakNarkomzem, 17 May 1932, SUIC'A, f. 660, op. 1, d. 2447, ll. 32–36.

143. Zakkraikom, Report on the collectivization campaign, 22 April 1932, SŠSSA-PA, f. 13, op. 9, d. 94, ll. 7–8; Beriia to Stalin, 21 November 1934, SŠSSA-PA, f. 13, op. 12, d. 95, ll. 1–3.

144. Report of the Orginstrootdel at Zakkraikom, 13 March 1932, SŠSSA-PA, f. 13, op. 10, d. 151, l. 5; Dadash Buniatzade, Report on the situation in Armenia, 27 April 1934, 27 April 1934, SŠSSA-PA, f. 13, op. 12, d. 13, ll. 1–2; report on cattle breeding, SŠSSA-PA, f. 13, op. 9, d. 186, l. 85.

145. Conference on Cattle Collectives at the Zakkraikom, 7 January 1932, SŠSSA-PA, f. 13, op. 10, d. 150, ll. 24–31.

146. Report on cotton cultivation in Tauz Raion, 16 January 1931, SŠSSA-PA, f. 13, op. 8, d. 192, ll. 4–7; Pirumov, Report to the Azerbaijani Narkomzem on construction work in Kazakh Raion, 20 February 1932, SŠSSA-PA, f. 13, op. 11, d. 177, ll. 1–2.

147. Ter-Sarkisov, Report of Ovtsevod Trest, 7 January 1932, SŠSSA-PA, f. 13, op. 10, d. 150, ll. 23–24.

148. Sarah Cameron depicts the horrific outcome of the famine in Kazakhstan as the result of long-term natural and social effects, as well as short-term political decisions (*Hungry Steppe*, 13–14). See also Kindler, *Stalins Nomaden*, 11–12; and Mehmet Volkan Kaşıkçı, "Making Sense of Catastrophe: Experiencing and Remembering the Kazakh Famine in a Comparative Context," *Journal of Contemporary History*, 58, no. 2 (2023): 223–46.

149. Dolidze, Report to the presidium of the Zakkraikom on the situation in Armenia, 27 April 1934, SŠSSA-PA, f. 13, op. 12, d. 13, ll. 9–10. Data from the 1937 census indicate an increase of about a third in the population of all three South Caucasian Republics compared to 1926, while the population of the North Caucasus, Ukraine, and especially Kazakhstan shrank. See Valentina Zhiromskaia, ed., *Vsesoiuznaia perepis' naseleniia 1937 goda: Sbornik dokumentov i materialov* (Moscow: Rosspen, 2007), 30–32.

150. Dolidze, Report to the Zakkraikom, SŠSSA-PA, f. 13, op. 12, d. 13, l. 7.

151. Cameron, *Hungry Steppe*, 177.

152. Buniatzade, Report on the situation in Armenia, SŠSSA-PA, f. 13, op. 12, d. 13, ll. 2–6.

153. Report from the Orgotdel to the TsK KP(b)A, 5 February 1930, SŠSSA-PA, f. 13, op. 8, d. 84, l. 41.

154. Kindler, *Stalins Nomaden*, 233; Botakoz Kassymbekova, "Humans as Territory: Forced Resettlement and the Making of Soviet Tajikistan, 1920–38," *Central Asian Survey* 30, no. 3–4 (2011): 358–59.

155. Cameron, *Hungry Steppe*, 89-96; Gosplan SSSR, *Piatiletnii plan*, 3:371; Niccolò Pianciola argues that economic regionalization is a major factor in explaining why the famine in early 1930 struck nonsedentary pastoral societies in Kazakhstan so much harder than in the Kyrgyz ASSR ("Stalinist Spatial Hierarchies," 86).

156. Beriia to Stalin, 21 November 1934, SŠSSA-PA, f. 13, op. 12, d. 95, l. 12.

157. Minutes of the pasture committees, 22-23 August 1934, HAA, f. 112, op. 1, d. 681, ll. 65-67.

158. Saparov, "Nagorno-Karabakh Conflict," 189.

159. Florian Mühlfried mentions this conscious neglect in the case of the Georgian highlands in *Being a State and States of Being in Highland Georgia* (New York: Berghahn, 2014), 57-60. Olivier Ferrando points to a similar policy in Tajikistan ("Soviet Population Transfers and Interethnic Relations in Tajikistan: Assessing the Concept of Ethnicity," *Central Asian Survey* 30, no. 1 [2011]: 42-43).

160. The long-lasting dispute between the villages of Alibegly (Azerbaijan) and Moseskend (Armenia) is another striking example: Report to the ZakTsIK Territorial Commission, 17 December 1928, SUIC'A, f. 607, op. 1, d. 213, l. 78.

161. Peyrat, "Soviet Federalism," 551; Peyrat, *Histoire du Caucase*, 173. In the 1930s, the Soviet economy was increasingly centralized, and the ZSFSR also lost much of its intermediary role.

162. Kaiser, *Georgian and Soviet*, 80-86; Saparov, "Nagorno-Karabakh Conflict," 191-93.

163. On nonsolutions in political conflicts, see Christine Bell and Jan Pospisil, "Navigating Inclusion in Transitions from Conflict: The Formalised Political Unsettlement," *Journal of International Development* 29, no. 5 (2017): 576-93.

6. How to Contextualize "Khrushchev's Gift"?

1. Vladimir Medinskii, "K chitateliam," in *Istoriia Kryma*, ed. S. Kodzov (Moscow: Olma, 2016), 6; A. Romanov, "Georgievskie tsveta snova nad Krymom: Vossoedinenie Kryma s Rossiei, 2014 god," in *Istoriia Kryma*, 456-58.

2. Minutes of the Cherviakov Commission, 27 November 1924, GA RF, f. 5677, op. 5, d. 26, l. 28.

3. Decision of the Cherviakov Commission, 23 January 1925, GA RF, f. 5677, op. 5, d. 26, l. 32. See also minutes of the Politburo, 11 December 1924, RGASPI, f. 17, op. 3, d. 480, l. 3; Cherviakov to Butsenko, 8 January 1925, TsDAVO, f. 1, op. 2, spr. 3143, ark. 3.

4. Central Administrative-Territorial Commission (TsATK) to the VUTsVK, 30 June 1925, TsDAVO, f. 1, op. 2, spr. 1808, ark. 79-80; minutes of the TsIK, 16 October 1925, GA RF, f. 3316, op. 17, d. 718, l. 159.

5. Demographic data for the territories to be transferred from the RSFSR to the UkrSSR on 1 March 1926, based on the 1920 census, DAKhO, f. 845, op. 3, spr. 677, ark. 50; transfer act for territories from Kursk Guberniia to Hlukhiv, Konotop, and Sumy Okruhy, 14 April 1926, TsDAVO, f. 1, op. 3, spr. 642, ark. 2-3; Pashkovskii, Report on the transfer of the Putivl' region to the UkrSNK, VUTsVK, and TsK KP(b)U, 26 March 1926, TsDAVO, f. 1, op. 2, spr. 2356, ark. 9-10.

6. Transfer act, 14 April 1926, TsDAVO, f. 1, op. 3, spr. 642, ark. 8-9.

7. *The Tale of the Campaign of Igor: A Russian Epic Poem of the Twelfth Century*, trans. Robert Craig Howes (New York: W. W. Norton, 1973), 33; demographic data for the territories to be transferred, DAKhO, f. 845, op. 3, spr. 677, ark. 50; Strelets, Report on the transfer of Putivl' Uezd, no date, TsDAVO, f. 1, op. 2, spr. 3256, ark. 2.

8. Butsenko to Enukidze, 24 February 1926, GA RF, f. 3316, op. 17, d.718, l. 255.

9. Enukidze to Butsenko, 10 March 1926, GA RF, f. 3316, op. 17, d. 718, l. 257; decision of the VTsIK, 15 March 1926, GA RF, f. 3316, op. 17, d. 718, l. 259.

10. Ryl'sk UIK to the Ukrainian People's Commissariat for Finance (Narkomfin), 7 March 1926, TsDAVO, f. 1, op. 3, spr. 645, ark. 4-5.

11. Note of protest from the Ukrainian delegation to the All-Union Commission for Raionirovanie, 10 March 1926, TsDAVO, f. 1, op. 3, spr. 645, ark. 13-14; Ukrainian delegation, Note of protest regarding the handling of the transfer, 14 April 1926, TsDAVO, f. 1, op. 3, spr. 642, ark. 29-30.

12. Butsenko to Avel' Enukidze, no date, TsDAVO, f. 1, op. 3, spr. 620, ark. 17.

13. I. Akulov, Report to the Politburo VKP(b), 11 December 1935, with handwritten notes by Stalin, GA RF, f. 3316, op. 65, d. 151, l. 5.

14. Decision of the Supreme Soviet UkrSSR, 15 October 1944, GA RF, f. 7523, op. 15, d. 101, l. 1; decision of the Supreme Soviet RSFSR, 18 October 1944, GA RF, f. 7523, op. 15, d. 101, l. 2; ukaz of the Supreme Soviet SSSR, 5 November 1944, GA RF, f. 7523, op. 15, d. 101, l. 4.

15. Transfer act for the Dar'ino-Yermakovka Rural Soviet from Rostov Oblast (RSFSR) to Roven'ky Raion (UkrSSR), 9 September 1945, GA RF, f. 385, op. 17, d. 434, ll. 9-10.

16. Andreas Kappeler, *The Russian Empire: A Multiethnic History* (London: Longman, 2001), 377-82; Müller, *Sowjetische Nationalitätenpolitik*, 135-37; Walter Sperling, *Vor den Ruinen von Grosny: Leben und Überleben im multiethnischen Kaukasus* (Berlin: Matthes & Seitz, 2023), 200-203.

17. Edgar Anderson, "How Narva, Petseri, and Abrene Came to Be in the RSFSR," *Journal of Baltic Studies* 19, no. 3 (1988): 204-10.

18. Decision of the Presidium of the Supreme Soviet SSSR on the transfer of Crimea from the RSFSR to the UkrSSR, 19 February 1954, GA RF, f. 7523, op. 57, d. 963, ll. 1-3.

19. Sometimes only formal decisions on territorial transfers are stored, as in the case of the Dzhetysai, Kirov, and Pakhtaaral' Raiony between Uzbekistan and Kazakhstan, 12 May 1971, Tsentral'nyi gosudarstvennyi arkhiv Respubliki Kazakhstan (hereafter TsGA RK), f. 698, op. 14, d. 779, l. 19.

20. Baberowski, *Verbrannte Erde*, 328-29; Fitzpatrick, *Everyday Stalinism*, 27.

21. Even though readers presume that the author of an autobiography tells his or her "truth," individual biases are by default part of the product. See Philippe Lejeune, *Le pact autobiographique* (Paris: Éditions du Seuil, 1975), 44-45; and Pierre Bourdieu, "L'illusion biographique," *Actes de la Recherche en Sciences Sociales* 62-63, no. 1 (1986): 69-72.

22. Vladimir Putin, "Address by the President of the Russian Federation," 22 February 2022, http://en.kremlin.ru/events/president/transcripts/67828;

Dmitrii Karaichev, "Mify o nezakonnosti peredachi Kryma v 1954 godu," *Zerkalo nedeli*, 11 January 2013, https://zn.ua/internal/mify-o-nezakonnosti-peredachi-kryma-v-1954-godu.html.

23. Documents on the solemn ceremonies on the occasion of the Pereiaslav anniversary in Kiev, May 1954, TsDAVO, f. 1, op. 16, spr. 490, ark. 92-111.

24. Jeffrey Burds, "Bor'ba s banditizmom v SSSR v 1944-1953 gg.," *Sotsial'naia istoriia: Ezhegodnik* (2000): 169-90; Grzegorz Motyka, *Ukraińska partyzantka, 1942-1960: Działalność Organizacji Ukraińskich Nacjonalistów i Ukraińskiej Powstańczej Armii* (Warsaw: Rytm, 2006), 424-52.

25. Gwendolyn Sasse, *The Crimea Question: Identity, Transition, and Conflict* (Cambridge, MA: Harvard University Press, 2007), 120-21; See also Korine Amacher, "La Crimée," in *Histoire partagée, mémoire divisée: Ukraine, Russie, Pologne*, ed. Korine Amacher, Andrii Portnov, and Eric Aunoble (Lausanne: Antipodes, 2021), 75; and Austin Charron, "Crimea's 1954 Transfer to Ukraine: A Practical yet Contested Union," in Ardeleanu and Palko, *Making Ukraine*, 244-48.

26. Oleh Bazhan et al., eds., *Krym v umovakh suspil'no-politychnykh transformatsii, 1940-2015: Zbirnyk dokumentiv ta materialiv* (Kiev: NAN Ukraïny, 2016), 96-169.

27. P. Knyshevskii, "Shtrikhi k portretu kremlevskoi galerei," *Novoe vremia*, no. 9 (1994): 54, cited according to Mark Kramer, "Why Did Russia Give Away Crimea Sixty Years Ago?," https://www.wilsoncenter.org/publication/why-did-russia-give-away-crimea-sixty-years-ago.

28. Hayden White, *Metahistory: The Historical Imagination in Nineteenth-Century Europe* (Baltimore: Johns Hopkins University Press, 1973), 34.

29. Paul R. Magocsi, *A History of Ukraine: The Land and Its Peoples*, 2nd ed. (Toronto: University of Toronto Press, 2010), 703; William Taubman, "The Khrushchev Period, 1953-1964," in *Cambridge History of Russia*, 3:283.

30. Kerstin S. Jobst, *Geschichte der Ukraine*, 2nd ed. (Stuttgart: Reclam, 2015), 47. This passage is an unchanged reproduction of the wording in the first edition of 2010 (212).

31. Jeremy Smith, "Leadership and Nationalism in the Soviet Republics, 1951-1959," in *Khrushchev in the Kremlin: Policy and Government in the Soviet Union, 1953-1964*, ed. Jeremy Smith and Melanie Ilic (London: Routledge, 2011), 79, 81; Ronald G. Suny, *The Soviet Experiment: Russia, the USSR, and the Successor States*, 2nd ed. (New York: Oxford University Press, 2011), 435.

32. One exception is I. Lezhnev, Expert opinion on territorial questions between the RSFSR and the UkrSSR for the TsIK, 18 June 1923, GA RF, f. 5677, op. 5, d. 20, l. 3.

33. Brian G. Williams, *The Crimean Tatars: From Soviet Genocide to Putin's Conquest* (London: Hurst and Co., 2015), 9-31.

34. Tsentral'noe statisticheskoe upravlenie, *Vsesoiuznaia perepis' naseleniia 1926 goda*, 5:11.

35. On the deportation of the Crimean Tatars, see Williams, *Crimean Tatars*, 89-115.

36. I. I. Babkov, *Iuzhno-ukrainskii i severo-krymskii kanaly i ikh vliianie na preobrazovanie prirody* (Leningrad: Vsesoiuznoe obshchestvo po raspredelenii politicheskikh i nauchnykh znanii, 1951), 14-15; L. I. Kukharenko, *Velikie*

stalinskie stroiki na Dnepre (Kiev: Izdatel'stvo KGU, 1952), 69; A. Zotiev and I. Mokhoshchekov, *Kanal izobiliia* (Simferopol': Krymizdat, 1964); Sasse, *Crimea Question*, 115–16.

37. Kliment Voroshilov, Address to the Presidium of the Supreme Soviet on 19 February 1954, *Pravda*, no. 58/12,991, 27 February 1954, 2.

38. Sharaf Rashidov, Address to the Presidium of the Supreme Soviet on 19 February 1954, *Pravda*, no. 58/12,991, 27 February 1954, 2.

39. Shtoulberg et al., "Soviet Regional Policy," 54–55.

40. Keller, *Russia and Central Asia*, 237–40.

41. Taubman, "Khrushchev Period," 274–76; Suny, *Soviet Experiment*, 418.

42. Sergei Khrushchev, *Trilogiia ob ottse* (Moscow: Vremia, 2010), 1:162–63.

43. Charron, "Crimea's 1954 Transfer," 246–48; Kramer, "Why Did Russia Give Away Crimea Sixty Years Ago?"

44. Zotiev and Mokhoshchekov, *Kanal izobiliia*, 15–18; Boyechko, Hanzha, and Zakharchuk, *Kordony Ukraïny*, 90–96.

45. Anton Troianovski and Malachy Browne, "Satellite Imagery Shows Ukrainian Water Flowing Again to Crimea, as Russia Nears Big Objective," *New York Times*, 8 June 2022, https://www.nytimes.com/2022/06/08/world/europe/crimea-water-canal-russia.html.

46. Dan Sabbagh et al., "The Disastrous Bursting of Ukraine's Nova Kakhovka Dam: And the Battle That Is to Come," *The Guardian*, 10 June 2023, https://www.theguardian.com/world/2023/jun/10/the-disastrous-bursting-of-ukraines-nova-kakhovka-dam-and-the-battle-that-is-to-come.

47. Pianciola, "Benefits of Marginality," 513–29.

48. "Postanovlenie Verkhovnogo Soveta Kazakhskoi SSR, 21 ianvaria 1956," *Kazakhstanskaia pravda*, no. 8541, 22 January 1956, 1.

49. Zhumabek Tashenev, "O peredache Bostandykskogo raiona i chasti zemel' Golodnoi stepi iz sostava Kazakhskoi SSR v sostav Uzbekskoi SSR," *Kazakhstanskaia pravda*, no. 19/8541, 22 January 1956, 4.

50. "Akt velikodushiia i bratstva," *Kazakhstanskaia pravda*, no. 24/11515, 29 January 1963, 1.

51. Dinmukhamed Kunaev, *Ot Stalina do Gorbacheva* (Almaty: Sanat, 1994), 156.

52. Taubman, "Krushchev Period," 278–79; Suny, *Soviet Experiment*, 417–19; Peterson, *Pipe Dreams*, 324–28.

53. Galina Shimyrbaeva, Interview with Ismail Yusupov on 21 April 2004, http://nomad.su/?a=15-200404220016.

54. Kunaev, *Ot Stalina do Gorbacheva*, 155.

55. Taubman, "Khrushchev Period," 290.

56. Kunaev, *Ot Stalina do Gorbacheva*, 170–71.

57. For a reevalution of the Brezhnev era, see Boris Belge and Martin Deuerlein, eds., *Goldenes Zeitalter der Stagnation? Perspektiven auf die sowjetische Ordnung der Brežnev-Ära* (Tübingen: Mohr Siebeck, 2014).

58. Ukaz of the Supreme Soviet of the Kazakh SSR on the incorporation of a part of Syr-Daria Oblast of the Uzbek SSR into the Kazakh SSR, 12 May 1971, TsGA RK, f. 698, op. 14, f. 779, l. 19.

59. Maike Lehmann, *Eine sowjetische Nation: Nationale Sozialismusinterpretationen in Armenien seit 1945* (Frankfurt am Main: Campus, 2012), 65–75; Mouradian, *De Staline à Gorbatchev*, 416–25; Saparov, "Nagorno-Karabakh Conflict," 192.

Conclusion

1. Werth, "Russia's Borders," 644.
2. Blauvelt, *Clientelism and Nationality*, 228.
3. Jeremy Smith, "New Borders, New Belongings in Central Asia: Competing Visions and the Decoupling of the Soviet Union," in *Empire and Belonging*, 184–86.
4. On the anti-Armenian sentiment among the Georgian intelligentsia, see Kaiser, *Georgian and Soviet*, 97–99.
5. Stalin, "O proekte konstitutsii Soiuza SSR," *Pravda*, no. 325/6931, 26 November 1936, 4.
6. Cherviakov to the Politburo RKP(b), 30 November 1924, TsDAVO, f. 1, op. 2, spr. 1808, ark. 10–14.
7. Rindlisbacher, "From Space to Territory," 99–100.
8. Broers, *Armenia and Azerbaijan*, 310–14.
9. Reeves, *Border Work*, 58–59; Alexander Morrison, "Stalin's Giant Pencil: Debunking a Myth about Central Asia's Borders," *eurasianet*, 13 February 2017, https://eurasianet.org/stalins-giant-pencil-debunking-a-myth-about-central-asias-borders.
10. Sasse, *Crimea*, 237; Cornell, "Autonomy," 269–72; Timur Dadabaev, "'We Want a State of Our Own!': Reconstructing Community Space in Bordering Areas of Central Asia," *Journal of Territorial and Maritime Studies* 2, no. 2 (2015): 15–17.

Glossary

1. With the constitution of 1936 the adjectives "Socialist" and "Soviet" switched places in all the designations of the federal entities of the Soviet state. As this book refers mostly to the era before 1936, the glossary prefers the order "Socialist Soviet Republic."

Bibliography

1. Gatagova et al., eds., Ts*K RKP(b)-VKP(b) i natsional'nyi vopros*.
2. Snapkovskii et al., *Gosudarstvennye granitsy Belarusi*.
3. Krzhizhanovskii, ed., *Voprosy ekonomicheskogo raionirovaniia SSSR*; Alampiev, *Ekonomicheskoe raionirovanie SSSR*.

Bibliography

The most important sources for this study were documents housed in the state and party archives of several countries located in the post-Soviet space. Until 2022, they were easily accessible. They reveal for the most part the negotiations between the various actors at different levels of hierarchy in all of the regions addressed here. For instance, the documents of the commissions related to the revisions of the Russian-Ukrainian border are almost completely preserved at the Russian and Ukrainian state archives (GA RF in Moscow and TsDAVO in Kiev). Most of the records of the Sredazbiuro surrounding the formation of the national territories in Central Asia are stored in the archive of the Communist Party (RGASPI) in Moscow, while documents concerning the establishment of the national territories in the South Caucasus are in a collection of ZSFSR records kept at the Central Archive of Contemporary History (SUIC'A) in Tbilisi. The files of the Zakkraikom are also stored in Tbilisi, but at the Archive of the Georgian Ministry of Internal Affairs (SŠSSA-PA). Statistical materials and ethnographic analyses are housed at the Russian State Archive of the Economy (RGAE). Even though all of these documents were fully accessible until 2022, they are not always organized in a way that makes it easy to use them. For example, documents concerning certain commissions, such as those led by Aleksandr Cherviakov and Saak Ter-Gabrielian, are spread out among different folders. Consequently, scholars have to piece together the various stages in the decision making as if it were a jigsaw puzzle—with some pieces (still) missing.

Some of the archival documents have been published. Most of Vladimir Lenin's writings were edited by the Institute of Marxism-Leninism in the 1960s and 1970s and printed in the *Complete Collected Works* (Polnoe sobranie sochinenii, *PSS*). With regard to the nationality question in the early Soviet state, the two volumes edited by L. Gatagova et al. between 2005 and 2009 are of particular value.[1] For certain territorial issues, such as the establishment of the border between the RSFSR and the BSSR, extensive volumes of documents have been compiled and edited by V. Snapkovskii et al.[2] The minutes of the party congresses and Lenin's and Stalin's collected works were already edited and published during the Soviet era. Despite their ideological biases, they can serve as a point of reference for the evolution of thinking within the Bolshevik leadership. The extensive publishing activity that occurred during raionirovanie in the 1920s has for the most part never been revisited. Notable exceptions are Gleb Krzhizhanovskii's anthology from 1957 and Pëtr Alampiev's critical compilation from the early 1960s.[3] The main documents produced during this debate have been largely ignored to this day.

Archives

ARAN   Arkhiv Rossiiskoi akademii nauk (Archive of the Russian Academy of Sciences, Moscow)

    f. 350   Kommunisticheskaia akademiia TsIK SSSR, 1918–1936

DAKhO   Derzhavnyi arkhiv Kharkivs'koï oblasti Ukraïny (State Archive of Kharkiv Oblast, Kharkiv)

    f. 203   Kharkovskii gubernskii ispolnitel'nyi komitet sovetov rabochikh, krest'ianskikh i krasnoarmeiskikh deputatov, 1919–1925

    f. 845   Kharkovskii okruzhnyi ispolnitel'nyi komitet sovetov rabochikh, krest'ianskikh i krasnoarmeiskikh deputatov, 1922–1930

DASO   Derzhavnyi arkhiv Sums'koï oblasti Ukraïny (State Archive of Sumy Oblast, Sumy)

    f. 32   Sums'kyi okruzhnyi vykonavchyi komitet, 1923–1930

GA RF   Gosudarstvennyi arkhiv Rossiiskoi Federatsii (State Archive of the Russian Federation, Moscow)

    f. 3316   Tsentral'nyi ispolnitel'nyi komitet SSSR (TsIK SSSR), 1922–1938

    f. 5677   Administrativnaia komissiia pri prezidiume VTsIKa, 1918–1938

    f. 6892   Komissiia Tsentral'nogo ispolnitel'nogo komiteta SSSR po raionirovaniiu, 1922–1928

GARO   Gosudarstvennyi arkhiv Rostovskoi oblasti (State Archive of Rostov Oblast, Rostov-na-Donu)

    f. R-98   Kraistatbiuro, Rostov-na-Donu, 1920–1934

    f. R-1485   Kraevoi ispolitel'nyi komitet iugo-vostoka, 1924; Severo-Kavkazskii kraevoi ispolnitel'nyi komitet, 1924–1934

HAA   Hayastani Azgayin Arkhiv (National Archives of Armenia, Yerevan)

- f. 112   Tsentral'nyi ispolnitel'nyi komitet Armianskoi SSR
- f. 113   Sovet narodnykh komissarov Armianskoi SSR
- f. 123   Narodnyi komissariat zemledeliia

NARB   Natsianal'ny arkhiŭ Respubliki Belarus' (National Archives of the Republic of Belarus, Minsk)

- f. 6   Tsentral'nyi ispolnitel'nyi komitet BSSR, 1919-1937

RGASPI   Rossiiskii gosudarstvennyi arkhiv sotsial'no-politicheskoi istorii (Russian State Archive of Socio-Political History, Moscow)

- f. 2   Lenin (Ul'ianov), Vladimir Ilich, 1871-1923
- f. 17   Tsentral'nyi komitet KPSS, 1898/1903-1991
- f. 62   Sredneaziatskoe biuro TsK VKP(b) (Sredazbiuro), 1922-1934
- f. 64   Kavkazskoe biuro TsK RKP(b) (Kavbiuro), 1920-1922
- f. 558   Stalin (Dzhugashvili), Iosif Vissarionovich, 1878-1953

RGAE   Rossiiskii gosudarstvennyi arkhiv ekonomiki (Russian State Archive for the Economy, Moscow)

- f. 634   Konstantin Egorov, 1897-1982
- f. 4372   Gosudarstvennyi komitet po planirovaniiu

SŠSSA-PA   sak'art'velos šinagan sak'meta saministros ark'ivi— partiuli ark'ivi (Archives of the Ministry of Internal Affairs of Georgia–Party Archive, Tbilisi)

- f. 13   Zakavkazskii kraevoi komitet (Zakkraikom), 1922-1937

SUIC'A   sak'art'velos uaxlesi istoriis c'entraluri ark'ivi (Central Archive of Contemporary History of Georgia, Tbilisi)

- f. 607   Zakavkazskii tsentral'nyi ispolnitel'nyi komitet (ZakTsIK), 1922-1936
- f. 612   Soiuznyi sovet Federativnogo soiuza sotsialisticheskikh respublik Zakavkaz'ia, 1922-1923
- f. 617   Sovet narodnykh komissarov ZSFSR, 1923-1937
- f. 631   Zakavkazskaia gosudarstvennaia planovaia komissia (ZakGosplan), 1924-1936
- f. 660   Zakavkazskii narodnyi komissariat zemledeliia (Zaknarkomzem), 1929-1936

TsDAHO   Tsentral'nyi derzhavnyi arkhiv hromads'kykh obiedan' Ukraïny (Central State Archive of Public Organizations of Ukraine, Kiev)

    f. 1   Tsentral'nyi komitet KP(b)U

TsDAVO   Tsentral'nyi derzhavnyi arkhiv vyshchykh orhaniv vlady ta upravlinnia Ukraïny (Central State Archive of the Highest Ukrainian State and Government Organs, Kiev)

    f. 1   Vseukraïns'kyi tsentral'nyi vykonavchyi komitet (VUTsVK), 1920–1935
    f. 2   Rada narodnykh komisariv Ukraïns'koi RSR
    f. 337   Ukrderzhplan

TsGA KR   Tsentral'nyi gosudarstvennyi arkhiv Kyrgyzskoi Respubliki (Central State Archive of the Kyrgyz Republic, Bishkek)

    f. 20   Ispolnitel'nyi komitet KAO, 1924–1927
    f. 21   Tsentral'nyi ispolnitel'nyi komitet Kirgizskoi ASSR, 1927–1937
    f. 949   Komissiia po raionirovaniiu, 1924–1930

TsGA RK   Tsentral'nyi gosudarstvennyi arkhiv Respubliki Kazakhstan (Central State Archive of the Republic Kazakhstan, Almaty)

    f. 698   Tsentral'noe statisticheskoe upravlenie

Primary Sources and Edited Document Volumes

Adigamov, A. "Zaiavlenie Bashrevkoma po voprosu o Tatarskoi Respublike." *Zhizn' natsional'nostei*, no. 5/61 (1920): 2.

Aleksandrov, Ivan. *Ekonomicheskoe raionirovanie Rossii*. Moscow: Tipografiia III Internatsional, 1921.

——. *Elektrifikatsiia i transport*. Rostov-na-Donu: Gosizdat, 1921.

——. *Osnovy khoziaistvennogo raionirovaniia SSSR*. Moscow: Ekonomicheskaia zhizn', 1924.

Amanzholova, Dina, T. Dalaeva, and G. Sultangalieva, eds. *Rossiia i Tsentral'naia Aziia: Konets XIX–nachalo XX veka. Sbornik dokumentov i materialov*. Moscow: Novyi khronograf, 2017.

Andropov, Yurii. *Izbrannye rechi i stat'ia*. Moscow: Izdatel'stvo politicheskoi literatury, 1983.

Babkov, I. I. *Iuzhno-Ukrainskii i Severo-Krymskii kanaly i ikh vliianie na preobrazovanie prirody*. Leningrad: Vsesoiuznoe obshchestvo po raspredeleniia politicheskikh i nauchnykh znanii, 1951.

Bauer, Otto. *Die Nationalitätenfrage und die Sozialdemokratie*. Vienna: Ignaz Brand, 1907.

Bazhan, Oleh, O. V. Bazhan, S. Blashchuk, H. Boriak, S. Vlasenko, and N. Makovs'ka, eds. *Krym v umovakh suspil'no-politychnykh transformatsii, 1940–2015: Zbirnyk dokumentiv ta materialiv*. Kiev: NAN Ukraïny, 2016.

Bukharin, Nikolai, and Yevgenii Preobrazhenskii, *Azbuka kommunizma*. Petrograd: Gosizdat, 1920.

Butsenko, Afanasii [Panas]. *K voprosu raionirovaniia Ukrainy*. Kharkiv: Gosizdat Ukrainy, 1925.

Christaller, Walter. "Wie ich zu der Theorie der zentralen Orte gekommen bin: Ein Bericht, wie eine Theorie entstehen kann, und in meinem Fall entstanden ist." *Geographische Zeitschrift* 56, no. 2 (1968): 88–101.

———. *Die zentralen Orte in Süddeutschland: Eine ökonomisch-geographische Untersuchung über die Gesetzmäßigkeit der Verbreitung und Entwicklung der Siedlungen mit städtischen Funktionen*. Jena: Fischer, 1933.

Chugaev, D., P. Avvakumov, and S. Gaponenko, eds. *Revoliutsionnoe dvizhenie v Rossii v avguste 1917 g: Razgrom Kornilovskogo miatezha*. Moscow: AN SSSR, 1959.

Dimanshtein, Semën, ed. *Revoliutsiia i natsional'nyi vopros: Dokumenty i materialy po istorii natsional'nogo voprosa Rossii i SSSR v XX veke*, vol. 3. Moscow: Kommunisticheskaia akademiia, 1930.

Dokumenty i materialy po vneshnei politike Zakavkaz'ia i Gruzii. Tiflis: n.p., 1919.

Egorov, Konstantin. "Ekonomicheskoe raionirovanie i administrativnaia reforma RSFSR." *Vlast' sovetov*, no. 4–6 (1922): 25–26.

———. *Ekonomika raionov SSSR: Po materialam raionnykh kontrol'nykh tsifr na 1927–1928 god*. Moscow: Gosizdat, 1928.

———. "Osnovy raionirovaniia RSFSR." In *Voprosy ekonomicheskogo raionirovaniia: Sbornik materialov i statei, 1917–1929 gg.*, edited by Gleb Krzhizhanovskii, 175–207. Moscow: Gosizdat, 1957.

———. *Raionirovanie SSSR: Sbornik materialov po raionirovaniiu s 1917 po 1925 god*. Moscow: Planovoe khoziaistvo, 1926.

Fel'dman, Grigorii. "Analiticheskii metod postroeniia perspektivnykh planov." *Planovoe khoziaistvo*, no. 12 (1929): 97–127.

Galkin, Yurii, ed. *Sbornik dokumentov o pogranichnom spore mezhdu Rossiei i Ukrainoi v 1920–1925 gg. za Taganrogsko-Shakhtinskuiu territoriiu Donskoi oblasti*. Moscow: Shcherbinskaia tipografiia, 2007.

Gatagova, L., L. Kosheleva, and L. Rogovaia, eds. *TsK RKP(b)-VKP(b) i natsional'nyi vopros*, 2 vols. Moscow: Rosspen, 2005–2009.

Glavnoe upravlenie geodezii i kartografii pri Sovete ministrov SSSR. *Armianskaia SSR*. Scale 1:50,000. Moscow: General'nyi shtab, 1973–1990.

Goliakov, Ivan, ed. *Sbornik dokumentov po istorii ugolovnogo zakonodatel'stva SSSR i RSFSR, 1917–1952 gg*. Moscow: Gosudarstvennoe izdatel'stvo iuridicheskoi literatury, 1953.

Gosplan SSSR. *Piatiletnii plan narodno-khoziaistvennogo stroitel'stva SSSR*. 3rd ed. 3 vols. Moscow: Planovoe khoziaistvo, 1930.

———. *Problemy rekonstruktsii narodnogo khoziaistva SSSR na piatiletie: Piatiletnii perspektivnyi plan na 5 s"ezde Gosplanov*. Moscow: Planovoe khoziaistvo, 1929.

Gosudarstvennaia komissiia po elektrifikatsii Rossii. *Plan elektrifikatsii RSFSR: Vvedenie k dokladu 8-mu s"ezdu sovetov*. Moscow: Gosudarstvennoe tekhnicheskoe izdatel'stvo, 1920.

Institut Marksizma-Leninizma pri TsK KPSS. *Dvenadtsatyi s"ezd RKP(b), 17–25 aprelia 1923: Stenograficheskii otchet.* Moscow: Izdatel'stvo politicheskoi literatury, 1968.

———. *Vos'moi s"ezd RKP(b), mart 1919 goda: Protokoly.* Moscow: Izdatel'stvo politicheskoi literatury, 1959.

———. *Vtoroi s"ezd RSDRP, iiul'–avgust 1903 goda: Protokoly.* Moscow: Izdatel'stvo politicheskoi literatury, 1959.

Iz istorii armiansko-gruzinskikh otnoshenii, 1918 god: Pogranichnye konflikty, peregovory, voina, soglashenie. Tiflis: n.p., 1919.

Karskii, Yefim. *Etnograficheskaia karta belorusskogo plemeni.* St. Petersburg: n.p., 1903.

Khronin, Vasilii, ed. *Materialy po voprosu o prisoedinenii k iugo-vostochnoi oblasti Taganrogskogo, Aleksandro-Grushevskogo i Kamensko-Ekaterininskogo raionov Ukrainy.* Rostov-na-Donu: Tipografiia Shtaba TsKVO, 1924.

Knipovich, Boris. *Metodologiia raionirovaniia.* Moscow: Gosizdat, 1921.

Korichev, S. "K voprosu ob ekonomicheskom raionirovanii RSFSR." *Zhizn' natsionalnostei* 147, no. 12 (1922): 4–5.

Komissiia TsIK UzSSR po raionirovaniiu. *Materialy po raionirovaniiu Uzbekistana.* Samarkand: UzTsIK, 1926.

Krzhizhanovskii, Gleb. *Ob elektrifikatsii.* Moscow: Gosizdat, 1921.

———, ed. *Voprosy ekonomicheskogo raionirovaniia SSSR: Sbornik materialov i statei, 1917–1929 gg.* Moscow: Gosizdat, 1957.

Kukharenko, L. I. *Velikie stalinskie stroiki na Dnepre.* Kiev: Izdatel'stvo KGU, 1952.

Kukushkin, Yu., and O. Chistiakov, eds. *Ocherk istorii sovetskoi konstitutsii,* Moscow: Politizdat, 1987.

Kunaev, Dinmukhamed. *Ot Stalina do Gorbacheva.* Almaty: Sanat, 1994.

Lenin [Ul'ianov], Vladimir. *Polnoe sobranie sochinenii.* 5th ed. 55 vols. Moscow: Izdatel'stvo politicheskoi literatury, 1958–.

Lizhnev-Fin'kovskii, P. Ya. "Uchastie zemleustroitelei v kul'turno-prosvetitel'noi rabote." *Zemleustroitel'* 1, no. 1 (1924): 6–8.

Maiberg, B. "Natsional'no-gosudarstvennoe razmezhevanie respublik Srednei Azii." *Izvestiia,* 11 September 1924, 2.

Narodnyi komissariat vnutrennikh del RSFSR. *Territorial'noe i administrativnoe delenie Soiuza SSR.* Moscow: NKVD, 1928.

Ordzhonikidze, V. *Temi SSR Gruzii: Ikh ekonomicheskie i finansovye vozmozhnosti.* Tiflis: GruzGosplan, 1926.

Ramzin, K. *Revoliutsionnoe dvizhenie Srednei Azii v obrazakh i kartinakh.* Tashkent: Saku, 1928.

Ratzel, Friedrich. *Politische Geographie.* Munich: Oldenbourg, 1897.

Rindlisbacher, Stephan, and Frank Grelka. Introduction to *'Our Work with the Masses Is Not Worth a Kopeck...': A Document Collection on German and Polish Rural Soviets in Ukraine during the NEP, 1923–1929,* edited by Stephan Rindlisbacher and Frank Grelka, 19–30. Wiesbaden: Harrassowitz, 2021.

Rudnyckyj, Stefan. *Ukraina und Ukrainer.* 2nd ed. Berlin: Kroll, 1915.

Shestnadtsatyi s"ezd Vsesoiuznoi Kommunisticheskoi Partii (b): Stenograficheskii otchet. Moscow: Gosizdat, 1930.

Skalov, G. "Ekonomicheskoe ob"edinenie sr.-aziatskikh respublik kak faktor natsional'noi politiki," *Zhizn' natsional'nostei,* no. 5 (1923): 40–45.

Snapkovskii, V. A. Velikii, V. Rashakevich, and A. Sharapo, eds. *Gosudarstvennye granitsy Belarusi: Sbornik dokumentov i materialov v dvukh tomakh*. 2 vols. Minsk: BGU, 2012-2013.
Stalin [Dzhugashvili], Iosif. *Sochineniia*, 38 vols. Moscow: Gosudarstvennoe izdatel'stvo politicheskoi literatury, 1946–.
Sul'kevich, Semën. *Administrativno-politicheskoe stroenie SSSR*. Part 1: *Izmeneniia administrativno-territorial'nykh deleniia SSSR za period s 1917 goda po 1924 god*. Leningard: Izvestiia TsIK SSSR i VTsIK, 1924.
Sultanbekov, B., ed. *Tainy natsional'noi politiki TsK RKP: Chetvertoe soveshchanie TsK RKP s otvetstvennymi rabotnikami natsional'nykh respublik i oblastei v g. Moskve 9–12 iiunia 1923 g. Stenograficheskii otchet*, Moscow: Insan, 1992.
The Tale of the Campaign of Igor: A Russian Epic Poem of the Twelfth Century, trans. Robert Craig Howes. New York: W. W. Norton, 1973.
Tamamshev, A. Z. *Porodnoe raionirovanie i osnovnye printsipy metizatsii krupnogo rogatogo skota v SSR Armenii*. Erivan': IRSKh, 1933.
Trainin, Ivan. "O plemennoi avtonomii." *Zhizn' natsional'nostei*, no. 2 (1923): 19-25.
Tsentral'ne statystychne upravlinnia USRR. *Natsional'nyi sklad sil's'koho naselennia Ukraïny*. Kharkiv: TsSU USRR, 1927.
Tsentral'noe statisticheskoe upravlenie. *Vsesoiuznaia perepis' naseleniia 1926 goda*, 56 vols. Moscow: TsSU, 1928.
———. *Vsesoiuznaia perepis' naseleniia 1926 goda: Kratkie svodki. Narodnost' i rodnoi iazyk naseleniia SSSR*. Moscow: TsSU, 1928.
Tsentral'nyi ispolnitel'nyi komitet SSSR. *Administrativno-territorial'noe delenie Soiuza SSR: Izmeneniia, proizshedshie s 1 noiabria 1931 g. do 1 iiulia 1932 g*. Moscow: Vlast' sovetov, 1932.
Upravlenie delami Sovnarkoma SSSR. *Sobranie uzakonenii i razporiazhenii pravitel'stva za 1917–1918 gg*. Moscow: n.p., 1942.
Vladimirskii, Mikhail. *Organizatsiia sovetskoi vlasti na mestakh*. Moscow: Gosizdat, 1919.
Wilson, Woodrow. *Essential Writings and Speeches of the Scholar-President*. Edited by Mario R. DiNunzio. New York: New York University Press, 2006.
Zaitsev, P. "Pochemu uprazdniaetsia okruzhnoe zveno v sisteme sovetskogo apparata." In *Ot okruga k raionu: Sbornik statei i ofitsial'nykh materialov*, 35-36. Moscow: Vlast' sovetov, 1930.
Zelenskii, Isaak, and Iosif Vareikis, eds. *Natsional'no-gosudarstvennoe razmezhevanie Srednei Azii*. Tashkent: Sredniaia Aziia, 1924.
Zhiromskaia, Valentina, ed. *Vsesoiuznaia perepis' naseleniia 1937 goda: Sbornik dokumentov i materialov*. Moscow: Rosspen, 2007.
Zotiev, A., and I. Mokhoshchekov. *Kanal izobiliia*. Simferopol': Krymizdat, 1964.

Secondary Literature

Abashin, Sergei. "Empire and Demography in Turkestan: Numbers and the Politics of Counting." In *Asiatic Russia*, edited by Tomohiko Uyama, 129-49.
———. *Natsionalizmy v Srednei Azii: V poiskakh identichnosti*. St. Petersburg: Aleteiia, 2007.

———. *Sovetskii kishlak: Mezhdu kolonializmom i modernizatsiei*. Moscow: Novoe literaturnoe obozrenie, 2015.
Abashin, Sergei, Kamoludin Abdullaev, Ravshan Abdullaev, and Arslan Koichiev. "Soviet Rule and the Delimitation of Borders in the Ferghana Valley, 1917–1930." In *Ferghana Valley: The Heart of Central Asia*, edited by S. Frederick Starr, Baktybek Beshimov, Inomjon I. Bobokulov, and Pulat Shozimov, 94–118. Armonk, NY: M. E. Sharpe, 2011.
Akiyama, Tetsu. *The Qïrghïz Baatïr and the Russian Empire: A Portrait of a Local Intermediary in Russian Central Asia*. Leiden: Brill, 2021.
———. "Why Was Russian Direct Rule over Kyrgyz Nomads Dependent on Tribal Chieftains 'Manaps'?" *Cahiers du monde russe* 56, no. 4 (2015): 625–49.
Alampiev, Pëtr. *Ekonomicheskoe raionirovanie SSSR*, 2 vols. Moscow: Izdatel'stvo ekonomicheskoi literatury, 1959–1963.
Altstadt, Audrey L. "The Baku City Duma: Arena for Elite Conflict." *Central Asian Survey* 5, no. 3-4 (1986): 49–66.
Amacher, Korine. "La Crimée." In *Histoire partagée, mémoire divisée: Ukraine, Russie, Pologne*, edited by Korine Amacher, Andrii Portnov, and Eric Aunoble, 67–81. Lausanne: Antipodes, 2021.
Amanzholova, Dina. "Ispytanie vlast'iu: Iz istorii formirovaniia biurokratii Kazakhskoi ASSR, 1920-e gg." *Cahiers du monde russe* 56, no. 4 (2015): 753–91.
Anderson, Benedict. *Imagined Communities: Reflections on the Origin and Spread of Nationalism*. 3rd ed. New York: Verso, 2003.
Anderson, Edgar. "How Narva, Petseri, and Abrene Came to Be in the RSFSR." *Journal of Baltic Studies* 19, no. 3 (1988): 197–214.
Ardeleanu, Constantin, and Olena Palko, eds. *Making Ukraine: Negotiating, Contesting, and Drawing the Borders in the Twentieth Century*. Montreal: McGill-Queen's University Press, 2022.
Ashimbaev, D. *Kto est' kto v Kazakhstane: Entsiklopedicheski slovar'*. 12th ed. Almaty: Credo, 2012.
Asschenfeldt, Friedrich, and Max Trecker. "From Ludendorff to Lenin? World War I and the Origins of Soviet Economic Planning." *Europe-Asia Studies* 76, no. 1 (2023): 10–28.
Baberowski, Jörg. *Der Feind ist überall: Stalinismus im Kaukasus*. Munich: Deutsche Verlags-Anstalt, 2003.
———. *Verbrannte Erde: Stalins Herrschaft der Gewalt*. Munich: C. H. Beck, 2012.
Baizakova, Zhulduz. "Border Issues in Central Asia: Current Conflicts, Controversies and Compromises." *UNISCI Journal*, no. 45 (2017): 221–34.
Baldauf, Ingeborg. "Some Thoughts on the Making of the Uzbek Nation." *Cahiers du monde russe et soviétique* 32, no. 1 (1991): 79–96.
Ball, Alan. "Building a New State and Society: NEP, 1921–1928." In *The Twentieth Century*, edited by Ronald G. Suny, 168–91. Vol. 3 of *The Cambridge History of Russia*. Cambridge: Cambridge University Press, 2006.
Barker, Thomas Mack, and Andreas Moritsch. *The Slovene Minority of Carinthia*. New York: Columbia University Press, 1984.
Baron, Nick. "The Mapping of Illiberal Modernity: Spatial Science, Ideology, and the State in Early Twentieth-Century Russia." In *Empire De/Centered*, edited by Sanna Turoma and Maxim Waldstein, 105–34.

———. "Nature, Nationalism, and Revolutionary Regionalism: Constructing Soviet Karelia, 1920–1923." *Journal of Historical Geography* 33, no. 3 (2007): 565–95.

———. "New Spatial Histories of 20th-Century Russia and the Soviet Union: Exploring the Terrain." *Kritika: Explorations in Russian and Eurasian History* 9, no. 2 (2008): 433–47.

———. *Soviet Karelia: Politics, Planning, and Terror in Stalin's Russia, 1920–1939*. New York: Routledge Curzon, 2004.

Baron, Nick, Luminita Gatejel, and Stephan Rindlisbacher. "'Drawing the Line': Border Commissions in Eastern Europe." *Journal of Modern European History* 22, no. 1 (2024): 2–9.

Baron, Nick, and Peter Gatrell. "Population Displacement, State-Building, and Social Identity in the Lands of the Former Russian Empire, 1917–23." *Kritika: Explorations in Russian and Eurasian History* 4, no. 1 (2003): 51–100.

Bartov, Omer, and Eric Weitz, eds. *Shatterzone of Empires: Coexistence and Violence in the German, Habsburg, Russian, and Ottoman Borderlands*. Bloomington: Indiana University Press, 2015.

Baumann, Fabian. *Dynasty Divided: A Family History of Russian and Ukrainian Nationalism*. Ithaca, NY: Cornell University Press, 2023.

Beissinger, Mark R. *Scientific Management, Socialist Discipline and Soviet Power*. London: Tauris, 1988.

———. "Soviet Empire as 'Family Resemblance.'" *Slavic Review* 65, no. 2 (2006): 294–303.

Bektursunov, Mirlan. "The Rise of the 'Lineage Proletariat': The Soviet State's Class Policy and Kyrgyz Lineage Society in the 1920s." *Ab Imperio*, no. 1 (2024): 97–125.

———. "'Two parts—one whole?' Kazakh-Kyrgyz Relations in the Making of Soviet Kyrgyzstan, 1917–24." *Central Asian Survey* 42, no. 1 (2022): 109–26.

Belge, Boris, and Martin Deuerlein, eds. *Goldenes Zeitalter der Stagnation? Perspektiven auf die sowjetische Ordnung der Brežnev-Ära*. Tübingen: Mohr Siebeck, 2014.

Bell, Christine, and Jan Pospisil. "Navigating Inclusion in Transitions from Conflict: The Formalised Political Unsettlement." *Journal of International Development* 29, no. 5 (2017): 576–93.

Bichsel, Christine. *Conflict Transformation in Central Asia: Irrigation Disputes in the Ferghana Valley*. London: Routledge, 2009.

Blais, Hélène. "An Intra-Imperial Conflict: The Mapping of the Border between Algeria and Tunisia, 1881–1914." *Journal of Historical Geography* 37, no. 2 (2011): 178–90.

Blank, Stephen J. *The Sorcerer as Apprentice: Stalin as Commissar of Nationalities, 1917–1924*. Westport, CT: Greenwood, 1994.

———. "The Transcaucasian Federation and the Origins of the Soviet Union, 1921–1922." *Central Asian Survey* 9, no. 4 (1990): 29–58.

Blauvelt, Timothy K. *Clientelism and Nationality in an Early Soviet Fiefdom: The Trials of Nestor Lakoba*. London: Routledge, 2021.

———. "'From Words to Action!' Nationality Policy in Soviet Abkhazia, 1921–1938." In *The Making of Modern Georgia, 1918–2012: The First Georgian Republic and Its Successors*, edited by Stephen F. Jones, 232–62. London: Routledge, 2014.

———. "Ideology Meets Practice in the Struggle for the Transcaucasus: Stepan Shaumyan and the Evolution of Bolshevik Nationality Policy." *Caucasus Survey* 8, no. 1 (2020): 81–92.

———. "Resistance and Accommodation in the Stalinist Periphery: A Peasant Uprising in Abkhazia." *Ab Imperio*, no. 3 (2012): 78–108.

Blauvelt, Timothy K., and Adrian Briscu. "Who Wanted the TDFR? The Making and the Breaking of the Transcaucasian Democratic Federative Republic." *Caucasus Survey* 8, no. 1 (2020): 1–8.

Blum, Mark E., and William Smaldone, eds. *Austro-Marxism: The Ideology of Unity*. 2 vols. Leiden: Brill, 2016–2017.

Borisënok, Yelena. *Fenomen sovetskoi ukrainizatsii: 1920–1930-e gody*. Moscow: Evropa, 2006.

———. *Stalinskii prokonsul Lazar' Kaganovich na Ukraine: Apogei sovetskoi ukrainizatsii, 1925–1928*. Moscow: Rodina, 2021.

———. "Ukraina i Rossiia: Spor o granitsakh v 1920-e gody." In *Regiony i granitsy Ukrainy v istoricheskoi perspekive*, edited by Leonid Gorizontov, 205–37. Moscow: Strategiia, 2005.

Borys, Jurij. *The Russian Communist Party and the Sovietization of Ukraine: A Study in the Communist Doctrine of the Self-Determination of Nations*. Stockholm: P. A. Norstedt, 1960.

Bourdieu, Pierre. "L'illusion biographique." *Actes de la recherche en sciences sociales* 62–63, no. 1 (1986): 69–72.

Boyechko, Vasyl', Oksana Hanzha, and Borys Zacharchuk. *Formuvannia derzhavnykh kordoniv Ukraïny 1917–1940 rr*. Kiev: AN URSR, 1991.

———. *Kordony Ukraïny: Istorychna retrospektyva ta suchasnyi stan*, Kiev: Osnovy, 1994.

Brinegar, Sara. "The Oil Deal: Nariman Narimanov and the Sovietization of Azerbaijan." *Slavic Review* 76, no. 2 (2017): 372–94.

Broers, Laurence. *Armenia and Azerbaijan: Anatomy of a Rivalry*. Edinburgh: Edinburgh University Press, 2019.

Brower, Daniel R. *Turkestan and the Fate of the Russian Empire*. London: Routledge, 2003.

Brown, Kate. *A Biography of No Place: From Ethnic Borderland to Soviet Heartland*. Cambridge, MA: Harvard University Press 2003.

Brubaker, Rogers. *Ethnicity without Groups*. Cambridge, MA: Harvard University Press, 2004.

———. *Nationalism Reframed: Nationhood and the National Question in the New Europe*. Cambridge: Cambridge University Press, 1996.

Bruski, Jan Jacek. "The Path to the Treaty of Riga: The Establishment of the Polish-Ukrainian Border, 1918–21." In *Making Ukraine*, edited by Constantin Ardeleanu and Olena Palko, 109–37.

Burbank, Jane. "Thinking Like an Empire: Estate, Law, and Rights in the Early Twentieth Century." In *Russian Empire*, edited by Jane Burbank, Mark von Hagen, and Anatolyi Remnev, 196–217.

Burbank, Jane, Mark von Hagen, and Anatolyi Remnev, eds. *Russian Empire: Space, People, Power, 1700–1930*. Bloomington: Indiana University Press, 2007.

Burds, Jeffrey. "Bor'ba s banditizmom v SSSR v 1944-1953 gg." *Sotsial'naia istoriia: Ezhegodnik* (2000): 169-90.
Bustanov, Alfrid K. *Soviet Orientalism and the Creation of Central Asian Nations.* New York: Routledge, 2015.
Buttino, Marco. "Central Asia, 1916-1920: A Kaleidoscope of Local Revolutions and the Building of the Bolshevik Order." In *The Empire and Nationalism at War*, edited by Eric Lohr, Vera Tolz, Aleksandr Semenov, and Mark von Hagen, 109-35. Bloomington: Indiana University Press, 2014.
———. *Revoliutsiia naoborot: Sredniaia Aziia mezhdu padeniem tsarskoi imperii i obrazovaniem SSSR.* Moscow: Zven'ia, 2007.
Cadiot, Juliette. "Kak uporiadochivali raznoobrazie: Spiski i klassifikatsii natsional'nostei v Rossiiskoi Imperii i v Sovetskom Soiuze, 1897-1939 gg." *Ab Imperio*, no. 4 (2001): 177-206.
———. *Le laboratoire impérial: Russie-URSS, 1860–1940.* Paris: Éditions CNRS, 2007.
Cameron, Sarah I. *The Hungry Steppe: Famine, Violence, and the Making of Soviet Kazakhstan.* Ithaca, NY: Cornell University Press, 2018.
Campbell, Ian W. "Nationalizing Violence in a Collapsing Empire: A View from the Steppe." *Ab Imperio*, no. 3 (2020): 98-113.
Caroe, Olaf. *Soviet Empire: The Turks of Central Asia and Stalinism.* London: MacMillan, 1967.
Carrère d'Encausse, Hélène. *The Great Challenge: Nationalities and the Bolshevik State, 1917–1930.* New York: Holmes and Meier, 1992.
Cattaruzza, Marina. *Italy and Its Eastern Border, 1866–2016.* New York: Routledge, 2016.
———. "The Making and Remaking of a Boundary: The Redrafting of the Eastern Border of Italy after the Two World Wars." *Journal of Modern European History*, 9, no. 1 (2011): 67-75.
———. "Das nationale Problem der Sozialdemokratie und der internationalen kommunistischen Bewegung, 1889-1953." In *Die Moderne und ihre Krisen: Studien von Marina Cattaruzza zur europäischen Geschichte des 19. und 20. Jahrhunderts*, edited by Sacha Zala, 243-60. Göttingen: V&R unipress, 2012.
Chamberlain, Lesley. *Lenin's Private War: The Voyage of the Philosophy Steamer and the Exile of the Intelligentsia.* New York: St. Martin's, 2007.
Charron, Austin. "Crimea's 1954 Transfer to Ukraine: A Practical yet Contested Union." In *Making Ukraine*, edited by Constantin Ardeleanu and Olena Palko, 238-60.
Chernev, Borislav. "Ukraine's Borders at the Brest-Litovsk Peace Conference, 1917-18." In *Making Ukraine*, edited by Constantin Ardeleanu and Olena Palko, 67-85.
Chioni Moore, David. "East, West, and South: Complex Asymmetries in Postcolonial/Post-Soviet Debates since 2001." *Ab Imperio*, no. 1 (2024): 49-54.
Chopart, Thomas. "Identifier, légitimer, stigmatiser: Les matériaux de la Délégation ukrainienne à la Conférence de la Paix de Paris, 1918-1920." *Matériaux pour l'histoire de notre temps* 113/114, no. 1 (2014): 180-85.

Clement, Victoria. *Learning to Become Turkmen: Literacy, Language, and Power, 1914–2014*. Pittsburgh: University of Pittsburgh Press, 2018.

Colomer, Josep M. *Great Empires, Small Nations: The Uncertain Future of the Sovereign State*. New York: Routledge, 2007.

Connelly, John. *From Peoples into Nations: A History of Eastern Europe*. Princeton, NJ: Princeton University Press, 2020.

Connor, Ulla. *Territoriale Grenzen als Praxis: Zur Erfindung der Grenzregion in grenzüberschreitender Kartographie*. Baden-Baden: Nomos, 2023.

Conquest, Robert. *The Last Empire*. London: Ampersand, 1962.

Conrad, Benjamin. *Umkämpfte Grenzen, umkämpfte Bevölkerung: Die Entstehung der Staatsgrenzen der Zweiten Polnischen Republik, 1918–1923*. Stuttgart: Steiner, 2014.

Cornell, Svante E. "Autonomy as a Source of Conflict: Caucasian Conflicts in Theoretical Perspective." *World Politics* 54, no. 2 (2002): 245–76.

Dadabaev, Timur. "'We Want a State of Our Own!' Reconstructing Community Space in Bordering Areas of Central Asia." *Journal of Territorial and Maritime Studies* 2, no. 2 (2015): 9–32.

Darrow, David W. "Census as a Technology of Empire." *Ab Imperio*, no. 4 (2002): 145–76.

David-Fox, Michael. *Crossing Borders: Modernity, Ideology, and Culture in Russia and the Soviet Union*. Pittsburgh: University of Pittsburgh Press, 2015.

Davion, Isabelle. "Teschen and Its Impossible Plebiscite: Can the Genie Be Put Back in the Bottle?" In *Beyond Versailles*, edited by Marcus M. Payk and Roberta Pergher, 38–58.

De Waal, Thomas. *Great Catastrophe: Armenians and Turks in the Shadow of Genocide*. Oxford: Oxford University Press, 2015.

Delaney, David. *Territory: A Short Introduction*. Malden, MA: Blackwell, 2005.

Demin, Iurii. "The Bolsheviks and the Soviet Socialist Republic of Iran, 1920–21: Moscow's Politics and the Ambitions of Regional and Local Political Actors." *Kritika: Explorations in Russian and Eurasian History* 25, no. 2 (2024): 273–98.

Derluguian, Georgi. *Bourdieu's Secret Admirer in the Caucasus: A World-System Biography*. Chicago: University of Chicago Press, 2005.

Di Fiore, Laura. "The Production of Borders in Nineteenth-Century Europe: Between Institutional Boundaries and Transnational Practices of Space." *European Review of History* 24, no. 1 (2017): 36–57.

Douds, Lara. *Inside Lenin's Government: Ideology, Power, and Practice in the Early Soviet State*. London: Bloomsbury, 2018.

Drozdov, Konstantin. "Belogorodchina v sostave Ukrainskoi derzhavy getmana P. P. Skoropadskogo: Okkupatsiia ili prisoedinenie?" *Belgorodskii kraevedcheskii vestnik*, no. 6 (2006): 11–35.

Duishembieva, Jipar. "'The Kara Kirghiz Must Develop Separately': Ishenaaly Arabaev (1881–1933) and His Project of the Kyrgyz Nation." In *Creating Culture in (Post) Socialist Central Asia*, edited by Ananda Breed, Eva-Marie Dubuisson, and Ali Iğmen, 13–46. Cham: Palgrave Macmillan, 2020.

Dullin, Sabine. *La frontière épaisse: Aux origines des politiques soviétiques, 1920–1940*. Paris: EHESS, 2014.

Edgar, Adrienne Lynn. *Tribal Nation: The Making of Soviet Turkmenistan*. Princeton, NJ: Princeton University Press, 2004.

Eisener, Reinhard. *Buchara im Strudel der Russischen Revolution: Auftakt und revolutionäres Umfeld, 1917–1919*. Potsdam: Thetis, 2023.

Ellman, Michael. *Socialist Planning*. 3rd ed. Cambridge: Cambridge University Press, 2014.

Erez, Manela. *The Wilsonian Moment: Self-Determination and the International Origins of Anticolonial Nationalism*. Oxford: Oxford University Press, 2007.

Fedtke, Gero. *Roter Orient: Muslimkommunisten und Bolschewiki in Turkestan, 1917–1924*. Cologne: Böhlau, 2020.

———. "Wie aus Bucharern Usbeken und Tadschiken werden: Sowjetische Nationalitätenpolitik im Lichte einer persönlichen Rivalität." *Zeitschrift für Geschichtswissenschaft* 54, no. 3 (2006): 214–31.

Ferrando, Olivier. "Soviet Population Transfers and Interethnic Relations in Tajikistan: Assessing the Concept of Ethnicity." *Central Asian Survey* 30, no. 1 (2011): 39–52.

Ferro, Marc. *Colonization: A Global History*. New York: Routledge, 1997.

Fink, Carole, *Defending the Rights of Others: The Great Powers, the Jews, and International Minority Protection, 1878–1938*, Cambridge: Cambridge University Press, 2004.

Fitzpatrick, Sheila, ed. *Cultural Revolution in Russia, 1928–1931*. Bloomington: Indiana University Press, 1978.

———. *Everyday Stalinism: Ordinary Life in Extraordinary Times. Soviet Russia in the 1930s*. Oxford: Oxford University Press, 1999.

———. *Stalin's Peasants: Resistance and Survival in the Russian Village after Collectivization*. New York: Oxford University Press, 1994.

Florin, Moritz. "Beyond Colonialism? Agency, Power, and the Making of Soviet Central Asia." *Kritika: Explorations in Russian and Eurasian History* 18, no. 4 (2017): 827–38.

Gabdulhakov, Rashid. "The Highly Securitized Insecurities of State Borders in the Fergana Valley." *Central Asia Fellowship Papers* 9 (2015): 1–10.

García-Álvarez, Jacobo, and Paloma Puente-Lozano. "Recent Geohistorical Research on Boundary-Making: Challenging Conventional Narratives on Borders and Modern State-Building." *Geography Compass* 16, no. 1 (2022): 1–14.

Gechtman, Roni. "A 'Museum of Bad Taste'? The Jewish Labour Bund and the Bolshevik Position Regarding the National Question, 1903–14." *Canadian Journal of History* 43, no. 1 (2008): 31–67.

Gerasimov, Ilya. "Narrating Russian History after the Imperial Turn." *Ab Imperio*, no. 4 (2020): 21–61.

Gerasimov, Ilya, Jan Kusber, and Alexander Semyonov, eds. *Empire Speaks Out: Languages of Rationalization and Self-Description in the Russian Empire*. Leiden: Brill, 2009.

Gerasimov, Ilya, Aleksandr Semenov, and Marina Mogil'ner. "Toward a Postnational History of Eurasia: Deconstructing Empires and Denationalizing Groupness." *Ab Imperio*, no. 1 (2023): 9–15.

Gerst, Dominik, Maria Klessmann, and Hannes Krämer, eds. *Grenzforschung: Handbuch für Wissenschaft und Studium*. Baden-Baden: Nomos, 2021.
Gerst, Dominik, and Hannes Krämer. "Methodologie der Grenzforschung." In *Grenzforschung*, edited by Dominik Gerst, Maria Klessmann, and Hannes Krämer, 121–40.
Gibson, Catherine. "Attuning to Emotions in the History of Border-Making: The Estonian-Latvian Boundary Commission in 1920." *Journal of Modern European History* 22, no. 1 (2024): 40–54.
———. *Geographies of Nationhood: Cartography, Science, and Society in the Russian Imperial Baltic*. Oxford: Oxford University Press, 2022.
Gilley, Christopher. *The 'Change of Signposts' in the Ukrainian Emigration: A Contribution to the History of Sovietophilism in the 1920s*. Stuttgart: ibidem, 2009.
Goff, Krista A. *Nested Nationalism: Making and Unmaking Nations in the South Caucasus*. Ithaca, NY: Cornell University Press, 2020.
Górny, Maciej. *Vaterlandszeichner: Geografen und Grenzen im Zwischenkriegseuropa*. Osnabrück: fibre, 2019.
Gorshenina, Svetlana. *Asie centrale: L'invention des frontières et l'héritage russo-soviétique*. Paris: Éditions CNRS, 2012.
Grant, Bruce. "An Average Azerbaijani Village, 1930: Remembering Rebellion in the Caucasus Mountains." *Slavic Review* 63, no. 4 (2004): 703–31.
Gregory, Paul R. *The Political Economy of Stalinism: Evidence from the Soviet Secret Archives*. Cambridge: Cambridge University Press, 2003.
Gullette, David. *The Genealogical Construction of the Kyrgyz Republic: Kinship, State and 'Tribalism'*. Leiden: Global Oriental, 2010.
Hallez, Xavier. "Le ralliement des Kazakhs au pouvoir soviétique, 1917–1920: Convictions politiques, système tribal et contexte russe." *Cahiers du monde russe* 56, no. 4 (2015): 705–52.
Happel, Jörn. *Nomadische Lebenswelten und zarische Politik: Der Aufstand in Zentralasien 1916*. Stuttgart: Steiner, 2010.
Hasanli, Jamil [Dzhamil' Gasanly]. *Sovetskii Azerbaidzhan: Ot ottepeli k zamorozkam, 1959–1969*. Moscow: Rosspen 2020.
Haslinger, Peter. "Dilemmas of Security: The State, Local Agency, and the Czechoslovak-Hungarian Boundary Commission, 1921–25." *Austrian History Yearbook* 46 (2018): 187–206.
———. *Der ungarische Revisionismus und das Burgenland 1922–1932*. Frankfurt am Main: Peter Lang, 1994.
Haugen, Arne. *The Establishment of National Republics in Soviet Central Asia*. New York: Palgrave Macmillan, 2003.
Haumann, Heiko. *Beginn der Planwirtschaft: Elektrifizierung, Wirtschaftsplanung und gesellschaftliche Entwicklung Sowjetrusslands, 1917–1921*. Düsseldorf: Bertelsmann, 1974.
Hausmann, Guido. "Das Territorium der Ukraine: Stepan Rudnyc'kyjs Beitrag zur Geschichte räumlich-territorialen Denkens über die Ukraine." In *Die Ukraine: Prozesse der Nationsbildung*, edited by Andreas Kappeler, 145–57. Cologne: Böhlau, 2011.
Hendl, Tereza, Olga Burlyuk, Mila O'Sullivan, and Aizada Arystanbek. "(En)Countering Epistemic Imperialism: A Critique of 'Westsplaining' and

Coloniality in Dominant Debates on Russia's Invasion of Ukraine." *Contemporary Security Policy* 45, no. 2 (2023): 171-209.

Herbert, Alexander, and Bryan Gigantino. "The Poverty of Cultural History: Decolonization, Race, and Politics in Post-Socialist Studies." *LeftEast*, 1 January 2024. https://lefteast.org/the-poverty-of-cultural-history-decolonization-race-and-politics-in-post-socialist-studies/.

Herrmann, Goetz, and Andreas Vasilache. "Grenze, Staat und Staatlichkeit." In *Grenzforschung*, edited by Dominik Gerst, Maria Klessmann, and Hannes Krämer, 68-88.

Hildermeier, Manfred. *Geschichte der Sowjetunion, 1917–1991: Entstehung und Niedergang des ersten sozialistischen Staates*. Munich: C. H. Beck, 1998.

Hirsch, Francine. *Empire of Nations: Ethnographic Knowledge and the Making of the Soviet Union*. Ithaca, NY: Cornell University Press, 2005.

———. "The Soviet Union as a Work-in-Progress: Ethnographers and the Category Nationality in the 1926, 1937, and 1939 Censuses." *Slavic Review* 56 no. 2 (1997): 251-78.

Hirschhausen, Ulrike von, and Jörn Leonhard. *Empires: Eine globale Geschichte, 1780–1920*. Munich: C. H. Beck, 2023.

Hovannisian, Richard G. *The Republic of Armenia*, 4 vols. Berkeley: University of California Press, 1971-1996.

Hutsalo, Liudmyla. "Reformuvannia ta likvidatsiia natsional'nykh administratyvnykh odynyts'." *Visnyk Akedemiï pratsi i sotsial'nykh vidnosyn Federatsiï profsilok Ukraïny*, no. 5 (2005): 146-50.

Ikhsanov, Anton. "Aleksandr Nikolaevich Samoilovich (1880-1938) i ego polevye informanty: Konstruirovanie turkmenskoi kul'turnoi identichnosti." PhD diss., HSE Moscow, 2023.

Jebsen, Nina, and Martin Klatt. "The Negotiation of National and Regional Identity during the Schleswig-Plebiscite Following the First World War." *First World War Studies* 5, no. 2 (2014): 181-211.

Jerram, Leif. "Space: A Useless Category of Historical Analysis." *History and Theory* 52, no. 3 (2013): 400-419.

Jeske, Martin. "Ein Imperium wird vermessen: Kartographie, Kulturtransfer und Raumerschließung im Zarenreich (1797-1919)." PhD diss., University of Basel, 2019.

———. *Ein Imperium wird vermessen: Kartographie, Kulturtransfer und Raumerschließung im Zarenreich, 1797–1919*. Berlin: De Gruyter, 2023.

Jobst, Kerstin S. *Geschichte der Ukraine*. Stuttgart: Reclam, 2010; 2nd ed. Stuttgart: Reclam, 2015.

Jones, Stephen F. "The Establishment of Soviet Power in Transcaucasia: The Case of Georgia, 1921-1928." *Soviet Studies* 40, no. 4 (1988): 616-39.

Kaiser, Claire P. *Georgian and Soviet: Entitled Nationhood and the Specter of Stalin in the Caucasus*. Ithaca, NY: Cornell University Press, 2023.

Kamenskii, A. "Tsentral'noe i mestnoe upravlenie i territorial'noe ustroistvo v kontekste reform XVIII veka." In *Administrativno-territorial'noe ustroistvo Rossii*, edited by A. Pyzhikov, 58-99.

Kappeler, Andreas. *The Russian Empire: A Multiethnic History*. London: Longman, 2001.

Karch, Brendan. "Plebiscites and Postwar Legitimacy." In *Beyond Versailles*, edited by Marcus M. Payk and Roberta Pergher, 16–37.
Karelin, Evgenii. "Zapadnaia oblast' Gosplana: Iz istorii ekonomicheskogo raionirovaniia strany 1920-e gody." *Rossiiskaia istoriia*, no. 2 (2010): 15–18.
Kaşıkçı, Mehmet Volkan. "Making Sense of Catastrophe: Experiencing and Remembering the Kazakh Famine in a Comparative Context." *Journal of Contemporary History* 58, no. 2 (2023): 223–46.
Kassymbekova, Botakoz. *Despite Cultures: Early Soviet Rule in Tajikistan*. Pittsburgh: Pittsburgh University Press, 2016.
———. "Humans as Territory: Forced Resettlement and the Making of Soviet Tajikistan, 1920–38." *Central Asian Survey* 30, no. 3–4 (2011): 349–70.
———. "On Decentering Soviet Studies and Launching New Conversations." *Ab Imperio*, no. 1 (2022): 115–20.
Kassymbekova, Botakoz, and Aminat Chokobaeva. "On Writing Soviet History of Central Asia: Frameworks, Challenges, Prospects." *Central Asian Survey* 40, no. 4 (2021): 483–503.
Kassymbekova, Botakoz, and Christian Teichmann. "The Red Man's Burden: Soviet Officials in Central Asia in the 1920s and 1930s." In *Helpless Imperialists: Imperial Failure, Fear and Radicalization*, edited by Maurus Reinkowski, 163–86. Göttingen: Vandenhoeck & Ruprecht, 2013.
Kauffman, Jesse. *Elusive Alliance: The German Occupation of Poland in World War I*. Cambridge, MA: Harvard University Press, 2015.
Keating, Jennifer. *On Arid Ground: Political Ecologies of Empire in Russian Central Asia*. Oxford: Oxford University Press, 2022.
Kegler, Karl R. *Deutsche Raumplanung: Das Modell der 'zentralen Orte' zwischen NS-Staat und Bundesrepublik*. Paderborn: Schöningh, 2015.
Keller, Shoshana. "The Central Asian Bureau: An Essential Tool in Governing Soviet Turkestan." *Central Asian Survey* 22, no. 2–3 (2003): 281–97.
———. *Russia and Central Asia: Coexistence, Conquest, Convergence*. Toronto: University of Toronto Press, 2020.
———. *To Moscow, Not Mecca: The Soviet Campaign against Islam in Central Asia, 1917–1941*. Westport, CT: Praeger, 2001.
Keményfi, Róbert. "Grenzen-Karten-Ethnien: Kartenartige Konstituierungsmittel im Dienst des ungarischen nationalen Raumes." In *Osteuropa kartiert/Mapping Eastern Europe*, edited by Jörn Happel and Christophe von Werdt, 201–14. Berlin: Lit, 2010.
Khalid, Adeeb. "Backwardness and the Quest for Civilization: Early Soviet Central Asia in Comparative Perspective." *Slavic Review* 56, no. 2 (2006): 231–51.
———. *Central Asia: A New History from the Imperial Conquests to the Present*. Princeton, NJ: Princeton University Press, 2021.
———. *Making Uzbekistan: Nation, Empire, and Revolution in the Early USSR*. Ithaca, NY: Cornell University Press, 2015.
———. "National Consolidation as Soviet Work: The Origins of Uzbekistan." *Ab Imperio*, no. 4 (2016): 185–200.
———. "Nationalizing the Revolution in Central Asia: The Transformation of Jadidism, 1917–1920." In *State of Nations*, edited by Terry Martin and Ronald G. Suny, 145–62.

———. *The Politics of Muslim Cultural Reform: Jadidism in Central Asia*. Berkeley: University of California Press, 1998.

Kharmandarian, Segvard. *Lenin i stanovlenie Zakavkazskoi Federatsii, 1921–1923*. Yerevan: Aiastan, 1969.

Khodarkovsky, Michael. *Russia's Steppe Frontier: The Making of a Colonial Empire, 1500–1800*. Bloomington: Indiana University Press, 2002.

Khomich, Sergei. *Territoriia i gosudarstvennye granitsy Belarusi v XX veke: Ot nezavershennoi etnicheskoi samoidentifikatsii i vneshnepoliticheskogo proizvola k sovremennomu 'status quo.'* Minsk: Ekonompress, 2011.

Khrushchev, Sergei. *Trilogiia ob ottse*, 3 vols. Moscow: Vremia, 2010.

Kindler, Robert. *Stalins Nomaden: Herrschaft und Hunger in Kasachstan*. Hamburg: Hamburger Edition, 2014.

Kirmse, Stefan. "Raumkonzepte von Zentralasien: Ein historischer Überblick." In *Die politischen Systeme Zentralasiens: Interner Wandel, externe Akteure, regionale Kooperation*, edited by Jakob Lempp, Sebastian Mayer, and Alexander Brandt, 19–39. Wiesbaden: Springer, 2020.

Kivelson, Valerie A., and Ronald G. Suny. *Russia's Empires*. New York: Oxford University Press, 2017.

Koichiev, Arslan. *Natsional'no-territorial'noe razmezhevanie v ferganskoi doline, 1924–1927 gg*. Bishkek: self-pub., 2001.

Kotkin, Stephen. *Magnetic Mountain: Stalinism as a Civilization*. Berkeley: University of California Press, 1997.

———. *Stalin*. 3 vols. London: Allen Lane, 2014–.

Kotsonis, Yanni, and David Hoffmann, eds. *Russian Modernity: Politics, Knowledge, Practices*. London: MacMillan, 2000.

Kramer, Mark. "Why Did Russia Give Away Crimea Sixty Years Ago?" https://www.wilsoncenter.org/publication/why-did-russia-give-away-crimea-sixty-years-ago.

Kravchenko, Volodymyr. *The Ukrainian-Russian Borderland: History versus Geography*. Montreal: McGill-Queen's University Press, 2022.

Kruglov, Vladimir. *Organizatsiia territorii Rossii v 1917–2007 gg.: Idei, praktika, rezul'taty*. Moscow: IRI RAN, 2020.

Kuromiya, Hiroaki. *Freedom and Terror in the Donbas: A Ukrainian-Russian Borderland, 1870–1990s*. Cambridge: Cambridge University Press, 1998.

———. *Stalin's Industrial Revolution: Politics and Workers, 1928–1932*. Cambridge: Cambridge University Press, 1990.

Kuzmany, Börries, Matthias Battis, and Oskar Mulej. "Accommodating National Diversity within States: Territorial and Non-Territorial Approaches since the Late 19th Century." *Nationality Papers* 50, no. 5 (2022): 851–52.

Kwiecińska, Elżbieta. "Poland's 'Civilizing Mission' and Ukrainian Statehood at the Paris Peace Conference." In *Making Ukraine*, edited by Constantin Ardeleanu and Olena Palko, 86–108.

Laba, Agnes. *Die Grenze im Blick: Der Ostgrenzendiskurs der Weimarer Republik*. Marburg: Verlag Herder-Institut, 2019.

Laruelle, Marlène. *Central Peripheries: Nationhood in Central Asia*. London: UCL Press, 2021.

Laycock, Jo. "Developing a Soviet Armenian Nation: Refugees and Resettlement in the Early Soviet South Caucasus." In *Empire and Belonging*, edited by Lewis H. Siegelbaum and Krista A. Goff, 97–111.

Lee, Eric. *The Experiment: Georgia's Forgotten Revolution, 1918–1921*. London: Zed, 2017.

Lefebvre, Camille. *Frontières de sable, frontières de papier: Histoire de territoires et de frontières, du jihad de Sokoto à la colonisation française du Niger, XIXe–XXe siècles*. Paris: Publications de la Sorbonne, 2015.

Lefebvre, Henri. *La production de l'espace*, 4th ed. Paris: Anthropos, 2000.

Lejeune, Philippe. *Le pact autobiographique*. Paris: Seuil, 1975.

Lehmann, Maike. *Eine sowjetische Nation: Nationale Sozialismusinterpretationen in Armenien seit 1945*. Frankfurt am Main: Campus, 2012.

Liber, George. "Korenizatsiia: Restructuring Soviet Nationality Policy in the 1920s." *Ethnic and Racial Studies* 14, no. 1 (1991): 15–23.

Light, Nathan. "Kyrgyz Genealogies and Lineages: Histories, Everyday Life, and Patriarchal Institutions in Northwestern Kyrgyzstan." *Genealogy* 53, no. 2 (2018): 1–26.

Lieven, Dominic. *Empire: The Russian Empire and Its Rivals*. New Haven: Yale University Press, 2001.

Loskutova, Marina. "Regionalisation, Imperial Legacy, and the Soviet Geographical Tradition." In *Empire De/Centered*, edited by Sanna Turoma and Maxim Waldstein, 135–56.

Löwis, Sabine von, and Beate Eschment, eds. *Post-Soviet Borders: A Kaleidoscope of Shifting Lives and Lands*. New York: Routledge, 2023.

Mace, James E. *Communism and the Dilemmas of National Liberation: National Communism in Soviet Ukraine, 1918–1933*. Cambridge, MA: Harvard University Press, 1983.

Magocsi, Paul Robert. *A History of Ukraine: The Land and Its Peoples*. 2nd ed. Toronto: University of Toronto Press, 2010.

Maier, Charles S. "Consigning the Twentieth Century to History: Alternative Narratives for the Modern Era." *American Historical Review* 105, no. 3 (2000): 807–31.

———. *Once within Borders: Territories of Power, Wealth, and Belonging since 1500*. Cambridge, MA: Harvard University Press, 2015.

Malysheva, E. P. "Administrativno-territorial'noe ustroistvo Svetskogo gosudarstva." In *Administrativno-territorial'noe ustroistvo Rossii*, edited by A. Pyzhikov, 202–41.

Mamoulia, Georges. *Les combats indépendantistes des Caucasiens entre URSS et puissances occidentales: Le cas de la Géorgie, 1921–1945*. Paris: L'Harmattan, 2009.

Markhuliia, Guram. *Turtsiia i armiano-gruzinskii vooruzhënnyi konflikt v oktiabre 1918 goda*. Tbilisi: baritoni, 2005.

Martin, Terry. *The Affirmative Action Empire: Nations and Nationalism in the Soviet Union, 1923–1939*. Ithaca, NY: Cornell University Press, 2001.

Martin, Terry, and Ronald G. Suny, eds. *A State of Nations: Empire and Nation-Making in the Age of Lenin and Stalin*. Oxford: Oxford University Press, 2001.

Masov, Rahim. *Istoriia topornogo razdeleniia*. Dushanbe: Irfon, 1991. Self-published in English as *The History of a National Catastrophe*, 2013.
Matveeva, Anna. "Divided We Fall . . . or Rise? Tajikistan–Kyrgyzstan Border Dilemma." *Cambridge Journal of Eurasian Studies*, no. 1 (2017): 1–17.
Maximenkov, Leonid. "Stalin's Meeting with a Delegation of Ukrainian Writers on 12 February 1929." *Harvard Ukrainian Studies* 16, no. 3–4 (1992): 361–431.
McDonald, Tracy. *Face to the Village: The Riazan Countryside under Soviet Rule, 1921–1930*. Toronto: University of Toronto Press, 2011.
Medinskii, Vladimir. "K chitateliam." In *Istoriia Kryma*, edited by S. Kodzov, 3–9. Moscow: Olma, 2016.
Michaluk, Dorota. "Emerging States and Border-Making in Times of War: Negotiating the Ukrainian-Belarusian Borders in 1918." In *Making Ukraine*, edited by Constantin Ardeleanu and Olena Palko, 163–88.
Mieczkowski, Z. "The Economic Regionalization of the Soviet Union in the Lenin and Stalin Period." *Canadian Slavonic Papers* 8, no. 1 (1966): 89–124.
Miles, William F. S. "Postcolonial Borderland Legacies of Anglo-French Partition in West Africa." *African Studies Review* 58, no. 3 (2015): 191–213.
Mirianašvili, Nat'ela. *sak'art'velos teritoriuli c'vlilebani amierkavkasiis respublikebt'an, 1918–1938 cc*. Tbilisi: universali, 2012.
Morrison, Alexander. "Bab'i Bunty in Semirech'e: Gender, Class, and Ethnicity in Central Asia during the First World War." *Revolutionary Russia* 36, no. 1 (2023): 34–55.
———. *The Russian Conquest of Central Asia: A Study in Imperial Expansion, 1814–1914*. Cambridge: Cambridge University Press, 2021.
Morrison, Alexander, Cloé Drieu, and Aminat Chokobaeva, eds. *The Central Asian Revolt of 1916: A Collapsing Empire in the Age of War and Revolution*. Manchester: Manchester University Press, 2020.
Motyka, Grzegorz. *Ukraińska partyzantka, 1942–1960: Działalność Organizacji Ukraińskich Nacjonalistów i Ukraińskiej Powstańczej Armii*. Warsaw: Rytm, 2006.
Mouradian, Claire. *L'Arménie*, 5th ed. Paris: Presses universitaires de France, 2013.
———. *De Staline à Gorbachev: Histoire d'une république soviétique. L'Arménie*. Paris: Éditions Ramsay, 1990.
Mühlfried, Florian. *Being a State and States of Being in Highland Georgia*. New York: Berghahn, 2014.
Müller, Daniel. "Die Armenier in den Kreisen Džebaril', Šuša und Dževanšir des Gouvernements Elizavetpol' nach den amtlichen 'Familienlisten' von 1886." In *Osmanismus, Nationalismus und der Kaukasus: Muslime und Christen, Türken und Armenier im 19. und 20. Jahrhundert*, edited by Fikret Adanir and Bernd Bonwetsch, 65–83. Wiesbaden: Reichert, 2005.
———. *Sowjetische Nationalitätenpolitik in Transkaukasien, 1920–1953*. Berlin: Köster, 2008.
Naganawa, Norihiro. "Officious Aliens: Tatars' Involvement in the Central Asian Revolution, 1919–21." *Kritika: Explorations in Russian and Eurasian History* 24, no. 1 (2023): 63–92.

———. "Tatars and Imperialist Wars: From the Tsar's Servitors to the Red Warriors." *Ab Imperio*, no. 1 (2020): 164–96.
Newman, David. "Boundaries." In *A Companion to Political Geography*, edited by John Agnew, Katharyne Mitchell, and Gerard Toal, 123–37. Malden, MA: Blackwell, 2008.
Nove, Alec. *An Economic History of the USSR, 1917–1991*. London: Penguin Books, 1992.
Núñez Seixas, Xosé M., ed. *The First World War and the Nationality Question in Europe: Global Impact and Local Dynamics*. Leiden: Brill, 2021.
———. "Wilson's Unexpected Friends: The Transnational Impact of the First World War on Western European Nationalist Movements." In *The First World War*, ed. Xosé M. Núñez Seixas, 37–64.
Obertreis, Julia. *Imperial Desert Dreams: Cotton Growing and Irrigation in Central Asia, 1860–1991*. Göttingen: V&R unipress, 2017.
Obiya, Chika. "When Faizulla Khojaev Decided to Be an Uzbek." In *Islam in Politics in Russia and Central Asia: Early Eighteenth to late Twentieth Centuries*, edited by Stéphane A. Dudoignon and Hisao Komatsu, 99–118. London: Kegan Paul, 2001.
Ohayon, Isabelle, and Tomohiko Uyama. "Mediators of the Empire in Central Asia, 1820–1928." *Cahiers du monde russe* 56, no. 4 (2015): 617–20.
Olimov, Muzaffar, and Saodat Olimova. "Integration vs Disintegration: State Borders and Border Conflicts in the Isfara Valley." In *Post-Soviet Borders*, edited by Sabine von Löwis and Beate Eschment, 187–205.
Osterhammel, Jürgen, and Jan C. Jansen. *Kolonialismus: Geschichte, Formen, Folgen*. 9th ed. Munich: C. H. Beck, 2021.
Paasi, Anssi. *Territories, Boundaries and Consciousness: The Changing Geographies of the Finnish-Russian Border*. Chichester: John Wiley and Sons, 1996.
Partlett, William, and Herbert Küpper. *The Post-Soviet as Post-Colonial: A New Paradigm for Understanding Constitutional Dynamics in the Former Soviet Empire*. Cheltenham: Edward Elgar, 2022.
Payk, Marcus M., and Roberta Pergher, eds. *Beyond Versailles: Sovereignty, Legitimacy, and the Formation of New Polities after the Great War*. Bloomington: Indiana University Press, 2019.
Payne, Matthew J. *Stalin's Railroad: Turksib and the Building of Socialism*. Pittsburgh: University of Pittsburgh Press, 2001.
Pelkmans, Mathijs. *Defending the Border: Identity, Religion, and Modernity in the Republic of Georgia*. Ithaca, NY: Cornell University Press, 2006.
Perović, Jeronim. *Der Nordkaukasus unter russischer Herrschaft: Geschichte einer Vielvölkerregion zwischen Rebellion und Anpassung*. Cologne: Böhlau 2015.
Peterson, James M., and Jacek Lubecki. *Globalization, Nationalism, and Imperialism: A New History of Eastern Europe*. Budapest: Central European University Press, 2023.
Peterson, Maya. *Pipe Dreams: Water and Empire in Central Asia's Aral Sea Basin*. Cambridge: Cambridge University Press, 2019.
Petronis, Vytautas. *Constructing Lithuania: Ethnic Mapping in Tsarist Russia ca. 1800–1914*. Stockholm: Stockholm University Press, 2007.
Peyrat, Etienne. *Histoire du Caucase au XXe siècle*. Paris: Fayard, 2020.

———. "Soviet Federalism at Work: Lessons from the History of the Transcaucasian Federation." *Jahrbücher für Geschichte Osteuropas* 65, no. 4 (2017): 529–59.
Pianciola, Niccolò. "The Benefits of Marginality: The Great Famine around the Aral Sea, 1930–1934." *Nationalities Papers* 48, no. 3 (2020): 513–29.
———. "Décoloniser l'Asie centrale? Bolcheviks et colons au Semireč'e, 1920–1922." *Cahiers du monde russe* 49, no. 1 (2008): 101–43.
———. "Stalinist Spatial Hierarchies: Placing the Kazakhs and Kyrgyz in Soviet Economic Regionalization." *Central Asian Survey* 63, no. 1 (2017): 73–92.
Pipes, Richard. *The Formation of the Soviet Union: Communism and Nationalism, 1917–1923*. 3rd ed. Cambridge, MA: Harvard University Press, 1997.
Porter, Andrew. *European Imperialism, 1860–1914*. New York: Palgrave Macmillan, 1994.
Pravilova, Ekaterina. *Finansy imperii: Den'gi i vlast' v politike Rossii na natsional'nykh okrainakh, 1801–1917*. Moscow: Novoe izdatel'stvo, 2006.
Pyzhikov, A., ed. *Administrativno-territorial'noe ustroistvo Rossii: Istoriia i sovremennost'*. Moscow: Olma-Press, 2003.
Rahimov, Mirzohid, and Galina Urazaeva. "Central Asian Nations and Border Issues." *Conflict Studies Research Centre* 10, no. 5 (2005): 1–23.
Rankin, William. *After the Map: Cartography, Navigation, and the Transformation of Territory in the Twentieth Century*. Chicago: University of Chicago Press, 2016.
Ratner, Steven R. "Drawing a Better Line: Uti Possidetis and the Borders of New States." *American Journal of International Law* 90, no. 4 (1996): 590–624.
Rebitschek, Immo. "State Building under Occupation: Pavlo Skoropadsky's Hetmanate in 1918." *Revolutionary Russia* 32, no. 2 (2019): 226–50.
Reeves, Madeleine. *Border Work: Spatial Lives of the State in Rural Central Asia*. Ithaca, NY: Cornell University Press, 2014.
Rhinelander, L. Hamilton. "The Creation of the Caucasian Vicegerency." *Slavonic and East European Review* 59, no. 1 (1981): 15–40.
Rice, Christopher. "Party Rivalry in the Caucasus: SRs, Armenians and the Baku Union of Oil Workers, 1907–08." *Slavonic and East European Review* 67, no. 2 (1989): 228–43.
Rindlisbacher, Stephan. "Between Proclamations of Friendship and Concealed Distrust: The Turkish-Soviet Border Commission, 1925–1926." *Journal of Modern European History* 22, no. 1 (2024): 55–68.
———. "Contested Lines: The Russio-Ukrainian Border, 1917–1929." In *Making Ukraine*, edited by Constantin Ardeleanu and Olena Palko, 189–209.
———. "From International Isomorphism to Traditionalist Iconography: Banknotes as an Alternative Approach to Soviet Chronology." *Jahrbücher für Geschichte Osteuropas* 70, no. 1–2 (2022): 100–130.
———. "From Space to Territory: Negotiating the Russo-Ukrainian Border, 1919–1928." *Revolutionary Russia* 31, no. 1 (2018): 86–106.
———. "National Forms with Economic Content? Gosplan's Expertise on Territorializing the Soviet State, 1921–1930." In *Spatial Entrepreneurs: Actors*

and *Practices of Space-Making under the Global Condition*, edited by Steffi Marung and Ursula Rao, 39–57. Berlin: De Gruyter, 2023.

———. "The Territorial Challenge in the Early Soviet State." In *Post-Soviet Borders*, edited by Sabine von Löwis and Beate Eschment, 51–66.

Rindlisbacher, Stephan, and Alun Thomas. "Paths Not Taken: How Did Nomadism Affect Border-Making during National Delimitation in Central Asia?" *Ab Imperio*, no. 2 (2023): 117–41.

Rolf, Malte. "Nationalizing an Empire: The Bolsheviks, the Nationality Question, and Policies of Indigenization in the Soviet Union, 1917–1927." In *First World War*, ed. Xosé M. Núñez Seixas, 65–86.

Romanov, Aleksandr. "Georgievskie tsveta snova nad Krymom: Vossoedinenie Kryma s Rossiei, 2014 god." In *Istoriia Kryma*, edited by S. Kodzov, 452–62. Moscow: Olma, 2016.

Rudling, Per Anders. *The Rise and Fall of Belarusian Nationalism, 1906–1931*. Pittsburgh: University of Pittsburgh Press, 2015.

Rupasov, Aleksandr, and Aleksandr Chistikov. *Sovetsko-finliandskaia granitsa, 1918–1938 gg: Ocherki istorii*. St. Petersburg: Avrora, 2016.

Sahach, Oksana. "Zminy v administratyvno-terytorial'nomu podili USRR na pochatku 20-kh rr. XX st." *Regional'na istoriia Ukraïny*, no. 4 (2010): 167–76.

Saparov, Arsène. *From Conflict to Autonomy in the Caucasus: The Soviet Union and the Making of Abkhazia, South Ossetia and Nagorno Karabakh*. London: Routledge, 2015.

———. "Nagorno-Karabakh Conflict: What's Next?" *Ab Imperio*, no. 3 (2023): 184–98.

Sasse, Gwendolyn. *The Crimea Question: Identity, Transition, and Conflict*. Cambridge, MA: Harvard University Press, 2007.

Schafer, Daniel E. "Local Politics and the Birth of the Republic of Bashkortostan, 1919–1920." In *State of Nations*, edited by Terry Martin and Ronald G. Suny, 165–90.

Schenk, F. Benjamin. "Mental Maps: Die Konstruktion von geographischen Räumen in Europa seit der Aufklärung." *Geschichte und Gesellschaft* 28, no. 3 (2002): 493–514.

———. "'A Sixth Part of the World': The Career of a Spatial Metaphor in Russia and the Soviet Union, 1837–2021." *Kritika: Explorations in Russian and Eurasian History* 24, no. 2 (2023): 349–80.

Schlögel, Karl. *Im Raume lesen wir die Zeit: Über Zivilisationsgeschichte und Geopolitik*. Munich: Carl Hanser, 2003.

———. *Petersburg: Das Laboratorium der Moderne, 1909–1921*. Frankfurt am Main: Fischer, 2009.

Scott, Eric R. *Familiar Strangers: The Georgian Diaspora and the Evolution of Soviet Empire*. Oxford: Oxford University Press, 2016.

Scott, James C. *Seeing Like a State: How Certain Schemes to Improve the Human Condition Have Failed*. New Haven: Yale University Press, 1998.

Shahvar, Soli, and Anatoly Mishaev. "The Re-Radicalization of Baku Provincial Workers in 1916." *Revolutionary Russia* 36, no. 1 (2023): 56–75.

Sharp, Alan. *The Versailles Settlement: Peacemaking after the First World War, 1919–1923*. 3rd ed. London: Palgrave Macmillan, 2018.

Shishkin, Philip. *Restless Valley: Revolution, Murder, and Intrigue in the Heart of Central Asia*. New Haven: Yale University Press, 2014.

Shtoulberg, Boris, Aleko Adamesku, V. Khistianov, and Murat Albegov. "Soviet Regional Policy." In *Regional Development in Russia: Past Policies and Future Prospects*, edited by Hans Westlund, Folke Snickars, and Aleksandr Granberg, 37-83. Cheltenham: Elgar, 2000.

Shul'gina, Ol'ga, "Administrativno-territorial'noe delenie Rossii v XX veke: Istoriko-geograficheskii aspect." Diss., MGPU Moscow, 2005.

Siegelbaum, Lewis H. *Soviet State and Society between Revolutions, 1918-1929*. New York: Cambridge University Press, 1992.

Siegelbaum, Lewis H., and Krista A. Goff, eds. *Empire and Belonging in the Eurasian Borderlands*. Ithaca, NY: Cornell University Press, 2019.

Siegelbaum, Lewis H., and Leslie P. Moch. "Transnationalism in One Country? Seeing and Not Seeing Cross-Border Migration within the Soviet Union." *Slavic Review* 75, no. 4 (2016): 970-86.

Simon, Gerhard. *Nationalismus und Nationalitätenpolitik in der Sowjetunion: Von der totalitären Diktatur zur nachstalinistischen Gesellschaft*. Baden-Baden: Nomos, 1986.

Slezkine, Yuri. "The USSR as a Communal Apartment, or How a Socialist State Promoted Ethnic Particularism." *Slavic Review* 53, no. 2 (1994): 420-21.

Smele, Jon. *The 'Russian' Civil Wars, 1916-1926: Ten Years That Shook the World*. London: Hurst and Co., 2015.

Smith, Jeremy. *The Bolsheviks and the National Question, 1917-1923*. London: St. Martin's, 1999.

———. "The Georgian Affair of 1922: Policy Failure, Personality Clash or Power Struggle?" *Europe-Asia Studies* 50, no. 3 (1998): 519-44.

———. "Leadership and Nationalism in the Soviet Republics, 1951-1959." In *Khrushchev in the Kremlin Policy and Government in the Soviet Union, 1953-1964*, edited by Melanie Ilic and Jeremy Smith, 79-93. London: Routledge, 2011.

———. "Nagorno Karabakh under Soviet Rule." In *The South Caucasus beyond Borders, Boundaries and Division Lines: Conflicts, Cooperation and Development*, edited by Mikko Palonkorpi, 9-25. Turku: Juvenes, 2015.

———. "New Borders, New Belongings in Central Asia: Competing Visions and the Decoupling of the Soviet Union." In *Empire and Belonging*, edited by Lewis H. Siegelbaum and Krista A. Goff, 182-98.

———. *Red Nations: The Nationalities Experience in and after the USSR*. Cambridge: Cambridge University Press, 2013.

Smith, Leonard V. *Sovereignty at the Paris Peace Conference of 1919*. Oxford: Oxford University Press, 2018.

Sperling, Walter. *Vor den Ruinen von Grosny: Leben und Überleben im multiethnischen Kaukasus*. Berlin: Matthes & Seitz, 2024.

Staliūnas, Darius, ed. "The Identification of Subjects According to Nationality: In the Western Region of the Russian Empire in 1905-1915." *Ab Imperio*, no. 3 (2020): 33-68.

———. *Spatial Concepts of Lithuania in the Long Nineteenth Century*. Boston: Academic Studies Press, 2016.

Sukhova, Ol'ga, and Ol'ga Filenkova. "Natsional'nyi vopros i raionirovanie v RSFSR v 1920-e-nachale 1930-kh godov: Upravlencheskie strategii i ikh realizatsiia. Po materialam Povolzh'ia." *Noveishaia istoriia Rossii*, no. 1 (2017): 62–77.

Suny, Ronald G. *The Baku Commune, 1917–1918: Class and Nationality in the Russian Revolution*. Princeton, NJ: Princeton University Press, 1972.

———. "Dialektika imperii: Rossiia i Sovetskii Soiuz." In *Novaia imperskaia istoriia postsovetskogo prostranstva*, edited by Ilya Gerasimov, G. Glebov, L. Kaplunovskii, Aleksandr Semënov, and Marina Mogil'ner, 163-96. Kazan: Tsentr issledovanii natsionalizma i imperii, 2004.

———. *Red Flag Unfurled: Historians, History and the Russian Revolution*. London: Verso, 2017.

———. *The Revenge of the Past: Nationalism, Revolution, and the Collapse of the Soviet Union*. Stanford, CA: Stanford University Press, 1993.

———. *The Soviet Experiment: Russia, the USSR, and the Successor States*. 2nd ed. New York: Oxford University Press, 2011.

Tagirova, Nailya. "Mapping the Empire's Economic Regions from the Nineteenth to the Early Twentieth Century." In *Russian Empire*, edited by Jane Burbank, Mark von Hagen, and Anatolyi Remnev, 125-38.

Taubman, William. "The Khrushchev Period, 1953-1964." In *The Twentieth Century*, edited by Ronald G. Suny, 268-91. Vol. 3 of *The Cambridge History of Russia*. Cambridge: Cambridge University Press, 2006.

Teichmann, Christian. *Macht der Unordnung: Stalins Herrschaft in Zentralasien 1920–1950*. Hamburg: Hamburger Edition, 2016.

Thomas, Alun. "The Caspian Disputes: Nationalism and Nomadism in Early Soviet Central Asia." *Russian Review* 76, no. 3 (2017): 502–25.

———. *Nomads and Soviet Rule: Central Asia under Lenin and Stalin*. London: Tauris, 2018.

———. "Revisiting the 'Transcaspian Episode': British Intervention and Turkmen Statehood, 1918-1919." *Europe-Asia Studies* 75, no. 1 (2023): 131–53.

Tohidipur, Timo. "Grenzen im Spiegel des Rechts." In *Grenzforschung*, edited by Dominik Gerst, Maria Klessmann, and Hannes Krämer, 297-315.

Turoma, Sanna, and Maxim Waldstein, eds. *Empire De/Centered: New Spatial Histories of Russia and the Soviet Union*. Farnham: Ashgate, 2013.

Urbansky, Sören. *Beyond the Steppe Frontier: A History of the Sino-Russian Border*. Princeton, NJ: Princeton University Press, 2020.

Uyama, Tomohiko, ed. "The Alash Orda's Relations with Siberia, the Urals, and Turkestan: The Kazakh National Movement and the Russian Imperial Legacy." In *Asiatic Russia*, edited by Tomohiko Uyama, 271-87.

———. *Asiatic Russia: Imperial Power in Regional and International Contexts*. London: Routledge, 2012.

Vechers'kyi, V. *Monastyri ta khramy Putyvl'shchyny*. Kiev: Nash chas, 2007.

Velychenko, Stephen. *Painting Imperialism and Nationalism Red: The Ukrainian Marxist Critique of Russian Communist Rule in Ukraine, 1918–1925*. Toronto: University of Toronto Press, 2015.

———. *State Building in Revolutionary Ukraine: A Comparative Study of Governments and Bureaucrats, 1917–1922*. Toronto: Toronto University Press, 2011.

Vermenych, Yaroslava, and Oleksandr Androshchuk. *Zminy administratyvno-terytorial'noho ustroiu Ukraïny XX–XXI. st.* Kiev: NAN Ukraïny, 2014.

Viola, Lynne. "The Aesthetic of Stalinist Planning and the World of the Special Villages." *Kritika: Explorations in Russian and Eurasian History* 4, no. 1 (2003): 101–28.

———. *Peasant Rebels under Stalin: Collectivization and the Culture of Peasant Resistance.* New York: Oxford University Press, 1999.

Voronovici, Alexandr. "Overlapping Spaces: Negotiating and Delineating the Ukrainian-Moldovan Border during the Interwar and Wartime Years." In *Making Ukraine*, edited by Constantin Ardeleanu and Olena Palko, 210–37.

Wehrhahn, Torsten. *Die Westukrainische Volksrepublik: Zu den polnisch-ukrainischen Beziehungen und dem Problem der ukrainischen Staatlichkeit in den Jahren 1918 bis 1923.* Berlin: Weissensee Verlag, 2004.

Werth, Nicolas. "Un état contre son peuple: Violences, répressions, terreurs en Union soviétique." In *Le livre noir du communisme: Crimes, terreur et repression*, edited by Karel Bartosek, Stéphane Courtois, Pascal Fontaine, Rémi Kauffer, Nicolas Werth, Jean-Louis Margolin, Andrzej Paczkowski, Jean-Louis Panné, Pierre Rigoulot, and Yves Santamaria, 45–313. Paris: Robert Laffont, 1997.

Werth, Paul W. *How Russia Got Big: A Territorial History.* London: Bloomsbury, 2025.

———. "Russia's Borders in East and West." *Kritika: Explorations in Russian and Eurasian History* 22, no. 3 (2021): 623–44.

White, Hayden. *Metahistory: The Historical Imagination in Nineteenth-Century Europe.* Baltimore: Johns Hopkins University Press, 1973.

Williams, Brian Glyn, *The Crimean Tatars: From Soviet Genocide to Putin's Conquest.* London: Hurst and Co., 2015.

Wolff, Larry. *Woodrow Wilson and the Reimagining of Eastern Europe.* Stanford, CA: Stanford University Press, 2020.

Xač'atryan, Karen, Hamo Suk'iasyan, and Geġam Badalyan. *Xorhrdayan Hayastani ev lġin-i tarack'ayin korustnerë 1920–1930-akan t'vakannerin.* Yerevan: HHGAA, 2015.

Yamamoto, Takahiro. *Demarcating Japan: Imperialism, Islanders, and Mobility, 1855–1884.* Cambridge, MA: Harvard University Press, 2023.

Yefimenko, Hennadii. "Die Grenzziehung zwischen der Sowjetukraine und Russland: Kriterien, Verlauf, Ergebnisse." *Nordost-Archiv* 27 (2018): 171–91.

———. "Vyznachennia kordonu mizh USRR ta RSFRR." *Problemy istoriï Ukraïny*, no. 20 (2011): 135–76.

Zaleski, Eugène, and Marie-Christine MacAndrew. *Planning for Economic Growth in the Soviet Union, 1918–1932.* Chapel Hill: University of North Carolina Press, 1971.

Index

Abdrakhmanov, Yusup, 97, 113, 124
Abkhazia, 127, 180
Akhalkalaki (region), 128, 132
Alash movement (Alash Orda), 17, 96, 102, 108, 124
Aleksandrov, Ivan, 37–40, 46, 57
Aleksei Mikhailovich (Tsar), 162
All-Russian Central Executive Committee. *See* VTsIK
All-Ukrainian Central Executive Committee. *See* VUTsVK
Andropov, Yurii, 191n44
Arabaev, Ishenaly, 96, 108, 113
Armenia (Armenian SSR): "pasture issue" 147–55; refugees arriving in, 131, 229–30n32; territory of, 94, 122, 126–32, 134–35, 154–55. *See also* Azerbaijan; border conflicts; border creation; border revisions; raionirovanie; ZSFSR
Arsen'ev, Konstantin, 35
Asfendiarov, Sandzhar, 106, 125
Atabaev, Kaigizys, 113
Austria-Hungary. *See* Habsburg Empire
Austromarxism, 14–15, 23, 30, 40, 67
autonomous oblasts and national republics: in Central Asia, 95, 99–102, 108, 112–16, 166; dissolution of, 60–61, 160, 173–74; formation of, 18, 20–27, 29–30, 166, 173; in relation to raionirovanie, 39–40, 43–44, 57; in the South Caucasus, 127, 132. *See also* federalism; nation and nationality; RSFSR; *specific places*
Azerbaijan (SSR): minorities, 10, 126; "pasture issue" 147–55; territory of, 94, 122, 126–32, 134–35, 154–55. *See also* Armenia; border conflicts; border creation; border revisions; raionirovanie; ZSFSR

Bagirov, Mir Dzhafar, 142
Baku, 22, 127–28, 131–32, 153; Baku Commune, 17, 128–29, 132
Bashkiria (Bashkordostan; Bashkir ASSR), 19–20, 22–24, 26, 44, 56, 174
Basmachi, 21, 95, 98–99, 221n26
Bauer, Otto, 14–15. *See also* Austromarxism
Belarus (Belarusian SSR), 46, 174–75; Belarusification, 28, 51; territory of, 51–52, 62, 70, 91. *See also* border revisions; raionirovanie; Politburo
Belgorod (town), 64, 73, 77
Beloborodov, Aleksandr, 71, 91, 117, 133–34
Beriia, Lavrentii, 153, 179–80
Berlin Conference (1884–1885), 4
Bessarabia. *See* Moldova
Borchaly (region), 128, 132
border conflicts (in USSR): Alagelliar (Armenia-Azerbaijan), 140–41, 171; Borisovka/Ohybne (UkrSSR-RSFSR), 88–89, 91–92, 176; Hungry Steppe (Mirzachul') (Uzbekistan-Kazakhstan), 111–12, 114, 167–69; Isfana Volost (Uzbekistan-Kyrgyzstan), 117, 120–21; Isfara Volost (Uzbekistan-Kyrgyzstan), 117–18; Khoromnoe (UkrSSR-RSFSR), 88, 92; Milove/Chertkovo (UkrSSR-RSFSR), 1–3, 9, 84–88, 91–92, 158, 176, 178, 181, 217n130; Miropol'e/Myropillia (UkrSSR-RSFSR), 82–84, 92, 178; Niuvadi (today Nrnadzor) (Armenia-Azerbaijan), 142–44; Osh (Uzbekistan-Kyrgyzstan), 108–9, 116–19; Sevakiar/Zor (Armenia-Azerbaijan) 144–46, 178; Shinikh Airum (Armenia-Azerbaijan), 135–41, 147, 177, 231n63; Sokh Valley (Uzbekistan-Kyrgyzstan), 117–21, 176, 181; Suliukta mines

INDEX 269

(Uzbekistan-Kyrgyzstan), 117–22, 178; Uch-Kurgan (Uzbekistan-Kyrgyzstan), 119–20, 226n136; Uspenskaia/Uspens'ka (UkrSSR-RSFSR), 84–88, 91–92; Yulduz-kak (Uzbekistan-Kyrgyzstan), 121–22; Znob' (UkrSSR-RSFSR), 81–84, 179

border creation (in USSR): Delimitation Commission for Central Asia (1924), 103–14, 154, 177; RSFSR-Ukraine (1917-1919), 64–65; South Caucasus, 128–30, 132–35, 231n53. *See also* raionirovanie

border revisions (in USSR): Cherviakov Commission (1924-1925), 68, 70–80, 82, 86, 91, 154, 157, 176–77; Crimea (1954), 156, 159–66, 171; Dar'ino-Yermakovka/Darïno-Yermakivka (1944-1945), 160, 170–71; Kul'besherov Commission (1927), 118–20; between Kazakhstan and Uzbekistan (1956-1971), 166–70; between Kyrgyzstan and Tajikistan (1938), 122–23; Petrovskii Commission (1925-1926), 116–17; Putivl' Volost (1926), 157–59, 161–62, 170–71, 178–79; between the RSFSR and Belarus, 51; between the RSFSR and Estonia (1947), 160; between the RSFSR and Georgia (1944-1957), 160; between the RSFSR and Latvia (1947), 160; Ter-Gabrelian Commission (1925-1928), 80–83, 157; Territorial Commission of the ZakTsIK (1923-1929), 134, 136–46, 154–55, 177, 230–31n49. *See also* Politburo

border survey, 87–88, 122–23, 132–46, 179

borot'bisty (left-wing Ukrainian Socialist Revolutionaries), 68, 80

Briansk (region), 69, 71, 73, 76, 82, 88

Broido, Grigorii, 102

Bukeikhanov, Alikhan, 96

Bukhara (Emirate; Soviet Peoples' Republic of), 24–25, 29, 55, 94–103, 112, 114–16, 122. *See also* border creation; Central Asia

Bukharin, Nikolai, 17, 20, 71

Bund (Jewish Socialist Party), 14

Buniat-Zade, Dadash, 140–41, 143, 150–51, 153

Butsenko, Panas (Afanasii): border revision between the UkrSSR and RSFSR, 69, 71–74, 76, 79–80, 83, 85, 89, 159, 211n24; Ukrainization, 68, 90; raionirovanie, 68

Catherine II (Empress, the Great), 76–77

Caucasian Viceroyalty (*namestnichestvo*), 40, 43, 45, 128. *See also* Armenia; Azerbaijan; Georgia; North Caucasus Krai; Russian Empire; South Caucasus; ZSFSR

census(es): of 1897, 74, 105, 109; of 1920, 74, 105–10, 157; of 1926, 6, 21, 64, 89, 126, 163

Central Asia (region), 7–10, 17, 21–22, 32, 35, 93–97, 123–26, 146, 152, 154, 166, 172, 175–81, 218n1. *See also* border conflicts; border revisions; Bukhara; Kazakhstan; Kirrespublika; korenizatsiia; Kyrgyzstan; Khorezm, raionirovanie; RSFSR; Tajikistan; Turkmenistan; Uzbekistan

Central Asian revolt of 1916, 94–95, 98, 105

Central Executive Committee of the USSR. *See* TsIK SSSR

Civil War, 3, 17–22, 25, 32, 36–37, 71, 175; in Central Asia, 21, 94–99; in the South Caucasus, 127–30; in Ukraine, 64–67

Checheno-Ingush ASSR, 160, 171–72

Cherviakov, Aleksandr, 70–74, 77, 79, 91, 154, 176

Chicherin, Georgii, 98

Christaller, Walter, 35

Chuprov, Aleksandr, 35

collectivization of agriculture, 58–60, 148, 151–53, 155. *See also* People's Commissariat of Agriculture; Cultural Revolution, nomadism

colonialism, 4–5, 22, 42, 94–95, 188–89n21–25

Communist Party (Bolshevik): VIII Party Congress (1919), 24; X Party Congress (1921), 27, 38; XII Party Congress (1923), 24, 28, 43, 72, 83; XV Party Congress (1927), 58; XVI Party Congress (1930), 58; in Belarus, 51; in Bukhara, 29, 96–97, 100–101, 114; Central Committee of, 24–26, 28, 31, 98, 102, 114–15; in Georgia, 26–27, 130–31, 153; factionalism in,

INDEX

Communist Party (*continued*)
4, 22, 26–27, 67–68, 90–91, 99, 104, 124, 130–31, 177, 211n24; governing practices, 20, 37, 80, 101, 130–31; ideology of, 3, 17–18, 30, 172; in Khorezm, 29, 96–97, 225n116; party discipline within, 4, 22, 24, 27–29, 62, 79, 104, 154, 175; Stalinism, 11, 58–61, 89–92, 122–25, 153–54, 159–61, 173–75; in Tajikistan, 115–16, 122; in Turkestan, 96–97, 100–101, 114; in Ukraine, 25, 67–68, 71, 73–74, 79, 89–92, 211n24; in Uzbekistan, 115–16, 122; in the ZSFSR, 130–32, 153–54. *See also* Politburo; *specific Bolsheviks*

Constitution of 1924 (USSR), 29, 85

Constitution of 1936 (USSR), 174

Cotton affair (1983–1984), 165

Crimea (transfer of 1954), 156, 159–66, 171, 179–80. *See also* border revisions

Cultural Revolution (1928–1931), 57, 207n140; bordering processes, 8, 90–91, 122, 159–60; collectivization, 150–53; decision making, 159–60, 179; raionirovanie, 57–61

Dagestan (ASSR), 30, 44

Dashnaktsutiun (Armenian nationalists), 128, 150

delimitation (*razmezhevanie*): definition of, 34. *See also* border conflicts; border creation; border revisions; nation and nationality

Dilizhan (Delizhan) (Region in Armenia), 135–42, 147

Donbas (region), 52, 65, 69, 72–74, 79–80, 84, 91, 159, 178

Donetsk-Krivoi Rog Soviet Republic, 19

Dosov, Vladimir, 57

Dublitskii, Vladimir, 50, 117–19

Eastern Europe (region), 6–8, 22, 125, 175, 178. *See also* border conflicts; border revisions; Moldova; raionirovanie; RSFSR; Ukraine

Eizmont, Nikolai, 68–69

empire: definition of, 3–5. *See also* colonialism; federalism; nation and nationalism, minorities; *specific empires*

Enver Pasha, 99

Erivan'. *See* Yerevan

Estonia (Estonian SSR), 10, 160

experts (professional expertise), 2, 4, 6–10, 16, 18, 21, 31, 36, 80, 87, 91, 116, 125, 134, 154, 172, 175–76, 178–79; definition of, 34; for GOELRO, 37–38; at Gosplan, 32–34, 38–46, 51, 54, 56–62, 67, 73–74, 76, 115, 176; at Narkomnats, 21, 33, 39, 42, 100, 102; regional expertise, 44–47, 49–52, 54–56, 61–62, 69–70, 72, 116–17, 119, 134, 143, 145–46; Russian imperial, 34–36, 61, 63, 75–76, 175; at TsIK, 87. *See also* border conflicts; border revisions; border survey; raionirovanie; *specific experts*

federalism, 20, 23–24, 172–73; in Central Asia, 98–99, 102; in the South Caucasus, 130–31, 133–35, 146–49. *See also* autonomous oblasts and national republics

Finland, 19–20, 45

Fitrat, Aburauf, 96

France, 4, 16, 43

Frunze (town). *See* Bishkek

Frunze, Mikhail, 98

Georgia (Georgian SSR), 25–26, 47, 49, 55–56, 128–32, 160, 174. *See also* border creation; raionirovanie; South Caucasus; ZSFSR

Georgian affair (1922), 26–27, 130–31

Germany, 15–16, 35, 43, 128, 174

Great Terror (1936–1938), 60, 90–91, 125, 153–54

GOELRO. *See* raionirovanie

Gosplan, 32, 198n1; planned economy, 36–38, 58–61, 176; first five-year plan (1928–1933), 58–60, 150–51, 166. *See also* experts; raionirovanie

Habsburg Empire, 14,16, 64–65

Hrushevs'kyi, Mikhailo, 70

Hummet (Muslim Social Democratic Party), 127

Islamov, Sharustam, 100, 105–6, 108–11, 113, 124

Izvestiia (newspaper), 72, 114

Jadids (Muslim reformers), 17, 21, 95–96, 124

Kabardino-Balkarian ASSR, 160

Kalinin, Mikhail, 31, 42, 80, 89, 141

INDEX

Kamenev, Lev, 26, 52
Karakalpak (AO, ASSR), 102, 113, 116, 166
Karklin, Oto, 104, 110-11, 113
Kars (region), 128, 130
Kas'ian, Sarkis, 139
Kavbiuro. *See* Zakkraikom
Kazakh (Region in Azerbaijan), 128, 132, 139-40, 147, 152
Kazakhstan (Kazakh ASSR, SSR), 60, 93, 116, 122, 153, 166-70, 174, 180, 226n123. *See also* border conflicts; border revisions; Kirrespublika
Kemal, Mustafa (Atatürk), 128, 130
KEPS, 36-37, 58
Kharkiv (region), 46, 53-54, 75
Kharkiv (town), 46, 65, 83, 91
Khiva. *See* Khorezm
Khmel'nyts'kyi, Bohdan, 162
Khodzhaev, Faizulla, 96, 100, 124
Khodzhaev, Said Ali, 116, 119
Khodzhanov, Sultanbek, 101-2, 104, 106-13, 124-25
Khodzhibaev, Abdurakhin, 108, 112, 116
Khorezm (Kanate of Khiva; Soviet Peoples' Republic of), 94-99, 102-3, 114. *See also* border creation; Central Asia
Khronin, Vasilii, 69, 72
Khrushchev, Nikita, 12, 61, 157, 160-63, 165, 168-69, 171
Khrushchev, Sergei, 165
Kiev, 46, 64-65
Kirrespublika (Kirgiskaia ASSR, 1920-1925), 98-100, 102, 108, 110, 112-13, 116, 220n24, 222n53. *See also* border revisions; Kazakhstan; korenizatsiia; raionirovanie
Kolchak, Aleksandr, 22
Komi (AO, ASSR), 23-24
korenizatsiia, 6, 24, 27, 172, 175-76; XII Party Congress, 28, 43, 72, 83; in Central Asia, 50, 95-97, 99-101; "Piedmont Principle," 6, 11, 77, 91, 176; in the ZSFSR, 131-32, 148-50; in Ukraine, 67-68, 89-92. *See also* autonomous oblasti and national republics; Communist Party; federalism; nation and nationality
Krzhizhanovskii, Gleb, 17, 37-38, 40, 52, 59
Kuban (region), 43, 70-71, 153, 163
Kuban affair (1932-1933), 60, 90-91
Kuibyshev, Valerian, 59

Kul'besherov, Biashim, 118-21
Kunaev, Dinmukhammed, 168-71
Kursk (region), 33, 39-40, 51-52, 64, 69-71, 73, 76-77, 80-83, 157-59
Kviring, Emanuïl, 79
Kyrgyzstan (Kara-Kirgiz AO, Kyrgyz ASSR, SSR), 49-51, 55, 60, 93, 113, 116-23, 166, 174-75, 178, 180-81. *See also* border conflicts, border revisions, raionirovanie
Kyrychenko, Oleksii, 165

Latsis, Martin, 17, 71, 76, 91
Latvia (Latvian SSR), 10, 160
Lenin (Ul'ianov), Vladimir: on Bolshevik rule, 20, 27, 31, 131; on "Great Russian chauvinism," 19, 27; on nationality question, 2, 14-15, 22, 32-33, 72-73, 99; on planned economy, 36-38; on self-determination, 10-11, 14-17, 25-26, 32, 83, 174. *See also* Communist Party; Marxism-Leninism
Lori (region), 128, 132

Magidovich, Iosif, 54-55, 116-17, 119, 221n26
Makharadze, Filipp, 46-47
Malenkov, Georgii, 165
Manuïl's'kyi, Dmytro, 25
Marxism-Leninism, 2-4, 14-15, 27, 30, 172-73. *See also* Communist Party
Mendeleev, Dmitrii, 35, 38
Mendeshev, Seitkali, 110, 118-19
Menshevik Party, 15; in Georgia, 128-29
Mezhlauk, Ivan, 101
minorities (national), 5, 10, 13, 16-19, 29-30, 51, 114, 127, 173. *See also* autonomous oblasts and national republics; korenizatsiia; nation-state; nation and nationality; Paris Peace Conference
Mirza-Galiev, Mukhamedkhafii, 116-17
Moldova (ASSR, SSR), 7, 30, 67
Molotov (Skriabin), Viacheslav, 83
Mongolia, 75, 175
Mukhiddinov, Abdukadyr, 116
Musavat (political party), 127

Nakhichevan (region), 128, 132
Nagorno-Karabakh (region), 127-28, 132, 141-42, 170, 179-81
Narkomnats. *See* People's Commissariat of Nationality Affairs

INDEX

Narkomzem. *See* People's Commissariat of Agriculture
nation-state, 3–5, 15–17. *See also* empire; minorities; nation and nationality; Paris Peace Conference, self-determination
nation and nationality (*natsiia, natsional'nost'*, and *narodnost'*): ambiguity of terminology, 22–23, 34, 63, 67, 97, 101–2, 105–10, 112, 220n24, 223n66; "backwardness" in relation to, 3, 5, 16, 18, 22–23, 28, 33, 101, 123–24, 132, 147, 149–50, 155, 176; crystallization of, 10, 22–23, 60–61, 67, 92, 101–3, 114–17, 122, 124, 126–28, 155; definitions of, 14, 67; ethno-national hierarchies, 5, 18, 23–24, 28, 101, 132, 147, 155, 173–75. *See also* self-determination
nationality question (in USSR), 2, 14, 18, 20, 28–30, 33, 40, 173, 191n44; Lenin on, 15, 26–27; Stalin on, 14–15, 25–27, 193n5. *See also* self-determination
national republics. *See* autonomous oblasts and national republics
New Economic Policy (NEP), 38, 58, 61, 68, 148
"new imperial history," 3, 9, 187n6. *See also* empire; nation-state
Nicholas II (Emperor), 17
NKVD. *See* People's Commissariat of Internal Affairs
nomadism (in USSR), 50, 101, 233n106, 234n108-9; Bolshevik approach to; 111, 147, 150–51; collectivization; 151–54, 236n148–49, 237n155; in relation to national delimitation, 102, 106–7, 111, 113–14; "pasture issue", 121–23, 147–54, 234n114, 234–35n122. *See also* nation and nationality
North Caucasus (region), 1–2, 44–45, 52, 68–72, 177–78. *See also* Caucasian Viceroyalty
North Crimean Canal. *See* Crimea

Orakhelashvili, Mamiia, 177
Ordzhonikidze, Sergo (Grigorii, Grigol), 26–27, 129–30, 132, 177, 179
Ottoman Empire. *See* Turkey

Paris Peace Conference (1919–1920), 5–6, 13, 15–17, 63, 77, 129–30, 175, 180. *See also* minorities; self-determination; Treaty of Sèvres; World War I

"pasture issue." *See* Armenia; Azerbaijan; nomadism
Peace of Riga (1921), 51, 63–64, 67
People's Commissariat of Agriculture (Narkomzem), 76, 131, 135, 140, 143, 148–52
People's Commissariat of Internal Affairs (NKVD), 23, 34, 71, 90–91
People's Commissariat of Nationality Affairs (Narkomnats), 21–23, 30, 32–33, 36–37, 39, 42–43, 100, 102
Peter I (Emperor, the Great), 45
Petrovskii, Grigorii, 116–17
Piatakov, Georgii, 71
Pishpek. *See* Bishkek
planned economy. *See* Gosplan
Poland, 5, 45, 51, 63–65, 67, 77, 90
Politburo (of the Communist Party), 20, 31, 175–78; on the borders in the South Caucasus, 126, 154; on the delimitation in Central Asia, 102–4, 114; on the RSFSR-Belarusian border, 51; on the RSFSR-Ukrainian border, 72, 79, 85, 91, 157. *See also* border conflicts, border revisions; Communist Party
Poloz, Mykhailo, 29, 68–69, 71–73, 80, 90
postcolonial theory, 4–5, 188–89n21–25. *See also* "new imperial history"
Pravda (newspaper), 79, 114
Putin, Vladimir, 2
Putyvl' (until 1926 Putivl'), 51, 77, 156–60, 170–71, 178–79

raionirovanie, 6–7, 11, 13, 31, 51–53, 60–62, 172, 175–77; abolition of the okruga (1930), 59–60; All-Union Commission of, 54–56, 115; in Armenia, 49, 55–56, 59–60, 206n129; in Azerbaijan, 55–56; Communist Academy, 57–58; definition of, 34–35; end of, 58–61, 208n157, 208n162; in Georgia, 47, 49, 55–56, 206n129; GOELRO, 37–38, 51, 61–62; in Kyrgyzstan, 49–50, 55; Section for Raionirovanie at Gosplan, 32, 38–40, 42–43; in the RSFSR, 42–45, 52, 69; in Tajikistan, 56; in Turkestan, 54–55, 100; in Ukraine, 39–41, 43, 45–49, 53–54, 56, 59, 69, 208n151; in Uzbekistan, 54–55; in the ZSFSR, 46–47, 55–56, 155, 204n85–86
Rakhimbaev, Abdulla, 100
Rashidov, Sharaf, 164–65
Renner, Karl, 14. *See also* Austromarxism

INDEX 273

Revolutions of 1917, 16–18, 172; in Central Asia, 94–97; in the South Caucasus, 128–29; in Ukraine, 63–65. *See also* Civil War
Romania, 16, 63, 67, 90
RSFSR (Russian Socialist Federative Soviet Republic): administrative-territorial structure, 23, 34, 36–40, 42–43, 45–46, 52, 59; formation of, 17–20. *See also* autonomous oblasts and national republics; border conflicts; border creation; border revisions; federalism; korenizatsiia; nation and nationality; raionirovanie
Rudzutak, Yan, 100, 114–15, 123
Russian Empire, 17–20, 22, 25, 64–65, 93, 128; administrative-territorial structure, 23, 32–35, 39–40, 44–46, 50, 52, 55, 61, 64–65, 75–76, 85, 128, 134–35, 206n125, 206n129; colonialism, 93–94; imperial rule, 93–96, 187n6
Russian Federation, 2, 4, 51, 156, 161–62, 166, 171, 173, 180–81
Ryskulov, Turar, 98–100, 124

Sapronov, Timofei, 23
Segizbaev, Sultan, 105–6
self-determination (national), 5–6, 13, 16–18, 27, 40, 43, 173–74; Lenin on, 14–16, 18, 26–27; plebiscites, 5–6, 13, 16–17, 64–65, 80, 96–97, 175; Stalin on, 25–27, 174; Wilson on, 15–16
Semënov-Tian'-Shanskii, Pëtr, 35
Semënov-Tian'-Shanskii, Veniamin, 35
Shakhty (until 1920 Aleksandrovsk-Grushevskii), 69, 72–74, 79–80, 84, 91, 159, 178
Shaumian, Stepan, 128
Shums'kyi, Oleksandr, 68, 90
Skoropadskii, Pavel, 64
Skrypnik affair (1932–1933), 60, 91–92
Skrypnyk, Mykola, 29, 60, 68, 90–91
Smirnov, Aleksandr, 76, 80
Socialist Soviet Republic of Lithuania and Belorussia (Litbel), 19, 21
South Caucasus (region), 7, 9–10, 17, 22, 24, 27, 60, 93–94, 99, 126–32, 154–55, 172, 174, 176–81. *See also* Armenia; Azerbaijan; border conflicts; border creation; border revisions; Caucasian Viceroyalty; Georgia; raionirovanie; ZSFSR
Soviet Union. *See* USSR
space. *See* territory

Sredazbiuro, 24, 99–104, 111–14, 123, 129, 177, 196n60. *See also* border revisions; Communist Party
Stalin (Dzhugashvili), Josef, 7–8, 18, 24, 31, 58–62, 77, 83, 91–92, 101, 151, 153, 155, 176; on internal borders, 52, 90, 122, 159–62, 164, 166, 179–80; on nationality question, 14, 25–29, 33, 104, 108, 173–74; on self-determination, 25–27, 174. *See also* Communist Party; Marxism-Leninism
Starobil's'k (region), 1–2, 75, 84–87
Sturua, Georgii, 143
Sultan-Galiev, Mirsaid, 22–23, 28
Sultan-Galiev affair (1923), 28, 68
Supreme Soviet of the USSR, 122, 160–61, 164. *See also* TsIK
Sverdlov, Yakov, 20
Switzerland, 56, 150

Taganrog (1920–1924 Tahanrih), 69, 72–73, 79–80, 84–85, 91, 159, 178
Tajikistan (Tajik ASSR, SSR), 56, 60, 93, 115–16, 122–24, 153, 175, 180. *See also* border conflicts; border revisions; nation and nationality
Tashenev, Zhumabek, 167
Tashkend, 93–94, 98, 100–101, 103, 105–6, 110–12, 114, 166–68
Tatarstan (Tatar ASSR), 26, 174
Tbilisi (until 1936 Tiflis), 26, 128–30, 133–34, 136–37, 139–44, 147–49, 154
Ter-Gabrielian, Saak, 29, 54–56, 80, 82–83, 91, 115
territory, 8–9, 91–92, 172–73, 191–92n46; colonial, 4–5, 180; national, 5–6. *See also* border conflicts; border revisions, raionirovanie
Tiflis. *See* Tbilisi
Trainin, Ivan, 100
Transcaucasian Central Executive Committee. *See* ZakTsIK
Transcaucasian Federation. *See* ZSFSR
Treaty of Kars (1921), 130
Treaty of Moscow (1921), 130
Treaty of Pereiaslav (1654), 161–62, 164–65
Treaty of Sèvres (1920), 129–30
Trotsky (Bronshtein), Leon, 28, 31, 71, 90
Thünen, Johann Heinrich von, 35
TsIK SSSR (Central Executive Committee of the USSR), 29, 31, 77, 80–89, 115–22, 141, 157, 159. *See also* Supreme Soviet
Turkbuiro. *See* Sredazbiuro

INDEX

Turkestan (Governor-Generalship, Krai, ASSR), 21, 24, 44–45, 94–104, 109, 111, 114, 124, 220n24, 222n53. *See also* border creation; korenizatsiia; raionirovanie

Turkey, 3, 16, 128–31, 148, 153

Turkkommisia. *See* Sredazbiuro

Turkmenistan (Turkmen SSR), 60, 93, 102, 105, 113, 116, 175. *See also* border creation

Ukraine (UNR, ZUNR, Ukrainian SSR), 7, 20, 25–26, 30, 32, 46, 60, 93, 153–54, 172; formation of, 17, 63–65; Ukrainization, 9–10, 28, 68, 89–90. *See also* border conflicts; border creation; border revisions; Crimea; korenizatsiia; raionirovanie

United Kingdom, 4–5, 16, 128–29

United States of America, 3, 16

Urals (region), 19–20, 43–44

USSR, 172–74; formation of, 25–27, 46; relation to the RSFSR, 31. *See also* autonomous oblasts and national republics; border conflicts; border creation; border revisions; Communist Party; federalism; korenizatsiia, Marxism-Leninism; nation and nationality; nationality question; raionirovanie

Uzbekistan (Uzbek SSR), 7, 55–56, 93, 100, 102–5, 107, 109–22, 124, 161, 165–71, 178, 180. *See also* border conflicts; border creation; border revisions; korenizatsiia; raionirovanie

Validov, Akhmet-Zaki, 22, 99

Vareikis, Iosif, 19, 104, 110–13, 124

Virgin Lands campaign, 164–70

Vladimirskii, Mikhail, 23, 40, 57–58

Volga German (Worker's Commune, ASSR), 19, 21–22, 173

Voronezh (region), 32–33, 39–40, 51–52, 64, 69, 71, 73–80, 88

Voroshilov, Kliment, 164

VSNKh, 36–37, 39, 58

VTsIK (All-Russian Central Executive Committee), 20, 29, 31, 38–43, 81–88, 117, 133, 159

VUTsVK (All-Ukrainian Central Executive Committee), 52, 68, 81–90, 159

Weber, Alfred, 35

Wilson, Woodrow, 15–16, 129–30

World War I, 4–5, 13–15, 36, 63, 94–95, 128, 133, 144, 148

World War II, 3, 157, 160, 162–63, 174

Yegorov, Konstantin, 33–34, 36, 60, 172; on administrative-territorial reforms, 37–38; on border revisions, 51, 73–74, 76, 91, 115; on centralization, 54, 58; on raionirovanie, 32, 34, 38–39, 42, 53–58, 62, 176

Yenukidze, Avel', 29, 31, 77–79, 88, 159

Yerevan (until 1936 Erivan'), 132, 140, 153

Yerzinkian, Aramais, 140–43, 153

Yusupov, Ismail, 168–69

Zakkraikom, 24, 26–27, 59, 126, 129, 131–32, 135, 148, 152–54, 177. *See also* border revisions; Communist Party

ZakTsIK (Transcaucasian Central Executive Committee): on borders, 131–46; on "pasture issue," 146–52. *See also* border revisions; nomadism; ZSFSR

Zengezur (region), 128, 132, 144

Zelenskii, Isaak, 104–14, 123–24, 154

Zhizn' natsional'nostei (journal), 23, 33

Zhordania, Noe, 129

Zinov'ev, Grigorii (Ovsei-Gershon Radomysl'skii), 28, 52

ZSFSR (Transcaucasian Federation, 1922–1936), 26, 44, 98–99, 102; dissolution of, 154, 174; formation of, 26–27, 130–31; social unrest in, 131, 134. *See also* Armenia; Azerbaijan; border creation; border conflicts; border revisions; Caucasian Viceroyalty; Georgia; korenizatsiia; raionirovanie

www.ingramcontent.com/pod-product-compliance
Lightning Source LLC
Chambersburg PA
CBHW021851230426
43671CB00006B/344